Praise for Volume I

"[This] volume catches Mussolini's spirit, his personality as no other book does." —*New York Evening Post*

"Auto-revelation, auto-inspiration, auto-intoxication at the highest pitch."
—*New York Herald Tribune Book Review*

"Mussolini's autobiography is as frank as it is arrogant. . . . [Readers] will not be able to repress a shiver."
—*Spectator*

"The most perfect piece of self-revelation I have ever seen. Like him or not, agree with him or not, here he is, Mussolini the man, the patriot, the leader."
—*Saturday Review of Literature*

Praise for Volume II

"Well translated and authoritatively introduced. . . . There is much here that should open the eyes of readers, for the Duce is disarmingly frank."
—*New York Times Book Review*

"Psychologically interesting as a portrait of a poseur, stripped of his trappings." —*Kirkus*

"[Ascoli's] perceptive and lively preface [is] a kind of balance sheet of the Fascist tragi-comedy. Mussolini's own story of his fall [includes] lies, half-lies, startling admissions, and insights. . . . Like a prisoner exhibited in a cage he can only strike attitudes: appeals to superstition; self-pity; historical wisdom; boastful cynicism; grotesque poses; contrition, with slyness; and, of course, explanations of how his predicament was once Napoleon's. It is hard to stop quoting from the Duce."
—*Nation*

"Remarkable. . . . There is a good deal of surprising candor." —*Atlantic*

"[A] fascinating narrative. . . . Ascoli's preface is a balanced and penetrating analysis of an adventurer."
—*Commonweal*

"[This book] has its undeniable fascination. . . . Its principal value, beyond a doubt, is the light it sheds upon Mussolini himself."
—*New York Herald Tribune Book Review*

"A discerning preface [by Ascoli] adds much to [the Duce's] discussion of his own fall. . . . [The] authorship gives it importance as an historical document."
—*Library Journal*

MY RISE AND FALL

by BENITO MUSSOLINI

Foreword to Volume I by Richard Washburn Child,
Former Ambassador to Italy

Volume II Edited, with a Preface, by Max Ascoli

NEW INTRODUCTION BY RICHARD LAMB

DA CAPO PRESS • NEW YORK

First Da Capo Press edition 1998

This Da Capo Press paperback edition of *My Rise and Fall*
brings together in one unabridged volume *My Autobiography*, originally
published in New York in 1928, and *The Fall of Mussolini: His Own Story*,
originally published in New York in 1948, with the addition of a new
introduction by Richard Lamb. *The Fall of Mussolini* is reprinted by
arrangement with Farrar, Straus & Giroux, Inc.

Published by Da Capo Press, Inc.
A Subsidiary of Plenum Publishing Corporation
233 Spring Street, New York, N.Y. 10013

INTRODUCTION

BENITO MUSSOLINI was a brilliant journalist and writer. Although something is lost in translation, both these volumes show, in Mussolini's own words, his vigor and contemporary views.

In *My Rise* (first published in English in 1928 as *My Autobiography*) Mussolini speaks of his parents and his early days before attaining power. However, he says nothing of his two early loves who profoundly influenced him. The first was Angelica Balbanoff, a revolutionary Socialist from an aristocratic Russian family who had revolted against her class. Mussolini met her while living a vagabond life in Lausanne. With her help he organized underpaid Italian immigrants working in Switzerland to claim a fair wage. She described Mussolini then as "ill dressed and unkempt . . . but full of enthusiasm with a completely indisciplined mind" and with a hatred of oppression.

Angelica was intelligent and well read. Attracted by his youthful good looks and bustling energetic mind always full of politics, she became Mussolini's mistress. Her intellectual companionship was a boon to Mussolini: she gave him countless books and arranged for him to attend stimulating lectures at the University of

Lausanne, which he describes in this volume. Mussolini quickly matured politically and developed a great admiration for Nietzche's insistence on the heroic virtues and the spirit of militarism. As his political skill increased, Mussolini acquired a reputation as a writer for Socialist publications and as a speaker at meetings. But when he organized a strike of building workers at Berne, he was expelled from the canton.

Although greatly influenced by Angelica, Mussolini did not become a Marxist. The moderate Socialism of Guiseppe Mazzini, the hero of the *Risorgimento* (the nineteenth-century Italian struggle to liberate all of northern Italy from Austrian rule), appealed more to him, together with Mazzini's plan to abolish both national frontiers and import duties. After serving as a conscript in the Italian army, Mussolini held posts as a school teacher at Tolmezzo in the Friuli (then part of Austria) and on the Italian Riviera, but he lost both appointments because of his unruliness.

However, so highly was he regarded that he was offered the post of Secretary to the Chamber of Labor at Trento in Austria. Here he met the Italian patriot Cesare Battisti (executed by the Austrians in 1916) and swiftly imbibed Battisti's doctrines and enthusiasm for the return of the Italian-speaking parts of the Tyrol to Italy; for the rest of his days Mussolini was a fervent Italian nationalist and patriot with a passionate desire to extend Italy's national boundaries. His fiery articles arguing for the return of the Tyrol to Italian rule soon caused the Austrians to deport him. He was acclaimed in left-wing circles with "the halo of a martyred revolutionary" and became Secretary to the Forli Socialist Party. There he edited the well-known Socialist weekly *Lotta di Classe* (*The Class Struggle*), often expressing extreme left-wing views and attacking the Catholic Church (a position he later regretted).

Mussolini was strongly opposed to Italy's declaration of war on Turkey in 1911. Giovanni Giolitti, the Italian prime minister, wanted to annex Tripoli from Turkey. The war was popular because the idea of an outlet for Italy's surplus rural population in a former part of the Roman Empire had considerable appeal. So active an opponent was Mussolini that he was arrested for trying to block the movements of troop trains. At the Socialist Conference at Reggio Emilia he was hailed as the rising star of the Socialist movement; a few weeks later he was, to the delight of Angelica Balbanoff, appointed editor of the main left-wing Milan newspaper *Avanti*. Luigi Barzini commented that at the time Mussolini was not only the most professional journalist of the day but "one of the best and most moving speakers in Italy paying little attention to the logic and truth of what he said provided it was energetic and stirring."

With Angelica as his advisor Mussolini made a success of *Avanti*, but World War I brought his editorship to an abrupt end. Mussolini was adamant that Italy must not honor the tripartite alliance and fight alongside Austria and Germany; the successful Anglo-French resistance on the Marne convinced him that Germany would lose. He became a vociferous supporter of Italian intervention on the Allied side. For this he was sacked and started *Il Popolo d'Italia* with funding from the French government and rich industrialists. As he confirms in his autobiography, this paper was his platform from 1914 until 1922. In *Il Popolo*, instead of urging the workers to start a class war against capitalism, Mussolini's articles were strongly nationalistic, appealing to patriots to complete the *Risorgimento* by annexing Trieste and the Trento from Austria. He was an important factor in Italy entering the war on the Allied side in May 1915.

During his time at *Avanti* Angelica Balbanoff had been a great help to Mussolini and much of the good sense of his articles was due to her. With his change of policy at *Il Popolo* Angelica considered him a renegade Socialist and would not speak to him. Instead, he fell in love with the beautiful Margherita Sarfatti, a rich Jewess and one of Italy's leading art critics as well as a political journalist. At *Il Popolo* she was his constant companion and a wise advisor. On foreign affairs she was anti-German and pro-British and pro-French. (By 1935, with a middle-aged spread, she had lost her charms for him, and then his foreign policy went awry.)

After serving with distinction at the front against Austria, Mussolini resumed the editorship of *Il Popolo* in October 1917 and campaigned for national unity, for a greater war effort, and for the suppression of Socialist and other newspapers that were advocating peace; as a result, the British government subsidized him. Although *Il Popolo* had been launched originally as a Socialist newspaper, by 1918 it sang a very different tune, condemning Marxism and scoffing at the rule of the proletariat. Sarfatti and Mussolini formulated a campaign glorifying Mussolini's part in bringing Italy into the war, and emphasizing the territorial gains to which Italy was entitled after the Allies' victory.

Meanwhile, Italy was descending into chaos with raging inflation, food shortages, and widespread strikes. Mussolini launched the Fascist Party in Milan in March 1919 (although in his autobiography he gives the impression that this occurred earlier) with the aim of restoring order. In the ensuing general election of November 1919 the Fascists—fighting on a left-wing and anti-clerical policy—received a derisory vote. Mussolini then bid for popularity and power by presenting the Fascists as the only force capable of checking the spread of Bolshevism. All over Italy, Socialist mobs were attacking trains, barracks, banks, and public buildings; local *soviets* were proclaimed in worker-occupied factories and, in some areas, control passed into the hands of Communists. Mussolini organized large gangs of black-shirt Fascists (mainly ex-service men) to attack the Communists and strikers, meeting violence with violence. This attracted support from the middle classes and the wealthy who saw Fascism as the best chance of saving Italy from a Bolshevik-style revolution.

Ignoring the Fascist violence, the Italian prime minister, Giolitti, made an electoral agreement with Mussolini to allow Fascist candidates a clear run in return for a promise of support in Parliament for the general election in May 1921. As a result, Mussolini and 34 other Fascists were elected. But the Fascist "black-shirts" continued their outrages with frequent bloody clashes with Socialists and Trade Unionists. Four prime ministers—Giolitti, Ivanoe Bonomi, Luigi Salandra, and Antonio Facta—negotiated with Mussolini, offering him and other Fascists posts in prospective coalition cabinets while ignoring the behavior of his disorderly bands of black shirts. They wanted to appoint Mussolini as Minister of the Interior and hoped to use Fascism to tame the rebellious working class. Eventually, Facta, the last prime minister before Mussolini, ordered the police and army to stop Mussolini's black shirts from marching on Rome, which the Fascists were threatening to do with enormous publicity. But at the last moment the cowardly King of Italy, fearing civil war, withdrew the orders and suppressed the proclamations.

There is considerable doubt whether Mussolini (who was being dissuaded by Margherita Sarfatti) would have risked the march on Rome if he had been faced with firm government opposition. In any event, the king telegraphed Mussolini in Milan offering him the prime ministership. The much-publicized "March on Rome" never took place and is a myth, because Mussolini travelled to Rome in a first-class sleeper, while the black-shirt bands made no move towards Rome until after he installed himself. It is difficult for Americans and British to understand how continuous violence and ever-escalating threats resulted in the Fascists being given power constitutionally. Nothing like that could have happened in Britain or America, where there is a long record of stable democratic government. To understand how the Fascists came to power without winning a majority in a general election one must look at the short history of parliamentary government in Italy.

The Italians like to express their political wishes not in the ballot box but by rowdy gatherings of citizens in the piazzas. Camille Cavour (the architect of Italy's unification into a single state in 1861) tried hard to import the British style of parliamentary government into Italy, but he failed. For the previous three centuries before Cavour there had been six large city-states—Naples, Tuscany, Papal States, Venetia, Piedmont, and Lombardy—each governed autocratically by monarchies of the European type. Only in Piedmont was there patriotism; the *Risorgimento* battles in 1848 were mainly a reaction against the rule of foreign despots. Therefore, when Italy established herself in 1861 as a united kingdom, she was essentially a union of the former city-states without any proper parliamentary or electoral experience.

Cavour had ingeniously managed to make a parliamentary cabinet system work in the small kingdom of Piedmont; he found the problem of cabinet rule for the larger nation of 1861 far more difficult. If he had lived, he might have accomplished wonders. Unfortunately, when the *Risorgimento* was complete in 1870, thirty years of economic distress, coupled with the high taxation necessary for creating a modern state, followed. Enormous sums were spent on much-needed new railways, but also on needless bureaucracy. The golden age after unification that the patriots of the *Risorgimento* had expected failed to materialize. Until the early 1900s there was no obvious return for all the new high taxes. Bureaucracy ran riot with inflated numbers of civil servants and railway officials, while parliamentary graft, state corruption, and inefficiency were widespread and blatant.

There was an economic recovery shortly before the outbreak of World War I, and, when the war was won, Italians again expected a new golden age. The reality was completely the reverse of their hopes, and this produced a wave of semi-Bolshevik reaction, which Lenin and Soviet propaganda fanned. The Socialists unwisely copied the Bolsheviks and exercised violence in place of the ballot box; down this path the Fascists soon followed.

Between 1919 and 1922 successively weak democratic prime ministers failed to restore order. The majority of Italian upper and middle classes began to believe only Fascism could conquer the crisis; it may well be that civil war was only narrowly averted by Mussolini becoming prime minister. To understand his rise to power in October 1922, one must always take into account the Italians' preference for the "'Politics of the Piazza" over the ballot box.

During the thirteen years from his attaining the prime ministership in 1922 to the Abyssinian War in 1935, Mussolini enjoyed a highly favorable image in America. He was looked on as a bulwark against the spread of Communism in Europe because of the way he overcame the chaos that had plagued Italy. Mussolini received massive press coverage in the United States with much praise for his regime; he cultivated American journalists in Rome and granted them all sorts of favors if they wrote pieces praising the results of Fascism. Mussolini could not write articles in English for American newspapers, but Margherita Sarfatti could, and did. She ghosted numerous articles for Hearst and United Press—all highly favorable to Mussolini and Fascism. This success prompted Mussolini to compose *My Autobiography*.

In Britain, Mussolini also enjoyed a consistently favorable reaction from all the right-wing newspapers, although the Socialist *Daily Herald* was highly critical (especially after his suppression of trade unions). On November 2, 1922, immediately after Mussolini came to power, Gialomo De Martino, the Italian ambassador in London, was able to cable to Rome that only the *Daily Herald* had commented negatively on the change in government, and that most circles, including the city of London, were pleased with the Fascists assuming power.

In his account of events Mussolini glosses over any guilt he may have felt over the assassination of Giacomo Matteoti, a member of Parliament and leading

Introduction

opponent of Fascism. He may not have been directly responsible, but undoubtedly his consistent encouragement of violence by Fascists was a key factor in the Socialist M.P.'s death. For a critical period it looked as if Mussolini would fall from power in the aftermath of the assassination. In his autobiography he reproduces nearly in full his famous speech on January 3, 1925, when he took the bull by the horns, suppressed all press criticism, and became a complete dictator flaunting the constitution. Until then, he had been the head of a Fascist-dominated coalition government.

In 1925 and 1926 Mussolini obtained diplomatic triumphs with the settlement of Italy's debts to the Allies arising from World War I. Italy's war debt to Britain was settled on the most generous terms by Winston Churchill, Chancellor of the Exchequer, who flouted the arguments of his Treasury advisors that Italy could afford to pay substantially more. This shows how much Churchill admired the Italian dictator. In Washington, Mussolini was equally successful in securing a similarly generous settlement of Italy's debt to the United States, evidence of the esteem in which America held him. Curiously, Mussolini does not blow his own trumpet over his adroit handling of Italy's war debts in his autobiography.

The first volume of *My Rise and Fall* concludes at the end of the 1920s, when Mussolini had firmly established Fascism as the popular government of Italy; he did not take up the tale again until his overthrow in 1943, after World War II had gone disastrously wrong for him. The intervening years were crucial ones for Mussolini, full of drama and—at first—triumph. The events that occurred from the early 1930s through the early 1940s—although not discussed by Mussolini directly—are nonetheless important for comprehending his decline and brutal death at the hands of his country-men.

ii

Two leading historians of Fascism clash over Mussolini. Renzo de Felice asserts that Mussolini was an intelligent ruler with massive popular support who handled the Ethiopian war well. Denis Mack Smith has bitterly criticized de Felice, claiming he overemphasizes Mussolini's popularity; Mack Smith's own books portray Mussolini as a mountebank who governed mainly by press statement. The truth is *Il Duce* was a highly intelligent and very popular ruler with a flair for government. His faults were his oscillations, over-quick reactions, and readiness to use violence, and—in the end—his greed to partake of the spoils of conquest with Hitler.

Mussolini's home policy was successful, although autocratic and undemocratic: he banned any parliamentary opposition ruthlessly and suppressed criticism from political opponents. His undoing was his foreign policy. Yet, guided by Margherita Sarfatti for the first twelve years of his rule, and apart from the atrocious incident of Corfu in 1923, he virtually aligned his foreign policy with Britain and became a close personal friend of Austen Chamberlain (Foreign Secretary from 1924 to 1929). When Hitler came to power in Germany in 1933, Mussolini despised and disliked him. At their first meeting in Venice the two dictators got on very badly, with Mussolini warning Hitler to keep his hands off Austria. When Nazis attempted a coup d'état in Vienna in 1934, Mussolini acted, helping the anti-Nazi right wing, led by Count Ernst Starhemberg, to suppress it and moving Italian troops to the Brenner Pass to be ready to intervene should the Austrian Nazis succeed. In 1935, in flagrant breach of the Versailles Treaty, Hitler announced conscription and the existence of a powerful air force. Once again, Mussolini took a stronger anti-Nazi line than Britain.

After protesting vigorously to Berlin, he organized the Stresa Conference, where the three victorious powers of World War I met in full agreement for the last time. Urged on by Mussolini, France, Britain, and Italy warned Hitler not to attempt again union between Germany and Austria, and agreed that League of Nations sanctions should be applied against Nazi Germany if she persisted with her illegal rearmament.

But, at Stresa, Mussolini fell into a deadly trap. He had assumed because of the silence of British Prime Minister Ramsay Macdonald and Foreign Secretary John Simon that Britain would allow him a free hand to invade Abyssinia. The British attitude had always been that Abyssinia, a backward country where slavery, drugs, and gunrunning were rife, should be within Italy's sphere of influence, while French Foreign Minister Pierre Laval had already promised Mussolini that the French would not oppose an Italian invasion. Unfortunately for Mussolini, in 1923 against British wishes Abyssinia had been made a member of the League of Nations. This had not bothered the British government until British supporters of the League of Nations suddenly unfurled the Peace Ballot in the summer of 1935. Ten million answered "Yes" to the question whether, if one nation violated the covenant by attacking another member state, the other states should combine together to compel the attacking nation to stop. (In the United States, which was not a member of the League, there was no such anti-Italian backlash.) The British government, now under Stanley Baldwin, panicked and reneged on Britain's virtual nod to Mussolini to pursue his invasion of Abyssinia.

When Mussolini invaded Abyssinia on October 5, 1935, Britain took the lead at Geneva in organizing economic sanctions against Italy. However, almost immediately, they assented to France's proposals, which would have given Italy the lion's share of Abyssinia. Mussolini was on the brink of accepting but, when he saw how hostile British public opinion was, he rejected them. This was a fatal mistake. Sanctions were ineffective; an oil sanction was mooted, but it too would have been useless as the United States was supplying Italy with all the oil she needed. The Abysinian War was short lived: in May 1936 it ended when Italian troops occupied the capital Addis Ababa. But grievous

Introduction

damage had been done to Italian relations with France and Britain.

Having scorned Hitler the previous year, Mussolini, in angry reaction against sanctions, started to move towards the Nazi camp. When Hitler—to the admiration of almost all Germans—once again spurned the Versailles Treaty and remilitarized the Rhineland in March 1936, Mussolini condoned the action. Without Italian support and faced with hesitation by Britain, France would not take military action to throw the Nazis out. The last great opportunity to stop Hitler dead in his tracks was irretrievably lost.

However, with Abyssinia firmly part of a new Italian empire Mussolini made strenuous efforts to make friends again with Britain. Frightened by Germany's massive rearmament, he feared that Hitler would annex Austria, which Mussolini still looked on as his sphere of influence. Unfortunately, Anthony Eden, the new British Foreign Secretary, had an implacable dislike for Mussolini and scorned his advances. Had Eden been more malleable, Mussolini could have been kept out of Hitler's grasp. The Führer flattered *Il Duce* and insinuated that he would abet Mussolini in his plan to claim Djibuti, Corsica, and Nice from France as well as a greater share in governing Tunisia. The Spanish Civil War, in which Italy gave much military aid to the dictatorial General Francisco Franco, fanned Eden's opposition to Mussolini, although the bulk of the British cabinet and the conservatives were on Franco's side.

Mussolini foolishly joined the Anti-Commintern Pact with Germany and Japan against Russia in November 1937, but he was far from happy about it. He was uneasy about Hitler, fearing a German attack on Austria and inwardly hankering after a firm alliance with Britain to restrain Hitler.

The Abyssinian War had made Mussolini more popular inside Italy. Italians felt they had at last received a handsome reward for their victory in World War I and an outlet in the sun for part of their surplus population. But Mussolini's overtures towards Hitler were unpopular and badly received also in Britain and even in America.

Then, in September 1938, came Munich. In an effort to prevent another world war from breaking out because of Hitler's demands on Czechoslovakia, British Prime Minister Neville Chamberlain entreated Mussolini to bring Hitler to a conference table where, instead of war, the carving up of Czechoslovakia would be decided. Mussolini complied. Hitler's demands were met and Mussolini was covered with glory as the man who had preserved the peace of Europe.

Like Neville Chamberlain, Mussolini thought that Hitler's territorial ambitions had been satisfied at Munich, but both were soon disappointed. Hitler would not honor the small print of the Munich Agreement from the start, and in March 1939 German troops occupied Prague and the whole rump of Czechoslovakia. Mussolini was aghast at this breach of faith and the downgrading of the Munich Agreement, which he looked upon as the pinnacle of his career. For a few days he thought he had made a mistake in supporting Hitler and contemplated whether or not to come to new accords with France and Britain, even sending an Italian diplomat to Paris to start negotiations.

Albania had been under Italian domination for many years, and an Italo-Albanina agreement had been drafted that would give Italy control of the country. At the last moment their king, Zog, made difficulties. Mussolini, urged on by his son-in-law and Foreign Minister Galeazzo Ciano, effected a military occupation of Albania in April 1939, deluding himself that this action made him the equal of Hitler.

The French and British reacted with an Anglo-French guarantee of the independence of Greece and Romania, and an offer of military aid to Turkey in the event of an attack. Mussolini was furious, seeing his path to expansion in the east blocked, and on the rebound he authorized Ciano to negotiate with German Foreign Minister Joachim von Ribbentrop for a binding military agreement. Within three weeks of the Anglo-French agreements with Greece, Romania, and Turkey, Ciano and Ribbentrop met in Milan and signed the "Pact of Steel" between Italy and Germany for military aid if either country went to war. It was an act of irresponsibility that was most unpopular within Italy.

Deviously, Ribbentrop gave assurances that Germany would on no account go to war for three years, although he knew Hitler was ready and willing that autumn. Mussolini feared war with France and Britain; he knew that air raids from nearby French airfields would devastate his key industries in Milan and Turin. Britain would cut off Abyssinia by closing the Suez Canal, and would threaten his hold on Tripoli by sea attacks on Italian naval convoys and by land attacks from Tunisia and Egypt. Mussolini knew that Hitler was about to demand Danzig and other territory from Poland, but had deluded himself that the German dictator would use only diplomatic means. Hitler never had any intention of honoring his commitment not to go to war for three years. Mussolini expected no war at all, hoping his demands at France's expense would be met by negotiation while he expanded Italian influence in Greece and Romania with the help of Hitler, who had shown how weak Britain and France were when confronted with territorial demands. Relations between Ciano and Ribbentrop became icy when Hitler told Ciano that, because of Polish provocation, Germany no longer adhered to the three-year period of peace.

Mussolini was shocked and infuriated when on August 23, 1939 Hitler secured a great diplomatic triumph with a non-aggression pact with the Soviet Union. It became obvious that a European war was about to break out because France and Britain had guaranteed the security of Nazi-threatened Poland. Mussolini was so alarmed that he wriggled out of his "Pact of Steel" commitment to fight by the side of Germany on the grounds that his armed forces had been so depleted by the

Abyssinian War and the Spanish Civil War that Italy could only fight if Germany supplied an impossibly high quantity of oil, raw materials, and weapons. Hitler accepted with good grace, and instead Mussolini promised to contain as many Anglo-French divisions as possible.

During the "Phoney War" of 1939 and the first part of 1940, Mussolini oscillated violently between the Nazis and the Allies. Hitler forewarned him that Germany would launch an attack against the West in the spring, but Mussolini was far from convinced that it would be successful. Even after German Panzer divisions had crossed the Meuse and threatened to overrun the Allied armies, Mussolini still believed the French might stage a second Battle of the Marne. Not until the French resistance on the Somme had been crushed and German armored divisions were roaming at will over France, would Mussolini declare war. Then he succumbed to greed, believing he could get his fingers on the booty without much fighting; he persuaded King Victor Emmanuel to agree. Both the king and *Il Duce* expected a very short war. They were to be bitterly disappointed.

The war went disastrously for Italy. Although France was down and out militarily, Mussolini insisted on Italian divisions attacking France's mountainous frontiers, where the Italians suffered heavy casualties without winning any ground. Then at armistice talks Mussolini demanded Italian occupation of France up to the Rhone, together with Corsica, Tunisia, and the Somali coast; military bases in Algiers, Oran, and Casablanca; and Beirut neutralized. Hitler would have

Introduction

none of this—he rejected all of Mussolini's requests. Britain was continuing the war and Hitler wanted to placate Vichy France so that the right-wing Pétain government would give no help to Britain. Thus, Mussolini had no booty with which to impress the Italian people; any eventual spoils would have to await a postwar peace conference.

In North Africa the Italian army suffered a crushing defeat when the British under General Archibald Wavell advanced with amazing speed into Italian Cyrenaica and captured more than 200,000 Italian troops, while in Greece (where Mussolini had attacked against Hitler's advice) Italian troops were ignominiously pushed back behind the frontier.

The war became desperately unpopular in Italy. However, when Hitler attacked the Soviet Union on June 21, 1941, Mussolini also declared war on the Soviet Union and sent Italian troops to fight alongside the Germans. There was a wave of enthusiasm for the war in Italy; the Church, strongly anti-Communist, blessed Italian troops leaving for Russia as if they were embarking on a crusade.

On December 7, 1941 the Japanese attacked Pearl Harbor, destroying or disabling most of the battleships there and killing 2,400 Americans. For a moment there was doubt whether Congress would allow America to fight Germany and Italy as well as Japan. Then Hitler and Mussolini made their biggest mistakes by declaring war on the United States. Until then the Italian community in America had shown no signs of militant anti-Fascism, but with Mussolini's declaration of war anti-Fascism dominated the country, with long-standing opponents of Mussolini having a field day. The Mediterranean was lost to Italy when in April 1943 Anglo-American troops captured Tunis. The Italian and German armies lost all their equipment and 240,000 soldiers became prisoners-of-war. Mussolini realized it was all over. He was ready to doublecross Hitler and made overtures to Britain for a separate peace, but his efforts encountered a wall of silence (demolishing the frequent claims in the Italian press that Churchill and Mussolini secretly communicated during the war). Anti-Fascists and monarchists also tried to negotiate with the Allies without success, being rebuffed by the "Unconditional Surrender" formula. Then, in July 1943, came the plot to overthrow Mussolini.

iii

The first volume shows Mussolini at his peak. *My Fall* (first published in English in 1948 as *The Fall of Mussolini: His Own Story*) reveals him at his nadir. If he had not fallen into the arms of Hitler, the Fascist period would have been hailed by most Italians as a golden era in Italian history (although many of the cultured class detested him, and his rule was hideously marred by violence and brutal suppression of opposition). Inheriting a crippled economy, he transformed it by judicious expenditure on public works, railways, roads, and industrial investment. Although he failed to

Introduction

do much for the rural population, he did halt inflation, and produced industrial peace and relative prosperity.

For his first thirteen years in power—apart from a few hiccups—Mussolini aligned Italian foreign policy with France and Britain, and earned the esteem of many American and European statesmen, including Winston Churchill, Austen Chamberlain, Ramsay Macdonald, Aristide Briand, and Gustav Stressemann. Franklin Roosevelt gave him qualified admiration as a bulwark against Communism (while Eleanor Roosevelt disliked him). Both American ambassadors to Italy, Richard Washburn Child (who encouraged Mussolini to compose the first volume and contributed a foreword) and Breckinridge Long, were steadfastly enthusiastic for Mussolini. Thanks mainly to the Hearst press Mussolini was extremely popular in the United States, especially amongst the Italian community. Mussolini enjoyed enormous popularity with his countrymen, but it sank when he allied Italy with the Nazis. After his anti-Semitic laws of 1938—showing how far he had fallen under Hitler's baneful influence—his unpopularity intensified.

Mussolini wrote the contents of the second volume while he was head of the puppet government at Salò in 1944. He had plenty of leisure for research and writing. He uses all his skills as a journalist and writer to justify his dramatic 21 years as dictator, showing considerable erudition and a sense of history. Despite its vitriol and self-justification his colorful language must evoke in most readers some small spark of sympathy for the former dictator, now a powerless puppet for Hitler. Mussolini understood too well that he had brought Italy to ruin and that he and the rump of the country were inexorably in the hands of Hitler, who had irrevocably lost the war. Total defeat was less than a year away.

Mussolini relates how he called a meeting of the Grand Fascist Council on July 24, 1943 to discuss the dire straits in which Italy found herself: Italian troops were refusing to fight the Allies in Sicily, and an invasion of the mainland by Anglo-American forces was obviously imminent. Dino Grandi, the former ambassador in London, had put forward a resolution covertly hostile to Mussolini. The king had promised, if it was passed, to use it as an excuse to topple the dictator. Mussolini, unaware of the danger, rashly allowed the resolution to succeed; the next day the king ordered Mussolini to be arrested and appointed Pietro Badoglio as prime minister. The king was a willing accomplice in the plot. Mussolini was kept prisoner; 45 days later, in accordance with an armistice agreed upon by the Allies, Badoglio declared that the war alongside Germany was over. The Italian people hailed the announcement with enormous joy, but chaos resulted. During the previous 45 days of Badoglio's rule German troops had poured into Italy with the connivance of the Badoglio government. Mussolini produces evidence from captured archives to show how blatantly warnings of the German danger were ignored. Fierce fighting broke out around Rome between Italian and German divisions. Unfortunately, although

Mussolini never knew, the Badoglio government had cowardly refused to allow the famous 82 US Airborne Division to land on Rome airfields on the night of September 8 simultaneously with the armistice. With their help the Italians could easily have repulsed the Germans. Even as it was, they were having the best of the struggle when Badoglio and the king decided cravenly to flee Rome, leaving the Italian army all over Italy to surrender ignominiously. Thousands of soldiers went home by rail, bicycle, or on foot, while the bulk were rounded up by the Germans and shipped off to Germany.

Mussolini quotes from his speech to the Grand Council. It is clear that by July 24 he considered the war lost. He recalls that until October 1942 he held high hopes of victory by "a great pincer movement with the Germans storming the Caucasus and Rommel's German-Italian armies conquering Egypt," but admits that all this is now over. *Il Duce*'s defeatist attitude contributed to the favorable vote on Grandi's motion. Of course, Mussolini did not give any hint that he was hoping to negotiate a separate peace with the Allies, because this information would have been passed on to the Germans with disastrous results.

By September 22, Mussolini was still being kept prisoner in a ski hotel on Gran Sasso mountain near Aquila, although the Germans were in full occupation of that part of Italy and could have sent a detachment to fetch Mussolini down by the funicular railway. Instead, Hitler ordered a spectacular glider landing on the mountain; Mussolini was borne away in triumph in a Storch aircraft by Otto Skorzeny amid enormous publicity. Mussolini recounts in detail his "escape," although he must have known perfectly well it was pure propaganda.

Mussolini pours vitriol on the architects of the July 25th plot, vilifying Badoglio and Grandi. But this did them little harm, as by then Grandi had retreated to Portugal, never to return to the political scene, and Badoglio had been deposed as prime minister. But his indictment of the king, describing him as not only a coward but a liar and traitor, damaged Victor Emmanuel in the eyes of the nation. This polemic contributed to the downfall of the House of Savoy after the war was over. Mussolini expresses his wish that he had eliminated the monarchy when he came to power in 1922. This is an interesting view, but there are considerable doubts whether he could have deposed the king back then. However, Mussolini is correct in declaring that by seizing dictatorial powers in January 1925 he considerably reduced the monarch's authority. Yet, King Victor Emmanuel alone brought him down on July 25, 1943.

Mussolini acknowledges the despair assailing him at Salò, where he had no choice except to execute Hitler's orders. He writes that Italy was "not even a nation" and admits that her rebirth would come only after total defeat, anticipating a new era of Fascism well in the future (on the lines of Napoleon III in 1848 recreating the 1814 empire of Napoleon I). He predicts that only when the spirit of ancient Romans once more breathes into the Italians of today would Italy become great again. Over fifty years later, Mussolini's final words retain a certain appeal; he was a realist who recognized that by July 1943 he was the most unpopular man in Italy because his countrymen considered him to be the architect of the hated war and of Italy's defeat. He admits that his broadcast to the Italian nation after his rescue by Hitler was the voice "of the most hated man" in Italy, while recalling with nostalgia the years from the 1929 Lateran Treaty to the Spanish Civil War.

Mussolini's poignant words to the German ambassador were "I have drained the poisoned chalice to the dregs." Greed had overcome him. He had made the fatal mistake of supping with the devil, when Hitler's successes in acquiring Austria and Czechoslovakia for Germany peacefully had convinced Mussolini that an alliance with Hitler would be more likely to produce territorial gains for Italy than friendship with France and Britain. His last months were blackened by the cruelty of the Verona Trials, when he condemned to death even his own son-in-law, Ciano, and by his barbaric orders that all captured partisans were to be shot out of hand.

No wonder after his death he was reviled in Italy and worldwide. He cannot be rehabilitated. Yet, there is stark tragedy in his fall from his peak of popularity in 1936 after his Abyssinian victory to his final friendless, powerless days. Lately new research has added much to our knowledge about Mussolini and his policies, but these two works in his own words—some truthful, some false—are still essential for any reassessment.

RICHARD LAMB
England
July 1998

Richard Lamb has written eight books on modern history, including War in Italy, 1943–1945: A Brutal Story *(also available from Da Capo Press) and, most recently,* Mussolini and the British.

CONTENTS

Contents

VOLUME 1
MY RISE

ILLUSTRATIONS

From a photograph by A. Badodi, Milan.

MUSSOLINI.

In his office at the Palazzo Chigi, the Ministry of Foreign Affairs. When listening intently this is his attitude and expression.

FOREWORD

By RICHARD WASHBURN CHILD

It is far from my purpose to elaborate the material in this book, to interpret it, or to add to it.

With much of the drama it contains I, being Ambassador of the United States at the time, was intimately familiar; much of the extraordinary personality disclosed here was an open book to me long ago because I knew well the man who now, at last, has written characteristically, directly and simply of that self for which I have a deep affection.

For his autobiography I am responsible. Lives of Mussolini written by others have interests of sorts.

"But nothing can take the place of a book which you will write yourself," I said to him.

"Write myself?" He leaned across his desk and repeated my phrase in amazement.

He is the busiest single individual in the world. He appeared hurt as if a friend had failed to understand.

"Yes," I said and showed him a series of headings I had written on a few sheets of paper.

"All right," he said in English. "I will."

It was quite like him. He decides quickly and completely.

So he began. He dictated. I advised that method because when he attempts to write in longhand he corrects and corrects and corrects. It would have been too much for him. So he dictated. The copy came back and he interlined the manuscript in his own hand—a dash of red pencil, and a flowing rivulet of ink—here and there.

When the manuscripts began to come to me I was troubled because mere literal translators lose the vigor of the man himself.

"What editing may I do?" I asked him.

"Any that you like," he said. "You know Italy, you understand Fascism, you see me, as clearly as any one."

But there was nothing much to do. The story came through as it appears here. It is all his and—what luck for all of us—so like him! Approve of him or not, when one reads this book one may know Mussolini or at least, if one's vision is clouded, know him better. Like the book or not, there is not an insincere line in it. I find none.

Of course there are many things which a man writing an autobiography cannot see about himself or will not say about himself.

He is unlikely to speak of his own size on the screen of history.

Perhaps when approval or disapproval, theories and isms, pros and cons, are all put aside the only true measure of a man's greatness from a wholly unpartisan view-point may be found in the answer to this question:

"How deep and lasting has been the effect of a man upon the largest number of human beings—their hearts, their thoughts, their material welfare, their relation to the universe?"

In our time it may be shrewdly forecast that no man will exhibit dimensions of permanent greatness equal to those of Mussolini.

Admire him or not, approve his philosophies or not, concede the permanence of his success or not, consider him superman or not, as you may, he has put to a working test, on great and growing numbers of mankind, programmes, unknown before, in applied spirituality, in applied plans, in applied leadership, in applied doctrines, in the applied principle that contents are more important than labels on bottles. He has not only been able to secure and hold an almost universal following; he has built a new state upon a new concept of a state. He has not only been able to change the lives of human beings but he has changed their minds, their hearts, their spirits. He has not merely ruled a house; he has built a new house.

He has not merely put it on paper or into orations; he has laid the bricks.

It is one thing to administer a state. The one who does this well is called statesman. It is quite another thing to make a state. Mussolini has made a state. That is superstatesmanship.

I knew him before the world at large, outside of Italy, had ever heard of him; I knew him before and after the moment he leaped into the saddle and in the days when he, almost single-handed, was clearing away chaos' own junk pile from Italy.

But no man knows Mussolini. An Italian newspaper offered a prize for the best essay showing insight into the mystery of the man. Mussolini, so the story goes, stopped the contest by writing to the paper that such a competition was absurd, because he himself could not enter an opinion.

In spite of quick, firm decisions, in spite of grim determination, in spite of a well-ordered diagrammed pattern and plan of action fitted to any moment of time, Mussolini, first of all, above all and after all, is a personality always in a state of flux, adjusting its leadership to a world eternally in a state of flux.

Change the facts upon which Mussolini has acted and he will change his action. Change the hypotheses and he will change his conclusion.

And this perhaps is an attribute of greatness seldom recognized. Most of us are forever hoping to put our world in order and finish the job. Statesmen with some idea to make over into reality hope for a day when they can say: "Well, that's done!" And when it is done,—often enough it is nothing. The bridges they have built are now useless, because the rivers have all changed their courses and humanity is already shrieking for new bridges. This is not an unhappy thought, says Mussolini. A finished world would be a stupid place—intolerably stupid.

The imagination of mere statesmen covers a static world.

The imagination of true greatness covers a dynamic world. Mussolini conceives a dynamic world. He is ready to go on the march with it, though it overturns all his structures, upsets all his theories, destroys all of yesterday and creates a screaming dawn of a to-morrow.

Opportunist is a term of reproach used to brand men who fit themselves to conditions for reasons of self-interest. Mussolini, as I have learned to know him, is an opportunist in the sense that he believes that mankind itself must be fitted to changing conditions rather than to fixed theories, no matter how many hopes and prayers have been expended on theories and programmes.

He has marched up several hills with the thousands and then marched down again. This strange creature of strange life and strange thoughts, with that almost psychopathic fire which was in saints and villains, in Napoleons, in Jeanne d'Arcs and in Tolstoys, in religious prophets and in Ingersolls, has been up the Socialist, the international, the liberal and the conservative hills and down again. He says: "The sanctity of an ism is not in the ism; it has no sanctity beyond its power to do, to work, to succeed in practice. It may have succeeded yesterday and fail to-morrow. Failed yesterday and succeed to-morrow. The machine first of all must run!"

I have watched, with a curiosity that has never failed to creep in on me, the marked peculiarities, physical and mental, of this man. At moments he is quite relaxed, at ease; and yet the unknown gusts of his own personality play on him eternally. One sees in his eyes, or in a quick movement of his body, or in a sentence suddenly ejaculated, the effect of these gusts, just as one sees wind on the surface of the water.

There is in his walk something of a prowl, a faint suggestion of the tread of the cat. He likes cats—their independence, their decision, their sense of justice and their appreciation of the sanctity of the individual. He even likes lions and lionesses, and plays with them until those who guard his life protest against their social set. His principal pet is a Persian feline which, being of aristocratic lineage, nevertheless exhibits a pride not only of ancestry but, condescendingly, of belonging to Mussolini. And yet, in spite of his own prowl, as he walks along in his riding-boots, springy, active, ready to leap, it seems, there is little else feline about him. One quality is feline, however—it is the sense of his complete isolation. One feels that he must always have had this isolation—isolation as a boy, isolation as a young radical, adventurer, lover, worker, thinker.

There is no understudy of Mussolini. There is no man, woman, or child who stands anywhere in the inner orbit of his personality. No one. The only possible exception is his daughter Edda. All the tales of his alliances, his obligations, his ties, his predilections are arrant nonsense. There are none—no ties, no predilections, no alliances, no obligations unpaid.

Financially? Lying voices said that he had been personally financed and backed by the industrialists of Italy. This is ridiculous to those who know. His salary is almost nothing. His own family—wife, children, are poor.

Politically? Whom could he owe? He has made and can unmake them all. He is free to test every officeholder in the whole of Italy by the yardstick of service and fitness. Beyond that I know not one political debt that he owes. He has tried to pay those of the past; I believe that the cynicism in him is based upon the failure of some who have been rewarded to live up to the trust put in them.

"But I take the responsibility for all," says he. He says it publicly with jaws firm; he says it privately with eyes somewhat saddened.

He takes responsibility for everything—for discipline, for censorship, for measures which, were less rigor required, would appear repressive and cruel. "Mine!" says he, and stands or falls on that. It is an admirable courage. I could, if I wished, quote instance after instance of this acceptance—sometimes when he is not to blame—of the whole responsibility of the machine.

"Mine!" says he.

And in spite of any disillusionment he has suffered since I knew him first, he has retained his laugh—often, one is bound to say, a scornful laugh—and he has kept his faith in an ability to build up a machine—the machine of Fascism—the machine built not on any fixed theory but one intended by Mussolini to run—above all, to run, to function, to do, to accomplish, to fill the bottles with wine first, unlike the other isms, and put the labels on after.

Mussolini has superstitious faith in himself. He has said it. Not a faith in himself to make a personal gain. An assassin's bullet might wipe him out and leave his family in poverty. That would be that. His faith is in

a kind of destiny which will allow him, before the last
chapter, to finish the building of this new state, this
new machine—"the machine which will run and has a
soul."

The first time I ever saw him he came to my residence
sometime before the march on Rome and I asked him
what would be his programme for Italy. His answer
was immediate: "Work and discipline."

I remember I thought at that time that the phrase
sounded a little evangelical, a phrase of exhortation.
But a mere demagogue would never choose it. Wilson's
slogans of Rights and Peace and Freedom are much
more popular and gain easier currency than sterner
phrases. It is easier even for a sincere preacher, to offer
soft nests to one's followers; it is more difficult to excite
enthusiasm for stand-up doctrines. Any analysis and
weighing of Mussolini's greatness must include recognition that he has made popular throughout a race of
people, and perhaps for others, a standard of obligation
of the individual not only exacting but one which in the
end will be accepted voluntarily. Not only is it accepted
voluntarily but with an almost spiritual ecstasy which
has held up miraculously in Italy during years, when
all the so-called liberals in the world were hovering over
it like vultures, croaking that if it were not dead it was
about to die.

It is difficult to lead men at all. It is still more difficult to lead them away from self-indulgence. It is still
more difficult to lead them so that a new generation, so
that youth itself, appears as if born with a new spirit,

Foreword xiii

a new virility bred in the bones. It is difficult to govern a state and difficult to deal cleanly and strongly with a static programme applied to a static world; but it is more difficult to build a new state and deal cleanly and strongly with a dynamic programme applied to a dynamic world.

This man, who looks up at me with that peculiar nodding of his head and raising of the eyebrows, has done it. There are few in the world's history who have. I had considered the phrase "Work and discipline" as a worthy slogan, as a good label for an empty bottle. Within six years this man, with a professional opposition which first barked like Pomeranians at his heels and then ran away to bark abroad, has made the label good, has filled the bottle, has turned concept into reality.

It is quite possible for those who oppose the concept to say that the reality of the new spirit of Italy and its extent of full acceptance by the people may exist in the mind of Mussolini, but does not spring out of the people themselves but it is quite untrue as all know who really know.

He throws up his somewhat stubby, meaty, short-fingered hands, strong and yet rather ghostlike when one touches them, and laughs. Like Roosevelt. No one can spend much time with him without thinking that after all there are two kinds of leaders—outdoor and indoor leaders—and that the first are somewhat more magnetic, more lasting and more boyish and likable for their power than the indoor kind.

Mussolini, like Roosevelt, gives the impression of an energy which cannot be bottled, which bubbles up and over like an eternally effervescent, irrepressible fluid. At these moments one remembers his playing of the violin, his fencing, his playful, mischievous humour, the dash of his courage, his contact with animals, his success in making gay marching songs for the old drab struggles of mankind with the soil, with the elements, with ores in the earth, and the pathways of the seas. In the somber conclusions of the student statesman and in the sweetness of the sentimentalist statesman there is little joy; unexpected joy is found in the leadership of a Mussolini. Battle becomes a game. The game becomes a romp. It is absurd to say that Italy groans under discipline. Italy chortles with it! It is victory!

He is a Spartan too. Perhaps we need them in the world to-day; especially that type whose first interest is the development of the power and the happiness of a race.

The last time I took leave of Mussolini he came prowling across the room as I went toward the door. His scowl had gone. The evening had come. There had been a half hour of quiet conversation. The strained expression had fallen from his face. He came toward me and rubbed his shoulder against the wall. He was relaxed and quiet.

I remembered Lord Curzon's impatience with him long ago, when Mussolini had first come into power, and Curzon used to refer to him as "that absurd man."

Time has shown that he was neither violent nor absurd. Time has shown that he is both wise and humane.

It takes the world a long time to see what has been dropped into the pan of its old scales!

In terms of fundamental and permanent effect upon the largest number of human beings—whether one approves or detests him—the Duce is now the greatest figure of this sphere and time. One closes the door when one leaves him, feeling, as when Roosevelt was left, that one could squeeze something of him out of one's clothes.

He is a mystic to himself.

I imagine, as he reaches forth to touch reality in himself, he finds that he himself has gone a little forward, isolated, determined, illusive, untouchable, just out of reach—onward!

CHAPTER I

A SULPHUROUS LAND

ALMOST all the books published about me put squarely and logically on the first page that which may be called my birth certificate. It is usually taken from my own notes.

Well, then here it is again. I was born on July 29, 1883, at Varano di Costa. This is an old hamlet. It is on a hill. The houses are of stone, and sunlight and shade give these walls and roofs a variegated color which I well remember. The hamlet, where the air is pure and the view agreeable, overlooks the village of Dovia, and Dovia is in the commune, or county, of Predappio in the northeast of Italy.

It was at two o'clock Sunday afternoon when I came into the world. It was by chance the festival day of the patron saint of the old church and parish of Caminate. On the structure a ruined tower overlooks proudly and solemnly the whole plain of Forli—a plain which slopes gently down from the Apennines, with their snow-clad tops in winter, to the undulating bottoms of Ravaldino, where the mists gather in summer nights.

Let me add to the atmosphere of a country dear to me by bringing again to my memory the old district of Predappio. It was a country well known in the thirteenth century, giving birth to illustrious families during the Renaissance. It is a sulphurous land. From it the ripening grapes make a strong wine of fine perfume. There are many springs of iodine waters. And on that plain and those undulating foothills and mountain spurs, the ruins of mediæval castles and towers thrust up their gray-yellow walls toward the pale blue sky in testimony of the virility of centuries now gone.

Such was the land, dear to me because it was my soil. Race and soil are strong influences upon us all.

As for my race—my origin—many persons have studied and analyzed its hereditary aspects. There is nothing very difficult in tracing my genealogy, because from parish records it is very easy for friendly research to discover that I came from a lineage of honest people. They tilled the soil, and because of its fertility they earned the right to their share of comfort and ease.

Going further back, one finds that the Mussolini family was prominent in the city of Bologna in the thirteenth century. In 1270 Giovanni Mussolini was the leader of this warlike, aggressive commune. His partner in the rule of Bologna in the days of armored knights was Fulcieri Paolucci de Calboli, who belonged to a family from Predappio also, and even to-day that is one of the distinguished families.

The destinies of Bologna and the internal struggles of its parties and factions, following the eternal conflicts and changes in all struggles for power, caused, at last, the exile of the Mussolinis to Argelato. From there they scattered into neighboring provinces. One may be

The house at Varano di Costa, in Predappio, where Mussolini was born.

sure that in that era their adventures were varied and sometimes in the flux of fortune brought them to hard times. I have never discovered news of my forbears in the seventeenth century. In the eighteenth century there was a Mussolini in London. Italians never hesitate to venture abroad with their genius or their labors. The London Mussolini was a composer of music of some note and perhaps it is from him that I inherit the love of the violin, which even to-day in my hands gives comfort to moments of relaxation and creates for me moments of release from the realities of my days.

Later, in the nineteenth century, the family tie became more clearly defined; my own grandfather was a lieutenant of the National Guard.

My father was a blacksmith—a heavy man with strong, large, fleshy hands. Alessandro the neighbors called him. Heart and mind were always filled and pulsing with socialistic theories. His intense sympathies mingled with doctrines and causes. He discussed them in the evening with his friends and his eyes filled with light. The international movement attracted him and he was closely associated with names known among the followers of social causes in Italy—Andrea Costa, Balducci, Amilcare, Cipriani and even the more tender and pastoral spirit of Giovanni Pascoli. So come and go men whose minds and souls are striving for good ends. Each conference seems to them to touch the fate of the world; each talisman seems to promise salvation; each theory pretends to immortality.

The Mussolinis had left some permanent marks. In

Bologna there is still a street named for that family and not long ago a tower and a square bore the name. Somewhere in the heraldic records there is the Mussolini coat of arms. It has a rather pleasing and perhaps magnificent design. There are six black figures in a yellow field—symbols of valor, courage, force.

My childhood, now in the mists of distance, still yields those flashes of memory that come back with a familiar scene, an aroma which the nose associates with damp earth after a rain in the springtime, or the sound of footsteps in the corridor. A roll of thunder may bring back the recollection of the stone steps where a little child who seems no longer any part of oneself used to play in the afternoon.

Out of those distant memories I receive no assurance that I had the characteristics which are supposed traditionally to make parents overjoyed at the perfection of their offspring. I was not a good boy, nor did I stir the family pride or the dislike of my own young associates in school by standing at the head of my class.

I was then a restless being; I am still.

Then I could not understand why it is necessary to take time in order to act. Rest for restfulness meant nothing to me then any more than now.

I believe that in those youthful years, just as now, my day began and ended with an act of will—by will put into action.

Looking back, I cannot see my early childhood as being either praiseworthy or as being more than normal in every direction. I remember my father as a dark-haired, good-natured man, not slow to laugh, with strong features and steady eyes. I remember that near the house where I was born, with its stone wall with moss green in the crevices, there was a small brook and farther on a little river. Neither had much water in it, but in autumn and other seasons when there were unexpected heavy rains they swelled in fury and their torrents were joyous challenges to me. I remember them as my first play spots. With my brother, Arnaldo, who is now the publisher of the daily *Popolo d'Italia*, I used to try my skill as a builder of dams to regulate the current. When birds were in their nesting season I was a frantic hunter for their concealed and varied homes with their eggs or young birds. Vaguely I sensed in all this the rhythm of natural progress—a peep into a world of eternal wonder, of flux and change. I was passionately fond of young life; I wished to protect it then as I do now.

My greatest love was for my mother. She was so quiet, so tender, and yet so strong. Her name was Rosa. My mother not only reared us but she taught primary school. I often thought, even in my earliest appreciation of human beings, of how faithful and patient her work was. To displease her was my one fear. So, to hide from her my pranks, my naughtiness or some result of mischievous frolic, I used to enlist my grandmother and even the neighbors, for they understood my panic lest my mother should be disturbed.

The alphabet was my first practice in worldly affairs and I learned it in a rush of enthusiasm. Without knowing why, I found myself wishing to attend school —the school at Predappio, some two miles away. It was taught by Marani, a friend of my father. I walked to and fro and was not displeased that the boys of Predappio resented at first the coming of a stranger boy from another village. They flung stones at me and I returned their fire. I was all alone and against many. I was often beaten, but I enjoyed it with that universality of enjoyment with which boys the world around make friendship by battle and arrive at affection through missiles. Whatever was my courage, my body bore its imprints. I concealed the bruises from my mother to shelter her from the knowledge of the world in which I had begun to find expression and to which I supposed she was such a stranger. At the evening repast I probably often feared to stretch out my hand for the bread lest I expose a wound upon my young wrist.

After a while this all ended. War was over and the pretense of enmity—a form of play—faded into nothing and I had found fine schoolmates of my own age.

The call of old life foundations is strong. I felt it when only a few years ago a terrific avalanche endangered the lives of the inhabitants of Predappio. I took steps to found a new Predappio—Predappio Nuovo. My nature felt a stirring for my old home. And I remembered that as a child I had sometimes looked at the plain where the River Rabbi is crossed by the old highway to Mendola and imagined there a flourishing town. To-day that town—Predappio Nuovo—is in full process of development; on its masonry gate there is carved the symbol of Fascism and words expressing my clear will.

When I was graduated from the lower school I was sent to a boarding school. This was at Faenza, the town noted for its pottery of the fifteenth century. The school was directed by the Salesiani priests. I was about to enter into a period of routine, of learning the ways of the disciplined human herd. I studied, slept well and grew. I was awake at daylight and went to bed when the evening had settled down and the bats flew.

This was a period of bursting beyond the bounds of my own little town. I had begun to travel. I had begun to add length after length to that tether which binds one to the hearth and the village.

I saw the town of Forli—a considerable place which should have impressed me but failed to do so. But Ravenna! Some of my mother's relatives lived in the plain of Ravenna and on one summer vacation we set out together to visit them. After all, it was not far away, but to my imagination it was a great journey—almost like a journey of Marco Polo—to go over hill and dale to the edge of the sea—the Adriatic!

I went with my mother to Ravenna and carefully visited every corner of that city steeped in the essences of antiquity. From the wealth of Ravenna's artistic treasures there rose before me the beauty and fascination of her history and her name through the long centuries. Deep feelings remain now, impressed then upon me. I experienced a profound and significant enlarging of my concepts of life, beauty and the rise of civilizations. The tomb of Dante, inspiring in its quiet hour of noon; the basilica of San Apollinare; the Candiano canal, with the pointed sails of fishing-boats at its mouth; and then the beauty of the Adriatic moved me—touched something within me.

I went back with something new and undying. My mind and spirit were filled with expanding consciousness. And I took back also a present from my relatives. It was a wild duck, powerful in flight. My brother Arnaldo and I, on the little river at home, put forth patient efforts to tame the wild duck.

CHAPTER II

MY FATHER

MY father took a profound interest in my development. Perhaps I was much more observed by his paternal attention than I thought. We became much more knit together by common interests as my mind and body approached maturity. In the first place I became fascinated by the steam threshing machines which were just then for the first time being introduced into our agricultural life. With my father I went to work to learn the mechanism, and tasted, as I had never tasted before, the quiet joy of becoming a part of the working creative world. Machinery has its fascinations and I can understand how an engineer of a railway locomotive or an oiler in the hold of a ship may feel that a machine has a personality, sometimes irritating, sometimes friendly, with an inexhaustible generosity and helpfulness, power and wisdom.

But manual labor in my father's blacksmith shop was not the only common interest we shared. It was inevitable that I should find a clearer understanding of those political and social questions which in the midst of discussions with the neighbors had appeared to me as unfathomable, and hence a stupid world of words. I could not follow as a child the arguments of lengthy debates around the table, nor did I grasp the reasons for the watchfulness and measures taken by the police. But now in an obscure way it all appeared as connected with the lives of strong men who not only dominate their own lives but also the lives of their fellow creatures. Slowly but fatally I was turning my spirit and my mind to new political ideals destined to flower for a time.

I began with young eyes to see that the tiny world about me was feeling uneasiness under the pinch of necessity. A deep and secret grudge was darkening the hearts of the common people. A country gentry of mediocrity in economic usefulness and of limited intellectual contribution were hanging upon the multitudes a weight of unjustified privileges. These were sad, dark years not only in my own province but for other parts of Italy. I must have the marks upon my memory of the resentful and furtive protests of those who came to talk with my father, some with bitterness of facts, some with a newly devised hope for some reform.

It was then, while I was still in my early teens, that my parents, after many serious talks, ending with a rapid family counsel, turned the rudder of my destiny in a new direction. They said that my manual work did not correspond to their ambitions for me, to their ability to aid me, nor did it fit my own capacities. My mother had a phrase which remains in my ears: "He promises something."

At the time I was not very enthusiastic about that conclusion; I had no real hunger for scholastic endeavor. I did not feel that I would languish if I did not go to a

Mussolini's mother and father, Rosa and Alessandro Mussolini.

normal school and did not prepare to become a teacher.
But my family were right. I had developed some capacities as a student and could increase them.

I went to the normal school at a place called Forlimpopoli. I remember my arrival in that small city.
The citizens were cheerful and industrious, good at bargaining—tradesmen and middlemen. The school, however, had a greater distinction; it was conducted by Valfredo Carducci, brother of the great writer Giosue Carducci, who at that time was harvesting his laurels because of his poetry and his inspiration drawn from Roman classicism.

There was a long stretch of study ahead of me; to become a master—to have a teacher's diploma—meant six years of books and pencils, ink and paper. I confess that I was not very assiduous. The bright side of those years of preparation to be a teacher came from my interest in reforming educational methods, and even more in an interest begun at that time and maintained ever since, an intense interest in the psychology of human masses—the crowd.

I was, I believe, unruly; and I was sometimes indiscreet. Youth has its passing restlessness and follies. Somehow I succeeded in gaining forgiveness. My masters were understanding and on the whole generous. But I have never been able to make up my mind how much of the indulgence accorded to me came from any hope they had in me or how much came from the fact that my father had acquired an increasing reputation for his moral and political integrity.

So the diploma came to me at last. I was a teacher! Many are the men who have found activity in political life who began as teachers. But then I saw only the prospect of the hard road of job hunting, letters of recommendation, scraping up a backing of influential persons and so on.

In a competition for a teacher's place at Gualtieri, in the province of Reggio Emilia, I was successful. I had my taste of it. I taught for a year. On the last day of the school year I dictated an essay. I remember its thesis. It was: "By Persevering You Arrive." For that I obtained the praise of my superiors.

So school was closed. I did not want to go back to my family. There was a narrow world for me, with affection to be sure, but restricted. There in Predappio one could neither move nor think without feeling at the end of a short rope. I had become conscious of myself, sensitive to my future. I felt the urge to escape.

Money I had not—merely a little. Courage was my asset. I would be an exile. I crossed the frontier; I entered Switzerland.

It was in this wander-life, now full of difficulties, toil, hardship and restlessness, that developed something in me. It was the milestone which marked my maturity. I entered into this new era as a man and politician. My confident soul began to be my support. I conceded nothing to pious demagoguery. I allowed myself, humble as was my figure, to be guided by my innate proudness and I saw myself in my own mental dress.

To this day I thank difficulties. They were more numerous than the nice, happy incidents. But the latter gave me nothing. The difficulties of life have hardened my spirit. They have taught me how to live.

For me it would have been dreadful and fatal if on my journey forward I had by chance fallen permanently into the chains of comfortable bureaucratic employment. How could I have adapted myself to that smug existence in a world bristling with interest and significant horizons? How could I have tolerated the halting progress of promotions, comforted and yet irritated by the thoughts of an old-age pension at the end of the dull road? Any comfortable cranny would have sapped my energies. These energies which I enjoy were trained by obstacles and even by bitterness of soul. They were made by struggle, not by the joys of the pathway.

My stay in Switzerland was a welter of difficulties. It did not last long, but it was angular, with harsh points. I worked with skill as a laborer. I worked usually as a mason and felt the fierce, grim pleasure of construction. I made translations from Italian into French and vice versa. I did whatever came to hand. I looked upon my friends with interest or affection or amusement.

Above all, I threw myself headforemost into the politics of the emigrant—of refugees, of those who sought solutions.

In politics I never gained a penny. I detest those who live like parasites, sucking away at the edges of social struggles. I hate men who grow rich in politics.

I knew hunger—stark hunger—in those days. But I

never bent myself to ask for loans and I never tried to inspire the pity of those around me, nor of my own political companions. I reduced my needs to a minimum and that minimum—and sometimes less—I received from home.

With a kind of passion, I studied social sciences. Pareto was giving a course of lectures in Lausanne on political economy. I looked forward to every one. The mental exercise was a change from manual labor. My mind leaped toward this change and I found pleasure in learning. For here was a teacher who was outlining the fundamental economic philosophy of the future.

Between one lesson and another I took part in political gatherings. I made speeches. Some intemperance in my words made me undesirable to the Swiss authorities. They expelled me from two cantons. The university courses were over. I was forced into new places, and not until 1922 at the Conference of Lausanne, after I was Premier of Italy, did I see again some of my old haunts, filled with memories colorful or drab.

To remain in Switzerland became impossible. There was the yearning for home which blossoms in the hearts of all Italians. Furthermore, the compulsory service in the army was calling me. I came back. There were greetings, questions, all the incidents of the return of an adventurer—and then I joined the regiment—a Bersaglieri regiment at the historic city of Verona. The Bersaglieri wear green cock feathers in their hats; they are famous for their fast pace, a kind of monotonous and ground-covering dogtrot, and for their discipline and spirit.

I liked the life of a soldier. The sense of willing subordination suited my temperament. I was preceded by a reputation of being restless, a fire eater, a radical, a revolutionist. Consider then the astonishment of the captain, the major, and my colonels, who were compelled to speak of me with praise! It was my opportunity to show serenity of spirit and strength of character.

Verona, where my regiment was garrisoned, was and always will remain a dear Venetian city, reverberating with the past, filled with suggestive beauties. It found in my own temperament an echo of infinite resonance. I enjoyed its aromas as a man, but also as a private soldier I entered with vim into all the drills and the most difficult exercises. I found an affectionate regard for the mass, for the whole, made up of individuals, for its maneuvers and the tactics, the practice of defense and attack.

My capacity was that of a simple soldier; but I used to weigh the character, abilities and individualities of those who commanded me. All Italian soldiers to a certain extent do this. I learned in that way how important it is for an officer to have a deep knowledge of military matters and to develop a fine sensitiveness to the ranks, and to appreciate in the masses of our men our stern Latin sense of discipline and to be susceptible to its enchantments.

I can say that in every regard I was an excellent soldier. I might have taken up the courses for noncommissioned officers. But destiny, which dragged me from my father's blacksmith shop to teaching and from teaching to exile and from exile to discipline, now decreed that I should not become a professional soldier. I had to ask for leave. At the time I swallowed the greatest sorrow in my life; it was the death of my mother.

One day my captain took me aside. He was so considerate that I felt in advance something impending. He asked me to read a telegram. It was from my father. My mother was dying! He urged my return. I rushed to catch the first train.

I arrived too late. My mother was in death's agony. But from an almost imperceptible nod of her head I realized that she knew I had come. I saw her endeavor to smile. Then her head slowly drooped and she had gone.

All the independent strength of my soul, all my intellectual or philosophical resources—even my deep religious beliefs—were helpless to comfort that great grief. For many days I was lost. From me had been taken the one dear and truly near living being, the one soul closest and eternally adherent to my own responses.

Words of condolence, letters from my friends, the attempt to comfort me by other members of the family, filled not one tiny corner of that great void, nor opened even one fraction of an inch of the closed door.

My mother had suffered for me—in so many ways. She had lived so many hours of anxiety for me because of my wandering and pugnacious life. She had predicted my ascent. She had toiled and hoped too much and died before she was yet forty-eight years old. She had, in her quiet manner, done superhuman labors.

She might be alive now. She might have lived and enjoyed, with the power of her maternal instinct, my political success. It was not to be. But to me it is a comfort to feel that she, even now, can see me and help me in my labors with her unequaled love.

I, alone, returned to the regiment. I finished my last months of military service. And then my life and my future were again distended with uncertainty.

I went to Opeglia as a teacher again, knowing all the time that teaching did not suit me. This time I was a master in a middle school. After a period, off I went with Cesare Battisti, then chief editor of the *Popolo*. Later he was destined to become one of the greatest of our national heroes—he who gave his life, he who was executed by the enemy Austrians in the war, he who then was giving his thought and will to obtaining freedom of the province of Trento from the rule of Austria. His nobility and proud soul are always in my memory. His aspirations as a socialist-patriot called to me.

One day I wrote an article maintaining that the Italian border was not at Ala, the little town which in those days stood on the old frontier between our kingdom and the old Austria. Whereupon I was expelled from Austria by the Imperial and Royal Government of Vienna.

I was becoming used to expulsions. Once more a wanderer, I went back to Forli.

The itch of journalism was in me. My opportunity was before me in the editorship of a local socialist newspaper. I understood now that the Gordian knot of Italian political life could only be undone by an act of violence.

Therefore I became the public crier of this basic, partisan, warlike conception. The time had come to shake the souls of men and fire their minds to thinking and acting. It was not long before I was proclaimed the mouthpiece of the intransigent revolutionary socialist faction. I was only twenty-nine years old when at Reggio Emilia at the Congress in 1912, two years before the World War began, I was nominated as director of the *Avanti*. It was the only daily of the socialist cause and was published in Milan.

I lost my father just before I left for my new office. He was only fifty-seven. Nearly forty of those years had been spent in politics. His was a rectangular mind, a wise spirit, a generous heart. He had looked into the eyes of the first internationalist agitators and philosophers. He had been in prison for his ideas.

The Romagna—that part of Italy from which we all came—a spirited district with traditions of a struggle for freedom against foreign oppressions—knew my father's merit. He wrestled year in and year out with endless difficulties and he had lost the small family patrimony by helping friends who had gone beyond their depth in the political struggle.

Prestige he had among all those who came into contact with him. The best political men of his day liked him and respected him. He died poor. I believe his foremost desire was to live to see his sons correctly estimated by public opinion.

At the end he understood at last that the old eternal traditional forces such as capital could not be permanently overthrown by a political revolution. He turned his attention at the end toward bettering the souls of individuals. He wanted to make mankind true of heart and sensitive to fraternity. Many were the speeches and articles about him after his death; three thousand of the men and women he had known followed his body to the grave. My father's death marked the end of family unity for us, the family.

CHAPTER III

THE BOOK OF LIFE

I PLUNGED forward into big politics when I settled in Milan at the head of the Avanti. My brother Arnaldo went on with his technical studies and my sister Edvige, having the offer of an excellent marriage, went to live with her husband in a little place in Romagna called Premilcuore. Each one of us took up for himself the torn threads of the family. We were separated, but in touch. We did not reunite again, however, until August 1914, when we met to discuss politics and war. War had come—war—that female of dreads and fascinations.

Up till then I had worked hard to build up the circulation, the influence and the prestige of the Avanti. After some months the circulation had increased to more than one hundred thousand.

I then had a dominant situation in the party. But I can say that I did not yield an inch to demagoguery. I have never flattered the crowd, nor wheedled any one; I spoke always of the costs of victories—sacrifice and sweat and blood.

I was living most modestly with my family, with my wife Rachele, wise and excellent woman who has followed me with patience and devotion across all the wide vicissitudes of my life. My daughter Edda was then the joy of our home. We had nothing to want. I saw myself in the midst of fierce struggle, but my family did represent and always has represented to me an oasis of security and refreshing calm.

Those years before the World War were filled by political twists and turns. Italian life was not easy. Difficulties were many for the people. The conquest of Tripolitania had exacted its toll of lives and money in a measure far beyond our expectation. Our lack of political understanding brought at least one riot a week. During one ministry of Giolitti I remember thirty-three. They had their harvest of killed and wounded and of corroding bitterness of heart. Riots and upheavals among day laborers, among the peasants in the valley of the Po, riots in the south—even separatist movements in our islands. And in the meantime, above all this atrophy of normal life, there went on the tournament and joust of political parties struggling for power.

I thought then, as I think now, that only the common denominator of a great sacrifice of blood could have restored to all the Italian nation an equalization of rights and duties. The attempt at revolution—the Red Week—was not revolution as much as it was chaos. No leaders! No means to go on! The middle class and the bourgeoisie gave us another picture of their insipid spirit.

We were in June then, picking over our own affairs with a microscope.

Suddenly the murder of Serajevo came from the blue.

In July—the war.

Up till that event my progress had been somewhat
diverse, my growth of capacity somewhat varied. In
looking back one has to weigh the effect upon one of
various influences commonly supposed powerful.

It is a general conviction that good or bad friends can
decisively alter the course of a personality. Perhaps it
may be true for those fundamentally weak in spirit
whose rudders are always in the hands of other steers-
men. During my life, I believe, neither my school
friends, my war friends, nor my political friends ever
had the slightest influence upon me. I have listened always with intense interest to their words, their suggestions and sometimes to their advice, but I am sure that
whenever I took an extreme decision I have obeyed only
the firm commandment of will and conscience which
came from within.

I do not believe in the supposed influence of books. I
do not believe in the influence which comes from perus-
ing the books about the lives and characters of men.

For myself, I have used only one big book.

For myself, I have had only one great teacher.

The book is life—lived.

The teacher is day-by-day experience.

The reality of experience is far more eloquent than
all the theories and philosophies on all the tongues and
on all the shelves.

I have never, with closed eyes, accepted the thoughts
of others when they were estimating events and realities
either in the normal course of things or when the situa-

tion appeared exceptional. I have searched, to be sure, with a spirit of analysis the whole ancient and modern history of my country. I have drawn parallels because I wanted to explore to the depths on the basis of historical fact the profound sources of our national life and of our character, and to compare our capacities with those of other people.

For my supreme aim I have had the public interest. If I spoke of life I did not speak of a concept of my own life, my family life or that of my friends. I spoke and thought and conceived of the whole Italian life taken as a synthesis—as an expression of a whole people.

I do not wish to be misunderstood, for I give a definite value to friendship, but it is more for sentimental reasons than for any logical necessity either in the realm of politics or that of reasoning and logic. I, perhaps more than most men, remember my school friends. I have followed their various careers. I keep in my memory all my war friends, and teachers and superiors and assistants. It makes little difference whether these friendships were with commanding officers or with typical workers of our soil.

On my soldier friends the life of trench warfare— hard and fascinating—has left, as it has upon me, a profound effect. Great friendships are not perfected on school benches, nor in political assemblies. Only in front of the magnitude and the suggestiveness of danger, only after having lived together in the anxieties and torments of war, can one weigh the soundness of a friendship or measure in advance how long it is destined to go on.

In politics, Italian life has had a rather short panorama of men. All know one another. I have not forgotten those who in other days were my companions in the socialistic struggle. Their friendship remains, provided they on their part acknowledge the need to make amends for many errors, and provided they have been able to understand that my political evolution has been the product of a constant expansion, of a flow from springs always nearer to the realities of living life and always further away from the rigid structures of sociological theorists.

My Fascist friends live always in my thoughts. I believe the younger ones have a special place there. The organization of Fascism was marked and stamped with youth. It has youth's spirit and it gathered youth, which, like a young orchard, has many years of productiveness for the future.

Though it appears that the obligations of governing increase around me every day, I never forget those who were with me—the generous and wise builders, the unselfish and faithful collaborators, the devoted soldiers of a new Fascist Italy. I follow step by step their personal and public fortunes.

Some minds appear curious as to what territories my reading has explored. I have never attached my name or my mind to a certain school, and as I have already said, I never believed that books were absolute and sure viaticums of life.

I have read the Italian authors, old and new—thinkers, politicians, artists. I have always been attracted by the study of our Renaissance in all its aspects. The nineteenth century, with its artistic and spiritual contrasts, classicism and romanticism and their contrasts, has held my attention. I have studied thoroughly the period of our history called *risorgimento* in its moral and political essence.

I have analyzed with great care all the development of our intellectual life from 1870 up to this moment.

These studies have occupied the most serene hours of my day.

Among foreign writers, I have meditated much upon the work of the German thinkers. I have admired the French. One of the books that interested me most was the "Psychology of the Crowd" by Gustave Lebon. The intellectual life of the Anglo-Saxons interests me especially because of the organized character of its culture and its scholastic taste and flavor.

But all that I have read and am reading is only a picture that is unfolded before my eyes without giving me an impression strong enough to make an incision in me. I draw out only the cardinal points that give me above all and first of all the necessary elements for the comparison of the essence of the different nations.

I am desperately Italian. I believe in the function of Latinity.

I came to these conclusions after and through a critical study of the German, Anglo-Saxon and Slavonic history and that of the world; nor have I for obvious reasons neglected the history of the other continents.

The American people, by their sure and active creative lines of life, have touched, and touch, my sensibility. For I am a man of government and of party. I endlessly admire those who make out of creative work a law of life, those who win with the ability of their genius and not with the intrigue of their eloquence. I am for those who seek to make technic perfect in order to dominate the elements and give to men more sure footings for the future.

I do not respect—I even hate—those men that leech a tenth of the riches produced by others.

The American nation is a creative nation, sane, with straight-lined ideas. When I talk with men of the United States it does not occur to me to use diplomacy for winning or persuading them. The American spirit is crystalline. One has to know how to take it and possibly win it over with a watchful responsiveness rather than with cunning words. As the reserves of wealth are gone now from the continents to North America, it is right that a large part of the attention of the world should be concentrated upon the activity of this nation that has men of great value, economists of real wisdom and scholars that are outlining the basis of a new science and a new culture. I admire the discipline of the American people and their sense of organization. Certainly every nation has its periods. The United States is now in the golden age. It is necessary to study these tendencies and their results, and this is not only in the interest of America but in the interest of the world.

America, a land harboring so many of our emigrants, still calls to the spirit of new youth.

I look to her youth for her destinies and the preservation of her growing ideals, just as I look to the youth of Italy for the progress of the Fascist state. It is not easy to remember always the importance of youth. It is not easy to retain the spirit of youth.

It was fortunate for me that in the trenches of the Carso—one of the bloodiest and most terrible spots of all the Allied battle fronts and in the vicissitudes of difficult experiences in the struggle with life, I did not leave my own youth behind.

CHAPTER IV

WAR AND ITS EFFECT UPON A MAN

I WRITE of war and my experience in and with war. I write of popular misconceptions as to war. I write of my convictions as to war. And I write of war from two points of view—the politics of the world and the reality of the trenches, where I have been and have learned the torture of pain.

It is impossible for me to show my development and feelings from war without showing how my nation entered war, felt war and accepted war. My psychology was the Italian psychology. I lived it and I cannot suppress it.

It was nonsense to believe that war came unheralded and as a new experience.

The European war, which suddenly burst out in 1914 during a period of apparent economic and moral peacefulness, was not a sudden return to barbarism, as many optimistic socialists and believers in democracy wished —and still to this day wish—people to believe. One must not forget that in 1904 and 1905 Russia fought with Japan a long, disastrous and exhausting war. In 1911 there was the Libyan war. In 1912 and 1913 two Balkan Wars had kept the awakened attention of Europe on the destinies of these nations. These wars had in them the characteristics of an extraordinary drama, as in the incident of Lule-Burgas and in the siege of Adrianople.

The real truth of the matter was that an intense spirit of war was all over Europe—in the air—and everybody breathed it. It was the imponderable; we were at the dawn of a new tragic period of the history of mankind. The beginning of that hard historic event, the World War, was at hand. The gigantic development drew in peoples and continents. It compelled tens of millions of men to live in the trenches, to fight inch by inch for years over the bloody theatre of tragic conflict. Millions of dead and wounded, victories and defeats, complex interests—moral or immoral—spirit of resentment and hate, bonds of friendship and disillusionments—all that chaotic and passionate world which lived and made the Great War was part of a cyclopic ensemble which is difficult to grasp, to define, to circumscribe in mere autobiographic memoirs like these.

When one thinks that Germany alone has already published on the war sixty official books, and considers many that the other nations have published or will publish, one may lose himself in the labyrinth of speculative thoughts. This tremendous chaos gave birth among the defeated nations to the dissolving intellectual scepticism from which sprang the philosophy of realities.

Therefore I proceed by impression, by remembrances. I force my memory to build up, in a logical line running parallel to my thoughts and actions, the rich picture and the innumerable interlocking events which took place in the most tortured period that humanity ever knew. I was intimately entwined with it.

The tragedy of Serajevo, the murder of the Archduke Francis Ferdinand, heir to the throne of Austria-Hungary, and his wife, created a panic in the public opinion of the whole of Europe. Remember that I was then editor of an internationalist-socialist daily. That which wounded the sensitiveness of the various nations was the lightning rapidity of the tragedy. I could see the mathematical efficiency of the organizations which made possible the plans and success of the murder in spite of all the exceptional precautions taken by the police of Austria-Hungary. I realized that Europe was in sympathy with the restlessness of Serbia against the old Hapsburg monarchy. After the annexation of Bosnia-Herzegovina by Austria, that region never had a minute's peace. The Serbian mentality, which worked —and still does—itself along the subterranean tunnels of secret societies, gave from time to time unpleasant surprises to Austria-Hungary, and the large empire was suffering from it. But no more than a thoroughbred is disturbed by flies.

The tragedy of Serajevo, however, appeared to me to be the last straw. Every one understood that Austria would act. Strong measures! All the embassies, all the different political parties of Europe, realized the gravity of the case and its terrible consequences. They went feverishly to work to find a possible solution. And we looked on!

In Italy the echo of the murder of Serajevo aroused

only curiosity and a thirst for more news. Even when the corpses of the archduke and his wife were taken into the Gulf of Triest, which was lighted up the whole night with tremendous torches, the impression on Italians, even those still under Austrian rule, was no deeper than it would have been in the presence of a spectacular epilogue of a theatrical tragedy.

Francis Ferdinand was an enemy of Italy. I thought that he always underestimated our race. He was not able to sense the heart throbs of the people of Italian blood still under his flag. He could not weigh the power of race consciousness. He was cherishing the dream of a monarchy melting three races together. Races, I knew, are difficult to melt. Francis Ferdinand enjoyed the display of his antipathy toward Italy. He took interest in the affairs of Italy only to seek a possible solution for the question of the temporal power of the Pope. It was said that in the secrecy of his court and among his religious advisers he contemplated the creation of a papal city in Rome with an outlet on the sea.

Though deeply a Catholic, like myself, he accepted of Christianity only the hard, familiar, autocratic ideals which were the base of the old despotism forming the platform of autocratic government, but were incapable of speaking to souls. In psychological makeup, this small, snarling archduke believed himself to be specially anointed by God to rule over subjects. He put fear in the hearts of smaller nations bordering his domain. His death gave surprise; it gave no sadness to us. For obvious reasons the pathetic end of the archduchess created feelings of a more sympathetic nature. We Italians are responsive, sympathetic.

The telegram of the Kaiser to the bereaved children fed the already dramatic tune and tempo of our impressions. I saw that Germany intended steadfastly to stand back of Austria for whatever action this nation was going to take toward Serbia. It was thought that Vienna would make a formal protest to Belgrade, but no one anticipated an ultimatum of such deadliness as fatally to wound the sensibility and the honor, as well as the very freedom, of that nation. All these currents I had to watch as the young editor of the *Avanti*.

The dictatorial form of the ultimatum, the style in which it was written, brought home to the world the shocking realization that war hung in the sky. We, in Italy, had to ask whether internationalism was having a success or whether it was an unreality. I wondered and reached a conclusion.

Embassies went feverishly to work; the political parties added the pressure of their weight to the diplomatic activities. The call to arms and the clamor of gathering armies put into second line the theoretical protests of socialist and international forces.

All of us in Italy who faced hard facts rather than mouthy theories heard the call of our country—a call of loneliness. Illusions burst like bubbles. Even the convention of French and German Socialists and the murder of Jaurès in Paris were but secondary episodes. To me they appeared as fringes of the mighty and dramatic conflict toward which day by day the various nations were being drawn by destiny.

I must not forget that a few months previous to the
Great War I had heard and noted a voice raised in the
French parliament painting with pessimistic colors the
inefficiency of the French Army, both from the view-
point of economic war and the lack of modern means of
defense and offense. Clemenceau, foaming at the mouth,
was present at this discussion. He said afterward that
never in his career as a politician since 1871 had he witnessed a more dramatic séance than this one in which
the French nation was compelled fully to realize the insufficiency of its army, lacking the very means needed
for a great conflict. That was a lesson. We do not forget it.

War was ripe. The tardy and weak intervention, both
known and secret, of the Pope and of the benevolent
nations outside the circle of the Allies had no weight.
They could not stop the procession of events. War
began the first of August, 1914. It was the full bloom
of summer. Under the deep shadow of the cloud the
people of old Europe stood in awe, but fascinated as one
is fascinated by a snake.

Italy a few years previously had renewed the Triple
Alliance Treaty. It had been a marriage without respect
and without trust, brought about more in order to coun-
terbalance military power than by political necessity.
There is small difference between security and military
alliance.

The alliance with Austria and Germany gave, however, to Italy a certain latitude and a certain freedom of
movement. The Marchese of San Giuliano, who was at

the head of the Ministry of Foreign Affairs, faced by
the Austrian ultimatum to Serbia and by the scheming
to bring about war at all costs, had to play fast to keep
Italy neutral. As a matter of fact, the treaty called only
for action if one or more of the nations of the Triple
Alliance was assaulted by a nation outside that alliance.
We were kept in the dark, as I well knew. That was
enough to break the pact—to free us from further obligations to that alliance.

One of the first courageous actions in which Italy
showed the measure of her independence and strength
was recognition of this. Meanwhile the intervention of
Russia in behalf of Serbia called also France against
Germany, the ally of Austria-Hungary.

I watched England. She was pondering deeply upon
the step to take; and then, in order to keep her supremacy, and also for the sake of her pride and the sake of
humanity, she moved her formidable war machinery and
quickened the organization of new armies to snatch from
Germany's grip the control of the old Continent.

Public opinion in Italy was deeply moved, facing
war, with its German invasion of East France. There
was the description, with horrid details, of German
methods, and above all the invasion of Belgium in spite
of every sense of right and humanity. The French Army
was helplessly forced back. The future, not of one nation but of many nations, was in the scale. Of this, in
my editorial office, I was always conscious. There was
also the feeling of a common culture which was com-
pelling us to forget past and present quarrels. I could

not bear the idea that my country might abandon those who were crushed under the weight of war and unwarranted misfortune.

Germany began to influence Italian public opinion with methods of propaganda that irritated the sensitiveness of our race. That enraged me. To direct this propaganda, a great diplomat, Prince von Bülow, who knew the Italian and Roman world intimately, was sent. His aim in Italy was to ensure its neutrality for good and all.

But our nation was turning toward war. I was helping. The Socialist party, which at that time had a certain weight in Italian life, due more to weakness of other political parties than to its own strength, was uncertain what attitude to take. There it wabbled. The majority in that party stood for an absolute neutrality —a neutrality without limit of time, pledge or dignity. In that party there were many who stood openly in sympathy with Germany. I did not. A handful of intelligent and strong-willed men began to ask themselves if it was really right for Italians to lend themselves to the political aims of the King of Prussia, and if that was good for the future of Italy and of the world. I, myself, asked that question in the newspaper *Avanti*. For obvious reasons it was read avidly by every class of citizens. The putting of that question was my most distinguished effort at journalism.

It was sufficient to cause a part of public opinion to turn toward the possibility of our standing side by side with France and England in the war. We could not, and should not, forget that there were certain sentimental reasons, besides the practical reasons, advising us to review in this general conflict the old decision concerning our eastern border, which had remained open since our war with Austria in 1886.

At night I walked to my family, to my home, with pregnant questions in my mind, with deepening determination, with hardening resolution. Above all, there was my own country. I saw that internationalism was crumbling. The unit of loyalty was too large. I wrote an editorial in which I said also how utterly foolish was the idea that even if a socialist state were created, the old barriers of race and historical contentions would not go on causing wars.

Italy's borders on the eastern side reached the Judrio, but the region of Trentino illegally held by Austria entered as a wedge between Lombardy and the Venetian provinces. Our deal with the empire of Austria-Hungary was still to be closed, because the borders prophesied by Dante were dear to every Italian heart. They were still and always would be along the line of the Brenner and of the Giulian and Illyrian Alps, including Fiume and Dalmatia.

Facing this new situation, every political man, including myself, began to examine his conscience. The mere mention of this problem was sufficient to make clear and evident the hidden travail of national consciousness. I was transformed in my thought.

"Now or never!" was the war cry of Cesare Battisti, whose noble spirit and final martyrdom by Austrian execution has made him immortal in Italian hearts.

Then there was the prophetic vision of that fiery revolutionary spirit, Filippo Corridoni. With their inspiration I began to drag with me a fraction of the Socialists in favor of war. I had with me rebels of many schools, who through the dregs of their struggles would in the end now stand once more upon the indestructible vitality of our race.

The Socialist Senedrium, seeing where I was going, took the *Avanti* out of my control. I could no longer preach, by that means, intervention of Italy in the war. I faced the Socialists in our conventions. I was expelled. I held public gatherings.

I created the Fasciti—a group of daring youths who believed that intervention could be forced. Do not doubt that their actions shook deeply our political framework, existing from the time of the independence of Italy up till 1914. I was their leader.

It is interesting to-day when democracy is challenged to recall that the Liberal Democratic pacifist group, headed by Giovanni Giolitti, a man of great influence in parliament and also a shrewd organizer of political schemes, was busy in the attempt to find a formula which would solve the problem of righting the borders of Italy, but which would save our country from the burden, the sacrifice and the loss of life that every war imposes. Giolitti promised that, even without war, Italy could obtain a great deal. This "great deal" awakened a feeling of sarcasm in the generous hearts of Italians. Naturally they are realists and the enemies of all forms of political bargaining.

Italians were looking beyond those peaceful concessions and those petty betterings of the borders. They did not believe in the sincerity of this scheming. I considered it weak statesmanship—the statesmanship of compromise. There were seers who saw in the European conflict not only national advantages but the possibility of a supremacy of race. In the cycle of time, again a dramatic period had come which was making it possible for Italy by the weight of its army to deal as an equal with the leading nations of the world.

That was our chance. I wanted to seize it. It became my one thought of intensity.

The World War began on July 28, 1914. Within sixty days I severed my official connection with the Socialist party. I had already ceased to be editor of the *Avanti*.

I felt lighter, fresher. I was free! I was better prepared to fight my battles than when I was bound by the dogmas of any political organization. But I understood that I could not use with efficient strength my convictions if I was without that modern weapon, capable of all possibilities, ready to arm and to help, good for offense and defense—the newspaper.

I needed a daily paper. I hungered for one. I gathered together a few of my political friends who had followed me in the last hard struggle and we held a war council. When money alone is concerned, I am anything but a wizard. When it is a question of means or of capital to start a project, or how to finance a newspaper, I grasp only the abstract side, the political value, the spiritual essence of the thing. To me, money is detestable;

what it may do is sometimes beautiful and sometimes noble.

A few friends, bristling with ideas and ardent with faith, almost immediately found small rooms, garret-like, in the narrow street of Paolo da Cannobio, near the Piazza del Duomo in Milan. Near by there was a printing establishment. Its owner agreed to publish our newspaper at a small cost. I was mad to tell Italy and Italians the truth—their opportunity!

We had no need for great means. We wanted a newspaper that would hold the city of Milan like a fortress, with editorial articles of such value that they would be reprinted or quoted by every Italian newspaper.

Thus—and how dramatically!—the number of our readers would be multiplied. That was my passion. Our offices were quickly furnished with a desk and a few chairs. I can never cease to have affection for that intellectual dugout, the journalistic trenches from which I began to fight. A contract was signed with the printing establishment—a contract that every week was in danger of smashing for the lack of the few thousand lire needed to pay our weekly expense. But we were living on an idea.

On November 15, 1914, the first number of the *Popolo d'Italia* appeared. Even now I call this new paper my most cherished child. It was only through it, small as was its beginning, that I was able to win all the battles of my political life. I am still its director.

I could write and I may write a thousand memories of this newspaper which was born in 1914 and remained my platform up to 1922. It was an instrument for the making of me. The name of the *Popolo d'Italia* will occur over and over again. Its story in any case may be told through my personality as a political man, as a newspaper man, as a believer in this war, as a soldier, as an Italian and as a Fascist.

My first article in the *Popolo d'Italia* turned a large part of public opinion toward the intervention of Italy in the war, side by side with France and England.

Standing by me and helping my work as newspaper man were the Fascisti. They were composed of revolutionary spirits who believed in intervention. They were youths—the students of the universities, the socialist syndicalists—destroying faith in Karl Marx by their ideals. There were professional men too—and the workingmen who could still hear the real voice of the country.

And now, while Italy remained out of the war, our first legions of volunteers were organized and went to France to fight. In the Argonne fell the two sons of Ricciotti Garibaldi, Bruno and Costante, nephews of the great Garibaldi, who conquered North Sicily and Naples for United Italy. The funeral of the two heroes took place in Rome and had solemn echoes all over Italy. Again the red shirts, once distinguished as the saviors of Italy, now in the land of France, testified to the indestructibility of Latinity.

The past quarrels—not long past—of Mediterranean interests were wiped out. The hostilities of the French during the time of our war in Libya were put aside. No one remembered the episode of the French ships *Ma-*

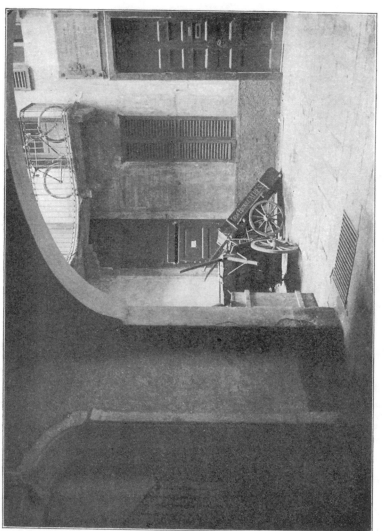

The first offices, in Milan, of the *Popolo d'Italia*, Mussolini's paper.

nouba and *Carthage*, which brought help to the Turks, who were fighting against us, in January, 1912. Everything was off. France was in danger, assaulted and invaded after the tragic rape of Belgium. This I preached and set forth. France was in danger!

Gabriele d'Annunzio, on the fifth of May, made his speech at Quarto dei Mille, near Genoa. Quarto dei Mille was the starting point of Garibaldi and his thousand northerners and other patriots who went down to Sicily to deliver Southern Italy from the yoke of the Bourbons. He, with superb eloquence, exhorted Italy to enter the war.

The spirit of the country was tuned up. The opposition of Giolitti brought about a quick decision. The crown, bound by parliamentary formulas and by the advice of its counsellors, wanting to follow strictly the literal and orthodox interpretation of the constitution, told the personal representative of the Kaiser that Italy as an old ally had been kept in the dark and thus betrayed.

The insurrection in Milan in favor of war, the strong feelings of the same flavor in Rome, Padua, Genoa and Naples, decided His Majesty Victor Emmanuel III to exclude Giovanni Giolitti and to reconfide to Salandra, who had tendered his resignation, the task of reconstituting a new ministry. I felt that I had had a part in winning this battle. Still a young unproved man, I had already a record of untrammeled freedom and power.

The new ministry spelled war. Thrown aside was the "great deal" of His Excellency Giolitti; the question now was to choose the right moment and the right way to jump into the war. We were breathing hard, our hearts were ready, we were awaiting the great hour. It came May 24, 1915. Can any one say what were my emotions at this moment of triumph?

I cannot try to narrate in one chapter all the events of the war on the Italian front. It is impossible. The war moulded me. I was forced into its dramatic unfolding in the circumscribed view-point of a mere soldier of the war. I will tell what touched me most as a soldier and indirectly as a political man.

I made up my mind to be the best soldier possible from the very day that I wore again the glorious uniform of gray-green of the regiment of Bersaglieri—the best shock troops of Italy—in which regiment I had already served during the time of my compulsory military service. I wanted to be a soldier, obedient, faithful to discipline, stretching myself with all my might to the fulfilment of my duty.

In this I felt that I succeeded. My political position brought me plenty of offers of privileges and sheltered places. I turned them down.

I wanted to create the impression of a complete and rigid consistence with an ideal. This was not a scheming on my part for personal gain; it was a deep need in my nature of what I believed and still hold on to as my life's dedication—namely, that once a man sets up to be the expounder of an idea or of a new school of thought, he must consistently and intensively live the daily life and fight battles for the doctrines that he teaches at any cost until victory—to the end!

Time has effaced many things; the easy spirit of forgetfulness has erased so much. Victory, which came after forty-one months of hard fighting, has awakened many deep resentments.

As soon as war was declared, as I have said, I asked the military authorities to accept my services as a volunteer. They answered that I could not be a volunteer. That was a tragedy. They said that they refused on the ground that an article of the military by-laws considered as possible volunteers only those who had been rejected for physical unfitness, or were exonerated for other reasons from compulsory military service. I could not be accepted as a volunteer. I was to wait my turn to be called to arms until the order from my superiors should be sent me. I was disconsolate.

Happily, my turn came quickly. On September first, only three months after Italy declared war, I donned the simple uniform of a private Bersagliere. I was sent to Brescia, in Lombardy, not far from the raids of airplanes, to drill.

Almost at once I was, to my great relief, despatched to the thick of the fighting on the high Alps. For a few months I underwent the hardest trials of my life in mountain trenches. We still had nothing to soften our hardships in the trenches or in the barracks. We were simply stumbling along. Short of everything—carrying on—muddling through! What we suffered the first months—cold, rain, mud, hunger! They did not succeed in dampening in the slightest degree my enthusiasm and my conviction as to the necessity and the inevitableness of war. They did not change the direction of one hair of my head, one thought in it.

I was chosen to be the amanuensis of headquarters. That I refused. I refused flatly. I amused myself instead by joining the most dangerous reconnoitering expeditions. It was my will and my wish. I gained through that. Within a few months I was promoted corporal by merit of war action, with a citation from my superior in these words: "Benito Mussolini, ever the first in operations of courage and audacity."

My political past, with the suspicions of cautious and sometimes unseeing authorities, still followed me; it was enough to keep my superiors from sending me to the training school for officers at Vernezzo. After one week of leave I went back to the trenches, where I remained for months. The same life, feverish, adventurous, desperate—and then typhoid fever sent me to the military hospital at Cividale. When I was better I was packed off to Ferrara for a brief, stupid period of convalescence. From there I again took my place on the high pinnacles of the Alps where at night one looking into the dark sky with its shimmering stars felt nearer to the great dome above.

My battalion was ordered to an advance post on the Carso—Section 144—to take up the offensive. I was then made one of the company of soldiers who had specialized in hand grenades. We lived only a few dozen yards from the enemy, in a perpetual and, it sometimes seemed, an eternal atmosphere of shell fire and mortal danger that would be our life forever.

After the first period of hardship I became perfectly and almost comfortably accustomed to all the terrible elements that life in the trenches involves. I read with hungry eagerness the *Popolo d'Italia*—my newspaper. I had left it in the hands of a few friends. Precipitously separated from it, as one leaves suddenly a beloved relative, I had given orders to keep alight the lamp of Italy's duty and destiny.

I commanded: "Continue always to call for war to the end."

I wrote often to my friends. Never did I let myself indulge in writing all my true feelings and opinions, because I was first of all a soldier, obeying. I found my recreation in the trenches studying the psychology of officers and troops. Later on that practice in observation became invaluable to me.

In my rough heart I held a persistent admiration for the soldiers from all corners of Italy. Many ordered to the eastern front were not convinced of the historical basis for the war; yet they knew how to obey their commanding officers with admirable discipline. Many of those officers were students of the colleges and universities. It was fine to see them striving to emulate the regulars and to prove that the old-time valor was still alive in the new Italian generation.

The fact was that war, with its heavy toll of man and materials, and with its terrific hardships, surprised us. It was far away from our Garibaldian conception of what war was. We were compelled, in breakneck haste, to modify our ideas, to change our systems of fighting and our methods of offense and defense. My heart was gladdened to see that the capacity for adaptability of our race brought marvellous and quick returns. The headquarters and all the auxiliary military organizations, particularly the medical, worked with a precision which I never have forgotten. But often, as I went over the political situation back of our armies, dark doubts were in my mind. The work and actions of the men in power and of the political organizations centred in Rome caused me deep fears. The parliamentary world seemed unable to free itself from its old faults.

The poisonous currents of non-intervention and neutrality were still spending their last strength upon us. They would not fairly face their defeat. I knew they were doing their utmost to minimize the energy and elasticity of our fighting efforts.

The foolish babblings and fears of the coffeehouse strategists, the slackers whose presence offended the families whose sons were in the war, contributed to depress the spirit of resistance. As a plain soldier, I could not understand how, for instance, Rumania could be dragged into the war with a few hundred machine guns. How could Greece be persuaded to march against the Turks, influenced by a classic dance that Isadora Duncan performed at the Piræus?

I was following, day by day, the movement of our army—the Battle of the Isonzo in 1916, the fights on the Alps. With less interest, I followed the fortunes of war in France, the unfortunate failure at the Dardanelles and the developments in the eastern section. As for Italy, never for a minute did I doubt that victory would finally come to us. Though war were to last longer than the longest estimate, though our economic power might totter under the effort and weight of the conflict, nevertheless I was sure of a final victory.

The Italian army in its various actions was led by a method of successive assaults, to shake the efficiency of the enemy. In spite of all the hardship, discipline remained intact throughout our lines. The invasion attempted on the plateaus of the Alps in 1916 was soon thrown back. The soldiers of the Carso, where I was, had all the appearance of seasoned veterans.

In such a gigantic drama, when thousands of our brothers fell, it is absurd to speak of oneself.

However, to prove once more what miseries were woven into the Italian life of politics, I was compelled from time to time to give out in the newspapers news concerning myself. This was in order to smash the suspicions of those persons who thought me hidden in some office, distributing mail and entertaining in my mind doubts of the possibility of our winning the war. I was compelled to offset this slander and to state over and over what I had done and what I was doing. I was then major corporal of the Bersaglieri and had been in the front line trenches from the beginning of the war up to February, 1917, always under arms, always facing the enemy without my faith being shaken or my convictions wavering an inch. From time to time I sent articles to the *Popolo d'Italia* exhorting to endless resistance. I pleaded for unshaken faith in final victory. For reasons of military discipline I used a *nom de plume*. Thus I found myself fighting in two ways—against the enemy without and in front of me and against the enemy of weak spirit within and behind me.

On the morning of February 22, 1917, during a bombardment of the enemy trenches in Sector 144—the sector of the hard-pressed Carso under the heaviest shell-fire—there happened one of those incidents which was a daily occurrence in trench life. One of our own grenades burst in our trench among about twenty of us soldiers. We were covered with dirt and smoke, and torn by metal. Four died. Various others were fatally wounded.

I was rushed to the hospital of Ronchi, a few miles from the enemy trenches. Doctor Piccagnoni and other surgeons took care of me with the greatest zeal. My wounds were serious. The patience and ability of the physicians succeeded in taking out of my body forty-four pieces of the grenade. Flesh was torn, bones broken. I faced atrocious pain; my suffering was indescribable. I underwent practically all my operations without the aid of an anæsthetic. I had twenty-seven operations in one month; all except two were without anæsthetics.

This infernal life of pain lasted until a furious bombardment burst into pieces one wing and part of the central building of my hospital at Ronchi. All the wounded were rushed to a far-away refuge, but my condition would not permit my removal. Unable to move, I remained for days under the intermittent fire of the enemy guns among the dirty, jagged ruins of the building. I was absolutely defenseless.

From a photograph by A. Badodi, Milan.

A photograph of Mussolini in the war, published in the *Popolo d'Italia*
Translation: The most recent snapshot of our editor and his captain taken at a
point of the extreme lines on the Carso.

In spite of all, my wounds began to heal. Better days and relief came. I received numberless telegrams of solicitude and once His Majesty the King called; his warm sense of humanity toward all soldiers and toward the victims of the war will never be forgotten by me or by Italy.

After some months I found myself in a war hospital in Milan. In August I began to walk with crutches, on which I swung about for many months. My limbs were too weak to support my weight.

I took my place as a fighter in my newspaper office. The acute situation created by the incredible and inconceivable failure of the Russian front was putting upon us new duties. It was necessary to face them. To all this there was added a subtle propaganda in the land. That despicable poison had as a slogan the vile sentence of a Socialist member of parliament: "We will desert the trenches before the winter comes."

There was need to fight to a finish these mysterious forces which were playing upon the sentiments and sufferings of the people. Soldiers, after a fortnight's furlough, were returning to the trenches in a sullen frame of mind. Life in the cities had all the characteristics of revelry. It was the psychological moment in which it was necessary to have the people feel highly the strength of authority. It was necessary that the government should stand up in its shoes.

I do not choose to make posthumous recriminations. The weakness of internal politics in 1917, the feeble parliamentary situation, the hateful socialistic propaganda, were certainly preparing the ground for events that could prove to be ruinous. And the blow came in October, 1917; it took the name of Caporetto.

Never in my life as an Italian and as a politician have I experienced a sorrow equal to that which I suffered after news of the defeat of Caporetto.

This episode, compared with other defeats in the various theatres of the Great War, certainly did not have an exceptional importance, but it was a terrific blow for Italians. This sudden breaking down of our front let a wedge of the enemy army penetrate into the high valley of the Isonzo. In the first rush of the war we had gone over the borders into old Austria, carrying on our warfare on enemy ground. We had withstood in 1916 the attack on the Alps of Asiago. We had conquered the plateau of Bainsizza. We had been ten times victorious on the Isonzo. Our sensitiveness and tormented souls were now shaken to the depths.

The moment was fearful. The Third Army, surrounded on the other side of the Isonzo, must be saved. It was imperative to stand at all costs on the Piave and to resist like stone on Mount Grappa to save the north of the Venetian provinces from being cut off from the rest of Italy. The rally of the army, followed by quick action, took place in almost no time. On Mount Grappa the Army of Iron withstood. On the Piave the enemy could not pass by. A new strength entered into play. One could feel it coming. A new spirit of war took its unfaltering stand. Once more we saw the enemy face to face, after losing Gorizia and two provinces, Belluno and Udine. We were deeply wounded, and we lived dramatic moments which seared my heart. But we may now be sure that Italy did not go through the tragic hours that many armies and other countries underwent. Compare with our disaster the general picture of the Great War—the loss of three provinces with the Battle of the Masurian Lakes, the invasion of Königsberg, the fourteen invaded departments of France and the flooding of Belgium.

I am proud that during that year of desperate moments my paper gave a higher note to the political life of the country. We raised the fighting spirit of the soldiers.

Helped by the mutilated, the wounded and the pro-war veterans, I began an active campaign of "Stand to a Finish." With fiery style I demanded on the part of the central government severe action against slackers and whosoever undermined the spirit of war. I called for the organization of a volunteer army. I asked for military rule in the north of Italy. I insisted on the suppression of socialist newspapers. I asked for a more humane treatment of the soldiers. I campaigned for war discipline—first behind us and all over the land, then at the front. This campaign developed by degrees in the news. paper, then in public meetings, in gatherings at the front. It brought results far beyond my highest hopes. The government seemed to be tugged after us by our efforts, toward resistance and victory.

Thus the winter went by. With the coming of the spring the whole Italian people stretched out their energies toward the front on the Piave and that on the Grappa.

At last! A spirit of national solidarity, deep and

alive, had become the common property both of the soldiers and of their families. A high spirit of duty and
sacrifice was the rule of life in our Italy!

We were ready in 1918 on the Piave with a heroic
army. The Arditi, the first shock troops, composed of
volunteers who went over the top with hand grenades
and daggers, was giving a unique dramatic appeal to
our aggressive spirit. In every one there was the deep
desire to efface the memory of the days of Caporetto.
We were to go back—back to where our brothers, dead
and alive, were waiting for us! The remembrance of
our dead, above all, was calling to us. Surely the wish
of our adversaries to cross the Piave could never be; it
was an idle hope, to be met and crushed by our own offensive.

Aviation continued to give service of reconnoitering
and bombardment. I could feel the soul of Italy stretching toward victory. Necessity had sharpened the more
brilliant minds. June came and with it the dawn of the
enemy's attack.

Our secret service succeeded in learning exactly the
time that the enemy would start his drive. Following
sound war strategy, our supreme command decided to
surprise the enemy, and just a few hours before the
enemy was ready to move a deluge of every description
fell on his front lines as well as the supporting lines behind. His plans were smashed. He threw bridges across
the Piave, but every one was destroyed. The Mon-
tello, which was once the key of that front and which the
enemy intended to take and use as a pincher against our

army, we held with dogged tenacity. There were oscillations for a few miles, but the battle raged on without a
stop. Our counter attacks came back always, again and
again and again. Thus after the first three days the
enemy felt that this time the Italians were like an unbreakable wall which they could not scale or batter
down!

Near Zenzon the adversary succeeded in crossing the
river as far as Monastie of Treviso, but a rapid counter
attack of a few of our brigades threw him back on the
Piave again. It turned into a disaster for the enemy, as
the river, flooded, washed away bridges and soldiers toward the sea. On the twenty-third of June, five days
after the beginning of the big battle, our supreme command assured Italy that our resistance was bound to
hold. I felt that it was a sure sign that victory was at
hand. I believe to this day that the Battle of the Piave
was one of the most decisive of the whole World War.

The enemy suffered loss beyond reckoning. About
100,000 Hungarians were sacrificed on the Piave. That
brought about deep resentment in Budapest. Among the
people of the various races in the Austrian Empire there
began discussions about the burdens that each nationality in that empire had to suffer. From them—the
enemies—each nationality felt that its treatment was
becoming intolerable.

News leaked out to us from Austria-Hungary. It
was clear that internal difficulties there were growing
every moment. The enemy's army, however, was still
holding together and under the goad of necessity was

sharpening the work of oppression on our two provinces which still remained under the weight of occupation and misfortune.

It was at this time, right after the spirit of exhilaration of victory, that I observed strange tendencies in the Italian political world. Evil activity was at hand. It needed to be exposed and suppressed. It was cloaked under the appearance of humanitarianism. It was planning to give a series of national rights to peoples who never had the consciousness and the dignity of nations —to peoples who had been for more than a century instruments of oppressing the Italian elements under Austria, under the instigation of the despotic empire. The sun of our victory was rising, but to be a complete victory, a victory that would carry our soldiers on the road to Vienna, it must not falter through false sentimentality.

This crisis was sufficient to inspire many great men still under the influence of antiquated and rusted democratic ideas to start discussions about the problems of racial differences. They always tended to favor our worst enemies. The spirit of our nationalism was attacked and dwarfed by sophisticated and pernicious applications of sentiment, irritating to our deepest feelings and to our most legitimate susceptibilities. Voices of the Italians began to say that every time Italy was on the verge of living its hour of joy, glory and victory there were always those who soiled the moment, and this often not in good faith.

Summer went by, and in October, 1918, our supreme

command, with fifty-one Italian divisions—to which were added three British, two French divisions, one American regiment and a few Czecho-Slovakian volunteers—determined to make a decisive and final drive on the Austrian front.

The strategic plan was a very wise one. The enemy's front was pierced at Sernaglia; our army rushed through the break. We started a surrounding movement, one to the left toward Trento, and one to the right toward Udine and the lower Piave. The ardent dash of our soldiers and the ability of our officers brought these movements to full success and crumbled to pieces the whole front of the enemy. The *War Bulletin* states the enormous number of prisoners, guns and war material that fell into our hands.

The army of Austria-Hungary was defeated. Its navy had suffered tremendous losses. We landed at Triest. We occupied Trento.

The final victory was not only a victory of a war. I saw more than that. It was a victory for the whole Italian race. After a thousand years we, awakened, were again giving a tangible proof of our moral and spiritual valor. We were living again on warlike tradition. Our love of country had bloomed again. We felt our formidable weight in the future of a new Europe. New generations of Italians rejoiced, for the Italian cities were once again rejoined to the country. Trento and Triest, as our race had wished so long, now were within the borders—the natural borders which Dante had prophesied and defined in the fourteenth century.

In every corner of the land the church-bells rang, saluting the new day. War, so long and so taxing, had ended!

It ended with a full undeniable victory of Italy in spite of the bankruptcy of Russia and of the abominable work of slackers and professional destroyers of ideals. For me, every family wore the badge of a dear one dead or wounded. Widows and orphans of war were proud to show the symbols of sadness and glory. We were in Trento and Triest. Fiume was half conquered, while Dalmatia was still in the scale.

Over Italy reigned almost supreme a spirit of pride and of serenity typical of those who have won. War had lasted longer than we thought, had diminished our wealth, had supposedly reduced to the minimum our future.

Victory, however, warmed our hearts and our souls. It exalted Italians and spurred them to higher work, honoring the dead as well as the living. From October to December, 1918, Italy seemed like a factory working in full blast in complete accord with progress. War had left, beyond its inevitable griefs, a deep poetical vein in our national life. No one sensed it better, no one seemed more a part of it, than I.

It was in this great historical moment immediately after a victory achieved with untold hardship that our young nation—younger as a nation than America—with traditions not yet seasoned by age, in spite of having thrown into the glowing brazier of the conflict men and wealth, was treacherously deceived. Its fundamental trustfulness was played upon in the making of the Treaty of Versailles.

This is the awful toll that Italy paid in the Great War—652,000 dead, 450,000 mutilated, 1,000,000 wounded. There is not in our country one single family which during the forty-one months of the war had not placed in the holocaust, on the altar of the country, a part of itself. I know every day, ten years later, that the mutilated, the wounded, the widows and orphans of war form a vast proportion of our population, inspiring the respect and homage of the multitude.

I never forget. We have gone through a thousand phases of internal troubles, from aberrations to a purifying revolution, yet—from Mount Stelvio to the sea, in our mountain cemeteries which the hand of time slowly effaces—there remains the most powerful citadel of the fortune of our nation and of our people. I never forget.

I had been the most tenacious believer in the war. I had fought with all my warm soul of Italian and soldier. I lived the joy of victory. I lived in the midst of the unrest of after-war. But in every event, happy or sad, I have always had as a touchstone, as a lighthouse, as a source of every advice and of deep wisdom, the memory of the dead. They are from every region and from every walk of life, even those who were under foreign yoke or emigrated to other countries. They gave their blood and were willing to offer the supreme sacrifice for the mother country. Until the time when a nation has the right of sitting with proud head among other nations, the surest sign of its strength, the highest title of its nobility, the vital food needed to reach greatness, will always be given by those who laid down their blood and life for their immortal country.

These are the marks that war made upon one's body, one's mind and one's soul.

Above all, it gave to one, who was still young, an understanding of the essences of mankind.

CHAPTER V

ASHES AND EMBERS

THE flame of war flickered and went out. But the years 1919 and 1920 that immediately followed the end of the war seemed to me the darkest and most painful periods of Italian life. Dark thunderclouds hung above our unity. The progress of Italy's unification was threatened. I watched the gathering storm.

Already disquieting events had menaced our national life. They were due to political happenings, even more than to an economic crisis. I point to the movement of the Sicilian Gasei in 1894 and the bloody demonstration in Milan in 1898. But these manifestations of rebellion were localized. Not one of them bore in it the virile germs of dissolution or of separatism. But I assert that the episodes of 1919 and 1920 had in them bacilli which if not treated heroically are deadly for the life of a civilized nation.

Everything was discussed again. We Italians opened the box of political problems and took apart the social clockwork. We pawed over everything from the crown to parliament, from the army to our colonies, from capitalistic property to the communistic soviet proposal for the federation of the regions of Italy, from schools to the papacy. The lovely structure of concord and harmony that we combatants and the wounded had dreamed that we would build after the luminous victory of October, 1918, was falling to pieces. The leaves were falling from our tree of idealism.

I felt that we were left without any cohesive force, any suggestive heroism, any remembrance, any political philosophy, sufficient to overcome and stop the factors of dissolution. I sensed the chills and heats of decay and destruction.

Already in January, 1919, the Socialists, slightly checked during the war, began, the moment the ink was drying on the armistice, their work of rebellion and blackmail. From Milan the socialistic municipality sent a special mission of help to the so-called brothers in Vienna. Sickly internationalism put forth its buds in this morbid springtime. At Triest the socialist Pittoni played an important part in the reorganization of the delivered city. In many Italian cities poor children of the old enemy Austrian and Hapsburg capital were asked to take precedence. It was a provoking sentimentality. A desire was already clear in the minds of subversives and of Liberal-Giolittians; it was to strike out of our memories the sense and feeling of our victory.

I knew those who whipped up our degeneration. They were German and Austrian spies, Russian agitators, mysterious subventions. In a few months they had led the Italian people into a state of marasmus. The economic crisis existing in every corner of the world could not be expected to spare Italy. The soldiers, like myself, returning from the war, rushed to their families. Who can describe our feelings? Such an imposing phenomenon as the demobilization of millions of men took place in the dark, without noise, in an atmosphere of throwing discipline to the winds. There were, for us, the troubles of winter and the difficulties of finding new garments and adjustments for peace.

We suffered the humiliation of seeing the banners of our glorious regiments returned to their homes without being saluted, without that warm cheer of sympathy owed to those who return from victorious war. Now it again appeared to me and to my friends as if there was in everybody an instinct to finish the game of the war, not with the idea of real victory but with content that we had lost as little as possible. Ears and spirits were ready to listen to words of peace, of humanity, of brotherhood between the nations. At night before sleep came I used to meditate and realize that we had no dam to stop this general decay of faith, this renunciation of the interests and destiny of a victorious nation. The sense of destruction penetrated very quickly and deeply the spirit of all classes. Certainly the central government was no dike to prevent the flood of weakness.

Politicians and philosophers, profiteers and losers— for at least many had lost their illusions—sharks trying to save themselves; promoters of the war trying to be pardoned; demagogues seeking popularity; spies and instigators of trouble waiting for the price of their treason; agents paid by foreign money in a few months threw the nation into an awful spiritual crisis. I saw be-

fore me with awe the gathering dusk of our end as a
nation and a people.

With my heart in tumult and with a deep sense of
bitterness corroding my soul, I could smell the danger.
Some audacious men were with me—not many. My action was at first tied to the urgent duty to fight against
one important and dark treason. Certain Italians,
blinded and having lost their memories, were led on by
some complicity and selfish desires among the Allies.
These Italians were actually setting themselves against
the mother country. Dalmatia, Italian in its origin, ardent as a saint in its faith, had been recognized to be ours
by the pact of London; Dalmatia had waited for the
victorious war with years of passion, and holding in its
bosom still the remains of Venice and of Rome, was now
lopped off from our unity. The politics of renunciation,
helped by foreigners, galloped forward. Wilson was the
distiller or supporter of theoretical formulas. He could
not comprehend Italian life or history. By his uncon-
scious aid this treason to us was nourished. Fiume, the
sacrificed town, whose people called desperately for
Italy in its manifestations in the public squares, who
sent pleading missions to our military chiefs, was occupied by corps of international troops. We were about to
lose another war trophy—the Austrian navy. Sesana,
twenty kilometers from Triest, was discussed as a possible frontier!

I said then that never in the life of any nation on the
day after victory had there been a more odious tragedy
than that of this silly renunciation. In the first months

of 1919, Italy, led on by politicians like Nitti and Albertini Salvemini, had only one frantic wish that I could see—it was to destroy every gain of victorious struggle. Its only dedication was to a denial of the borders and soil extent of the nation. It forgot our 600,000 dead and our 1,000,000 wounded. It made waste of their generous blood. These leaders wanted to satisfy foreign impulses of doubtful origin and doctrines brewed of poisons. This attempt at matricide of the motherland was abetted by Italians of perverted intellect and by professional socialists. Toward both, later on, the Fascist revolution showed so much forbearance that it was more than generosity.

I was snatched up in this fight against the returning beast of decadence. I was for our sacred rights to our own territories. Therefore I had to neglect in a degree the petty internal political life that was floundering in bewilderment and wallowing in disorder. On the international playground the stake was higher. One had to remain on the field to save what could be saved. As to internal politics, I knew very well that a strong government would quickly put in order the Socialists and the anarchists, the decadents and wreckers and the instigators of disorder. I knew at first hand their soul. It has always been the same at all times, in all ages—it is the spirit of coward wolves and ferocious sheep.

And thus one day, a few months after the Armistice, I saw at Milan a fact more disquieting and more important than I thought possible. I saw a Socialist procession, with an endless number of red flags, with thirty bands, with ensigns cursing the war. I saw a river in the street made of women, children, Russians, Germans, and Austrians, flowing through the town upward and downward from the popular quarters to those of the centre, and finally dispersing at one of the most central points of the town, at the amphitheater of the Arena. They had had numerous meetings. They clamored for amnesty for the deserters! They demanded the division of the land!

Milan was then considered, more than now, the city where the pulse of the working nation could be felt. Milan, where I had labored with ideals, had experienced in 1914 and in the first months of 1915 epic days for the war. The city always had a strong and gallant spirit. In it citizenship was more active than in many other parts of the country. It had known how to prepare itself with dignity to sustain war effort. And now, after the triumph, even this town, the town of the 10,000 volunteers, seemed to yield itself to a disease.

This procession I said was an evidence of the deep mire in which all the classes of the population were sinking, especially those belonging to the *populari*. As the procession passed through the streets the bourgeois— the shopkeepers, the hotel keepers—hastily closed their windows and doors. They pulled down the roller blinds.

"There," said I, "are eyes closing with the weariness of anxiety and fear."

Naturally enough, the revolutionists, observing their effect, puffed up with new braggart triumph. Not a single force, *interventista* or any other, set foot in the street to stop the irresponsibles. The beloved tricolor flag of Italy was taken as a mark. It was hastily taken off balconies!

I remember an episode in the shame of those days; a woman, a school-teacher in the popular quarters, ran to the defense of the Italian flag. Risking her life, she stood with blazing eyes against a herd of communists. You may be sure that in the period of redemption and resurrection, when we stood upright again, the golden medal for valor was bestowed on this woman of saintly courage.

The *Popolo d'Italia,* of which I was the founder and editor, lived then its life of intense polemics. Every day was a battle. The little street of Via Paolo da Conuobio was constantly blocked by police or by detachments of *carabinieri* and soldiers. All the staff were guarded whenever we appeared in public. One could understand that the government was anxious about us. The authorities wanted to control all that the *Popolo d'Italia* was doing and to curb all agitation for virile methods in the political struggle. The censorship was re-established exclusively and solely for the *Popolo d'Italia.* Through a back-door channel a disgusting Socialist deputy tried also to bring about an inquiry. His proposal was ridiculed out of the door.

I wrote, on the next day after the Procession of the Defeat of Milan, an article the title of which was taken from a famous polemical book of Giordano Bruno— "Against the Return of the Beast."

That article was published in the *Popolo d'Italia* on

the eighteenth of February and ended in these precise words:

If the opposition to a war that is not only finished but was victorious is now a pretext for an ignoble doubt, then we who are not ashamed to have been *interventiste*, but feel the glory of our position, will shout to the heavens, "Stand back, you jackals!" No one shall separate the dead. They constitute a sacred heap, as big as a gigantic pyramid that touches the skies, a heap that belongs to nobody; nobody can give or take away from the dead. They do not belong to any party; they belong to the eternal motherland. They belong to a humanity too complex and too august to be put into any wine club or into the back room of some co-operative. This political stew is supremely ignominious. Must we be forced to defend our dead from filthy profanation? Oh, Toti! Roman! One man! Thy life and thy death is worth infinitely more than the whole Italian socialism! And you files on parade—innumerable heroes that wanted the war, knowing how to want war; who went to war knowing what was war; who went to death knowing what it meant to go to death—you, Decio Raggi, Filippo Corridoni, Cesare Battisti, Luigi Lori, Venezian, Sauro, Rismondi, Cantucci— you thousands and thousands of others that form the superb constellation of Italian heroism—don't you feel that the pack of jackals is trying to rummage your bones? Do they want to scrape the earth that was soaked with your blood and to spit on your sacrifice? Fear nothing, glorious spirits! Our task has just begun. No harm shall befall you. We shall defend you. We shall defend the dead, and all the dead, even though we put dugouts in the public squares and trenches in the streets of our city.

That was a warning blast—a trumpet call. Many, hit in the face, fled. Some around us, trembling, thought of the danger that they might get into on account of such a polemic. But some others—not many—gathered around the old banner of my newspaper.

It was necessary to organize our resistance, to take care in discussions of international character, to strengthen our position on the front of internal politics, to be guarded from false friends, to fight false pacifists and to confound the false humanitarians. We had to make a general assault upon all that bundle of various degenerate tendencies, diverse in their appearance but absolutely identical in their utter failure to understand the logical and absolute meaning of the victory in war.

Our delegation in Paris was in a sorry strait. The ability and the injustice of some of the Allied statesmen had almost strangled it. Owing to our internal situation, it was impossible for our delegation to take a firm stand with feet well-planted. The regions to be restored to Italy were in a state of restlessness that made many of us anxious.

What a grave moment! An action of a handful of us on the public square was not sufficient; there were so many different fronts where one had to fight. We who were to defend Italy from within had to create one more unbreakable unity of strength, a common denominator of all the old pro-war partisans and loyalists, of all those who felt, like myself, desperately Italian. Then it was that I decided, after days and nights of reflection, to make a call through the medium of my newspaper for a full stop in the stumbling career toward chaos.

And on the twenty-third of March, 1919, I laid down the fundamental basis, at Milan, of the Italian *fasci di combattimento*—the fighting Fascist programme.

The first meeting of the Italian battle Fascists took place on the Piazza S. Sepolero in Milan. It was in a hall offered to us by the Milan Association of Merchants and Shopkeepers. The permission was granted after a long discussion among the managers of the association. Common sense prevailed in the end; a guaranty was given that no noise or disorder would occur. On that condition we got what we wanted.

The meeting was of a purely political character. I had advertised in the *Popolo d'Italia* that it would have for its object the foundation of a new movement and the establishment of a programme and of methods of action for the success of the battle I was intending to fight against the forces dissolving victory and the nation.

I prepared the atmosphere of that memorable meeting by editorials and summonses published in the *Popolo d'Italia*. Anyhow, the ones that came were not numerous. One of my fighting friends of good will was in the hall and he took the names of those who were willing to sign up. After two days of discussion, fifty-four persons signed our programme and took the pledge to be faithful to the fundamental basis of our movement.

I speak of movement and not of party, because my conception always was that Fascism must assume the characteristics of being anti-party. It was not to be tied to old or new schools of any kind. The name Italian Fighting Fascisti was lucky. It was most appropriate to a political action that had to face all the old parasites and programmes that had tried to deprave Italy. I felt that it was not only the anti-socialist battle we had to fight; this was only a battle on the way. There was a lot more to do. All the conceptions of the so-called historical parties seemed to be dresses out of measure, shape, style, usefulness. They had grown tawdry and insufficient—unable to keep pace with the rising tide of unexpected political exigencies, unable to adjust to the formation of new history and new conditions of modern life.

The old parties clung in vain to the rattling programmes. These parties had to make pitiful repairs and tinkerings in an attempt to adapt their theories as best they could to the new days. It was therefore not sufficient to create—as some have said superficially—an anti-altar to the altar of socialism. It was necessary to imagine a wholly new political conception, adequate to the living reality of the twentieth century, overcoming at the same time the ideological worship of liberalism, the limited horizons of various spent and exhausted democracies, and finally the violently Utopian spirit of Bolshevism.

In a word, I felt the deep necessity of an original conception capable of placing in a new period of history a more fruitful rhythm of human life.

It was necessary to lay the foundation of a new civilization.

To this end—through every day's observation of events and change, morning and evening, in vigor and in weariness—I aimed all my strength. I had a perfect and sure consciousness of the end I was driving at. This was my problem—to find the way, to find the moment, to find the form.

Those discussions over which I presided and dominated strengthened some of my conceptions that still conserve to-day the freshness of the original idea. Later, in this review of my life until now, I shall take up some of the details of the evolution of our plans. At our meetings there were present various elements—syndicalists, old interventionists, demobilized officers still in uniform, and many *arditi*, those brave grenade-and-knife shock troops of the war.

The Italian *arditi* were a creation of the war. The idea was born in Garibaldi's impetuous, fighting vigor and dash, and finds its remote origin in the heroic city militias that flourished in many parts of Italy at the happy time of the townships—the communes. The *arditi* rendered first-class service during the war. They were our troops of assault, of the first rush. They threw themselves into the battle with bombs in hands, with daggers in the teeth, with a supreme contempt for death, singing their magnificent war hymns. There was in them not only the sense of heroism but an indomitable will.

This typically Italian formation lived on after the war. The first fighting Fascisti were formed mostly of decided men. They were full of will and courage. In the first years of the anti-socialist, anti-communist struggle, the *arditi* war veterans played an important rôle. I was several times nominated their chief and still hold the title of honorary president of the *Arditi* association, which has assumed now a purely relief character, with the idea of maintaining intact its spirit of civic and military virtues.

Those who came to the meeting for the constitution of the Italian Fascisti of Combat used few words. They did not exhaust themselves by laying out dreams. Their aim seemed clear and straight-lined. It was to defend the victory at any price, to maintain intact the sacred memory of the dead, and the admiration not only for those who fell and for the families of those who were dead but for the mutilated, for the invalids, for all those who had fought. The prevalent note, however, was of anti-socialist character, and as a political aspiration, it was hoped a new Italy would be created that would know how to give value to the victory and to fight with all its strength against treason and corruption, against decay within and intrigue and avarice from without.

There are some who profess not to understand what Fascismo had as its intent, and some who believe that it grew without a gardener. I was certain at the time that it was necessary to fix, without any possibility of equivocation, the essential brand of the new movement. For this reason I made three planks for our platform. The first was the following:

The meeting of the twenty-third of March sends its first greeting and reverent thought to the sons of Italy who died for the greatness of their country and for the freedom of the world; to the mutilated and to the invalids, to all those who fought, to the ex-prisoners who fulfilled their duty. It declares itself ready to uphold with all its energy the material and moral claims that will be put forward by the associations of those who fought.

The second declaration pledged the Fascisti of Combat to oppose themselves to the imperialism of any other countries damaging to Italy. It accepted the supreme postulates of the League of Nations regarding Italy. It affirmed the necessity to complete the stability of our frontiers between the Alps and the Adriatic with the claim of annexation of Fiume and of Dalmatia.

The third declaration spoke of the elections that were announced for the near future. In this motion the Fasci di Combattimento pledged themselves to fight with all their means the candidates that were milk-and-water Italians, to whatever party they belonged.

Finally we talked of organization—the organization that would be adapted to the new movement. I did not favor any bureaucratic cut-and-dried organization. It was thought wise that in every big town the correspondent of the *Popolo d'Italia* should be the organizer of a section of the Fasci di Combattimento, with the idea that each group should become a centre of Fascist ideas, work and action. The first expenses—amounting to a few thousand lire—were covered by the feeble resources of the *Popolo d'Italia.* A central committee was formed to guide the whole movement.

It is amusing for me to recall that this meeting remained almost unnoticed. The stupid irony of the Socialists and the narrow-minded incomprehensiveness of the Italian Liberal party could not grasp its significance.

The *Corriere della Sera,* that great liberal newspaper, dedicated to this news about twenty lines in its columns!

The internal situation in Italian politics and Italian policy continued to be nebulous and full of uncertainty.

Disillusion and the shattering of ideals could be noticed, even among those who had fought. A sense of weariness dominated all classes—every one. The Church, which had put herself apart during the great European conflict, now started activity in order to have her voice listened to at the peace negotiations and to have a say about all the questions that interested the nations that had taken part in the war.

So far as our national life was concerned, the Church limited her action to the creation of the Partito Popolare—the so-called Popular, or Catholic, party. It was faithful to some important programme points regarding the family and religion and the nation. It represented at that time an attempt to stop the prevalent diffusion of those Bolshevik ideas of socialistic parliamentary systems that were then disintegrating Rome and the provinces. But the Partito Popolare itself ran off the rails and jumped the fences; it tried to compete with the Socialists themselves. Of little and doubtful patriotic faith, it ran square against the Fascisti and the *interventisti*. The Popular party, along with the others, was too much in a hurry to close the parenthesis of the war.

Political riots, disturbances and strikes took place alternately in a kind of sickly rotation in every Italian city.

It is necessary for me to review the conditions which we faced. Orlando, president of the council, was incapacitated by temperament to dominate the internal situation, just as he was unable to be a master in foreign

affairs. His work was contradictory, full of false sentimentality and failure to comprehend the real interests
of Italy. Not knowing French, and ignorant of the
treaties concluded with the Allied nations, Orlando, in
spite of the presence of Sonnino, was a disastrous influence during the peace negotiations at Versailles. Wilson, so far as Italy was concerned, was ambiguous—so
much so that on the twenty-third of April the Italian
delegation had to leave Paris. It returned on the fifth
of May—a dubious situation. In June, after a vote of
the chamber, the Orlando cabinet retired. In the meantime—also in June—serious clashes took place at Fiume
between French sailors and Italian soldiers.

Never did Italy have a man so damaging to the Italian interests and programmes as he who came next
—Nitti.

He was and remains a personality that is the negation of any ideal of life and of manly conflict. He has
a fairly good knowledge of finances. He is impudent
in his assertions. He is intensely egocentric. He always wants to play the most important part in cabinets, whether he is president of the council or simply a
minister.

His first act when he came into power was the granting of an amnesty. This amnesty was followed by two
others. The first had a character of general principle
and I approved it, but by granting the two others Nitti
committed a great moral crime, for he abolished the difference between those who wore the ensigns of valor in
sacrifice and those who had basely betrayed the nation

during the war and even had gone over to the enemy!

All the work of Nitti was fish-bait for the approbation of the Socialists. He conceived the ambition of holding the presidency of a future Italian republic. His measures, which wore demagogic dress, did not prevent disorders or devastations sometimes brought about with the cost of lives. He never would face Bolshevism and the dissolutive forces in the open field. He had a decree issued and signed by the King establishing the price of bread; he had it withdrawn on the next day and replaced by another decree, also signed by His Majesty.

There was no point in the national life that he failed to bring up for discussion. All this puffed up the Socialists. They laughed in their sleeves as they foresaw a strong political success for them at the elections. The elections had to take place under the proportional system! The Socialists would become, through the election battle, masters of Italian political life!

It seemed to me that the season was our summer of torment and resolve.

In June, 1919, the Treaty of Peace with Germany was consummated at Versailles. The event for Europe was the end of a nightmare. The continual disillusionments, the reservations and the protests of Germany and the diatribes between the Allies constituted a permanent danger and a reason for anxiety for many nations. The conclusion of the treaty was therefore for them a liberation.

For Italy, on the contrary, it was a complete shattering of ideals. We had won the war; we were utterly defeated in the diplomatic battle. We were losing—except Zara—the whole of Dalmatia, our land by tradition and history, by manners and costumes, by the language spoken and by the ardent and constant aspirations of the Dalmatians toward the mother country. Fiume, most Italian of cities, was contested. The colonial problem was resolved for us in an absolutely negative way. To a nation like ours, powerful and prolific, that has a need of raw materials, of outlets, of markets and of land, on account of the exuberance of its population, only some insignificant rectifications of frontiers were granted when the glut of colonial spoil was passed around.

I could feel the discontent oozing down through our masses and infecting the *combattenti* themselves. Once more Italy, who had thrown into the conflict men, means, patrimony and youth, went out of a peace settlement with empty hands and manifold disillusions.

The Nitti government, with its continuous note of pessimism, was doing no better than to describe our situation as near to bankruptcy, economic as well as political! Nitti himself, his newspapers and his acolytes, tried to make the Italian people believe that the Versailles Treaty was for us the best result obtainable. A sense of humiliation had crawled over our whole peninsula, but many there were who did not want to resign themselves to accept the tragic facts. No one knows better than I that many meditated, in sullen silence, most desperate actions.

The government was watching the turn of the psychological tide, while in the practical field it did not know what to do except to prepare and revise the mechanism of an election law by a vicious proportional system. In the field of destruction it reached an unbelievable decision to demobilize the aviation camps, and to cap the climax, in August, 1919, the report of the Commission of Inquiry on the painful episode of Caporetto was published.

I thought to myself, "This is fat on the fire!" The *Avanti,* a socialist newspaper that for the time being was published in three editions—one at Turin, one at Rome and one at Milan—had started a ferocious campaign against the army. On account of a strike of typographers, the *Avanti* was the only newspaper published in Rome for two months! During street demonstrations, officers, merely because they were in uniform, were insulted and assaulted. Charity toward the dignity of the nation prevents my presentation of episodes that now make the worst blackguards blush. The few Fascisti that had accomplished an act of faith in March, 1919, now met in all their work enormous difficulties. They were isolated, attacked, spied upon, sometimes by the subversives, sometimes by the government.

Every day in the *Popolo d'Italia* I wrote about the painful bath of fire of the *combattenti,* about the inflamed pride of the volunteers, about the necessity of concord, about the sordid hostility of the government that did not feel the beauty and the greatness of the sense of patriotic heroism. Gabriele D'Annunzio, the poet, who lived in Rome, wrote that his approbation "of my good shots was trembling with admiration."

Victory was losing her laurel leaves every day in spite of all. The national parliament was discussing and approving the new election laws. Disorders and blackmailing of the government were on the daily calendar. The debates had a character of pettiness and gossip and the flavor of a base world that knew nothing of war, virtue or heroism.

"Elections! Elections! Elections!" thought I. "These constitute the only subject that is able to rise to its feet in the Italian parliament!"

Incidents had taken place at Fiume between Italians and French sailors, and the population of that city did not hide its growing hostility toward the Allies. The latter therefore planned to have the city garrisoned by a mixed corps of their troops. So Fiume, a city purely of virile Italian stamp, had a mosaic of troops. It was the summit of inefficiency and, what is more, of stupidity.

D'Annunzio, who was trembling in his solitude, told me that he contemplated with grim brooding the taking of Fiume by force. There was no other way of salvation. Everything seemed to be lost. There were only a handful of men with the poet. But they were the most trustworthy elements of our army. They were old volunteers. They were Fascists who felt once again in the incandescent atmosphere of the streets of Rome and other cities the poetry of the war and of the victory. They started, armed, from Ronchi.

The occupation of Fiume, at the moment when the English sailors were getting ready to evacuate it, was rapid and startling. The government, as soon as it knew the truth, wanted to rush to offset the raid. It meditated a blockade, it sent thunder against the rebels. But D'Annunzio and his legionaries, having prepared their action in silence, now threw down a gauntlet of audacious challenge to the Nittian triflings.

Gabriele d'Annunzio, before starting from Ronchi, wrote me the following letter:

Dear Companion: The dice are on the table. To-morrow I shall take Fiume with force of arms. The God of Italy assist us!

I arise from bed with fever. But it is impossible to delay. Once more the spirit dominates the miserable flesh.

Sum up the article that the *Gazetta del Popolo* will publish; give the end in full.

Sustain the cause without stint during the conflict.

I embrace you,

11 September, 1919.   GABRIELLE D'ANNUNZIO.

The Italian atmosphere, so long checked and humiliated, exploded like Vesuvius after the announcement of the new D'Annunzio gesture. Again we heard the tune of high sentiments of fraternity and of enthusiasm. Again we felt the spirit of May, 1915. The best of our manhood felt the breath of poetry that came from this sacred liberation carried on in the face of the policy of the Nittian government.

The Fascisti were amongst the ardent legionaries of Fiume, while at home they were leading resistance against the defeatists, old and new. The Italian colonists all over the world—these colonists who had followed with anxiety and with unspeakable fright the negotia-

tions of Versailles—sent money in great quantity for
D'Annunzio's expedition. Fiume felt an intuition of its
salvation. There were manifestations of frantic enthusiasm. Audacity had repaired injustice; the city was
strongly held, so that it could resist by force of arms and
with courage all the Nittian or international interference.

The president of the council, Nitti, in parliament on
this occasion, took an ignoble attitude. He summoned
up the dangerous idea of protest by a general strike. By
his ambiguous language he invited the classes which
leaned toward socialism, and especially the Socialists
and radicals themselves, to agitate for street demonstrations against D'Annunzio's enterprise.

Nitti, after conversations with Trumbic, the Jugo-
Slav minister, saw all his tangled and slimy net of
humiliating understandings going to pieces through the
will of a few brave boys.

Nitti thought and acted only as a consequence of
physical fear. Attacked full front and exasperated in
his mad and miserable dream, he plotted with every
means to overcome the resistance of the Fiumean legionaries. The soldiers were declared deserters. The city was
blockaded so that economic pressure would squeeze the
spirit of the citizens. Parliament was closed and the elections were fixed for November 16, 1919, under the
troublesome proportional system.

The elections re-established, for a moment, an apparent truce. Every party wanted to measure the masses
and the groupings. The Socialists, who were speculating

Commander Gabriele d'Annunzio.

on the misfortunes of the war and were pointing to the danger of another war due to the D'Annunzian enterprise, were the favorites. The Church, which in politics always has an ambiguous attitude, urged on the activity of the priests in the villages so that the Partito Popolare, which had been created originally by the lay Catholics, in service of the church policy, might play the preponderant part in parliament. The Liberals, Democrats and some radicals built up a block that passed under the name of the Forces of Order. They were changeable forces, without any ideal base and without precise aims. They were another grouping among groupings whose futilities I had observed for years.

I wanted the Fascisti to try alone the chance of the elections. We did not ally ourselves with any other party, even with the nearest to them—the Nationalists. The atmosphere was against us, but it was necessary to count our own heads. It was necessary to know, even through the means of elections, what point had been reached by the Italian nation in moral disintegration and in moral reawakening as a victorious nation. I created an electoral committee with little means, but with ample courage. I ordered meetings for the principal towns of Italy and especially in Milan.

I remember so vividly the meeting on the Piazza Beligioioso. How typical it was! The place was a lonesome corner of old Milan, where from a camion that was used for a tribune on a dark night, by the light of torches, I addressed a big, closely pressed crowd. They were people not only from Milan but from other towns.

The Fascisti of Bologna, of Turin, of Rome and of Naples had in fact sent their representatives in order to have precise rules and sure orders for the impending electoral battle.

I made on this occasion some declarations of principles that still stand in the Fascist line. They have served me as a guide in all my political actions.

I said that revolutions were not to be denied *a priori;* that they might be discussed. I said that the Italian people could not copy Russian Bolshevism. We have in the history of our political struggles our own elements of greatness of concept. These have given to the spirit of the time all the strength of their Italian genius and the qualities of their Italian courage.

"If a revolution," said I, "has to take place, it is necessary to make one typically Italian, on the magnificent dimensions of the ideas of Mazzini and with the spirit of Carlo Pisacane."

I had already in my mind, clear and strong, the concept of complete rebellion against the decrepit old state that did not of itself know how to die.

The elections of the sixteenth of November took place and the Fascisti were beaten. I faced, and all of us faced, complete defeat. Not one of us had the necessary votes to become a member of parliament. Some Nationalists saved themselves in Rome and were later excellent interpreters of the national idea in the wallow of general bewilderment. At Milan, I was a long way off from the number of votes necessary to be elected. It was tragic, our record, but in the passage of time it is amusing and may be remembered by all losers.

Our uneasiness was now profound. The crowd was anti-Fascist. Under the skin of the population a sad illusion was being fed; in their minds a dark hope was stirring. The coming of Bolshevism! The plan for seizing the means of production, the installation of the soviets in Italy!

The *Avanti* had already published the general scheme and its details. My defeat did not bother me out of any personal consideration. It gave me a clear and precise idea of the desperateness of our situation. The Socialist newspaper wrote on that occasion a short notice about me: "A dead body has been fished up from the Naviglio." It was said in this note that in the night, in the modest Naviglio canal that cuts Milan in two, a dead body had been picked up. According to the documents they said it could be identified as the dead body of Benito Mussolini—his political corpse. They did not say that its eyes were gazing ahead.

Amidst the general feast of their victory the Socialists did not forget to imitate a regular funeral. This parade passed through the streets with a coffin, surrounded with burning candles. There were ribald psalms on the air. The strange procession, however, showed the distress and shoddiness of its ranks; it passed up and down the city of Milan—a city that had become now the absolute property of the Socialists. The procession passed under the windows of my house, where my family was living in anxiety amidst the general anxieties and with violence trembling in the air. I have not forgotten the episode, but I always see it in its frame—the frame of the misery and of the threadbareness of the paraders.

The elections had given 150 seats to the Socialists in parliament. They were themselves frightened by their staggering success. The situation was saved by the South of Italy—always more faithful to men than to organized mass parties.

The victory, of course, swelled up in most Socialists a desire to dominate. It distended their impudent abuse of power. Enormous processions with red flags, howling in the streets, strikes called not for protest but for celebration, occupied a whole week.

At Milan a crowd of 30,000 demanded that the red flag should be exposed on the Municipal building. During the cock-crowing over victory, all institutions, rules and regulations and orderly life were upset.

Nobody thought about work. That last of all! Only an audacious handful formed by Fascisti, *arditis* and Fiumean elements resisted the intoxication. An incident was provoked because of this. Bombs were thrown, a few were killed and many wounded. A commission of Socialist members of parliament, headed by Filippo Turati, marched up the stairs of the Prefetura, the governor's office of Milan, to claim my arrest and the arrest of the Fascisti chiefs.

That was an episode of political partisanship useless and evil. The authorities showed weakness and fear. They wanted to give satisfaction to the Socialists. But my clear and straight-lined political action did not suffer from this abuse of power. Having been let out after only one day of imprisonment, I consulted with my associates as to the whole work before us. What should we do now? How could we act before the damage to Italy became irreparable?

The electoral tragedy had broken up our central committees. Many of us had been arrested; many, threatened, had disappeared. Little by little, calm having been restored, I rewove at the *Popolo d'Italia* the fabric of our cause and tried to build again the structure of our organization. In various meetings I explained the gravity of the Italian situation. I spoke independently of the particular attitude of the Fascisti.

The victory of the Socialists was a danger, not so much because of the fact itself as because of the phenomenal retreat to their holes of all the weak and the incapables which followed the day after the Socialist victory. That victory crushed the Liberals and the Democrats. For some time a low furtive literature of propaganda had spread stories about disquieting episodes in the defeated German and Austrian countries. This literature spun narratives about professors obliged to become servants and scullions, Russian princesses engaged as ballet dancers, generals who were selling matches on the streets. All this put together with the Socialist victory produced a wave of fright in all classes, and I could see a serious fact of corruption and political paralysis. The old parties had been beaten by pussyfoot socialism. That socialism had no aim. It was victorious only through cowardice in the others and because of the general uneasiness in the population. Certainly it did not win on any declaration of a great faith.

I did not fold under the smallest edge of my flag.

From my editor's office that was getting barer and barer, to my readers that were getting fewer and fewer, I addressed the most bitter and severe exhortations to resist, resist, resist.

I made a little fortress out of the editor's office. The newspaper was sequestrated and censored every day; but notwithstanding difficulties and lack of means, I succeeded in keeping the little paper alive. I was throttled by the skinny hand of poverty. I could have sold out, but I held on.

So that I might be completely withdrawn from circulation, various messengers of the Nittian government came to me advising me to go and study the autonomous republics of Southern Russia. I understood the double game. They acted with me as they acted with D'Annunzio when they advised him to try the flight from Rome to Tokio. But D'Annunzio was now still resisting at Fiume, and I, with my newspaper, was renewing and reassembling the dispersed ranks of the Fascisti. I held meetings constantly. Not for a moment did I cease my activity. It cannot be said that I failed to look the triumphant beast in the face.

One day, just after the elections, I had to go personally because of postal regulations to the money-order window of the main post office in Milan. I was to receive some considerable contributions that Italians from oversea colonies were sending for the Fiume enterprise. In the huge buildings of the Central Post Office one could still see visible signs of the elections—the murmur of the discussions, the stenciled inscriptions on the walls were all there. I presented myself with my brother, Arnaldo, at the window of the money-order office.

The Bolshevik clerk, with evident irony, said I had to make myself known. He did not know any "certain Benito Mussolini." A short discussion arose that attracted other Bolshevik elements, who amused themselves by affirming that nobody knew Benito Mussolini. The development of this discussion, impudently provoking, was stopped by an old clerk of the post office, a faithful servant of the state who certainly was not intoxicated by the Socialist success.

He said, "Pay this money transfer. Do not be silly. Mussolini has a name that is not only known now here but will be known and judged all over the world."

I have never learned the name of this gentleman. He was straight and fair.

Some symptoms of reaction against the Socialist victory were to be noticed now. One day at the editor's office of the newspaper, facing the anxieties of my associates and the doubts of some half-hearted ones in my service, I felt it necessary to disclose my own hopes and faiths:

"Don't fear. Italy will heal herself from this illness. But without our watchfulness it might be deadly. We will resist! Resist! I should say so! Indeed, within two years I will have my turn!"

CHAPTER VI

THE DEATH STRUGGLE OF A WORN-
OUT DEMOCRACY

I HAVE little doubt that all inefficient party and parliamentary governments die from the same causes and with the same, typical mannerisms of decay.

I have watched one die and have been present to hear the raucous drawings of its last breaths. But these were times which tried the souls of us. We saw passing before our eyes the dreadful panorama of chaos and of evil forces which had broken into a gallop, ridiculous to behold, tragic beyond words to one who loved his country. Above all, these forces were trivial and insincere.

The political elections of November 16, 1919, had painted and glossed over Italian political life with a mere veneer of quiet. Not one of the weighty problems of domestic or foreign policy for which a quick, brave solution was needed had yet even been put under the microscope for study. Everything was boiled up in the joust of political parties. There was the usual seething of inconsequential prophecy about the new ministerial combinations.

The Socialists dominated the scene. They contin-

ually harassed the government, while it was concerned
on account of the attitude of the extreme left—communists.

The occasion of the crown speech, at the beginning
of the twenty-first legislature, was upon us. For this
ceremony there had been some worry on the part of
Nitti. He tried to hold the Socialists in check. But they
could not help showing their cold hostility to the king.
I was told in advance that they would refuse to be present in the hall during the king's speech.

On the day of the opening of the chamber, when the
king was solemnly entering the Hall of Parliament,
what was the demonstration? The Socialists made a
parade of their pinks in their buttonholes and went out
in groups, singing the Hymn of Workers and the In-
ternationale. With them, making a clumsy show of
doubtful political taste, filed the Republicans, the In-
dependents, and members of the Left.

The speech of the crown did not take a clear position
against the subversive forces which were menacing nothing less than our whole national unity. It forgot the
question of Fiume—a torch which held out a flame for
our national spirit. The speech even renounced some
sovereign prerogatives. It conceded a good share of the
crown patrimony, in behalf of the war veterans, combatants and wounded, for they also were full of evident
signs of restlessness. Furthermore, in a period when
foreign policies were in a snarl and the economic crisis
serious indeed, I could see little else besides the petty
shifts and maneuvers of parliamentary cloakrooms and

corridors in the same old disgusting struggle to grab places in the Ministry.

During the first three months the Ministry of Nitti fell three times at the chamber. It outlived itself and then succeeded itself.

The *Stampa,* an old Piedmont newspaper, liberal in character, began to be willing to indict the war. It began an attempt to carry in triumph the very man who was the breeder and teacher of neutrality—Giovanni Giolitti. The Church, together with the Popular party, wanted to draw the utmost profit from the abnormal situation. The Socialists revealed themselves very badly prepared for their victory. Victory had only set them down in a marsh of trouble; I knew that they could not create an equilibrium between the communists and the extreme right. On one side it was the nation; on the other politics—inefficient, empty politics.

Meanwhile Gabriele d'Annunzio, in Fiume, was resisting with his legionaries the flatteries of political secret agents who, we all knew, were pouring into Fiume, and was resisting also the blockade. Fascism was again setting in order its disunited ranks, after the electoral defeat of November 16, 1919, and the light was everywhere dim and the atmosphere murky with selfish, small, cowardly breathings.

Nevertheless, we began to see our way through.

To reorganize the ranks of Fascism was not a matter of impossible difficulty, because the Fasci di Combattimento—Bundles of Fight—had learned discipline and enthusiasm; we could stand our shocks from mere electoral vicissitudes. And on the other hand, some strategic leadership began to show itself at Florence, where, in October, 1919, there was held the first international meeting of the Italian Fasci di Combattimento. What a characteristic meeting! The adherents were obliged to defend the liberty of assembling by the voice of the revolver. Florence, a city with a tradition of kindness and hospitality, received the Fascists with violent hostility. Ambushes! Provocations! Nevertheless, the meeting was held. Our friends were able to control the place. By great energy they broke down resistance and suppressed the unprovoked violence of our opponents.

The meeting of Florence wrote the real problem of government across the sky. On October ninth, by way of starting that sky writing, I made an unadorned speech. I made clear appeal to the subversive forces of the nation. On the next day, after a sharp, needle-pointed speech by the poet F. T. Marinetti, the secretary, Pasella, presented a resolution in which the Fasci di Combattimento claimed the right to formulate for Italy a fundamental transformation of the state. It was a clearly defined programme of political convenience and expediency, aiming to create an absolutely new social and economic state.

I have interpreted and carried out that purpose. If the end I now seek is to disclose the paths which have led to the development of the self I am, then surely it was during this period of training and test, of trial and error, that the most significant guideposts may be found.

The programme of the Fasci was approved to a man.

There, indeed, was the disclosed warning of the Fascist régime to come. To the régime's problem, however, there was being added—and sharp it was—the problem of the syndicates. For that reason, during the afternoon sitting of October tenth, I myself proposed a resolution which declared "adhesion to the movement of economic deliverance and autonomy of the worker." We sent a greeting "to all those numerous groups of proletarians and employes who are not willing to submit to the leadership of political parties composed and controlled chiefly by little and big mediocrity which is now trying, by impoverishing and mystifying the masses, to gain applause and salaries." I often wonder if other nations do not feel the same.

The whole spirit of that meeting, which closed with a greeting for Fiume, was such as to rivet the old conception of the irreconcilable character of the fight.

I arrived at Florence, coming from Fiume, where I had gone by airplane. There had been a long, affectionate and definite heart-to-heart talk with Gabriele d'Annunzio about all that needed to be done in Italy. On my journey back, the plane, on account of the *bora*—a violent wind of the Upper Adriatic—was obliged to come down on the aviation field of Aiello, in the province of Udine. Chafing under the delay, I continued my journey to Florence by train, where I came just in time to preside at the meeting and to take what may be called a lively part in our resistance against the violence of our opponents. At bottom, I was the most harassed in spirit of all who were there. But to the eyes of the glowing crowd I was a patriot, a preacher of resistance, he who succeeded, through the violent articles written from day to day in the *Popolo d'Italia*, in beginning the smashing of Bolshevism. The meeting was ended in Fascist style; we swore to see one another again; we promised ourselves victory at any price.

I set out from Florence by auto, to go to Romagna. The machine was driven by Guido Pancáni, well known in Florence in his capacity of war volunteer and airplane pilot—a great athlete. In the same machine there were also the brother-in-law of Pancáni, Gastone Galvani, and Leandro Arpinati, of the railway workshops of Bologna, since then well known in the political clubs. When we came to Faenza the auto stopped before the Orpheum Coffee Shop, where I met and greeted some old friends of mine. On continuing the trip, the auto, driven at full speed, crashed into a railway crossing with closed gates. Under our terrible impact the first iron railing was broken to bits and the auto was hurled over the rails onto the second barrier. We were all, with the exception of the driver, Pancáni, flung yards away, like toy men. I, who came out unhurt, and Arpinati, who had been lightly bruised, went shouting for help for our two friends, who were groaning in agony. People arrived, the injured men were laid down in our auto, which, dragged by oxen, conveyed the two wounded to the hospital of Faenza. During the surgical treatments I also helped the two patients. I did what I could to comfort them. Finally I departed again by train to Bologna. The incident might have had greater consequences, but fortune assisted me; I felt that the hatred of our adversaries had been my talisman.

Already I have told how, after the electoral defeat of November 16, 1919, some of my friends were terrified and others asserted how useless it was to go against the stream. They said—for there are always minds of this type—that it was much better to come to an agreement with the opposition, which in those days held all strategic political positions and dominated the parliament. Compromise, negotiation and agreements were offered me.

I rejected flatly any agreement whatever. I did not admit even one moment's thought of coming to a covenant with those who had repudiated our Italy in war and now were betraying her in peace. Not many understood me—not even those close to me. Two of my editors on the *Popolo d'Italia,* my newspaper, asked permission to leave. They made their excuses on the grounds that they had moved from their political streets and house numbers. They even accused me of having helped myself—during the electoral fight—with funds gathered by the *Popolo d'Italia* in the cause of smarting Fiume. So I have seen myself—a bitter experience —obliged to defend myself from those who had been my friends.

I appeared before the convention of the Lombardian journalists, demanding opportunity to hear and be heard as to the charges made. My justification was ample and precise. The board was forced by the facts to do me justice. And afterward, without waiting for the hour of my triumphs, the self-same slanderers, it is fair to say, made honorable amends for their errors.

But meanwhile, taking a pretext from this episode, there was launched against me the furious wrath of the Socialists and of the members of the Popular party, led by the priests. Ferrets were sent to smell into my life. Soldiers and police were bribed. Secret inquiries were made into my every-day routine, into all my acts, all my beliefs. The deluded, the rejected, the unmindful— all whom my upright and fierce soul had fired at in some way or another—gathered against me. They could do nothing. In spite of the length and breadth of the investigation, up high and down low, no dragon was dredged out of my pool. As for the disposition of the funds for the Fiume campaign, and other unworthy calumnies, I published in my newspaper documents and testimony which could never be refuted.

The conclusion arrived at then has been and always will be the same until I cease to exist: on the score of integrity there is no assault to be made upon me. My political work may be valued more or less, this way or that, and people may shout me up or howl me down, but in the moral field it is another matter. Men must live in harmony with the faith by which they are pushed on; they must be inspired by the most absolute disinterestedness. True men, in politics, must be animated by the humane and devout sense; they must have a regard, a love toward and a deep vision regarding their own fellow creatures. And all these qualities must not be defiled by dissimulations or rhetoric or flatteries or compromises or servile concessions. On this ground, at least, I am proud to know myself as one not to be suspected

—even by myself—and feeling that my inmost moral fiber is invincible.

I believe that this, above all else, has been the stuff and fabric of my strength and of my success.

The beginning of 1920 found Italy engaged with a most difficult international situation. While in Paris the diplomats were sordidly debating, the bleeding wound of Dalmatia was yet open, and in it was D'Annunzio at Fiume. The Socialists, to be sure, had obtained a boisterous electoral victory, but they proved from day to day more and more impotent and incapable of maintaining their positions in government with dignity. The most temperate were overturned by the extremists. There was the gorgeous myth of Lenin! The Italian Liberal party had resigned all its prerogatives. The ministry was living from day to day, at the mercy of political extortions, of blackmail, of those who wanted special favors. There was turbulence in parliament and uproars of political nature on the streets.

Under such conditions it was necessary to struggle, even though sometimes victory seemed very difficult and almost unattainable. I started the year by an article entitled "Let's Navigate." I said: "Two religions are to-day contending with each other for the sway over the world—the black and the red. From two vaticans depart to-day encyclical letters—from that of Rome and from that of Moscow. We declare ourselves the heretics of these two expressions. We are exempt from contagion. The issue of the battle is of secondary importance to us. To us the fight has the prize in itself, though it be not crowned by victory. The world now has some strange analogy with that of Julian the Apostate. The Galileo with the red hair! Will he be a winner again? Or will the winner be the Mongol Galileo of the Kremlin? Will there be realized the upsetting of all valiant and virile thought?

"These questions weigh upon the uneasy spirits of our contemporaries.

"But in the meantime it is necessary to steer the ship! Even against the stream. Even against the flow. Even if shipwreck is waiting for the solitary and haughty bearers of heresy."

There was little time to spare for dwelling upon these highbrow controversies. Events were tumbling over themselves in a most troubled way. In the month of January, after harsh discussion, it appeared impossible to avoid a threatened railway strike. Soon after, the general strike of the post and telephone employees burst out and lasted six days. It disorganized not only the private interests of citizens but also state communications. It cut off the shuttle of thoughts in a moment made even more delicate by the international situation. The *Avanti,* the official newspaper of the Socialist party, of which I had once been editor, wrote on that occasion that the post, telegraph and telephone offices were a luxury of modern times; that the ancient peoples had been great even without telegraphic apparatus. Who knows whether this gibberish came from a mocking spirit or from the kind of confirmed idiocy with which extremists are afflicted? The stated cause of the agitations was always economic, but in truth the end was wholly political; the real intention was to strike a blow full in the face of the state's authority, against the middle classes and against disciplined order, with a view to establishing the soviets in Italy. That was the plain purpose behind all the ornaments and masks. It is little realized how easily a combination of disorders can put a whole nation—by control of its exchanges and its communications and cities —in the hands of a tyrannous minority.

In the midst of general hardships and of cowardice, of grumbling of impotents, of the vaporings of dull critics, I, almost alone, had the courage to write that the state's employees, if they were right in view of the feebleness of the government, were wrong, in any case, toward the nation. To inflict upon a people the mortification of an ill-advised strike, to trample upon the rights of the whole, meant to lead men from modern civil life back again to tribal conflict.

"These dissensions," I wrote in my paper on January 15, 1920, "are between function and government. The sufferer who suffers after having paid, the sufferer, with the inevitable prospect of paying more, is the Italian nation—the word 'nation' understood in the sense of human collectivity." And further on I added: "The material damages of a strike of this kind are enormous, incalculable. But the moral damages at home and abroad are still greater. The moment chosen for the strike gives to the strike itself the true and proper character of a support to Allied imperialism. This is the culminating moment of the negotiations in Paris. This is the moment in which there is the one question—to get, finally, a peace. Why didn't the postal, the telegraph and telephone operators wait two weeks more, until the return of Nitti from Paris? Was it just 'written,' was it just 'fatal,' that the ultimatum to the government should fall due on the thirteenth? All this confirms the sinister political character of the act."

As God pleased, on January twenty-first, the post and telegraph strike was ended, but already there had begun, on the nineteenth of January, a railway strike. It was a useless strike. The leaders of red syndicalism had been willing to proclaim it at any price, even when it was against both the sentiment and the interest of the workmen themselves. I defined this strike as "an enormous crime against the nation." The country was in desolation. Italy was in the claws of disorder and violence; the foreigners left our charming resorts and byways; the withholding of credit grew general among bankers, while catastrophic rumors held sway over the international world, entangling more and more our diplomatic negotiations.

In the midst of the most unbridled egoism, the Fascists firmly held their places during the strikes of the public services. I will not forget that some groups of our men, inspired by faith, thoroughly did their duty during these agitations. They faced with firm boldness the insults and threats of their striking fellow countrymen.

Meanwhile, in the face of the righteous indignation of public opinion, some Socialists began to feel timid. They tried to separate their responsibility from that of the leaders who had proclaimed the strike. On that occasion, in the *Popolo d'Italia* of January twenty-first, I published an article entitled "Too Late!" I thrust into the light—with words that later on revealed themselves prophetic—the real situation of socialism.

"The Turatians," I wrote—"and by this word we intend all those who in Filippo Turati, the leader of the Right, recognize their chief—should have been awakened before. Now the car is thrown upon the steep slope and the reformist's brake is creaking, but it does not hold; nay, it exhausts the strength of those who are dragging on the lever. At the bottom there is the impregnable massive wall against which the car will break to pieces. Out of the ruin will come wisdom. This was said also by the French fabulist, La Fontaine:

À quelque chose malheur est bon: à mettre un sot à la raison.

"It would be preferable, nevertheless, that the blockheads might restore their reason without plunging the nation into destruction and misery."

The railway strike was protracted up to January twenty-ninth, and all the time diplomatic discussions were bringing us to disastrous compromises in our foreign policy. About this time, into the aridity of the disputes of classes there was thrust an event colored with highest idealism. It was arranged that the suffering children of Fiume should be brought to Milan. They had been enduring the hardships of a blockaded town, without economic resources; they were at the mercy of their own distress. Already the children of Vienna, the sons of our enemies, had obtained in Milan kind treatment.

Was it not admissible that there should be found love and pity for the Italian infants of Quarnero? The episode of kindness, brought about by the Fascists with the consent of the Fiume command, resounded throughout Italy. Great manifestations of joy greeted these children at every junction or way station of their journey. The censors of the press, however, prevented us from writing of the triumphal journey of these children. It was all part and parcel of a programme systematically to slander our spirit, which always stamped the political handicraft of Nitti, like an ugly hall-mark on a leaden spoon.

This man, in order to justify his vile and inept diplomacy, dared to deliver in the chamber a speech on the Fiume question with a friendly intonation toward the Slavians, at the very time that Wilson was pressing his even stranger project to create of Fiume and Zara two isolated, detached, aborted free cities under the control and the authority of the League of Nations!

On the next day, February eighth, my newspaper bore on the first page the following head-line: "The Abominable Speech of H. E. Cagoia—The Snail." By this surname Gabriele d'Annunzio had stamped F. S. Nitti and the term had become popular. Following the head-line was a short editorial of mine, entitled "Miserable." In it, after having set forth again in a few words the painful history of the negotiations in Paris, I concluded:

The truth is that Nitti is preparing to go back again. He goes to Paris in order to give away his shirt. Before the stubborn Juglo-Slavian irreconcilableness our Cagoia knows

nothing better than to wail, weep and—yield. The whole tone
of his speech is vile, dreadfully vile. Not in vanquished Germany, nor in Austria, has there been so vile a Minister as
Nitti. If there had been one, he could not have lasted. This
one is the Minister of runaways, of autolesionists; he is the
Minister of Modigliani, the man of peace at any price. By
trying to remember continually that the objectives of Italy
were Trento and Triest, Cagoia offers arms to the Jugo-
Slavian resistance.

The peace of 1866, in comparison, is a masterpiece with
that offered by His Indecency. On his next journey to Paris,
Cagoia will make another renunciation. Zara? Valona? Who
knows? Quite likely. It is not impossible that he will yield
Gorizia too. Perhaps also Monfalcone. And why not the line
of Tagliamento? Maybe only by this price can we hope for
the friendship of Jugo-Slavia!

Before such infamy we feel that it would be preferable to
be citizens of the Germany of Noske than subjects of the
Italy of Cagoia.

We have before us days of dolor and shame; worse than
those of Caporetto, worse than those of Abba Carima!

We will recover our strength, but first there is some one
who will be forced to pay.

The domestic policies and the foreign policies pursued
by the government of that time did not fail to provoke
some stiff discussions among those newspapers that were
reflecting the varied tendencies of national life. The
Stampa, at the head of which was Senator Frassati, who
some time later was to be selected as ambassador to
Berlin, was one of my targets. I violently attacked it
because of the programme it adopted. It gave itself airs
as if it would be the redeemer of our fatherland. It is
necessary to remember that Senator Frassati had been
against the entrance of Italy into the World War. He

always stood apart during the most bleeding and tragic periods of Italian life. Consequently, he was the least capable of taking a pose as redeemer of our fatherland at the time when peace was to be concluded with the enemies after the victorious end of our war.

The *Corriere della Sera,* representing and interpreting the thought of a great flow of so-called liberal public opinion, was defending arbitration for Fiume and Dalmatia, proposed by Wilson and supported by the prose of Albertini, who followed a pernicious policy inspired by Salvemini and Nitti. The *Avanti,* the red publication, availed itself of all these polemics and of the slanders against me to libel me in general before the whole of public opinion. And all this campaign, vain and ineffectual, was even supported by the press of the Popular party. But more important, it was employed against the raising of Fascism and against the war victory.

Strikes were characterized by violent, disgraceful clashes between police and soldiers and the citizens; the interminable parliamentary discussions were marked by fist fights on the floor of the chamber. These were pitiful spectacles, humiliating not only to citizenship and to government itself but to the whole fabric of our political life.

In the short cycle of a few months there had been three ministerial crises, but Nitti always came back to power. The question, as always in a democracy gone drunk with compromise of principles, was one of mutual concessions, and very heavy ones. Miserable. Useless. Nobody was thinking of the rebuilding of social order in a nation which had won a bloody war and which had to face the fact that it was living in the presence of a world of moving realities.

Fascism, unique lighthouse in a sea of cowardice, of compromise and of foggy, plum-colored idealism, had engaged itself in battles; it was overpowered by mere blind multitudes. I was the bull's-eye of the target of the government of Nitti. He unloosed against me all his hounds, while his journalists tired themselves in vain to note down my contradictions in political matters. The Socialists, mindful of my moral and physical strength, covered me with their vengeance and their ostracism. At least, they roamed at a distance. They were cautious and far off the trail of real things.

During one of the many evenings when Milan was at the mercy of these scoundrels, I found myself surrounded and isolated in a café of the Piazza del Duomo, the central hub of the Lombardian metropolis. While I was sipping a drink, waiting for Michele Bianchi, a hundred Socialists and loafers hemmed in the café and began hurling abuses and insults at me. I had been recognized. Perhaps they intended, in their collective wrath, to give me a beating in order to place on my person the vengeance they had long since had in mind. The crowd, growing in numbers, became more and more menacing, and so the owner of the café and the female cashier hastened to pull down the shutters. She invited me, according to the fashion of those disorderly times, to go out because I was endangering their interests. I did not wait for a second invitation. I am used to facing the rabble without fear. The more there are of them, the more a man can move toward them with a sure courage which, to some, may appear as an affectation. I cannot say that there was any reluctance on my part to face these cowards.

I looked at the leaders and said, "What do you want of me? To strike me? Well, begin. Then be thereafter on guard. For any insult of yours, any blow, you will pay for dearly."

I remember the picture of that wolf pack. They were silent. They looked furtively at one another. The nearest withdrew, and then suddenly fear, which is as contagious as courage in any crowd of people, spread among the group. They backed away; they dispersed and only from a distance flung their last insults.

I recite this incident because it was typical of the usual occurrence in the life of a Fascist. But it must be remembered that in other cases the end was quite different—beatings, knife thrusts, bullets, assassinations, atrocities, torture and death.

In these days there began to develop a contest between General Diaz, victor of our last campaign, and Nitti.

The London pact, which had given Italy certain promises, broke down. The Adriatic coast-line was in a state of complete insecurity. Absurd rumors spread in the diplomatic clubs. The danger of seeing the Jugo-Slavians settled along the whole Adriatic shore had caused a bringing together in Rome of the cream of our unhappy regions. Students, professors, workmen, citizens

—representative men—were entreating the ministers
and the professional politicians. There was an appeal
from all the groups representative of the best Italian
life in behalf of Dalmatia. All these forces of righteous-
ness, on the occasion of the anniversary of Italy's entry
into war, organized a Dalmatian parade, with the object of dedicating, in the name of the fatherland, their
indestructible loyalty to their country.

Then, in the capital, came about an episode which is
still vivid in our memories. It raised general indignation. The Royal Guards, a new police corps, created
exclusively to serve the designs of the Nittian régime,
took the parade by storm. They fired gunshot volleys.
Many victims dropped and some fifty were wounded.
This was the most unworthy episode that ever happened under the sky of Rome within any memory. And
as if this assault and outrage were not sufficient, the
Dalmatians living in Rome were arrested, including the
women. Very few dared to raise their protests. Supine
victims and bullying authorities were the fashion. In the
chamber certain deputies, among whom were the nationalist writer, Luigi Siciliani, and Egilberto Martire,
moved interpellations which found no echo. From the
columns of the *Popolo d'Italia* I spread far and wide
my contempt. I hurled anathema against the system by
which a whole people were disgraced. My cry had some
echoes in the senate—in that senate where in historic
hours some great name always rose up to defend the
dignity, the right and the nobility of the Italian people.

A group of senators, at the head of whom was the Generalissimo Diaz, presented the following motion:

The senate regrets the methods of government which, by tolerating a want of discipline destructive of the state's power, diminishes the glorious victory of our arms and the admirable resistance of our people. It threatens any co-operative work for the prosperity of the unified fatherland and the peaceful attainment of every civil progress. These are methods opposite to Italian tradition, and they have culminated in the violent repression of a patriotic manifestation on May twenty-fourth with the arbitrary arrest of Dalmatians and Fiumeans, guests of Rome.

Among the signatures, with the name of Diaz, were to be seen the names of the Senator Attilio Hortis, a celebrated historian, of Admiral Thaon de Revel, and of many personalities of high Italian culture. The signers were sixty-four, among whom were the four vice-presidents of the senate.

The motion, in addition to its hint to awake Italian tradition, had strength and vigor, and disdain for the outrage done to the Italian war victory. The leader of that disdain, before all others, was Armando Diaz. The generalissimo bore about him the glory of Vittorio Veneto. He saw from day to day that his fine and lofty idealism as soldier and chieftain was fading away.

The Nitti government—part and parcel of a decadent party and futile parliamentary system—the Nitti government, bearing the stamp of mere pandering for favor and burned with the brand of politicians scrambling for power without regard for the nation and without brave idealism—fell ingloriously for the third time.

Giolitti came back.

After so many humiliations and oscillations, parliament and the political system had revealed itself as an assembly wholly unworthy to control or guide the destinies of a people. At the third fall of Nitti, Giolitti, of whom it may be said that he made the premiership a profession, came back upon the scene. His return gave some of us the impression that he was a kind of a receiver in bankruptcy for so-called self-government.

Justice requires our recognition of a great rectitude in the private life of Giolitti; we cannot say so much for his rectitude in his political character. He was a dissolver. He never gave evidence of believing in the deep idealistic springs and streams of Italian life. As a creature of the bureaucracy, he trusted the whole Italian problem to the vicissitudes of democratic and parliamentary pretense and artificiality. Thus, owing to his temperament, he held off during the war. Soon after the victory he returned to the political scene like a man who had to wind up a business. That business he was liquidating had been certainly the most bloody and yet no doubt the most magnificent and, in idealism, the most successful in our history as a united people.

The disclosed purposes of the Giolitti ministry as to domestic policy were good. After the most unhappy Nittian mire, public opinion was induced to accept new pilots without hostility. Foreign agents, provoking elements, supported also by some domestic political compromises, were inciting the Albanian population against us. This noble land, which is but twelve hours distant from Bari, and which had always absorbed an influx of our civilization, this land in which some sparks of modern civil life had gleamed only because of the influence we exercised there—all at once revolted against our garrison. We had been at Valona with sanitary missions since 1908, and since 1914 we had had military there. We had built there the city, the hospital, the magnificent roads which were a refuge for the Serbian army, routed in 1916. In Albania we had sacrificed millions of lire and had devoted thousands of soldiers to maintain her in efficiency and to give the little state a future and a well-ordered existence.

I knew and urged that it was useless to expect any decided Albanian policy from Giolitti. The domestic situation, which continued troubled, deprived him of energy or mind to devote to foreign policy. At that time the Honorable Sforza was Minister of Foreign Affairs; that was quite enough to accomplish the last vandalism in the Adriatic question. Meanwhile our military garrison was obliged to quit Valona, owing to the ineptitude of our government.

We entered another phase of defeatism.

In 1920 there was adopted among the railway employees the systematic practice of preventing the movement of trains carrying soldiers, carabinieri or policemen. Sometimes a similar policy extended also to the clergy. Against this inconceivable abuse of power, I alone protested. The Italian people were suffering passively from a stupid conception of their opportunities and from blindness which closed their eyes to their own power and pride. Those who dared to resist and were critical of the bureaucracy or of government policy were persecuted by the government itself.

There was the incident of the station master of Cremona, Signor Bergonzoni, which fell within my observation. He, by an energetic act, ordered the railway men subject to his authority to hook onto a train a car conveying some troops to Piacenza. For this episode, exhibiting the most ordinary case of regularity in routine, the Railway Syndicate, dominated by Socialists, demanded of the Ministry of Public Works the dismissal of the station master, Bergonzoni. And because the ministry by its firmness rejected this demand of the syndicate, Milan, which had nothing to do with all this matter, had imposed upon it a railway strike lasting thirteen days. Milan, a city of 900,000 inhabitants, choked by an enormous traffic, found itself incommunicado from its suburbs and the whole world. It was thrown back on the use of stage coaches, autos, camions, and was obliged to use even the small boats along the Naviglio River.

Milan, our greatest modern city, was in the power of political anarchy. Those same military forces who would have been able easily to take the situation in hand and dominate it were put at the mercy of the local authorities. They were even obliged to ask the authorities for the flour to make bread for the troops! The stations, situated at the boundaries of the district of

Milan, had in store heaps on heaps of goods; of course these stores decayed or deteriorated and were at the mercy of ware-house and freight-car robbers. At length, after thirteen days, on the morning of June twenty-fourth and after a meeting on behalf of the striking railway employees during which there was a fusillade of firearms, with dead and wounded, the railway men, overpowered by the indignation which had spread through the whole body of citizens, were convinced that it was better to return to work. But the state's authority was dead; it was now ready for the grave.

The Giolitti ministry muddled amid a quantity of financial difficulties. Giolitti himself hoped to be able to appease the Socialists with the project of general confiscation of all war profits, and still more with a plan to institute a strong tax on hereditary succession. This latter measure, wholly socialistic, would have annihilated the family conception of a patrimonial line. It would have threatened the rights of an owner to bequeath to his heirs his riches with his name. It had consequences which were not only economic but also moral and social. Capital as an institution is only in its infancy; the right of disposal is necessary to foster the functioning and development of this instrument of ambition, of human welfare and of civilization.

In international policy, Count Sforza, Minister of Foreign Affairs, concluded the agreement of Spa, signed the protocol of Tirana with the renunciation of Valona and Albania, signed the weak treaty of Sèvres with Turkey, and prepared by fits and starts to attempt an end also of the question of Fiume. This last happened at the conclusion of the treaty of Rapallo.

The application of the pact of London, by which Dalmatia was assigned to Italy, seemed to have been twisted without a single justifiable reason into something not to be argued. And Senator Scialoia, a gentleman of the old stamp, said amid the weak voices of the senate that the London treaty "has continually been tricked out of force and effect by those who are themselves Italians."

Believing with all my being that it was necessary to stop the flood of decadence in our foreign policy, I began to use our Fascisti organization and the *Popolo d'Italia.* I tried to raise some dikes. It was difficult to hold back the dirty water. There was a tendency to go toward communism whatever the cost. The power of Lenin—I admit it—had assumed a quality of potency only paralleled in mythology. The Russian dictator dominated the masses. He enchanted the masses. He charmed them as if they were hypnotized birdlings. Only some time afterward did the news of the dreadful Russian famine, as well as the information furnished by our mission which had gone to Russia to study Bolshevism, open the eyes of the crowd to the falsity of the Russian paradise-mirage. Enthusiasm ebbed away little by little. Finally Lenin remained only as a kind of banner and catchword for our political dabblers.

The aviation fields of Italy had been closed, the machines were being dismounted. There had been, however, some attempts to engage in civil aviation. One of the most unhappy and dramatic episodes of that time came out of the sky above Verona. Returning from a trip to Venice, a big airplane fell upon the city. The mishap caused the death of sixteen persons, including the pilots. Among the dead there were several journalists from Milan. The tragedy affected all Italy. Mourning was general. But to my horror the authorities seized this opportunity to abandon discussion of aviation and to dismantle the few machines, motors and wings which were left.

It was just at that period that I wanted to take lessons to become a pilot. The machine which crashed in Verona had been guided by a neighbor of my birthplace, Lieutenant Ridolfi. His body was carried to the churchyard of Forli. I had gone to Forli for a rest, with some political friends. My reception in my own home district had been cold and even hostile. My efforts to be agreeable and my willingness to learn to fly just after Ridolfi had lost his life seemed to be quite wasted. Anything in those days that did not have a material value seemed to be superfluous. Those were years when men's hearts were gray. For the same reason the state for which Gabriele d'Annunzio was preparing a durable form in Fiume did not catch the imagination of mankind.

But I did not give up. I repeated my flights. I flew over Mantua with the staff of the *Popolo d'Italia*. I was determined to show in action that aviation ought not to disappear from our vision of Italian possibilities and progress, to be won, if necessary, at the cost of hardships. I gave an example personally every time I had the chance, and my friends did likewise.

The growing exaltation of the bewitched masses and

the incredible weakness of the government culminated
at the beginning of September with the occupation of
the factories on the part of the metal workers. The occupation of the factories was to be an example of Bolshevism in action. The doctrine to be illustrated was
the taking possession of the means of production. The
workmen, with their childish understanding, and much
more the chiefs who were betraying them—and well
aware of their treachery as they did so—pretended that
they were able to administer directly, without an order
from any one planned beforehand, all the workshops,
all the processes, and even the sales of the output. In
truth, though it is not commonly realized, they did
nothing but make some side arms, such as daggers and
swords. They lost not less than twenty-one days in
forced leisure and childish manifestations of hatred and
impotence.

The occupation once begun, the managers, the owners, and the employes of the establishments were se-
questered by the workmen. The trade-marks and factory
signs were taken away, while upon the roofs and the
doors of the factories the red banners with the sickle
and hammer, symbol of the soviets, were hoisted with
cheers. In every establishment a committee was formed
subject to a socialist-communist set of by-laws. Tele-
phones were used to threaten all who were keeping out
of the movement and who, like us of the *Popolo d'Italia*,
were setting out to war against this grotesque sovietist
parody.

The seizure of the factories was accompanied by the

most ferocious acts. At Turin, the old capital of Piedmont, which had such glorious monarchical and military traditions, the red court of justice worked with all its might. Mario Sonzini, a nationalist and patriot, who had gone over to Fascism among the first, was arrested by the workmen and given a cruel and grotesque revolutionary trial. He was riddled by bullets and his body was then thrown into a ditch. Somebody had a kind Christian thought and threw him into the smelter ovens, but, as these were extinguished and as cold as industry itself, somebody else thought to put an end to the poor martyr by beating and kicking out what remained of life. Sonzini's guilt was only that he was a Fascist. The same fate befell others. To this kind of inhuman brutality not even the women were strangers. Apparently a bestial type of cruelty had taken hold of men and women drunk with licentiousness.

The newspaper *Avanti* on that occasion reported this barbarous murder as follows:

It may happen in life for one to be nationalist, to pass to Fascism, to reflect the tendencies of order and to be, nevertheless, arrested and shot to death; this is an average stroke of destiny.

The occupation of the factories in several Italian towns was merely an opportunity for violent demonstrations. There were dead at Monfalcone, there were dead in Milan and there were dead in other towns on the peninsula.

Our credit abroad had been extinguished like a

puffed-out candle. Even after the conclusion of peace, there was little thought any longer devoted to a rehabilitation of our nation. One could feel a clear sensation of collapse. The printing press began to spew out paper money. It was necessary to increase circulation; it was necessary to have recourse to inflation to prevent our economic life from going into complete ruin. After ten years, we are still feeling the burden of the consequences of that inauspicious period.

The exigencies of such artificial finance hastened the wreck. I denounced the peril in a series of articles in a debate with Meda, a member of the chamber, a man believed to be erudite in public finance. I can say now that nobody in that murky time had the ability to indicate any clear course to the Italian people; in financial matters we were going straight toward utter ruin—and playing an accompaniment on the strings of his foreign policy, Sforza was continuing his series of renunciations. He arrived at Rapallo and from that moment Fiume was doomed to become a detached, exiled city lying on a bed of thorns.

On November fourth the celebration of the anniversary of our victory gave opportunity for slight symptoms of reawakening. Rome and Milan both had extensive patriotic demonstrations. All Italy celebrated. I did.

But that was transitory. Almost at once affliction came in those mournful incidents—the tragedy of the Palace d'Accursio in Bologna, that of the Palace Estense in Ferrara, and the Bloody Christmas in Fiume.

In Bologna there was a bold handful of Fascists led by Arpinati. We were aware that the Socialists were preparing, in the red city and through the whole valley, pompous demonstrations to celebrate the installation of the new city government of Bologna, composed for the most part of reds. On November twenty-first, quantities of red banners were hoisted on the high towers of the City Hall Palace as well as on the private buildings. There had been planned also the release of flocks of pigeons to bring the greetings of the Bologna Socialists to their comrades of other places. The whole town was in the hands of the Socialists. They were on the point of adopting a constitution of the soviets. The city government minority, composed of elements of good order, with Fascists and combatants, was present at the meeting. This was considered by the reds as a provocation and a challenge.

The Fascist group of Bologna, which had its headquarters in a street called Marsala, organized several squads to defend the public order at any price. In the afternoon the Fascists were being singled out for continuous and increasing insults and provocations. The Fascio—the organization of the Fascisti—by placards made it plain that it was resolved not to be bull-dozed, and it warned the women and children to keep at home behind locked doors. It was foreseen that the streets of Bologna might witness a tragedy. This firm attitude of the Bologna Fascists, guided by Arpinati, whipped up the Socialists, not only because they felt themselves no longer able to do as they pleased but also because physi-

cal fear had taken possession of their leaders all up and
down the line. I say categorically that fear and cowardice have always been typical characteristics of the
Socialist party in Italy.

At the moment when about thirty Fascists formed in
tiny squads and tried to go from Indipendenza Street,
the open space crowded with the Socialists, there came
a general scattering and a disordered shouting and
clamor. A portion of the terrified crowd poured over to
the City Hall and entered the courtyard. The Socialists,
barricaded there as in a fortress, blinded by their own
base fears, supposed that all the fugitives were Fascists; they feared that the City Hall might be invaded;
therefore they threw from above, upon the crowd, hand
bombs with which they had armed themselves.

This increased the general terror in the crowd. Many
of the people ran off, tearing up their tickets of the Socialistic organizations.

While these events were going on around the palace
and in the courtyard, in the Hall of the City Council
there exploded a sudden tragedy. The red members of
the council, frightened by the apprehension of a Fascist invasion, thronged for the most part toward the
exit. Some of them, however, preferred joining the public, composed of red elements; some flung themselves
against the little group of the council conservatives. The
first shots were now heard in the hall. The guards, not
to be caught, threw themselves upon the ground. The
few minority councilors—among whom were the advocate Giordani and advocates Oviglio, Biagi, Colliva,

Manaresi—firmly kept their places, offering a conspicuous mark for wrath whipped up by fear. Somebody
fired. The bullet missed Oviglio by a miracle. But a second shot killed Lieutenant Giordani, a *bersagliere,*
mutilated in war, hated for his record by the reds.
Meanwhile, the organizers of the bloody riot were continuing to hurl bombs, as if they had gone out of their
minds, into the square crowded with people, and they
hit fugitive Socialists under the impression that their
victims were Fascists. Horrible was the carnage and the
butchery.

Something of the same kind happened a little later
at Ferrara on the occasion of a great Socialistic manifestation which was to have taken place in the historic
castle of the Estensi. A column of Fascists, advancing
to the spot of the meeting, met a fusillade of lead. The
Fascists left on the ground three dead and numbers of
wounded. Ferrara, the red, Ferrara, in which all mu-
nicipalities and the province were in the hands of the
Socialists; Ferrara, which had threatened to arrest its
own prefect—passed hours in anxiety. The same exasperated passion of Bologna seized the noble province
of the Estensi. I felt, however, that one could catch a
glimpse of tragedies which were mere preludes to certain revolution. What revolution?

I called to Milan the responsible chiefs of the Fascist
movement, the representatives of the Po Valley, of Upper Italy, of the towns and countrysides. Those present
were not many, but they were men resolved to take any
risk. I made them understand, as I had suddenly un-

derstood, that through newspaper propaganda, or by example, we would never attain any great successes. It was necessary to beat the violent adversary on the battle-field of violence.

As if a revelation had come to me, I realized that Italy would be saved by one historic agency—in an imperfect world, sometimes inevitable still—righteous force.

Our democracy of yesterdays had died; its testament had been read; it had bequeathed us naught but chaos.

CHAPTER VII

THE GARDEN OF FASCISM

IN certain contingencies violence has a deep moral significance.

In our land a leading class was neither present nor living. The Liberal party had abdicated everything to the Socialists. There was no solid, modern, national unity.

Ignorance was still astride the workmen and peasant masses. It was useless to attempt to blaze a trail by fine words, by sermons from chairs. It was necessary to give timely, genial recognition to chivalrous violence. The only straight road was to beat the violent forces of evil on the very ground they had chosen.

With us were elements who knew what war meant. From them was born the organization of Italian Bundles of Fight. Many also volunteered from our universities. They were students, touched by the inspiration of idealism, who left their studies to run to our call.

We knew that we must win this war too—throw into yesterday the period of cowardice and treachery. It was necessary to make our way by violence, by sacrifice, by blood; it was necessary to establish the order and discipline wanted by the masses, but impossible to obtain them through milk-and-water propaganda and through words, words and more words—parliamentary and journalistic sham battles.

We began our period of rescue and resurrection. Dead there were, but on the horizon all eyes saw the dawn of Italian rebirth.

The unhappy year of 1921 was closed with the tragic dissolution of the Fiume drama. After the Treaty of Rapallo, by which Fiume was doomed to be a separate body, the Italian resistance in Fiume made itself more decided than ever. D'Annunzio declared that, whatever the cost, he would not abandon the city which had suffered so long and painfully to keep alive and keep pure its Italian soul.

I, too, had been living this drama, day by day. D'Annunzio and I had been close together since the first days of the campaign. Now for more than a year I had been accustomed to receive his brotherly letters. They brought to me the breath of the passion of Fiume. Since the first moment of the occupation of the holocaust city the poet had disclosed to me his firm will to fight. Significant evidence is found in a letter which D'Annunzio had sent me on September 14, 1919, transmitting to me, for my newspaper, one of his most virile messages. He wrote:

My dear Mussolini: Here are two lines in a hurry. I have been working for hours. My hand and my eyes are aching. I send my son, Gabriellino, brave companion, to bring you this manuscript. Look out for any needed correction, and thank you. This is only the first act of a struggle that I will see to the end after my own style. In the event that the censorship should be bold enough to interfere, please publish the letter with the white intervals showing where words are omitted. Then we will see what we shall see.

I will write you again. I will come. I admire your constancy and the strength of your well-directed blows. Let me clasp your hand. Yours,

GABRIELE D'ANNUNZIO.

From July to December the situation in Fiume grew more and more difficult. In the face of the determined attitude of D'Annunzio, Giolitti—to be faithful to the engagements assumed at Rapallo by Count Sforza—resolved to blockade the city. The results of the blockade were dubious; therefore the government made up its mind to occupy the city by a military expedition. They chose Christmas, because there were two holidays during which newspapers did not appear. Italian soldiers were being hurled against an Italian city, against a handful of audacious legionaries, ardent-souled Italians, the combatants of D'Annunzio's brothers. Blood was on the streets. There were even dead. All Italy was saturated with deep indignation.

Thereafter a sense of remorse and conciliation took the upper hand. A formula was found. D'Annunzio gave up his authority to a committee of citizens and left Fiume. It had been held by him during sixteen months with invincible faithfulness. Now it was requisite to intrust its destinies to its best citizens and to the events which were maturing, inexorably. I wrote at that time a message which found an echo in all Italian hearts:

Beneath all the verbosity and the shuttle of mere words, the drama is perfect; horrible, if you choose, but perfect. On

one side is the cold Reason of State determined to the very
bottom, on the other the warm Reason of the Ideal ready to
make desperate, supreme sacrifices. Invited to make our
choice, we, the uneasy and precocious minority, choose
calmly the Reason of the Ideal.

A few days later, on January 4, 1921, I commem-
orated the dead of the Legion of Ronchi by one of the
most fervid articles I ever wrote. It ended with the following words:

They are the latest to fall in the Great War, and it is not
in vain! The Italian tricolored banner hails them, Italian
earth covers them. Their graves are a shrine. There all factions and divisions are obliterated. The dead of Carnaro bear
witness that Fiume and Italy are one, the same flesh, the
same soul. The opaque ink of the diplomats will never undo
what has been sealed by blood forever.

Hail then to the Ronchi Legion, to the Duce—the leader,
D'Annunzio—to his living who return and to his dead who
never will.

They have remained to garrison the snowy mountains—
Nevosso!

The iron necessity of violence already had been confirmed. Every one of us felt it. Now came the moment
to move to action with a clear sense of the definite issue.
The formation of squads and battling units which I had
drawn up by intuition had been accomplished. I had
given them, in precise directions, well-specified tasks
within clean limits. They began their work of discipline
and retaliation.

Our violence had to possess impetuosity. It had been
trained to be loyal, as were the legions of Garibaldi, and

above all chivalrous. The Central Committee of the Italian Bundles of Fight co-ordinated, under my direction, the whole work of the local executives and of the action squads, not only in the provinces but even in the towns. Valiant and vigorous elements joined us from the universities. Italian schools are enriched by the glorious names of students who quitted their halls for political life and Fascism. These eager boys left, without regret and without wavering, a merry existence to face mortal dangers during punitive actions against betrayers of our country. Later on, to these heroes of bold youth I ordered the awarding of degrees *ad honorem;* they had given their blood freely so that their nation might be saved. Among them was the best type of Italian young manhood, who by disciplined methodical action, full of impetus, as were the actors, met and destroyed the social-communist spiders which in the web of foolishness and ignorance were exterminating every life germ of the Italian people. Wherever there popped up a vexation, a ransom, a case of blackmail, an extortion, a disorder, a reprisal—there would gather the Fascist squads of action. The black shirt—symbol of hardihood—was our uniform of war.

The Liberal-Democratic government quite naturally put difficulties in the way of the Fascist movement. It relied principally on the royal guards—Guardia Regia —blind instrument of anti-national hatred. But we, who had sane courage, resource and ability, accepted the fact of facing ambush, traps and death. When instead we were taken to prison, we remained there long periods waiting for trial. I had an effect on my soldiers which seemed to me almost mystical. The boys saw in me the avenger of our wronged Italy. The dying said, "Give us our black shirts for winding sheets." I could not remain unmoved when I knew that their last thoughts were of "Our native land and the Duce." Love and songs bloomed. A revival of youth, filled with Italian boldness, swamped by its virile male beauty the unrestrained rages of the irresponsibles, painted out the fear of the Socialists, obliterated the ambiguity of the Liberals. The poesy of battle, the voices of an awakening race were multiplying, in those years of revival, the energies of our nation.

Our dead were innumerable. Italy's imps, the red dabblers, our organization of so-called Freemasons who were steeped in political intrigue, already were seeing the danger, menacing to them, of the coming of Fascism. Therefore they used every means to put us down; they created their snares and ambushes more and more carefully and built their pitfalls more and more cunningly. Every day both the public streets and the open rural fields of Italy were smeared with the blood of frightful conflicts. Sundays, holidays and any occasions for gatherings seemed particularly marked out for attack.

I restrained our own violence to the strict limit of necessity. I enforced that view-point with lieutenants and with the rank and file. At times they obeyed me with regret and pain. They were thinking of companions treacherously murdered. But they always submitted to my orders against reprisals. They accepted my authority voluntarily and completely. If I had had a mind to do so, I could have ordered a pitched battle. The boys would have leaped at the chance; they were looking to me as to a chief whose word was law.

There were evidences of such a deep attachment to me that I felt lifted up and refined by it. It created in me a deep sense of responsibility. Among the episodes I remember the death of a young man, twenty years old, the Count Nicolo' Foscari, treacherously stabbed to death by a communist dagger. This fine boy died after two days of agony. In the agony of the wound and at the point of death, he wanted to have always near him my photograph. He declared himself glad and proud to die and through me he knew how to die.

I was calloused to political battles. My inclination, however, has always been against all but chivalrous battles. I understood the sadness of civil strife; but in desperate political crises, when the bow happens to be too much bent, the arrow either flies off or the cord breaks. In a few months of action and violence we had to win no less than fifty years lost in empty parliamentary skirmishes, lost in the marshes of little political intrigues, lost in the wretchedness of an atmosphere defiled by selfish interest and petty personal ambition, lost in the maze of attempts to treat government as if it were a jam pot to attract the flies.

In 1921 I tried a political agreement and truce with our adversaries under the protection of the government. The utter incomprehension of the Socialists and Liberals was enormous. My gesture, prodigal and generous, created solely by me, served only to raise new fogs, miasmas and equivocations. The truce had been signed by the Socialists but not by the communists. The latter continued the open struggle, helped in every way by the Socialists themselves. A generous experiment in pacificism had been quite useless. Socialism had corrupted Italian life. There would be always some irreconcilable antagonists, and so the struggle, after a short parenthesis, was taken up again. It lasted until the final outcome, but its renewal was the beginning of the great political battle of 1921.

I will not set forth all the deadly frays of this year. They have gone into the past. But in the houses of my men are burning perennially the votive lamps of the survivors and on their hearths is the living memory of the fallen. The Fascist legions are of every age and of every condition. Many died when the victory was as yet uncertain, but the God of just men will guide all the fallen to eternal light and will reward the soul who lived nobly and who wrote in blood the goodness and ardor of his faith.

The first months of 1921 were characterized by an extreme violence in the Po Valley. The Socialists came to the point where they were even willing to shoot at the funeral processions of the Fascists. It happened even in Rome. It was at that time that in Leghorn there was held the congress of the Socialist party. A schism broke out. On that occasion the autonomous Communist party was created, which afterward in all the manifestations of Italian political life played such a loathsome part.

I knew—and it was evident to every one in spite of concealment—that the new Communist party was inspired and supported and even directed from Moscow. We were invaded just as other lands have since been invaded.

At Triest, a city dear to every Italian, which had always kept alive the flame of faith and enthusiasm, a great Fascist meeting was held. At the head of the Triest Fascists was Giunta, a member of the Italian Chamber and an ardent and valiant Fascist from the first call to action. He knew, in various circumstances, how to raise formidable barriers against this Slavic inroad and against the stupidity of the men who had taken authority in Triest. The gathering was held at the Rossetti Theatre. There I spoke. I set forth our fundamental principles, not only for the Fascists but for all those who were interested in a new and complete Italian policy. After a panoramic examination of the knotty problems which at that time were vexing Italian foreign policy, I demanded a complete, definite withdrawal of the Rapallo Treaty by which Sforza and Giolitti had signed away Fiume. I acknowledged, none the less, the impossibility of setting oneself, at that moment, against the tragic consequences of the treaty—the fruit of a long disintegration fostered by those who had led us into a morass.

"The fault of the renunciation," I affirmed, "is not to be attributed entirely to the negotiators at the last hour; the renunciation had been perpetrated already in parliament, in our journalism, even in a university where a professor has published books—translated, of course, at Zagabria—in order to demonstrate according to his style of thinking that Dalmatia is not Italian!

"The Dalmatian tragedy lies in this ignorance, this bad faith and utter incomprehension. We hope to put a stop to these grotesque errors by our future work. We will know, love and defend Italian Dalmatia.

"The treaty signed, it was possible to make it void by one of the following means: Either a foreign war or by insurrection at home. Both are absurd! It is impossible to excite the man in the street against a treaty of peace after five years of bloody calvary. Nobody is able to perform a miracle!

"It was possible to awake in Italy a revolution in favor of the intervention, but in November, 1921, it was not possible to think of a revolution in order to annul a peace treaty which, good or bad, has been accepted by ninety out of every hundred of Italians."

Having delineated clearly the uncertain and transitory position in which Italy found herself at that time in respect to the Fiume tragedy and herself, having shown the impossibility of creating a revolution which would have been premature and condemned to failure, I laid down and fixed by firm, precise tacks and nails what was to be the political programme of the Fascists in 1921.

"From these general premises," I said, "it follows that the Italian Bundles of Fight should ask:

"First, that the treaties of peace be re-examined and modified in parts which are revealed as inapplicable or the application of which can be a source of hatred and incentive to new wars;

"Second, the economic annexation of Fiume to Italy and the guardianship of Italians living in Dalmatian countries;

"Third, the gradual disengagement of Italy from the group of the Occidental plutocratic nations by the development of our productive forces at home;

"Fourth, an approach once again toward the nations of Austria, Germany, Bulgaria, Turkey, Hungary, but with dignified attitude, and safeguarding the supreme necessities of our north and south boundaries;

"Fifth, the creation and intensification of friendly relations with all peoples of the Near and Far East, not excluding those which are ruled by the soviets.

"Sixth, the recognition in colonial policy of the rights and necessities of our nation;

"Seventh, the reform and renewal of all our diplomatic representatives abroad by elements with special university training;

"Eighth, the building up of Italian colonies in the Mediterranean sea as well as those beyond the Atlantic by economic and cultural institutions and rapid communications."

I concluded my speech by an ardent affirmation of faith.

"It is destiny," I said, "that Rome again takes her place as the city that will be the director of the civilization of all Western Europe. Let us commit the flame of this passion to the coming generations; let us make of

Italy one of the nations without which it is impossible
to conceive the future history of humanity."

The year 1921 was the centenary of Dante. I was
dreaming, in the name of Alighieri: "The Italy of to-
morrow, both free and rich, all-resounding, with seas
and skies peopled with her fleets, with the earth everywhere made fruitful by her plows."

Later on, in a meeting of Lombardian Fascists, I indicated some landmarks of the Fascist battle. In a
speech that I made to my friends in Milan I affirmed
that by its fatiguing work Fascism was preparing men
of a spirit suited to the task of an imminent to-morrow
—that of ruling the nation.

Already in germination through all these affirmations,
there was growing the definite intention of preparing by
legal action, as well as by violence, for the conquest of
power.

The Socialists and Communists, though debating between themselves on doctrinarian questions, vied with
one another to show themselves more anti-Fascist than
the others. The Communists had no scruples. Every day
they gave proof of their contempt for law, and they evidenced a foolish disregard for the strength of their adversaries.

At Florence, during a parade of patriotic character,
there had been an attempt at a communist insurrection.
Bombs were thrown, isolated Fascists were pursued. It
happened on this occasion that a very young Fascist
named Berta was horribly murdered. The unhappy boy,
surprised upon a bridge of the Arno River, was beaten
to a bloody pulp and thrown from the parapet into the

water. As the poor victim, by a dull instinct of self-preservation, clung to the railing bars with his fingers, the Communists rushed upon him and beat his hands until our martyr, whose jellied hands were slackening their grip, finally let go and was plunged into the Arno. His body was whirled about in the current.

This single episode of incredible ferocity gave evidence of how deeply Communist outrage had penetrated into Italy. As if that were not enough, soon afterward there occurred the butchery of Empoli, where two camions were loaded with marines and carabineers. The proof of the degenerative ferocity of the Communists was provided by the corpses of the poor victims, for their inert bodies were treated as jungle savages treat the corpses of their victims.

This was not confined to any one province. At that time there happened also the trap and massacre of Casale Monferrato, where among the dead were two old Sardinian drummers and where Cesare Maria de Vecchi, a brave companion, was wounded. At Milan isolated Fascists were singled out and attacked by stealth. One of our most beloved friends, the very young Aldo Sette, was murdered with all the accompaniment of savagery.

But on the twenty-third of March occurred the culminating episode of premeditated horror, with dreadful consequences. The Communists caused a bomb to explode in the Diana Theatre in that city. It was crowded with peaceful citizens attending an operatic performance. The bomb sent twenty persons to sudden death. Fifty others were mutilated. All Milan gave itself up

to anguish and anger and to chills of vengeance. There
was no possibility of checking public sentiment. Squads
of Fascists assaulted for the second time the newspaper
Avanti and it was burned by them. Others tried also to
assault the Workers' Chamber, but a strong military
garrison barred the Fascists from an attack.

The action squads turned their activity into the suburbs, firmly held both by Communists and Socialists.
The swift, decisive action of the Fascists served to drive
from their nests and put to flight the subverters of civil
order. The political authority was powerless; it could
not control the disorders and disturbances. On the twenty-sixth of March I concentrated all the Fascists of
Lombardy. They filed off, marching compactly in columns, through the principal streets of Milan. It was a
demonstration of strength not to be forgotten. At last
over the horizon I had brought defenders of civil life,
protectors of order and citizenship. There had come a
spirit of revival for all good works. The martyrs of the
Diana and the Fascist victims were the best inspiration.
A whole people might now be united in the name of the
Roman Littorio, under the direction of Italian youth—
a youth which had won the war and now would again
attain the serene peace of the spirit and the rewards of
fruitful virtue, of discipline, work and fraternity.

Unforgettable were the demonstrations for the victims
of the dastardly bomb at the Diana. It was from that
day on that there began the progressive crashing down
and crumbling of the whole structure of Italian subversive elements. Now they were driven like rats to their

holes and were barricaded in the few forts of the Workers' Chambers and of the district clubs.

I led a life of intense activity. I managed the *Popolo d'Italia* and every morning I was able to give the political text for the day, not only to Milan but to the principal cities of Italy in which the political life of the nation found its sources. I led the Fascist party with a firm hand. I must say that I gave some very strict orders. I had an ear open to all who came to Milan with communications about our organization in the various provinces. I watched the activity of our enemies. I guarded for the Fascists the clear, clean stream of purpose. I maintained the freedom necessary for our elasticity of movements. I wished not to mix or adulterate such a pure and strong faith as the Fascist faith. I wished not to blend that ardent youth which was the essential soul of Fascism with old elements of trade and barter, combinations, coalitions, parliamentary compromises and the hypocrisies of Italian liberalism.

Among the many vicissitudes which have accompanied my existence I have always kept an invincible passion for flying. At that period, so tumultuous, so colored by dramatic hues, every morning found me on a bicycle going and coming some eighteen miles to take lessons in aviation. My teacher was Giuseppe Radaelli, a modest and brave aviator, full of passion for flight and happy to have a chance to teach me the difficult craft of being a good pilot.

One morning I took a seat in a plane with Radaelli. The first flight came off without incident. During the

second flight, on the contrary, the motor for some reason stalled, just at the moment when we were executing
the maneuver of coming down. The machine veered
sidewise and after gliding on one wing, precipitated
us onto the field from a height of about forty metres.
The pilot came off with some light wounds on the fore-
head. I had several about the head which would require
two weeks to heal. After an emergency treatment at
the field I was treated more thoroughly by Dr. Leonardo Pallieri at the Guardia Medica of Porta Venezia.
That incident, which might have had marked consequences to my life, was, thanks to the kind treatment
by my personal friend, Dr. Ambrogio Binda, passed off
as nothing.

This incident, however, gave me the opportunity to
measure how many Italians were following my affairs.
I got almost a plebiscite of warm sympathy from all
over the land. I rested, suffering, for some days, and
then I took up my usual activity at the *Popolo d'Italia*,
knowing that Italy no longer disregarded the part I
was to play.

On the day of the carnage at the Diana and of the
consequent reprisals, while spirits were kindled and irritated, a certain Masi, sent by the anarchists of Piombino, came to Milan to attempt my life. He presented
himself at my house, rang the bell and boldly climbed
the stairs. He was a strange creature of extraordinary
mien. My daughter Edda went to open the door.

The unknown man asked for me. He was sent to the
Popolo d'Italia, but went below and waited for me on

the large public square of Foro Bonaparte. When he saw me he came toward me at first rapidly, and then slowly he wavered. He asked me in a halting voice if I was Professor Mussolini, and when I said I was he added that he wanted to speak to me at some length.

The strange behavior of the individual with the grim eye made me understand that I found myself in the presence of a madman. I said that I did not give audience in the street; I told him that I received at the *Popolo d'Italia*, where in fact he came half an hour later, asking to be introduced to me. I consented at once and willingly. Masi—who, I repeat, was a young man with burning eyes—as soon as he came into my presence appeared embarrassed. He said he wanted to speak to me. His behavior was so curious that I asked him to tell me promptly and sympathetically what he wanted to say.

After a moment of hesitation he told me that he had been chosen by lot, in a drawing by the anarchists of Piombino, to murder me treacherously with a Berretta pistol. Later, having been caught in some doubts, he had resolved to come and confess everything to me, to hand me the weapon with which he had intended to kill me and to put himself at my mercy. I listened to him, but I said not a word.

Taking the revolver from his hands, I called the chief clerk and telephone operator of the newspaper, Sant' Elia, and intrusted to him that unhappy man, so ensnared by anarchy and frightened by the consequences of his dreams. I wanted Sant' Elia to accompany him to Triest, with a letter of introduction to the Fascist

Giunta. Soon afterward, however, the police—informed by what means I know not of the episode—arrested the anarchist of Piombino as he went away. This was the one clever piece of detective work performed at that time by the Milan police. They had utterly failed to trace out the dynamiters of the Diana even two months after the crime.

Oh, many had meditated upon my funeral! And yet love is stronger than hatred. I always felt a power over events and over men.

Giolitti in those days was in a most difficult parliamentary situation. On the political horizon there had appeared a political constellation of first magnitude—it was Fascism. Facing this fact, the president of the council of that epoch deemed it opportune to measure the parties on the basis of parliamentary suffrage, and he announced the elections for the month of May.

After a preliminary discussion the various parties which were pledged to order, in opposition to Socialist communism, found it expedient to go into the elections as a body, which could be defined as a national bloc.

In the centre of the bloc—the only motivating and encouraging force—was Fascism. All other parties kept their complexions as subverters in political and economic matters. The Socialist party presented itself separated from the Communist party, while the Popular party, which always claimed an inspiration of ecclesiastical, religious character, moved on the field alone, leaning heavily upon the political influence of the country vicars.

In order to make myself acquainted with the real efficiency of our party, I started reconnoitering in several provinces. I received an enthusiastic welcome at the beginning of April in Bologna, a fortress of socialism and a barometer indicating the level of the whole Po Valley. Bologna greeted me in a jubilation of colors, with parades, fanfares of welcome and speeches favoring Italian resurrection. The butchery of the Palace of Accursio was still too fresh and red in memory. Fascism was in a hot fervor; therefore my presence could not fail to whip up in all the young men a singular strength of will, hope and faith.

From Bologna I went to Ferrara, another stronghold of socialism. And there again there was waiting for me an unforgettable demonstration of strength. Bologna and Ferrara are two magnificent towns, centres of regions exclusively agricultural. In those days I could measure by my youth and intimate knowledge the strength, the mentality, the ways of thinking and the longing for order of the workers of the land. I understood that their thinking had lost its way, but it was not dominated by red propaganda. At bottom their mentality is that of people wise and praiseworthy, who have always been, at the crucial moments, the bulwark of the fortunes of the Italian race.

The electoral struggle lasted exactly a month. During that period I made but three speeches—one in Bologna, once in Ferrara and one in Milan, on the Place Borromeo. Contrary to what happened during the political elections of 1919, I succeeded this time in getting a plurality not only in Milan but also in the districts of Bologna and Ferrara. Great demonstrations of joy followed the news. Furthermore, all Fascism in the electoral field was gaining in undoubted strides.

In November, 1919, I had not succeeded in getting more than 4,000 votes. In 1921 I was at the head of the list with 178,000 votes. My election to the Italian Chamber caused a great rejoicing among my friends, my colleagues, my assistants. To all my faithful sub-editors, Giuliani, Gaini, Rocca, Morgagni and others, I recalled the episode of 1919, when I said to my discouraged and perplexed assistants that within the space of two years I would have my revenge. The prophecy had proved true within two years. A new moral atmosphere was being breathed by every stratum of our population. Though not many Fascists entered the parliament, the few represented in themselves a tremendous force for the new destinies of Italy.

At Montecitorio, the House of Parliament, in order to follow the rules of the chamber, the Fascists formed their own group. There were only thirty-five representatives. It was numerically a small group, indeed, but it was composed of men with good livers and excellent courage.

During the session I made few speeches. I think I spoke five times and that was all. Certainly I tried in all cases to give my oratory a spirit and to make it stick to realities. Certainly I confined it to a devotion to the interests of Italian life. I put aside parliamentary triflings and the tin sword play of parliamentary politicians.

In a speech made on the twenty-first of June, 1921, I criticised without reserve the foreign policy of the Giolitti ministry. I put on a firm, realistic basis the question of Northern Italy, the Upper Adige. I pointed out the feebleness of the government and of the men placed in authority over the new provinces. One of these, Credaro, was "bound also by means of the symbol of the political compass and triangle to the immortal precepts" of false liberalism—to wit, he was swayed by that Masonry which in Italy was representing a "web of foreign and internationalistic ideas." Therefore, I affirmed solemnly: "As the government of Giolitti is responsible for the miserable Salata and Credaro policy in the Upper Adige, I vote against him. Let us declare to the German deputies here in our present Italian parliament that we find ourselves at the Brenner Pass now, and that at the Brenner we will remain at any price." I took up again the hot, impassioned subject of Fiume and Dalmatia. I assaulted violently the shameful foreign policy of Sforza, leading our land to humiliation and ruin.

I spoke of our domestic policy. I stripped the covering from the Socialists and Communists and made them face Fascism. I pointed out with irony the fact that, among others, with the Communists stood Graziadei, who, at other times, had been my opponent when he was a Socialist reformer. I exposed to the light the utter lack of principles to be found in representatives who dipped their paws into this or that party group or programme solely for the purpose of gaining petty power or personal gain.

The speech, which had only the purpose of clarification, gave some needed hints as to our political action as Fascists in destruction of the methods and principles of our adversaries. To my surprise it created a deep impression. It had a vast echo outside the chamber and was undoubtedly among the factors which finally doomed the Giolitti ministry, like all the rest, to topple over like a drunken buzzard.

I was not alone in the parliamentary struggle. The group was helping me valiantly and with ability. Already the Deputy Federzoni, since then a distinguished official of the Fascist state, had started a review and revision of the whole work of Count Sforza, Giolitti's Minister of Foreign Affairs, and particularly of the Adriatic policy. There had been dramatic sessions in which the work of the aforesaid minister not only was put under a strict and inexorable examination, according to both the logic and conscience of Fascism, but was examined in the light of the negotiations and treaties, open or secret, which the parliament had to know and approve.

After various parliamentary ups and downs, the Giolitti ministry fell and was followed by that of Bonomi —a Socialist who arrived at being a Democrat through varied captious reasonings. He tried to set up a policy of internal pacification. He was interested in the truce between Fascists and Socialists, of which I have already told the meagre results. Just at the moment when Bonomi was developing this political fabric came the tragic episode of the massacre of Sarzana. There not less than eighteen Fascists fell. Then came the butchery of Modena, where the Royal Guards shot into a parade of Fascists, leaving some ten dead and many wounded. The home policy had not found as yet, one could mildly say, any perch of stability. I constantly was unfolding my active task as leader of the party, as journalist and politician.

I had a duel of some consequence with Ciccotti Scozzese, a mean figure of a journalist. He was the long hand of our Italian political Masonry. Among other various imperfections, one might say he had that of physical cowardice. Our duel was proof of it. After several assaults the physicians were obliged to stop the encounter because of the claim that my opponent had a heart attack. In other words, fear had set him all aflutter. Shortly before that duel I had another with Major Baseggio over some parliamentary squabble.

I think I have some good qualities as a swordsman— at least I possess some qualities of courage, and thanks to both, I always have come out of combat rather well. In those combats having a chivalrous character, I endeavor to acquit myself in a worthy manner.

Finally in November, 1921, I convoked in Rome a large congress of the Fascists of the whole of Italy. The moment had arrived to emerge from the first phase, in which Fascism had had the character of a movement outside the usual political divisions, into a new phase, in which the organic structure of a party, which had been made strong both by firm political intrenchment and by the growth of central and local organization, should be crystallized.

The Italian Bundles of Fight had been inspired by an impetuous spirit. They possessed therefore an organization of battle rather than a true and proper organization of party. It was now necessary to come to this second phase in order to be prepared to be a successor of the old parties in the command and direction of public affairs. The congress at the Augusteo—the tomb of Augustus and now a concert hall in Rome—had to agree on the terms for the creation of the new party. It had to fix both the organization and the programme.

That was a memorable meeting. Thanks to the number of the followers and the quickness and solidity of the discussions, it showed the virility of Fascism. My point of view won an overwhelming victory in that meeting. The Italian Bundles of Fight were now transforming themselves. They were to receive the new denomination of Fascist National party, with a central directory and supreme council over the provincial organizations and the lesser Fascist sections which were to be created in every locality. On that occasion I wanted with all my desire to strip from our party the personal character which the Fascist movement had assumed because of the stamp of my will. But the more I wished to give the party an autonomous organization and the more I tried, the more I received the conviction from the evidence of the facts that the party could not have existed and lived and could not be triumphant except under my command, my guidance, my support and my spurs.

The meeting in Rome gave a deep insight into the fundamental strength of Fascism, but especially for me it was a revelation of my personal strength. But there were several unpleasant incidents. There had been some men killed in Rome. The workers' quarter of Rome was hostile to us. The work of the congress had, however, its full and normal development, and the parade of Fascists at last filed off in battle array through the streets of Rome. It served notice to everybody that Fascism was ripe as a party, and as an instrumentality with the heart and the means to battle and to defend itself.

The Bonomi ministry developed its pacification policy in the midst of difficulties of all kinds. The time and the moment were rather murky. The year 1921 presented difficulties which would have made any politician shiver. On the horizon a line of clarification was to be discerned, but the sky was nevertheless still heavy with old clouds.

About the end of this formless, gray year, awaiting a great dawn, occurred an event in the financial world which threw a shadow of sorrow over the whole land. This was the crash of the Banca Italiana di Sconto. The collapse was felt particularly in the southern part of Italy by the humble classes who had deposited their savings in that bank. This great banking institution had been born during the war and had done notable service for the organization of our efficiency, but in the postwar period it could not bear the burden of its engagements. The big banking organization, in which the laboring populations of the South and of Upper Italy were interested so deeply, crumbled on itself, giving all the postwar Italian financial policy a sensation of dismay and failure. Ignorance, foolishness, fault, levity? Who knows?

Certainly our credit as a power and as a rebuilding force in comparison with foreign countries diminished enormously. To the faults of our domestic policy was added now, in the eyes of the world, a plutocratic and financial insufficiency.

From the broils of financial chaos and in the maze of debates which ensued, Fascism kept itself aloof. It delayed not to consider the past, but chose to determine carefully a sound, wise and foreseeing monetary policy for the nation.

For the first time I found myself squarely challenged by the gigantic problem of public finance.

For me it was a new airplane—and there was no competent instructor anywhere on our field.

CHAPTER VIII

TOWARD CONQUEST OF POWER

FINANCE, the proper use and easy flow of capital, and the development of the banking structure of a nation must not be underestimated when one has to face the clear responsibility of building a state or of leading a people out of chaos.

The noisy crash of the great Banca Italiana di Sconto in Italy revealed, as I have said, a deep weakness in our economic structure. After the war it was clear that many banking and industrial enterprises were out of adjustment and must disappear or be succeeded by stronger institutions.

There were struggles between opposing groups of capitalists. These created a cynical attitude among the modern middle class; at the same time it was shown that our capitalistic industrial group resented the vice of having no comprehensive plan. We needed a strong capitalistic tradition, rigorous experience; we found that in the whir of events it was difficult to perceive who was right and who would probably be able to save himself, when the pressure came and a test of strength was made.

The other nations, who saw deeply into this strange cauldron through the cold eyes of their financiers, made dark prophecies as to our economic life. The Italian government itself did not know how to behave in its money affairs, and, not finding anything better, did as is often done in such circumstances—began to print money. That contributed to render a situation which was already bad and complicated, grotesquely worse.

In January, 1922, the Inter-Allied Conference was held at Cannes in southern France. It was a very good junket and it was made more pleasant by the fine hospitality of the French. I went there to serve my newspaper, the *Popolo d'Italia*. What an excellent occasion it was to distract public opinion from our internal crisis, at least temporarily! We could examine thoroughly, instead of domestic thorns, problems of international character!

At Cannes I wanted to interview the great world politicians—responsible men. I would have liked, from a full survey, to have informed Italian public opinion as to the various ingredients which we could find in the pudding of our international situation. The Cannes conference was the overture to the opera of the conference in Genoa. Italy should have selected her own policy. It should have been one which would not betray vital interests arising from our most urgent historic and political necessities.

At any rate because of these considerations, I decided to go to Cannes. I collected ten thousand lire for necessary expenses. My brother, Arnaldo, went to convert them at a money changer and brought me the equivalent in French money, which amounted to no more than five thousand, two hundred francs. Though I had followed the course of foreign exchange this little personal experience made a deep impression. It made me realize an angular fact; the Italian currency had lost nearly half of its value in comparison to French currency! It was a grave symptom. It was a humiliation. It was a blow to the self respect of a victorious nation, a vexing weathervane; it indicated our progress toward bankruptcy! Up leaped the thought that this situation must be cured by the vital strength of Fascism. It was one of our opportunities; the desperate developments unfortunately had not compelled the government, or political parties, or parliament itself to act. The monstrosity of inflation instead gave to everybody a fatuous, inconsistent, artificial sense of prosperity.

The Cannes conference had no importance; it was a preface for Genoa. It was clothed in an atmosphere of indifference. International meetings had followed each other with tiresome regularity here and there in resorts of Europe which appeared pleasant places to hold meetings. The last reunions had lost interest and were, instead of being important, the object of newspaper satire and of mocking "couplets" in comic reviews. To me, however, the sojourn at Cannes gave a means of extracting personally, from a direct and realistic examination of peoples and events, deep and well-rooted conclusions.

The Cannes conference had provoked a sudden ministerial crisis in France. Briand, whom I interviewed in the course of these days, resigned without waiting for a vote of the Chamber of Deputies. And I, in an article of January 14th, 1922, entitled "After Cannes," having given due weight to the numerous sharp interrogation marks of the international situation, concluded:

"The unsolved problems, questionings and challenges could be ranged in line to infinity. It is urgent, instead, to take note of the most important lesson of the French crisis. It is a bitter verification. It will bring the masses of the populations who suffer morally and economically to say in their hearts, 'These gentlemen are either without conscience, or they are powerless and flabby. They either have no wish to make peace or they are not able to make it. A Europe in such terrible spiritual and economic conditions as those of the present must embark on reason or sink. The Europe of to-morrow, broken in divisions of impoverished peoples, may become a colony: two other continents are already high up on the horizon of history!' "

To the plight disclosed by the wide picture of the European horizon unfolding to my eyes, was to be added that due to our domestic troubles, always growing a little worse.

I have always spoken as a journalist, as a politician, as a deputy, of the existence of two Italies. One appeared to me freed from servitude. It was noble, proud, loyal, devoutly dedicated by a bloody sacrifice of war, resolved to be always in the first rank to defend the right, the privilege and the great name of the Italian people. On the other side, however, I saw another Italy, dull to any consciousness of nobility and power, indifferent to origin and traditions, serving obscure "isms," a slave to apathetic tendencies, cold, egotistic, incapable of gallantry, dead to sacrifice.

In a thousand hardships, in numerous fights, those two Italies were arrayed by immutable destiny one against the other; their opposition was revealed in bloody manifestations, typical of the fierce and final struggle between the Fascisti and their enemies. To see in its right light the character of this antithesis, let us examine some of the typical episodes.

In Pistoia, for instance, a brave officer, Lieutenant Federico Florio, who fought valiantly during the War and who had followed D'Annunzio in Fiume, was treacherously murdered by a deserter anarchist, Cafiero Lucchesi. It was a crime premeditated by a craven to strike down a gallant man. This criminal outrage filled the souls of the Fascisti with utter indignation. The last words of our martyr were simple and solemn, "I am sorry now I will not be able to do something else for my Country." No more. Then the agony came. I felt that such sacrifices cemented indissolubly the unity of Fascism.

"A formidable cement!" I wrote in my paper. "It binds the Fascisti legions; a sacred and intangible bond keeps close the faithful of the Littorio. It is the sacred bond of our dead. They are hundreds. Youths. Mature men. Not a party in Italy, nor any movement in recent Italian history can be compared to Fascism. Not one ideal has been like the Fascist—consecrated by the blood of so many young souls.

"If Fascism were not a faith, how did it or could it

give stoicism and courage to its legions? Only a faith
which has reached the heights, only a faith can suggest
those words that came out from the lips of Federico
Florio, already bloodless and gray. Those words are a
document; they are a testament. They are as simple and
as grave as a passage from the Gospel.

"The Fascisti of all Italy must receive and meditate
these words—in silence—but unceasingly marching, always more determined—toward the goal! No obstacle
will ever stop them."

All of us had full realization of the command and the
impulse which came from the dead. When faith leaps
out of the hearts of martyrs it carries irresistibly the
sure impression of nobility, and brands men with the
symbol of its eternal greatness.

The groups of the Fascisti, their meetings, their compact parades, and their services in patriotism had as
ideal leaders our martyrs, invincible knights of the Fascist faith and passion. We called them by name, one by
one, with firm and sure voice. At every name, the comrades answered, "Present." This was a simple rite; it
had all the value and the affirmation of a vow.

Quite an opposite symptom of the two contrasting
Italies was plainly manifested in the politics displayed
by the two senators, Credaro and Salata, who were in
border zones, as high commissioners of the government. These two men seemed to ask from the natives
who were not of Italian blood a kind of mercy and
tolerance for the fact that they themselves were Italians.
No demand of the German-speaking people on the

frontier was considered unjustified. Little by little, following that policy of cowardice and servitude, we renounced our well-defined rights, sanctified by the blood spilled by volunteer heroes. Already in June, 1921—as I said in the preceding chapter—without mincing words I had denounced and ridiculed in the presence of all the chamber of parliament the work done by Credaro and Salata. Their destructive, eroding activity, however, continued. The Fascisti, confronted by successive proofs of such innate and inane weakness, were roused; they accused the two governors with violent words. On January 17th, 1922, at the meeting held in Triest, the Fascisti demanded the recall of Salata and the suppression of the central office for the New Provinces. That campaign succeeded in making its own way some time afterward. In fact the two senators, Credaro and Salata were recalled even though they were replaced by the government. But the consequence of their errors were to be suffered for a weary time. Quite differently, with pride and dignity, would the black shirts have garrisoned the sacred limits of the Brenner and the Nevosso.

In that period of bitter charges, counter charges, debates and squabbles, while the European horizon was still filled with thunder storms, came the death of the Pontiff Benedict XV, Giacomo della Chiesa, of a noble family of Genoa. He passed away January 22nd, 1922. He had ruled the Church in the stormiest period of the war, following Pius X, the kind-hearted patriarch of Venice, who distinguished his pontificate by a strong battle against the fads of political and religious modernism.

Benedict XV did not leave in our souls a sympathetic memory. We could not, if we tried, forget that in 1917, while people were struggling, when we had already seen the fall of Czarism and the Russian revolution with the defection of the armies on the eastern front, the Pontiff defined the war with the unhappy expression, "a useless massacre." That phrase, inconceivable in such a terrible moment, was a blow to those who had faith in sacrifice for an ideal and who hoped the war would correct many deep-rooted historical injustices. Besides, war had been our invention; the Catholic Church had ever been a stranger to wars, when she did not provoke them herself. And yet, the ambiguous conduct of the Pope amid the fighting nations is considered nowadays by some zealous persons who are deficient in critical sense and blind to historical consciousness, as the maximum of equity and the essence of an objective spirit.

But that attitude and its expression had, for us Italians, a very different value. It served to make evident an anomalous phase of Italy's situation—that is, the position of the Pontiff in Rome during a period in which Italy was engaged in a terrible struggle. For that reason, on the death of Benedict XV, the succession to the pontificate took on at that moment a particular importance for the future.

There is a saying in our country which is applied to the most extraordinary events to imply that the most complex things can be reduced to very simple terms. The expression is, "When a Pope is dead, another one is made." There is no comment to be made on that simple statement. But to succeed to the throne of St. Peter, to become the worthy substitute for the Prince of the Apostles, to represent on earth the Divinity of Christ, is one thing; the weight and value of a conclusion reached by an elective assembly is another. In view of the relationship that existed between the State and the Church in Italy one can easily understand that there could be reasons for apprehension, as well as deep interest in the results of the Conclave. The eyes of all the Catholic world were turned toward Rome. Great vexations stirred all the European chanceries; secret influences were penetrating deep places; they were trying to suppress and overpower each other.

Spectators and diplomats of every country in the world were spell bound by the complexities at the very moment that preparations for the Conclave were being made, when all Rome was getting ready to wait patiently in the Plaza of St. Peter's during the balloting.

Meanwhile in Italy there arose a debate on the political effects of Benedict XV. Various prophecies were made as to his successor; the journalistic row that went on had never been surpassed. Many problems of vast consequences were superficially treated.

The fall of the Bonomi ministry, attributed to inefficiency in domestic politics and to the fall of the Banca Italiana di Sconto, was really due to the failure of a commemoration for Pope Benedict XV from the national parliament.

I had already on various occasions disclosed to the Fascisti, whom I considered and consider always the aristocracy of Italy, that our religious ideal had in itself moral attributes of first importance. I had affirmed the necessity of condemning the unfruitful conception, absurd and artificial, of affected or vicious anti-clericalism. That tendency not only kept us in a situation of moral inferiority as compared with other peoples, but also divided the Italians in the religious field into various schools of thought. Above all it exposed us to such corrupting, sinister and tortuous power as that of international Masonry of a political type, as distinguished from the Masonry known in the Anglo-Saxon countries.

I had wanted to show that the problem of the relations between the State and the Church in Italy was not to be considered insoluble, and to explain how necessary it was to create, after a calm and impartial objective examination, an atmosphere of understanding, in order to give to the Italian people a basis for a life of harmony between religious faith and civil life.

The Fascisti, as intelligent people worthy of the epoch in which they were living, followed me in the new conception of religious policy. To it was attached our war against Masonry as we knew Masonry in Italy. It was a war of fundamental importance and Fascism was almost unanimous in a determination to fight it to the end.

Let us not forget that the Masons of Italy have always represented a distortion, not only in political life, but in spiritual concepts. All the strength of Masonry was directed against the papal policies, but this struggle represented no real and profound ideal. The secret society from a practical point of view rested on an association of mutual adulation, of reciprocal aid, of pernicious nepotism and favoritism. To become powerful and to consummate its underhanded dealings, Masonry made use of the weaknesses of the Liberal governments that succeeded each other in Italy after 1870 to extend its machinations in the bureaucracy, in the magistracy, in the field of education, and also in the army, so that it could dominate the vital ganglions of the whole nation. Its secret character throughout the twentieth century, its mysterious meetings, abhorrent to our beautiful communities with their sunlight and their love of truth, gave to the sect the character of corruption, a crooked concept of life, without programme, without soul, without moral value.

My antipathy for that disgusting form of secret association goes back to my youth. Long before, at the Socialist congress of Ancona in 1914, I had presented to my comrades the dilemma: Socialists or Masons? That point of view had won a complete triumph, in spite of the strong opposition of the Mason-socialists.

Later, in Fascism, I made the same gesture of strength. It took courage. I obeyed the positive command of my conscience, and not any opportunism. My attitude had nothing in common with the anti-Masonic spirit of the Jesuits. They acted for reasons of defense. After all, their inner organization as a religious society is almost completely unknown.

For my direct, methodical and consistent course of policy the hate of the Masonic sect persecutes me even

now. Masonry of that type has been beaten in Italy,
but it operates and conspires behind mask of the international anti-Fascism. It utterly fails to defeat me. It
tries to throw mud at me, but the insult does not reach
its mark. It machinates plots and crimes, but the hired
assassins do not control my destiny. It goes gossiping
about my weaknesses, and the supposed organic afflic-
tions of my body, but I am more alive and stronger than
ever.

This is a war without quarter, a war of which I am a
veteran. Every time that I have wanted to cauterize
difficult situations in Italian political life, every time
that I have wanted to give a sincere, frank and loyal
moral rectitude to the personnel in politics, I have always had against me our Masonry! But that organization, which in other times was very powerful, has been
beaten by me. Against me it did not and cannot win.
Italians won this battle for me. They found the cure for
this leprosy.

To-day in Italy we breathe the open air; life is exposed to the light of day.

When Bonomi fell, the King consulted with many
minds. I too was called twice to the Quirinal, his official
palace, where conferences are held. Obvious reasons of
reserve forbid me to make known what I said to the
Sovereign. This political crisis took on abnormal aspects. We groped in the dark. The number of men in
the political field who were fit to fill a minority was very
limited. They looked toward Orlando, then toward De
Nicola, but nobody wanted to accept the responsibility

of forming a ministry under the prevailing conditions. They were obliged to go back to Bonomi, who fell for the second time on the "via crucis" when he presented himself again at the chamber.

New consultations and new suggestions were made. Always the same names were given: Orlando, De Nicola, Bonomi. The picture presented that degree of helplessness which has afflicted so many democracies, and which has enabled many countries to vie with each other in the humiliating and derisive boast that they have had more governments and ministries than years of existence! The requirements for leadership were unchanged—the ability to compromise principles and sometimes even integrity, to barter and negotiate with palavering artistry in an effort to build another shaky structure which would perpetuate the whole depressing system. This system may be dear to the heart of doctrinaires. It was quite another affair in practice.

The "Popular" or "Catholic" party, following its bad political instinct, which caused it to be ultra conservative under cover and revolutionary in the street and in parliament, vetoed any return of Giolitti. The posture of the "popolari" was quite unique. Unfortunately they controlled a strong group in the chamber. While they refused to accept the responsibility of power, they bluepencilled Giolitti and denied support to Bonomi. They rendered the composition of any ministry well-nigh impossible even as a makeshift.

In spite of repeated consultations the same names always came to the surface. It was such a stagnation as comes finally to weak democracies. It was tearing to pieces political logic, common sense, and, unfortunately, also Italy herself.

At last the Facta ministry was formed. This mediocre selection of a member of parliament, closely bound to Giolitti, was made as the only anchor of safety in an absurd extravaganza. Every day we went down one step on the stairs of dignity. Nevertheless, because of the conditions, and because Facta undertook a burden that nobody else wanted, I did not hesitate to declare in my paper that the new cabinet, colorless as it was, might function to some end. I was prepared to say that it could represent, if nothing else, a will to go on, at least in the affairs of ordinary routine administration. It is bad enough to suffer a government which creates nothing; it is even worse to suffer a system of politics which cannot of itself create even an administration!

Facta was an old veteran of parliament and I feel sure that he was a gentleman stamped out by the old die. Respectful of the third rate political morals of the men of his age, he had only one devotion. That was for his teacher, Giolitti. Facta had been a discreet Minister of the Treasury in other times. He had not, as even his friends admitted, the strength and authority needed to draw up a ministry at a serious moment. He had to face the gas and smoke of the struggle between parties, of the pretensions of the "popolari," of the growing strength of Fascism, and, finally, a delicate international situation abroad.

It was in just such ways that the old "liberal" Italy

with its petty dealing with problems, its little parliamentary pea-shooting, its unworthy plots in corridor and cloak rooms, ante-rooms and sidewalk cafés, for puny personal power, its recurring crises, its journalistic bickerings, was breaking the real Italy. Italy, with its struggling co-operatives, its inadequate rural banks, its mean and superficial measures of economy, its incapable and improvident charity! Italy, in its position of humble servant, with napkin on arm to wipe other mouths at international conferences! Italy, prolific and powerful! Italy, like a mother able to supply, even for foreign ingratitude, laborious sons to make fruitful other soils, other climates, other cities and other peoples! Such was her leadership; such was her plight!

Facta was the man who fully represented that old world. Facta was the first to be surprised that he had suddenly found so many admirers. He often said that he failed to understand why he should be at the head of the Italian government. This timid member of parliament forgot that all these people around him who gave him by their mouthings a sensation of strength and influence were only the survivors of an old Liberal-Democratic world, incapable of living, outdated, shipwrecked, clinging for safety to the last Liberal planks of compromise.

But the powerful machine of Fascism was already in motion. Nobody could step into its path to stop it, for it had one aim: to give a government to Italy.

In these days there were some attempts at Fascist secession and schism. I removed them with a few strokes

of the pen and a few measures taken within. I was
troubled less by mistaken disaffections than by a single
grave incident in Fiume. There a renegade Italian, Za-
nella, nursed and nourished an ignoble anti-Italian plot.
The Fascisti imposed banishment upon him. This evil
representative of the autonomists and of the Jugo-Slavs
was obliged to leave the unhappy city which without
Italy would never have been able to put its lips to the
cup of peace.

At this time Charles of Hapsburg died, after having
twice tried vainly to seize again the crown of Saint
Stephen. The nemesis of history completed its work and
took away from the Hapsburg line the last possibility
of return. In Italian history this reigning house had represented always a most unfortunate influence. It had
been invariably adverse to our solidarity.

Without attracting deep attention or intelligent public interest, living this way and that, up and down by
alternate hopes and crises, optimisms and weary de-
spairs—came the Conference of Genoa.

On the first of that May was celebrated the so-called
Festival of Labor. Unfortunately the only distinctions
given this festival were an increased outburst of Socialist
and Communist attacks and ambushes. Even the anniversary of the declaration of war, May 24th, was saddened by blood. Solemn celebrations were held throughout Italy, but in Rome the Communists dared to fire at
the parade which was doing honor to Enrico Toti, the
Roman who, besides his life, had hurled against the fugitive enemy also his crutches. One person fell dead and
there were twenty-four wounded.

As if that was not enough the Alliance of Labor, a hybrid coalition of all the anti-Fascist groups, proclaimed a general strike.

It was too much! There was no sign of any act of energy from the government. Without hesitation I ordered a general mobilization of the Fascisti. I affirmed on my word of honor that we would break the back of the attempt of the red rabble. "We are sure to smash, *we say crush*, this bad beast once for all."

Considering the timid behavior of the middle classes and of the government, this virile decision, taken after full analysis, with full determination and full responsibility, served as a cold douche for the socialists and the reds. The Fascist mobilization came like lightning.

On the same day the strike ended.

While the public streets, squares and fields were being put in order by the energetic intervention of the Fascisti, in the parliament at Montecitorio the usual intrigues went on. There was oscillation of plans and programmes. These ranged from proposals of a dictatorship to collaboration with the reds! In the general marasmus there came on July 12th a statement from the Minister of the Treasury, Peano, which marked for me the maximum of our anxiety.

The budget of the nation had a deficit of six billions and a half. It was a terrific figure for Italy. It was a situation impossible for our economic structure to bear. To errors in foreign and domestic policy was added financial chaos. Minister Facta in record-breaking speed had demonstrated his incapacity in every way. I made

a speech in parliament on July 19th, 1922, in which I
specifically and flatly withdrew from the ministry the
votes of the Fascist group. After having demonstrated
the equivocal position of the Socialists, who wanted to
collaborate with the government so that they might
blackmail it the better, and of the "popolari" who
wrongly considered themselves supreme rulers of the
situation, I said these clear and sharp words to the
Premier himself:

"Honorable Facta, I tell you that your ministry cannot live because it is unbecoming from every point of
view. Your ministry cannot live, I might better say
vegetate, or drag its life along, thanks to the charity of
all those who sustain you. The traditional rope in the
same manner sustains the not less traditional hanged.
After all, your makers are there to testify to the character of your ministry; you have been the first to be
surprised into the presidency of the council."

I went on then to examine the disheartening mistakes of the Facta policies and I concluded by asserting
that Fascism by getting away from the parliamentary
majority, had accomplished a "gesture of high political
and moral modesty. . . ." "It is impossible to be part
of the majority," I added, "and at the same time act
outside as Fascism is now forced to act."

These words excited a brisk stir of mumbles, exclama-
tions, and comments, which went to a higher pitch when
I added:

"Fascism will make its own decisions. Probably it will
soon say if it wants to become a legitimate party, for

that means a government party, or if it will instead be a party of insurrection. In the latter case it will no longer be able to be part of any governmental majority. Consequently it will not be obliged to sit in this chamber."

I gave in that way, not only to the dying Facta ministry, but also to any other new government, an energetic and unmistakable warning. I had put up the signboard of my intentions and declared in the open where I stood.

On that day the Facta ministry fell. And immediately they began to grope in the dark again, trying to find a successor. Orlando, Bonomi, Facta, Giolitti. Again these were the names mouthed about.

By process of deductions and eliminations the name finally hit upon was Meda. He was the Popular party deputy from Milan, and the chief of the "popolari" deputies who with their secret, sinister tactics kept any ministry under their power. Meda, who had already been a minister, made his gesture of refusal and renunciation because of fear. That was our paradox—nobody in Italy, amid this so-called strength of the constituted order, which included priests and radicals, wanted or was able to assume responsibility of power. Whatever claims "liberalism" and "democracy" had for power, now at least nobody would touch the treasure.

In this situation the socialists cheerfully blackmailed the nation, while the Fascisti were silently preparing the yeast and the bread, the will and the weapons for an insurrection of national dignity.

While the conferences to find ways out of the crisis went on slowly, at the moment of inability to constitute a government there came about in Italy an almost inconceivable situation. All the strength of the left party, not only those openly subversive, but also the organization of the Labor Confederation, the Socialist parliamentary group, the Democratic groups, and the Republicans, staged a general strike all over Italy. Its character was typically and solely anti-Fascist. Its pretense was to save the liberty of the people, threatened by Fascism!

This galaxy of political elements, more despicable than riffraff, these inert, wasteful, hopeless forces which in the past had massacred every liberty and had trampled in every imaginable way on our morals, our peace, our efficiency, and our order, could not have done a more illogical, a more unjust, a more offensive and provocative act toward Fascism and the Italian people.

The days marked by these sinister forces were days in which I made irrevocable decisions. Our development brought by degrees a political and a military reserve strength, which was to bring us in the end to the March on Rome and the conquest of power.

As an answer to the anti-Fascist provocation, I ordered another general mobilization of the Fascisti. The council of the "Fasci Italiani di combattimento" was ordered to sit permanently. The Fascist technicians were to be brought together to continue the work in the public services. The "squadristi" were to disperse subversive organizations. The Fascisti of Milan assaulted the *Avanti*, which was considered the lair of our opponents. They burned the offices. They occupied the street-car barns. They began to make the public services operative in spite of the declared strike.

To crush a strike the government was powerless, but a new strength had been substituted for the government! The Fascisti, well armed, occupied the electric stations in order to prevent acts of sabotage. It was necessary to destroy forever all the nerve centres of disorder. The Fascisti did it.

In Milan alone three young black shirts lost their lives. Of these, two were university students. We had many wounded boys.

The trial of strength, however, was successful. The enemies of Italy were taken with convulsions. They tossed responsibilities back and forth in foolish oratorical and literary battles. The life of the people had come back to a normal rhythm. Fascism had revealed a profound strength, one able to dominate our Italy of tomorrow, not only in the sense of mere force, but in determination, fundamental wisdom, character and unselfish patriotism.

Our antagonists were defeated, confused and humiliated. One of those who called themselves interpreters of the liberal idea recognized—how generous!—that Fascism was now a power which could not be neglected. The *Corriere della Sera*, the serious and in some ways admirable Milan newspaper—which had always used its circulation to become the speaking trumpet for the spirit of moribund, middle class mediocrity—had given, in the past, a sort of halo to Filippo Turati, the Socialist leader. Now it felt that it was necessary to give a bit of space to recognize the right of Fascism to participation in the government. The unsettled crisis went lumbering along. I was again called by the King. I had some interviews with Orlando. One after another all the projected combinations fell apart and were put aside like old rejected castings. So, wearily, they came back to Facta. He sent one of his emissaries to me and asked me under what conditions the Fascisti would accept places in the new government. I sent back word by the messenger that Fascism would ask for the most important offices.

I was urged to take a position in the Cabinet, but how absurd! Naturally I had to stay out of the coalition so that I could maintain my freedom to criticise, and if need be to take action. My claims, however, for Fascist representation were judged immoderate. The ill-starred Facta ministry was launched without us, but as the ship took the water the nation's sole greeting was a mutter of contempt and indifference.

Friends and enemies both looked only toward Fascism. It was the one element that sparked interest in the life of the Italian people.

I had made up my mind to lead the black shirts myself. I already had crystallized my determination to march on Rome.

The situation admitted of no other solution.

I called to Milan on October 16th a general who had special fitness and who was saturated by real Fascist faith. I made a scheme of military and political organization on the model of the old Roman legions. The Fascisti were divided by me into "principi" and "triari." We created, after conferring with the high leaders, a slogan, a uniform, and a watchword. I knew perfectly the Fascist and anti-Fascist situation in every region of Italy. I could march on Rome along the Tyrrhenian sea, deviating toward Umbria. From the south the compact formations of Puglie and Naples could join me. The only obstacle was a hostile zone, which centred in Ancona. I called Arpinati and other lieutenants of Fascism and ordered them to free Ancona from social-communist domination. The town, which was known to be in the hands of the anarchists, was conquered by maneuvres carried out in perfect military fashion. There were some dead and wounded. Too bad! But now the remnants of the anti-Fascist forces were destroyed. Anti-Fascism was now concentrated in Rome; it was driven back to its barrack on Montecitorio, where parliament sat.

A new sunshine broke over the multitudes of our provinces. We could all breathe with full lungs. The brave effort of Fascism was now rising with the flood tide of its full efficiency. Critics of reputation, historians of wide-world fame, studious people from every part of the earth were beginning to regard with quickening interest the movement I had created and dominated and was leading toward victory.

While I was penning some editorials against representatives of the sceptics, I wrote: "Fascism is to-day in the first stage of its life: the one of Christ. Don't be in a hurry; the one of Saint Paul will come."

I was preparing then every minute the details of the conquest of Rome and of power. I was certainly not moved by any mirage of personal power, nor by any other allurement, nor by a desire for egotistical political domination.

I have always had a vision of life which was altruistic. I have groped in the dark of theories, but I groped not to relieve myself, but to bring something to others. I have fought, but not for my advantage, indirect or immediate. I have aimed for the supreme advantages of my nation. I desired finally that Fascism should rule Italy for her glory and her good fortune.

I cannot, for obvious reasons, discuss all the measures, even some of the most simple, that I took in this period. Some are of political and secret character about which reserve is absolutely necessary. The *Popolo d'Italia,* my paper, without attracting too much attention from outsiders and from my enemies, had become the headquarters of the spiritual and material preparation for the March on Rome. It was the hub of our thought and action. The military and the political forces both obeyed my command. I weighed all the plans and proposals. Having made my own plan at last I gave the necessary orders. Then there began extensive preparatory maneuvres, such as the occupation of Trento, of Ancona and of Bolzano—places which might threaten our strategy.

I wanted to inform myself about the state of mind

of the Fascisti, about their efficiency and their determination. Accordingly I went to make four important speeches in different parts of Italy. In those speeches I set forth the policies of to-morrow. I defined the ultimate goal of Fascism. It was candidly stated. It was the conquest of power. I didn't want to ingratiate myself with the masses. I have always spoken with naked candor and even with brutality to the multitudes. That is a distinct contrast to the contemptible courtship made for their favor by the political parties of every time and every land.

On September 17th, 1922, for instance, one month before the March on Rome, I wrote that it was necessary to "throw down, from the altars erected by the 'Demos,' His Holiness *the Mass!*"

The Fascisti meetings which I attended were held in Udine, which is in northern Italy, in Cremona, which lies in the valley of the Po, in industrial Milan and in Naples, the centre of southern Italy. I wanted to be personally acquainted with the spirit of those districts, each with a nobility of its own. I was acclaimed as a conqueror and a saviour. This flattered me, but be sure that it did not make me proud. I felt stronger, and yet realized the more that I faced mountains of responsibility. In those four cities, so different and so far one from the other, I saw the same light! I had with me the honest, the good, the pure, the sincere soul of the Italian people!

I assembled the Central Committee of the Fasci Italiani di Combattimento—the Bundles of Fight—and we came to an accord on the outlines of the movement, which was to lead the black shirts triumphantly along the sacred roads to Rome.

Speaking in those days at the Circolo Sciesa of Milan I said to my trusted men that we finally had come to the "sad sunset of Liberalism, and to the Fascist-dawn of a new Italy."

CHAPTER IX

THUS WE TOOK ROME

A ND now we were on the eve of the historic march on the Eternal City.

Having completed my survey and estimate of conditions in the provinces, having listened to the reports of the various chiefs of the black shirts, having selected the plans of action and having determined in a general way upon the most favorable moment, I called together in Florence the chiefs of the Fascist movement and of the squads of action. There were Michele Bianchi, De Bono, Italo Balbo, Giuriati, and various others. Some one at that quiet conference suggested the mobilization of the black shirts for November 4th, the anniversary of the Victory. I rejected that proposal, for it would have spoiled a day of commemoration by introducing the element of revolutionary activity.

It was necessary to give our movement the full advantage of opportunity and to make it spark and detonate. It was necessary to weigh, besides the military aspects, the political effects and values. We had to consider, finally, the painful possibility of a violent suppression, or a failure spreading from some slip to all of our plans. We were obliged to determine beforehand all the hows and whens, the details of the means, with what men and with what aims the Fascist assault could most wisely be launched.

The Fascist meeting in Naples, which was advertised as our second great congress, with its display of discipline and of speech-making, served to hide the beginnings of the real mobilization. At a fixed moment the squads of action of all Italy were to be in arms. They would have to occupy the vital nerve centres—the cities, and the post offices, the prefectures, police headquarters, railroad stations, and military barracks.

Detachments of Fascisti were to march along the Tyrrhenian Sea, toward Rome, led by chiefs, all of them brave former officers. The same movement was to take place on the Adriatic side, from which direction was to be launched on Rome the strength of the low Romagna, Marche and Abruzzi districts. That plan required that we should free Ancona from the social-communist dominion. This had been done. From middle Italy the squadrons already mobilized for the meeting at Naples were also to be directed upon Rome. They were supported by groups of Fascist cavalry under the command of Caradonna.

The moment the Fascist mobilization and campaign was decided and actually began operation, martial law, the stern rules and orders of Fascism both for officers and privates, were to be enforced.

The political powers of our "National Directorate" were turned over to a military quadrumvirate of action in the persons of Generals De Bono, De Vecchi, Italo

Balbo and Michele Bianchi. I presided over the quad-rumvirate and I was the Duce (the leader) and had the ultimate responsibility for the work of the four men— a responsibility for which I was fully pledged not only to the Fascisti but to Italy.

We selected as general concentration headquarters the town of Perugia, capital of Umbria, where many roads flow to a centre and from which it is easy to reach Rome. In case of military and political failure we could, by crossing the Appennine range, retire to the Valley of the Po. In any revolutionary movement of history that zone has always been properly considered the key-stone of any situation. There our domination was abso-lute and undisputed. We selected the watchword; we fixed the details of the action. Everything had to be re-ported to me—in the offices of the *Popolo d'Italia*. Trusted Fascist messengers wove webs like scurrying spiders. All day long I was issuing the necessary or-ders. I wrote the proclamation which was to be ad-dressed to the country on the eve of action. We knew from very faithful unforgettable friends that the army, unless exceptional circumstances arose, would maintain itself on a ground of amiable neutrality.

At the historic congress at Naples, after my open-ing speech, which traced the outlines of the Fascist ac-tion in the state and assigned to Naples the title "Queen of the Mediterranean," the general discussion contin-ued in academic tone, without a definite aim except that of gaining time. The leader in that dissembling and sham discussion was Michele Bianchi, one of the qua-

drumvirate for the march on Rome. At that time he
had already revealed a notable political mind. De Bono
and Balbo, who had great authority over the squadrons
of action, joined the general headquarters in Perugia.

I went from the adjourned congress back to Milan.
During the trip I had an opportunity to see many
friends and to make additional preparations. I had important conversations regarding that particular drive
which had to be organized in Milan, as in other centres
of the Lombardy district. In order not to arouse the
suspicion of the police, for I was always surrounded by
spies, I assumed the attitude of an indifferent person
without a worry or trouble in the world. This was somewhat difficult, for I had to spend precious time in trying the speed of a new car, and in other workaday com-
ings and goings. In the evenings I went to the theatres.
I pretended to have a great spirit of activity in my editorial writing and newspaper management.

But suddenly, when I knew that everything was
ready, I issued from Milan, through the *Popolo d'Italia,*
by means of independent publications, and through the
correspondents of all the Italian newspapers, my proclamation of revolution. It had been signed by the quadrumvirate. Here is the text of the memorable document:

"Fascisti! Italians!
"The time for determined battle has come! Four years ago
at this season the national army loosed the final offensive
which brought it to Victory. To-day the army of the black
shirts again takes possession of that Victory, which has
been mutilated, and, going directly to Rome, brings Victory

again to the glory of that Capitol. From now on 'principi' and 'triari' are mobilized. The martial law of Fascism now becomes a fact. By order of the Duce all the military, political and administrative functions of the party management are taken over by a secret Quadrumvirate of Action with dictatorial powers.

"The army, the reserve and safeguard of the Nation, must not take part in this struggle. Fascism renews its highest homage given to the Army of Vittorio Veneto. Fascism, furthermore, does not march against the police, but against a political class both cowardly and imbecile, which in four long years has not been able to give a Government to the Nation. Those who form the productive class must know that Fascism wants to impose nothing more than order and discipline upon the Nation and to help to raise the strength which will renew progress and prosperity. The people who work in the fields and in the factories, those who work in the railroads or in offices, have nothing to fear from the Fascist Government. Their just rights will be protected. We will even be generous with unarmed adversaries.

"Fascism draws its sword to cut the multiple Gordian knots which tie and burden Italian life. We call God and the spirit of our five hundred thousand dead to witness that only one impulse sends us on, that only one passion burns within us—the impulse and the passion to contribute to the safety and greatness of our Country.

"Fascisti of all Italy!

"Stretch forth like Romans your spirits and your sinews! We must win. We will.

"Long live Italy! Long live Fascism!

"THE QUADRUMVIRATE."

At night there reached me the first news of bloody clashes in Cremona, Alessandri and Bologna, and of the assaults on munition factories and upon military barracks. I had composed my proclamation in a very short and resounding form; it had impressed the whole of the Italian people. Our life was suddenly brought into an ardent atmosphere of revolution. News of the struggles that were taking place in the various cities, sometimes exaggerated by the imaginations of reporters, gave a dramatic touch to the revolution. Responsible elements of the country asserted that as a result of this movement there would at last be a government able to rule and to command respect. The great mass of the population, however, looked out astonished, as it were, from their windows.

None of the subversive or liberal chiefs showed himself. All went into their holes, inspired only by fear. They understood quite thoroughly that this was the striking of our hour. Every one felt sure that the struggle of Fascism would have a victorious outcome. I could sense this even from far away. The air was full of it. The wind spoke of it. The rain brought it down. The earth drank it in.

I put on the black shirt. I barricaded the *Popolo d'Italia.* In the livid and gray morning Milan had a new and fantastic appearance. Pauses and sudden silences gave one the sensation of certain great hours that come and go in the course of history.

Frowning battalions of Royal Guards scouted the city and the monotonous rhythm of their feet sounded ominous echoes in the almost deserted streets.

The public services functioned on a reduced and meagre scale. The assaults of the Fascisti against the barracks and on the post offices were cause for fusillades of shots, which gave to the city a sinister echo of civil war.

I had provided the offices of my newspaper with everything needful for defense against attack. I knew that if the government authorities desired to give a proof of their strength they would have directed their first violent assault at the *Popolo d'Italia*. In fact, in the early hours of the morning, I saw trained upon the offices and upon me the ugly muzzles of the mitrailleuses. There was a rapid exchange of shots. I had my rifle charged and went down to defend the doors. The neighbors had barricaded entrances and windows and were begging for protection.

During the firing bullets whistled around my ears.

A major of the Royal Guard finally asked for a truce in order to talk with me. After a brief initial conversation, we agreed that the Royal Guard should withdraw as far as two hundred metres and that the mitrailleuses were to be removed from the middle of the street and placed at a crossing of the street, about a hundred metres away. With that sort of armistice began for me the day of October 28th!

At night a group of deputies, senators, and political men of Milan, the best-known and most responsible figures of the Lombard parliamentary world—among whom were senators Conti, Crespi and the deputy De Capitani—came to the offices of the *Popolo d'Italia* to ask me to desist from a struggle which they asserted would be the beginning of a violent, grave and reprehensible civil war. They proposed to me a sort of armistice and a truce with the central government. Perhaps a ministerial crisis might save, they said, the situation and the country.

I smiled back at the parliamentarians because of their innocence. I answered them in words like these:

"Dear sirs, there is not the slightest question of any partial or total crisis or of substitution of one ministry for another. The game I have undertaken has a wider and more serious character. For three years we have lived in a caldron boiling with small battles and devastations. This time I will not lay down weapons until a full victory is concluded. It is time to change the direction not only of the government, but also of the whole of Italian life. There is no question of a struggle of parties in parliament, but here is a question— we want to know if we Italians are able to live an autonomous life or are to be slaves of our own weakness, not only toward foreign nations, but also in our own affairs? War is declared! We will carry it to the bitter end. Do you see these communications? Well, the struggle is blazing all over Italy. Youth is in arms. I am rated as a leader who precedes and not one who follows. I will not humiliate with arbitration this page of the marvellous resurrection of Italian youth. I tell you that it is the last chapter. It will fulfil the traditions of our country. It cannot die in a compromise."

I then showed my visitors a letter, which I had received at dawn from Commander Gabriele d'Annunzio. I had sent a brief message to the redeemer of Fiume, who had been with us since the first moments of the darkest struggle. It was brought to him by the Generals Giampietro and Douhet, and Eugenio Coselschi. D'Annunzio, toward whom some vague hopes of the politicians had vainly turned, had immediately answered in these terms:

"DEAR MUSSOLINI:

"I received to-night the three messengers, after a hard day of work.

"In this book, so many times interrupted, are gathered the truths that the one-eyed man discovers in retirement and meditation. I think that Italian youth must now recognize them and follow them with purified heart.

"It is necessary to gather together all the sincere forces and start them toward the great goals that are fixed for Italy by her eternal destinies.

"From virile patience and not from restless impatience will salvation come to us.

"The messengers will tell you my thoughts and my intentions, free from all vague colorings.

"The King knows that I am still the most faithful and eager soldier of Italy.

"Let him stand against the adverse destinies, which must be faced and defeated.

"Victory has the light eyes of Pallas.

"Do not blindfold her.

"*Sine strage vincit,*

"*Strepitu sine ullo.*   "GABRIELE D'ANNUNZIO."

After having read the letter of D'Annunzio to these Lombard politicians I sent them away with the declaration that if I was left with only one man, or indeed all alone, I would not abandon the fight until I had obtained the final decisive ends as I had outlined them to my associates.

The logical clearness, the stout, rigorous, coherent reasons I had given impressed those who had come to offer conciliation, compromise, concessions.

I think that one of them must have immediately sped off to inform the premier, Facta, that nothing could be done with me.

Poor Facta, instead of being preoccupied with his shortcomings, was wondering how and to whom he could announce this real crisis among the sham crises. The chamber was closed at that time. Where could he turn?

Any one can see that in all events, even in solemn events, the grotesque and the ludicrous are always to be found, and sometimes prosper under the very shadow of great and tragic happenings.

The last of the Liberal governments of Italy wanted to make its final gesture. It addressed to the country a declaration phrased in the following terms:

"Seditious manifestations are appearing in some of the Italian provinces, brought about in such a way as to hamper the normal functioning of the powers of the State, and are of such nature as to throw the Country into serious trouble.

"The Government has tried its utmost to reach an agreement, with the hope of bringing back peace to all minds and to assure a peaceful solution of the crisis. Facing, however, a revolutionary attempt, it has the duty of maintaining public order by any means and at any price. Even though its resignations have been presented, it will fulfil this duty for the safety of citizens and the safety of free constitutional institutions.

"Meanwhile the citizens must maintain their calm and

must have faith in the measures of public security that have been adopted.

"Long live Italy! Long live the King!"

"Signed: FACTA, SCHANZER, AMENDOLA, TAD-
DEI, ALESSIO, BERTONE, PARATORE, SOLERI,
DEVITO, ANILE, RICCIO, BERTINI, ROSSI,
DELLO SBARBA, FULCI, LUCIANI."

At the same time the ministers, considering the situation created in the country, put their portfolios at the disposition of the president of the council, Facta. This man sought advice from several friends in Rome. As a result he offered a decree to proclaim martial law, which the King, in his profound wisdom, flatly refused to sign.

The Sovereign understood that the revolution of the black shirts was the conclusion of three years of struggle and of fighting; he understood that only with the victory of one party could we reach pacification and that order and progress in civil life which are essential to the harmony of the Italian people.

Out of respect for the most orthodox constitutional forms, the King allowed Facta to follow the rules of the Constitution. We had then resignations, designations, consultations, communications, charges, and so on and so on. At this moment came a sinister maneuvre that impressed me as being ominous. The National party of the right, which had a great similarity of outlook with the Fascisti, although it had not the same system of campaign, advanced some singular claims by means of emissaries.

The National right asserted in fact that it was the

keystone of the situation. Salandra, who was the most typical representative of the group, was disposed to sacrifice himself and to take upon his back the cross of power. This was to be understood as an aid for the Fascisti. I protested energetically against such a solution, which would have perpetuated compromise and error. Fascism was under arms, it was dominating the centres of national life, it had a very well-defined aim, it had followed deliberately an extra-parliamentary path and it could not allow its victory to be mutilated or adulterated in such a manner. That was my exact answer to the mediators of the union between the National right and Fascism. No compromise!

The struggle continued with the objectives I had mapped out. It is impossible in the pages of an autobiography to present the entire picture of the revolutionary events in those days. I distinctly remember that with every hour that passed I had more poignantly the sensation of triumphantly dominating the Italian political situation. The adversaries were confused, scattered, speechless. The Fascisti in compact files were already near the gates of Rome and were expecting me to go to the head of their military formations to march with them into the Capital.

On the afternoon of the 29th I received a very urgent telephone call from Rome on behalf of the Quirinal. General Cittadini, first aide-de-camp of His Majesty the King, asked me very kindly to go to Rome because the King, having examined the situation, wanted to charge me with forming a ministry. I thanked General

Cittadini for his kindness, but I asked him to give me the same communication by telegram. One knows that the telephone may play dirty tricks at times. General Cittadini, after having first objected that my request was not usual under the Court regulations, took into consideration the abnormal and informal situation, and agreed to send me the same invitation by telegram. In fact after a few hours an urgent message arrived. It was of a personal character.

This was it:

"On. Mussolini, Milan,
"His Majesty the King asks you to come immediately to Rome for he wishes to offer you the responsibility of forming a Ministry. With respect,   "GENERAL CITTADINI."

This was not yet victory, but the progress made was considerable. I communicated directly with the headquarters of the revolution in Perugia and with the various commands of the black shirts in Milan. I gave out, by means of an extra edition of the *Popolo d'Italia*, the news of the command I had received.

I was in a terrible state of nervous tension. Night after night I had been kept awake, giving orders, following the compact columns of the Fascisti, restricting the battle to the knightly practices of Fascism.

A period of greater responsibilities was about to begin for me; I must not fail in my duty or in my aims. I gathered all my strength to my aid, I invoked the memory of the dead, I asked the assistance of God, I

called upon the faithful living to assist me in the great
task that confronted me.

That night of October 31st, 1922, I left the direction
of the *Popolo d'Italia* and turned my fighting journal
over to my brother, Arnaldo. In the number of November 1st I published the following declaration:

"From now on the direction of the *Popolo d'Italia* is intrusted to Arnaldo Mussolini.

"I thank and salute with brotherly love all the editors,
collaborators, correspondents, employees, workers, all those
who have assiduously and faithfully labored with me for the
life of this paper and for love of our Country.

"Rome, October 30th, 1922.   "Mussolini."

I parted with regret from the paper that had been
the most constant and potent factor in our victory. I
must add that my brother, Arnaldo, has been able to
maintain the editorship with dignity and capacity.

When I had intrusted the paper to my brother I was
off for Rome. To the zealous people who wanted to get
me a special train to go to Rome to confer with the
King, I said that for me a compartment in the usual
train was quite enough. Engines and coal should not be
wasted. Economize! That is the first and acid test of a
true man of government. And after all I could only
enter Rome at the head of my black shirts, then camp-
ing at Santa Marinella in the atmosphere and the shin-
ing rays of the Capital.

The news of my departure sped all over Italy. In
every station where the train stopped I found a gathering of the Fascisti and of the masses who wanted to

bring me, even through the pouring rain, their cheers and their good-will.

Leaving Milan was painful. That city had given me a home for ten years; to me it had been prodigal in the satisfaction it had afforded; it had supported me in every stress; it had baptized the most wonderful squads of action of Fascism; it had been the scene of historical political struggles. Now I was leaving it, called by destiny and by a greater task. All Milan knew of my going, and I felt that even in the feeling of joy for a departure that was a symbol of victory, there was also a shade of sadness.

But this was not the hour for sentimentality. It was the time for quick, sure decisions. After the kisses and farewells of my family I said good-by to many prominent Milanese, and then I went away, speeding into the night, to take counsel with myself, to refresh my soul, to listen to the echoes of voices of friends and to envisage the wide horizons of to-morrow's possibilities.

The minor episodes of that trip and of those days are not important. The train brought me into the midst of the Fascisti; I was in view of Rome at Santa Marinella. I reviewed the columns. I established the formalities for the entrance into Rome. I established connections between the quadrumvirate and the authorities.

My presence redoubled the great enthusiasm. I read in the eyes of those young men the divine smile of triumph of an ideal. With such support I would have felt inspired to challenge, if need be, not only the base Italian ruling class, but enemies of any sort and race.

In Rome an indescribable welcome awaited me. I did not want any delay. Even before making contacts with my political friends I motored to the Quirinal. I wore a black shirt. I was introduced without formalities into the presence of His Majesty the King. The Stefani agency and the great newspapers of the world gave stilted or speculative details about this interview. I will limit myself, for obvious reasons of reserve, to declare that the conference was characterized by great cordiality. I concealed no plans, nor did I fail to make plain my ideas of how to rule Italy. I obtained the Sovereign's approbation. I took up lodgings at the Savoy Hotel and began to work. First I made arrangements with the general command of the army to bring militia into Rome and to have them defile in proper formation in a review before the King. I gave detailed and precise orders. One hundred thousand black shirts paraded in perfect order before the Sovereign. They brought to him the homage of Fascist Italy!

I was then triumphant and in Rome! I killed at once all unnecessary demonstrations in my honor. I gave orders that not a single parade should take place without the permission of the General Fascist Command. It was necessary to give to everybody from the first moment a stern and rigid sense of discipline in line with the régime that I had conceived.

I discouraged every manifestation on the part of army officers who wanted to bring me their plaudits. I have always considered the army outside and above every kind of politics. The army must, in my opinion,

King Victor Emmanuel III and Mussolini.

be inspired by absolute and conscientious discipline; it must devote itself, with the deepest will, only to the defense of frontiers and of historical rights. The army is an institution which must be preserved inviolate. It must not suffer the slightest loss in its integrity and in its high dedication.

But other and more complex problems surged about me at that moment. I was in Rome not only with the duty of composing a new ministry; I had also firmly decided to renew and rebuild from the very bottom the life of the Italian people. I vowed to myself that I would impel it toward higher and more brilliant aims.

Rome sharpened my sense of dedication. The Eternal City, "caput mundi," has two Courts and two Diplomacies. It has seen in the course of centuries imperial armies defeated under its walls. It has witnessed the decay of the strong, and the rise of universal waves of civilization and of thought. Rome, the coveted goal of princes and leaders, the universal city, heir to the old Empire and the power of Christianity! Rome welcomed me as leader of national legions, as a representative, not of a party or a group, but of a great faith and of an entire people.

I had long meditated my action as a man of party and as a man of government. I had carried these thoughts as I walked by day and even as I slept by night. I had won and could win more. I could have nailed my enemies to the wall, not only metaphorically but in very fact if I had wished—those enemies who had slandered Fascism and those whom I hated for having betrayed Italy in peace as they had betrayed her in war.

The atmosphere was pregnant with the possibility of tragedy. I had mobilized three hundred thousand black shirts. They were waiting for my signal to move. They could be used for one purpose or another. I had in the Capital sixty thousand armed men ready for action. The March on Rome could have set tragic fires. It might have spilled much blood if it had followed the example of ancient and modern revolutions. This was for me a moment in which it was more necessary than ever to examine the field with calm serenity and with cold reason to compare the immediate and the distant results of our daring action when directed toward definite aims.

I could have proclaimed a dictatorship, I could have formed a dictatorial ministry composed solely of Fascisti on the type of the Directory that was formed in France at the time of the Convention. The Fascist revolution, however, had its unique characteristics; it had no antecedent in history. It was different from any other revolution also in its capacity to re-enter, with deliberaate intent, legal, established traditions and forms. For that reason also, I knew that the mobilization should last the shortest possible time.

I did not forget that I had a parliament on my hands; a chamber of deputies of sullen mind, ready to lay traps for me, accustomed to an old tradition of ambiguity and intrigue, full of grudges, repressed only by fear; a dismayed senate from which I could obtain a disciplined respect but not an eager and productive collaboration. The Crown was looking on to see what I would do, following constitutional rules.

The Pontificate followed the events with anxiety. The other nations looked at the revolution suspiciously if not with hostility. Foreign banks were anxious for news. Exchange wavered, credit was still vacillating, waiting for the situation to be cleared. It was indispensable first of all to give the impression of stability to the new régime.

I had to see, oversee and foresee everything. I slept not at all for some nights, but they were nights fecund in action and ideas. The measures that immediately followed in the first twenty-four hours of my government bear witness.

Another problem arose from the character of the revolution. Every revolution has in it, besides the great mass of human impact and the conscientious and unselfish leaders, two other types—adventurers and melancholic intellectuals who might be called, by a synthetic expression, ascetics of revolution. When the revolution is over, the mass, which often is moved by the simple intuition of a great historical and social reality, goes peacefully back to its usual activities. It forms the laborious and disciplined leaven of the new régime. The conscientious and unselfish leaders form the necessary aristocracy of rulers. But the ascetics and the adventurers are a dead burden. The first would like to see overnight a perfect humanity, without faults. They do not understand that there is no revolution that can change the nature of men. Because of their Utopian illusions the ascetics are never contented; they waste their time and other men's energies in sophistry and doubts just when it is necessary to work like fiends in order to go forward. The adventurers always identify the fortune of the revolution with their own fortune; they hope to gain personal advantage from the victory and they harbor resentment when their wishes are not satisfied, and clamor for extreme and dangerous measures.

Now I had to defend the Fascist victory from the ascetics and the adventurers. The adventurers, however, sank rapidly in the Fascist revolution, because it was different and on a higher plane than any other revolution.

But I felt it my constant duty to examine and to ponder, in such a grave moment, every step I made.

First of all in the pressure of events, I desired to assure regularity to the country and to constitute a new government. Order came quickly. There were only a few sporadic incidents of violence, inevitable under such conditions. I felt the necessity of safeguarding Facta, and I called ten black shirts who had each been much decorated for bravery for the purpose of accompanying Facta to Pinerolo, his native town, under their word of honor. They kept their promise. "Nobody"—that was the order—"should touch a hair, mock or humiliate Facta." He had given to the country his only son, who died in an airplane accident during the war, and Facta deserved respect for that and more.

I forbade reprisals against the leaders of the oppositions. It was only by my great authority that I averted the destruction, not only rhetorical but also actual, of my most rabid enemies. I saved their skins for them. At the same time, in the space of a few hours, I constituted a new ministry. I discarded, as I said, the idea of a Fascist dictatorship, because I wanted to give to the country the impression of a normal life free from the selfish exclusiveness of a party. That sense of instinct for equilibrium accompanies me fortunately in the gravest, the most strenuous, and the most critical moments. I decided then, after having weighed everything, to compose a ministry of a nationalist character.

I have had the feeling, as I had then, that later there would become inevitable a process of clarification; but I preferred that it should come forth spontaneously from the succeeding political events.

But that was the last generous gesture that I ever made toward the old Italian ring of parties and politicians.

In the new ministry, among ministers and undersecretaries of state, were fifteen Fascisti, three Nationalists, three Liberals of the right, six "Popolari" and three Social Democrats. I was generous toward the Liberals of the right, whose peculiar maneuvre in order to pick up for their profit the results of the Fascist revolution had been quite recent. Among the "Popolari" and Social Democrats I selected those who gave promise of national spirit and who did not intrigue with subversive popularism or with socialism.

I kept for myself, with the Presidency of the Council, the office of the Interior and assumed ad interim that of Foreign Affairs. I gave to Armando Diaz the Ministry of War and I promised to give him an army worthy of the country and the victor of Vittorio Veneto. I called Admiral Thaon de Revel for the Navy and Federzoni for the Colonies.

The complete formation of the ministry was as follows:

Benito Mussolini, Deputy, *Presidency of the Council, Domestic and "interim" of Foreign Affairs* (Fascist).

Armando Diaz, General of the Army, *War*.

Paolo Thaon de Revel, Admiral, Senator, *Navy*.

Luigi Federzoni, Deputy, *Colonies* (Nationalist).

Aldo Oviglio, Deputy, *Justice* (Fascist).

Alberto De Stefani, Deputy, *Finances* (Fascist).

Vincenzo Tangorra, Deputy, *Treasury* ("Popolare").

Giovanni Gentile, Professor, *Public Instruction* (Liberal of the Right).

Gabriello Carnazza, Deputy, *Public Works* (Democrat).

Giuseppe DeCapitani, Deputy, *Agriculture* (Liberal of the Right).

Teofilo Rossi, Senator, *Industry and Commerce* (Democrat).

Stefano Cavazzoni, Deputy, *Work and Social Providence* ("Popolare").

Giovanni Colonna di Cesaro', Deputy, *Posts and Telegraphs* (Social Democrat).

Giovanni Giuriati, Deputy, *Liberated Provinces* (Fascist).

Under Secretaries of State

Presidency: Giacomo Acerbo, Deputy (Fascist).

Domestic: Aldo Finzi, Deputy (Fascist).

Foreign: Ernesto Vassallo, Deputy ("Popolare").

War: Carlo Bonardi, Deputy (Social Democrat).

Navy: Costanzo Ciano, Deputy (Fascist). *With the Commisariat of Commercial Marine.*

Treasury: Alfredo Rocco, Deputy (Nationalist).

Military Assistance: Cesare Maria De Vecchi, Deputy (Fascist).

Finances: Pietro Lissia, Deputy (Social Democrat).

Colonies: Giovanni Marchi, Deputy (Liberal of the Right).

Liberated Provinces: Umberto Merlin, Deputy ("Popolare").

Justice: Fulvio Milani, Deputy ("Popolare").

Instruction: Dario Lupi, Deputy (Fascist).

Fine Arts: Luigi Siciliani, Deputy (Nationalist).

Agriculture: Ottavio Corgini, Deputy (Fascist).

Public Works: Alessandro Sardi, Deputy (Fascist).

Post and Telegraph: Michele Terzaghi, Deputy (Fascist).

Industry and Commerce: Gronchi Giovanni, Deputy ("Popolare").

Labor and Social Providence: Silvio Gai, Deputy (Fascist).

When the ministry was completed I wrote the following paper of demobilization, signed by the quadrumvirate:

"Fascisti of all Italy!

"Our movement has been rewarded by Victory. The leader of our party has assumed the political powers of the State, both for domestic and for foreign affairs. Our Government, while it consecrates our triumph with the names of those who were its creators on land and sea, assembles, with the purpose of national pacification, men from the other parties, because they are attached to the cause of the Nation.

"The Italian Fascism is too intelligent to desire a greater victory.

"Fascisti!

"The supreme quadrumvirate of action, turning back its powers to the direction of the party, salutes you for your marvellous proof of courage and discipline. You have shown your merit in the future of the country.

"Disperse in the same perfect order in which you gathered for the great trial, destined—we firmly believe—to open a new epoch in Italian history. Go back to your usual work, because Italy now needs to work peacefully to reach its better day.

"Nothing must trouble the powerful stride of the Victory that we won in these days of proud passion and sovereign magnitude.

"Long live Italy. Long live Fascism!

"THE QUADRUMVIRATE."

Then I sent a telegram to D'Annunzio and I distributed an energetic circular to all the Prefects of the Kingdom and to the lesser authorities. The telegram to D'Annunzio said:

"Assuming the hard task of giving discipline and internal peace to the Nation, I send to you, Commander, my affectionate greetings for you and for the destinies of the country. The valiant Fascist youth which gives back a soul to the Nation will not blindfold Victory. Mussolini."

The text of the circular sent to office-holders was the following:

"From to-day, intrusted with the confidence of His Majesty the King, I undertake the direction of the Government of the Country. I demand that all authorities, from the highest to the least, discharge their duties with intelligence and with complete regard for the supreme interests of the Country.

"I will set the example.

"The President of the Council and Ministry of the Interior. Signed: Mussolini."

Finally I announced for November the 16th a meeting of the chamber of deputies, to render an account of what I had done, and to announce my intentions and programme.

It was an exceptional meeting. The hall was filled to overflowing. Every deputy was present. My declarations were brief, clear, energetic. I left no misunderstanding. I stated sharply the rights of revolution. I called the attention of the audience to the fact that only by the will of Fascism had the revolution remained within the boundaries of legality and tolerance.

"I could have made," I said, "of this dull and gray hall a bivouac for corpses. I could have nailed up the doors of parliament and have established an exclusively Fascist government. I could have done those things, but—at least for a time—I did not do them."

I then thanked all my collaborators and pointed with sympathy to the multitude of Italian laborers who had aided the Fascist movement with their active or passive solidarity.

I did not present one of the usual programmes that the past ministries used to present; for these solved the problems of the country only on paper. I asserted my will to act and to act without delaying for useless oratory. In the field of foreign politics I squarely declared the intention of following a "policy of dignity and national utility."

On every subject I made weighty declarations that showed how Fascism had already been able to assay and analyze and solve varying and urgent problems, and to fix the future outlines of government. Finally I concluded:

"Gentlemen:

"From further communications you will know the Fascist programme in its details. I do not want, so long as I can avoid it, to rule against the Chamber; but the Chamber must feel its own position. That position opens the possibility that it may be dissolved in two days or in two years. We ask full powers because we want to assume full responsibility. Without full powers you know very well that we couldn't save one lira—I say one lira. We do not want to exclude the possibility of voluntary co-operation, for we will cordially accept it, if it comes from deputies, senators, or even from competent private citizens. Every one of us has a religious sense of our difficult task. The Country cheers us and waits. We will give it not words but facts. We formally and solemnly promise to restore the budget to health. And we will restore it. We want to make a foreign policy of peace, but at the same time one of dignity and steadiness. We will do it. We intend to give the Nation a discipline. We will give it. Let none of our enemies of yesterday, of to-day, of to-morrow cherish illusions in regard to our permanence in power. Foolish and childish illusions, like those of yesterday!

"Our Government has a formidable foundation in the conscience of the Nation. It is supported by the best, the newest Italian generations. There is no doubt that in these last years a great step toward the unification of spirit has been made. The Fatherland has again found itself bound together from north to south, from the continent to the gen-

erous islands, which will never be forgotten, from the
metropolis of the active colonies of the Mediterranean and
the Atlantic Ocean. Do not, Gentlemen, address more vain
words to the Nation. Fifty-two applications to speak upon
my message to Parliament are too many. Let us, instead
of talking, work with pure heart and ready mind to assure
the prosperity and the greatness of the Country.

"May God assist me in bringing to a triumphant end my
hard labor."

I do not believe that, since 1870, the hall of Monte-
citoro had heard energetic and clear words. They burned
with a passion deep in my being. In that speech there
was the essence of my old and my recent wrestling with
my own mind and my own soul. More than one deputy
had to repress the rancour generated by my deserved
reproaches; but my exposition in parliament was rewarded by the approval of the whole of Italy. I was
looking beyond that old hall of parties of petty power
and of politicians. I was speaking to the entire nation.
It listened to me and it understood me!

My political instinct told me that from that moment
there would rise, with increasing truth and with increasing expansion of Fascist activity, the dawn of new history for Italy.

And perhaps dawn on a new path of civilization. . . .

CHAPTER X

FIVE YEARS OF GOVERNMENT

MY revolutionary method and the power of the Black Shirts had brought me to tremendous responsibility of power. My task, as I have pointed out, was neither simple nor easy; it required large vision, it gathered to it continually more and more duties.

An existence wholly new began for me. To speak about it makes it necessary for me to abandon the usual form of autobiographic style; I must consider the organic whole of my governmental activity. From now on my life identifies itself almost exclusively with thousands of acts of government. Individuality disappears. Instead, my person expresses, I sometimes feel, only measures and acts of concrete character; these do not concern a single person; they concern the multitudes, they concern and permeate an entire people. So one's entire life is lost in the whole.

Certainly I know that I took the direction of the government when the central power of the state was sinking to the bottom. We had a financial situation that Peano of the Liberal party had summarized with an astounding figure: six billions of deficit! Individually the people fed on expedients. Progressive inflation and the printing presses gave to everybody the old illusion of prosperity. It created an unstable delusion of well-being; it excited a fictitious game of interests. All this had to be expiated when faced by the severe Fascist financial policy.

Abroad our political reputation had diminished progressively. We were judged as a nation without order and discipline, unable either to prosper or produce. The chronic infection of disorder had withdrawn from us the sympathies of countries better equipped than we were. Worse yet, it had increased the haughtiness and the contempt of many of our enemies.

The Italian school system, in its complex formation, university, middle and lower schools, had turned its energies into purely abstract, theoretical functions; it had withdrawn more and more from a real world, a modern world, and from the fundamental problems of national life; it had been inert as a guide to civil duties. Schools and pulpits should always show the way to ascending peoples.

There still lived, in the national mechanism, strange and hateful regional political formations; these used to bring our solidarity into question, if not into peril. The activities of the government in terms of services, improvements and appropriations were guided and affected, not by real natural necessities, but by the desire to ingratiate this or that population, or region. The treasury was tapped by this base policy of politics—electoral strategy.

A bureaucracy already suffering from elephantiasis

increased its distention, generating that spirit of trouble, those characters of instability, of intolerance, of slight love of duty, which are typical of all great accumulations of functionaries, especially when the latter are not well paid, and do not see their moral prestige supported and built up by the authority of the state and by precise and clear definition of individual responsibility.

We still had, as a consequence of our generous struggle, the Fascist squadron formations. They might become, in the new conditions of life, a danger threatening public order and legality.

The army and the navy lived apart from the great problems of national life. As a matter of fact, though this is good in many respects, it is not good when they are set aside in an almost humiliated formation. Aviation was in disorder. It was difficult to give it new strength. One must not forget, when considering aviation, that Nitti had forbidden flight, not only for military planes, but also for private planes. His command was to demobilize aviation, and to sell the motors as well as the airplanes. It was a kind of premeditated murder of a nation which really did not want to be strangled.

In the meantime there assembled in Rome all the arms and legs of anti-Fascism, in all its gradations. The political parties, at first dismayed by the revolution of the Black Shirts and my advent to power, began to revive. They began to find courage to pursue again the general trend of political parties in the equivocal atmosphere of the parliamentary corridors at Montecitorio. The Italian press was, for the greater part, tied to old groups and to old political customers.

It was necessary to reorganize all civil life, without forgetting the basic need of a supervisory force. It was necessary to give order to political economy, to the schools, to our military strength. It was necessary to abolish double functions, to reduce bureaucracy, to improve public services. It was necessary to check the corrosion and erosion of criticism by the remnants of the old political parties. I had to fight external attacks. I had to refine and improve Fascism. I had to divide and floor the enemies. I saw the vision that I must in every respect work to improve and to give tone to all the manners and customs of Italian political life.

It was also imperative not to neglect the ten millions of Italians emigrated beyond the frontiers. We had to give faith again to the zones on our borders. We had to assist in bringing modern improvements and stimuli to the life of the southern regions, and to get in touch with all the men of the healthy and strong provinces, wherever they were.

Infinite then were the problems and the worries. I had to decide everything, and I had a will firm enough to summon up all the political postulates that I had enunciated and sustained with pen and paper, in meetings and in my parliamentary speeches. This was not only a problem of strength to last, to endure, to stand erect in any wind, but also, above all, a problem of will.

I abandoned everything that kept me tied to the fortunes of my newspapers; I parted from everything that could have the slightest personal character. I devoted myself wholly, completely, exclusively, to the work of reconstruction.

To-day there is no change. I want to be a simple, devoted servant of the state; chief of a party, but, first, worthy head of a strong government. I abandoned without regret all the superfluous comforts of life. I made an exception only of sports which, while making my body alert and ready, succeed in creating healthy and happy intervals in my complex life of work. In these six years—with the exception of official dinners—I have never passed the threshold of an aristocrat's salon, or of a café. I have also almost entirely abandoned the theatre, which once took away from me useful hours of evening work.

I love all sports; I drive a motor car with confidence; I have done tours at great speed, amazing not only to my friends, but also to old and experienced drivers. I love the airplane; I have flown countless times.

Even when I was kept busy by the cares of power, I needed only a few lessons to obtain a pilot's license. I once fell from a height of fifty metres, but that did not stop my flying. Motors give me a new and great sensation of strength. A horseback ride on a magnificent sorrel is also for me a joyous interruption, and fencing, to which I devote myself, often with remarkable physical benefit, gives me the greatest satisfaction. I ask of my violin nothing more than serene hours of music. Of the great poets, such as Dante, of the supreme philosophers, such as Plato, I often ask hours of poetry, hours of meditation.

Mussolini walking along the seashore, May 1, 1928.
From a photograph presented to Mr. Richard Washburn Child.

No other amusement interests me. I do not drink, I do not smoke, and I am not interested in cards or games. I pity those who lose time, money, and sometimes all of life itself in the frenzy of games.

As for the love of the table; I don't appreciate it. I do not feel it. Especially in these last years my meals are as frugal as those of a pauper. In every hour of my life, it is the spiritual element which leads me on. Money has no lure for me. The only things at which I aim are those which identify themselves with the greatest objects of life and civilization, with the highest interests, and the real and deep aspirations of my country. I am sure of my strength and my faith; for that reason I do not indulge in any concession or any compromise. I leave, without a look over my shoulder, my foes and those who cannot overtake me. I leave them with their political dreams. I leave them to their strength for oratorical and demagogic exertion.

Italy needed what? An avenger! Her political and spiritual resurrection needed a worthy interpreter. It was necessary to cauterize the virulent wounds, to have strength, and to be able to go against the current. It was necessary to eliminate evils which threatened to become chronic. It was necessary to curb political dissolution. I had to bring to the blood stream of national life a new, serene and powerful lymph of the Italian people.

Voting was reduced to a childish game; it had already humiliated the nation for entire decades. It had created a perilous structure far below the heights of the duties of any new Italy. I faced numberless enemies. I created new ones—I had few illusions about that! The struggle, in my opinion, had to have a final character: it had to be fought as a whole over the most diverse fields of action.

To express this character of completeness of the whole struggle, I must be able to set it forth in a clear, evident way; it is necessary for me to set forth in sub-divisions the different fields in which action was demanded of me and out of which evolved the most significant facts of my governmental life. Deeds and actions, more than any useless subjective expressions, write my true autobiography—from 1922 till 1927.

I never had any interval of uncertainty; fortunately, I never knew those discouragements or those exaltations which often are harmful to the effectiveness of a statesman. I understood that not only my prestige was at stake, but the prestige, the very name of the country which I love more than myself, more than anything else.

I was anxious to improve, refine and co-ordinate the character of the Italians. Let me state what my domestic policies have been, what was charted and what was achieved. From petty discords and quarrels of holiday and Sunday frequency, from many-colored political partisanships, from peasant strifes, from bloody struggles, from the insincerity and duplicity of the press; from parliamentary battles and maneuvres, from the vicissitudes of representative lobbies, from hateful and useless debates and snarling talk, we finally climbed up to the plane of a unified nation, to a powerful harmony—dominated, inspired and spiritualised by Fascism. That is not my judgment, but that of the world.

After my speech of November 16th, 1922, in the chamber of deputies, I obtained approval for my declaration by 306 votes against 116. I asked and without difficulty obtained full powers.

I issued a decree of amnesty which created an atmosphere of peace. I had to solve the problem of our armed Fascist squadrons. I always have had great influence with my soldiers and with the action squads, which in every part of Italy had given proof of their valor, their gallantry, and their passionate faith. But now that Fascism had reached power, these formations were, in such a situation, no longer desirable.

On the other hand, I could not suddenly wipe out or simply direct toward the fields of sport these groups of men who had for me a deep, blind, and absolute devotion. In their instinct, in their vibrant conviction, they were led not only by strength and courage, but by a sense of political virtue. And as the perils had not entirely disappeared, it was imperative to guard the citadel of the Black Shirt's triumph. I decided then to create a Voluntary Militia for National Security and Defence. Of course its duties had to be well defined. It must be commanded by seasoned veterans and chiefs who, after having fought the war, had known and experienced the struggles of the Fascist resurrection.

I proclaimed that with Fascism at the wheel everything illegal and disorderly must disappear. The decision to transform the squads of action to Voluntary Militia for National Security undoubtedly was one of political wisdom; it conferred on the régime not only authority, but also a great reserve strength.

The organization of the Grand Council, a body exquisitely political, was one of my major aims after my coming to power. I faced the necessity of creating a political organization typically Fascist, one which would be outside and above the various old political mechanisms dominating and misruling our national life. Every day I needed clear answers to questions arising—I needed a body of reference. In all my complex work as chief of the government, I could not forget that I was also chief of the party that for three years had fought in the squares and streets of Italy—not merely to gain power, but above all to meet the supreme task and the supreme necessity of infusing a new spirit into the nation.

The Grand Council had to be the propelling element of Fascism, with the hard and delicate task of preparing and transforming into legal enactments the work of the Fascist revolution. There were no—and there are none now—heterogeneous elements in the Grand Council, but virile Fascists, ministers, representatives of our deepest currents of public opinion, men of expert knowledge and of interests. The Grand Council has always succeeded. I preside over it, and let me add, as a detail, that all the motions and the official reports which have appeared in the papers in concise form, have been written by my hand. They are the product of long meditations in which Italian life and the position of Italy in the world have been examined and dissected by the Fascist soul, spirit and faith. The Grand Council, which today I want framed in the legislative institutions of the régime, has rendered in its first five years a magnificent, unparalleled service.

One of the problems which presented itself first of all was that of the unification of the police forces. We had the ordinary police, with the different branches of political and judiciary police; the Royal Carabinieri, and, finally, the body of the Royal Guards. This last institution, created by Nitti, was made up of demobilized elements and was a useless organization finding its place somewhere between the carabinieri and the usual forces of public security. I decided immediately to suppress the Royal Guards. That suppression in the main was not attended by unfortunate incidents. In some cities, such as Torino and Milano, there were riots and attempts at resistance. I gave severe orders. I called into my office or telephoned to the chiefs responsible for certain local situations. I ordered them to fire, if necessary. In six hours everything was calm again. The instant dissolving of an armed body of forty thousand men cost only four dead and some tens of wounded. The officers were incorporated into other organizations, or took up activities according to their own wishes; the privates reached their districts and homes without further trouble.

Our Italian form of political Masonry, which at first had seemed to have adjusted itself to the new conditions, submitting to the advent of Fascism to power, now began a stupid and deceitful warfare against me and against Fascism. In a meeting of the Grand Council I proclaimed the impossibility for Fascisti of membership at the same time in Masonry. As a leader of the ranks of socialism I had already pursued the same anti-Masonic policy. We must not forget that this shady institution with its secret nature has always had in Italy a character typical of the briber and blackmailer. It has nothing of protection, humanitarianism, benevolence. Every one, even those who were benefited, are convinced that Italian Masonry has been nothing more than a society for mutual aid and for reciprocal adulation of its members. Every one knows that it has diffused in every way a worship of self-interest, and methods of privilege and intrigue, neglecting and despising rights and prerogatives of intelligence and morality. My struggle against Masonry was bitter; I carry the tangible signs of it still, but it constitutes for me, for my sincerity, and my probity, one of the most precious titles of merit.

In 1923, after negotiations carried on with unwavering constancy, I united Italian Nationalism with Fascism. For a certain time an identical vision had been shared by these two organizations about everything concerning the ends and aims of our national life. Political developments, however, had led them along separate paths. Now that victory had been concluded and the better elements of Nationalism were already collaborating with the new régime, the unification was more than a wise move; it was also an act of political sincerity. Black Shirt and Blue Shirt—the latter was the uniform of the Nationalists—united in a perfect accord of chivalry and political loyalty. This new and deep unity permitted us to enjoy the prospect of more favorable auspices for a new future, one worthy of that great Italy which had been prophesied, desired and finally created by Nationalism and Fascism.

In April, 1923, in Turin, there assembled the national congress of the "Popular Party." It was a verbose and academic meeting, not very different from the other political congresses that for decades had hypnotized Italian public life. They naturally discussed the policies of the Fascist régime for a long while and, after various divergencies of opinion, the majority of those assembled voted in favor of a middle-ground position with an anti-Fascist leaning.

Among the members of my ministry there were some of the "Popular Party"; they found themselves, after the meeting, in a difficult and delicate situation. I naturally put before them the problem of giving thought to their opportunity of staying in the Fascist government in the new state of things created by the attitude of their party. There were some explanations. Differing opinions alternated, but, in order to initiate that process of political clarification that I had foreseen as inevitable, I advised the members of the government of the Popular party to give up their places so that they could avoid dissensions between their parliamentary group and the Fascist party.

This process of clarification I had foreseen as soon as I went into power. The climate and altitude of Fascism was not adapted to all minds of that time. There were still many dissenters. Many people fed on the illusory hope that they would be able to influence and bend the methodical and straight courses laid out by Fascism. For this purpose, I was approached by those who were skilled in twistings, turnings and slidings. Naturally, they always found me as resistant as flint.

In 1923, for the first time, our Labor Day passed without incident; the people worked calmly, without regretting that old date which now in Italy had lost every meaning. Later on I wanted to get in touch with the public opinion of Italy and to measure how deep Fascism had penetrated the masses. First I went to Milan and to Romagna. Afterward I went to Venice, Padua, Vicenza, Sicily and Sardinia; finally I journeyed to Piacenza and Florence. I found everywhere warm, vibrant enthusiasm, not only among my lieutenants and the Black Shirts, but also among all of the Italian people. That people finally was sensing that it had a government and a leader.

The Black Shirts, the makers of the revolution, hailed me as a leader with the same changeless enthusiasm they had shown when I was only the chief of the party and when I was developing that programme of journalistic attack which had added so much to my popularity. The Italian temperament at times is much more adapted to faction than to action. But now my old comrades were just as near to me in their daily tasks and their regimental discipline. Their attitude not only made me proud but moved me deeply. I could not ignore this warm youth so full of ardor, and I was quite decided not to sacrifice it to compromises with an old world which was destined to disappear. The population felt that it had recovered a real liberty; they had experienced liberation from the continuous blackmail of parties which deluded the masses. They blessed my political work. And I was happy.

It was in this period that the campaign of the opposition opened again. Not being able to beat me on the field of conciliation and compromise, the opposing elements, led by the *Corriere della Sera,* began a series of depressing prophecies and calamity howling. They launched deceitful attacks and spun their polemic webs. I put into effect, however, a new electoral law, because I did not want to fall into the pitfalls of our old proportional representative system. I had alienated the "Populars," the Democrats, and some of the Liberals. The reforming of the school, about which I will have more to say, had invited some hostilities.

Meanwhile, we had anti-Fascist assaults and ambushes. This was a stormy year. It must be regarded as a period of settling and one of difficulty. I had to guard Fascism from internal crises, often provoked by intrigue and trickery. I succeeded in this by being always inexorably opposed to those who thought they could create disturbances and frictions in the party itself. Fascism is a unit; it cannot have varying tendencies and trends, as it cannot have two leaders on any one level of organization. There is a hierarchy; the foundation is the Black Shirts and on the summit is the Chief, who is only one.

That is one of the first sources of my strength; all the dissolutions of our political parties were always born not from ideal motives but from personal ambitions, from false preconceptions or from corruption, or from mysterious, oblique and hidden forces which I could always identify as the work of our Italian Masonry. I took account of all this. I resolved not to yield a hairbreadth. When the more urgent legislative problems had been settled by parliament I decided to dissolve the chamber, and after having obtained extension of full powers, I announced elections for April 6th, 1924.

This signal for elections was sufficient to calm political agitations of dubious character. All the parties began their stock-taking and the revision of their forces. All got ready to muster the greatest number of votes and to send to the chamber the greatest possible number of representatives.

An election may be considered a childish play, in which the most important part is played by the elected. The "Honorables," to be able to become so, do not overlook any sort of contortion, of demagogy and compromise. Fascism did not want to submit to the usual forms of that silly farce. We decided to create a large National list on which places had to be found not only for known, tried and faithful custodians and trustees of Fascism, but also for those who in the active national life had been able to uphold the dignity of their country. Fascism by this policy gave full proof of great political wisdom and probity. It even tolerated men of opposing or doubtful position because they could serve. In the National list were included ex-presidents of the Council, such as Orlando, and of the Chamber, such as

De Nicola; but the main body of the list was made up of new elements. It was, in fact, composed of two hundred veterans, ten gold medals, one hundred and fourteen silver medals, ninety-eight bronze medals, eighty mutilated and war invalids, thirty-four volunteers. The majority of the list was drawn from the aristocracy of the war and the victory.

The Socialists, divided from the Communists, sharpened their weapons, and so did the Populars. But from the ballot boxes of April 6th there flowed a full, irrevocable, decisive victory for the National list. It obtained five million votes against the two millions represented by all the other lists put together. My policy and our régime was supported by the people. I then could be indulgent toward our adversaries, instead of pressing them harder, as I might have done.

I directed that political battle staying in Milan. I attached no great importance to the results of the electoral struggle, but it interested me as an expression of the support and the enthusiasm which, in every Italian city, had already been given to the National Fascist list. This indorsement by the people encouraged my thesis and my governmental work. Having gone back to Rome I was received as a returning victor, and, from the balcony of the Palazzo Chigi, while I saluted the people and the city of Rome, I congratulated the new and greater Italy, in which men of good faith were all in harmony.

This was my synthesis: Let Parties die and the Country be saved.

On May 24th, with unusual solemnity, came the opening of the Twenty-seventh Legislature. His Majesty
the King made a very impressive speech. The hall had
the appearance of a great occasion. For petty political
reasons, the elements which denied the country and belittled Italian life determined to stay away. The in-
auguration of the Twenty-seventh Legislature, however, did not lose anything in its fulness and moral
value. Particularly well received were the veterans,
some of whom were very much decorated. Now there
stirred, in that old chamber, so used to mean and petty
political intrigues, a breath of new life; there was present a heroic sense of the new soul of Italy, a sense of a
living aspiration for greatness.

All these things irritated the Socialists. In their hearts
they had hated the war, had debased our victory. The
old parliamentary world could not adjust itself to this
magnificent gathering of youth. The congenital coward-
liness of Montecitorio, the seat of parliament, would
certainly refuse homage to the bravery symbolized by
these golden medals!

The deep dissension between the new and the old
Italy was revived again at Montecitorio. This dissension persisted in the atmosphere of parliament even
after it had been beaten and overcome by Fascism in
the squares and streets of Italy and in the hearts of the
nation. In the historic meeting of May 24th, 1924, that
sad antipathy was to have its epilogue. Not by mere
chance had I chosen the precise date of our entrance into
the war.

After some days the usual parliamentary discussions began. The seating of new deputies roused violent diatribes. The Socialists, who were absent from the ceremony of May 24th, had again taken up their posts of combat. The atmosphere was red-hot. I knew that it would be necessary to give a different tone to all our political life, especially to parliamentary life—there was no use my cherishing illusions about that. With very great patience I succeeded in appeasing the first tumultuous meetings. Nothing proved more effective in elevating the plane of the discussion than a speech delivered on June 6th by the blind veteran, Carlo Delcroix. On June 7th I answered all the opponents exhaustively. I denounced their maneuvres. I remember that I admonished every one in the name of Fascist martyrdom and in the name of the peace of souls, to attend solely to productive activities. I added: "We feel that we represent the Italian people and we declare that we have the right to scatter to the winds the ashes of your spites and of our spites, so that we may feed with powerful lymph, in the course of years and centuries, the venerable and intangible body of the country."

I felt the necessity of making in parliament a high appeal for calm, for a sense of balance and justice. I was animated by a deep and sincere desire for peace. But the success of my words was apparent only; in the ardors of the parliamentary political struggle scenes unworthy of any assembly took place.

The Socialists had been hit in their most sensitive spots; they had been slammed against reality. They were outnumbered, amazed by the rush of Italian youth, dismayed by the new direction events were taking. All the new political realism was in full antagonism to their leanings; they were beaten and they felt it. In such a situation, the Socialists wanted as a last resort to squeeze out some way of avoiding surrender, at least, in parliament.

Skillful and astute in every political art, they protracted without end all the annoyances they could devise. It was a game played with the deliberate aim to destroy and tear down. In this subtle work of exasperation, Matteotti, the deputy, distinguished himself above all others. He was a Socialist from the province of Rovigo, whose arrogant spirit held tenaciously to the principle of political dissolution. As a Socialist he hated war. In this attitude he reached a degree of absurdity even beyond that attained by any other Socialist. In the tragic period after the defeat at Caporetto, he had set himself against our Venetian refugees. Matteotti denied shelter to those unhappy people who fled from the lands then invaded by the enemy and in which the Austrians were committing every sort of violence. He said that they ought to remain under Austrian domination!

To this parliamentary battle of polemics he now brought his whole bag of tricks and devices. Being a millionaire, he considered socialism as a mere parliamentary formula. It is to be remembered, however, that he was an ardent fighter, well able to irritate his adversaries in the whirlwind of the struggle, but he was far from being able seriously to imperil the assembly and to silence such a party as the Fascist. Matteotti was not a leader. In that same Socialist party there were individuals who surpassed him in powers of debate, in talent, and in coherence. In his electoral districts he had had violent fights with the Fascists, and in the chamber he had at once revealed himself as a most zealous and pugnacious opponent.

One day Matteotti disappeared from Rome. Immediately it was whispered about that a political crime had been committed. The Socialists were looking for a martyr who might be of use for purposes of oratory, and at once, before anything definite could possibly be known, they accused Fascism. By my orders, we began a most painstaking and complete investigation. The government was determined to act with the greatest energy, not only for the sake of justice, but also to stop, from the very first moment, the spread of any kind of calumny. I threw the Prefect and Police Chief of Rome, the Secretary of the Interior, Finzi, and the Chief of the Press Office, Cesare Rossi, into the task of clearing up the mystery. Activity on the part of the police for the discovery of the guilty persons was ordered without stint. Very soon it was possible to identify the guilty. They were of high station. They came from the Fascist group, but they were completely outside our responsible elements.

The sternest proceedings were instituted against them without limit or reservation. Severe measures were taken—so severe indeed that in some cases they proved to be excessive.

The suspects were arrested at once. Among the responsible elements, those who had had relations with the guilty ones, merely because they were under suspicion retired, though innocent, from public life. No threat of restraint was laid on the authorities, the police and the courts.

All this should have stilled the storm.

On the contrary. This dramatic episode was destined to disturb the austere serenity that I had imposed on myself and on every one, in the general policy of the country. Though we were still living in an atmosphere incandescent with passion, with polemics and violent battles, it seemed hardly possible that only a few days after the opening of the Twenty-seventh Legislature, a group of men of position could carry through an enterprise which, begun as a jest, was to conclude in a tragedy. I always have had harsh and severe words for what happened. But despite the faithful and energetic behavior of the central government, there now burst out an unparalleled offensive against Fascism and against its leader. The opposition in the chamber gave the first signal of an attack in grand style. I perceived and foresaw immediately the ignoble game, which grew, not from any love for the poor victim, but solely from hate for Fascism. I was not surprised. In the chamber, when weak men already were hesitating, I said:

"If it is a question of lamenting, if it is a question of condemning, if it is a question of regretting the victim, if it is a question of pressing our prosecution of all the guilty and those responsible, we here repeat that this will be done calmly and inexorably. But if from this very sad happening some one seeks to draw an argument for anything but a wider reconciliation of all men on the basis of an accepted and recognised need of national concord—if any one should try to stage upon this tragedy a show of selfish political character for the purpose of attacking the government, it must be known that the government will defend itself at any cost. The government, with undisturbed conscience, sure of having already fulfilled its duty and willing to do it in the future, will adopt the necessary means to crush a trick which, instead of leading to the harmony of Italians, would trouble them with the deepest dissensions and passions."

These words did not penetrate minds already hardened. And there happened exactly what I had foreseen; the opposition threw themselves on the corpse of Matteotti in order to poison the political life of Italy and to cast calumnies on Fascism both in Italy and abroad.

The course of Italian public life from June till December, 1924, offered a spectacle absolutely unparalleled in the political struggle of any other country. It was a mark of shame and infamy which would dishonor any political group. The press, the meetings, the subversive and anti-Fascist parties of every sort, the false intellectuals, the defeated candidates, the soft-brained cowards, the rabble, the parasites, threw themselves like ravens on the corpse. The arrest of the guilty was not enough. The discovery of the corpse and the sworn statement of surgeons that death had not been due to a crime but had been produced by trauma was not enough.

Instead, the discovery of the corpse in a hedge near Rome, called the Quartarella, unstopped an orgiastic research into the details which is remembered by us under the ignominious name of "Quartarellismo."

Fortunes were built on the Matteotti tragedy; they speculated on portraits, on medals, on commemorative dates, on electric signs; a subscription was opened by subversive newspapers and even now the accounts are still open.

The opposition parties and their representatives in the chamber retired from Montecitorio and threatened not to participate further in legislative work; to this movement and to those who espoused it was given, by false analogy with the well-known event of Roman history, the name of Aventino. But the Aventino group was here reduced to a grotesque parody, in which hate and nakedness of power now reunited men of the most diverse political complexions. They ranged all the way from Socialists to Liberals, from Democrat-Masons to Populars, who pretended to be called Catholics. Clandestine meetings were held. They abused in every way the liberty of the press and of assembly, in order to destroy Italian life. Fanatical elements waited hour after hour for Fascism to be overthrown. In the background of this ignoble dramatic farce, there stood out the figure of senator Albertini, the happy owner of the newspaper. This man was willing to scrape in the garbage, to listen to all the dirty rogues, to collect the most men-

dacious pamphlets, trying somehow, sometime, somewhere, to hit at me and at Fascism.

I did not have a moment of doubt or discouragement.
I knew the attitudes, postures and poses of these adversaries. I knew that if they could they would have
ignobly used the corpse of the Socialist deputy as an
anti-Fascist symbol and flag. But their ghoulish politics passed the bounds of my imagination. Besides these
speculators, there were those on the timid and flabby
fringes of Fascism. They let themselves be led astray
by the political atmosphere. They did not perceive that
an episode is not the stuff of which history should be
made. In the name of a sentimental morality, they were
willing to kill a great moral and political probity and
knife the welfare of an entire nation.

In this situation there were also many repentant Mag-
dalenes, and many, impelled by the sad habit of many
Italians to consider as pure gold the acts and the work
of any opposition, hid their Fascist insignia and, trembling, abandoned the Fascist nation, already grown red-
hot from a thousand attacks and counter-attacks of its
adversaries.

We were going back into the depths of a revolutionary period, with all the excesses of such an abnormal
time, all its spites, troubles, and explosions. An atmosphere was formed in which many magistrates, often under Masonic influence, could certainly not give equitable and faultless judgments. Various parties beyond
the borders were giving help to the Socialists at home.
It was then clear to what extent anti-Fascism was still

abroad in certain international zones where Democracy, Socialism and Liberalism had consolidated their weight of patronage, blackmail and parasitism.

All this might have created for a moment, in certain political atmospheres, the illusion that the government had weakened. In December, 1924, at the end of that painful three months, some were calculating the days of life of our ministry. A great hope sprang up in the hearts of the politically hungry. There was, in fact, a miserable maneuvre on the part of the three former presidents of the council; they were able to delude themselves and others. But these professional political men have so little practical sense that they could not understand that with one breath I could have given an order to the Black Shirts which would have overturned once and for all their fancies and their dreams.

The swelled frogs waited for their triumph. The corrupt press gave the maximum of publicity to the calumnies, to incitation to commit crimes and to spread defamation. The Crown, supreme element of equilibrium, was violently menaced with blackmail and worse. As ever, there were adventurers who were eager to speculate on any turn in the tide of events in order to create again for themselves a political rebirth. This base and pernicious crew I, for my part, have always eliminated from the sphere of activity and position controlled by me.

As if all this were not enough, in that dark December of 1924, to complete the picture, Cesare Rossi, the former chief of the press office, tried a rascally trick.

This man, cast out from Fascism because he was implicated in the Matteotti affair, prepared a memorial which was a tissue of lies and libels. He aimed to involve the régime in guilt, and consequently to involve me. Everything that had happened or was happening in Italy he endeavored to put on my doorstep. This memorial, written by such a man, pretended to present a "moral indictment" of me. But in that field I cannot be attacked; every attempt of this sort is empty. I was informed beforehand of the plot that Rossi was going to attempt; I knew the contents of his memorial and the day on which it was to be printed in the papers of the opposition. I put an end to the miserable maneuvre. I published the memorial in a friendly paper; in this way I indicated that I gave no value to it. It was a jest and a delusion. The theatrical stroke fell on emptiness; the bubble swelled by slanders flattened like a pricked balloon.

The contemptible game lasted six months. The half-hearted had sunk beneath the surface; the singers of the doleful tunes felt their throats becoming parched. The speculators were now disgusted with themselves. In that period a former minister, decorated with the Collare dell'Annunziata, the highest order of Italy's sovereign, alligned himself with the cult of Republicanism and with the worst elements of the Socialists!

I held the Fascist party firmly in my hand during this period. I curbed the impulses of some Fascists who wanted violent reprisals with a clear order: "Hands in the pockets! I am the only one that must have his hands

free." In Florence and Bologna, however, there occurred episodes of extreme violence. I understood then
that it was time to speak and act.

In all that time I credit myself with the fact that I
never lost my calm nor my sense of balance and justice.
Because of the serene judgment that I endeavor to summon to guide my every act, I ordered the guilty to be
arrested. I wanted justice to follow its unwavering
course. Now I had fulfilled my task and my duty as a
just man. Now against my adversaries I could play my
own game—in the open.

When the menace of a general strike in the Province
of Rome arose, I ordered the Florentine legions of the
Militia to parade in the streets of the Capital. The
armed Militia with its war songs is a great agent of per-
suasion. It is an argument. In September, 1924, I had
visited the most intense zones of the Tuscan Fascism;
I went among the strong populations of the Amiata,
among the workers and peasants, among the miners of
the province of Siena. On that occasion, while opponents
hourly awaited my fall—and that was also the secret
hope of many enemies beyond the borders—I delivered
to the Fascists an audacious sentence in which I sounded
an affirmation of strength and victory:

Of our adversaries, I said, "we will make a litter for
the Black Shirts."

The opposition press made a great fuss about these
words; but their chattering had no importance. That
became clear on January 3rd, 1925. On that day, when
Rome was already full of the exiled from the provinces

and of those who tremblingly awaited the conclusion
of the political struggle, I made in parliament this
speech, which certainly was not lacking in reserve:

Gentlemen,

The speech I am going to make before you might not be
classed as a parliamentary speech. It may be possible that,
at the end, some of you will find that this speech is tied, even
though a space of time has elapsed, to the one I pronounced
in this same hall on November 16th. Such a speech can lead
somewhere, but it cannot lead to a political vote. In any
case let it be known that I am not looking for this vote. I do
not want it; I have had plenty. Article 47 of the Statute
says: "The Chamber of the Deputies has the right to accuse
the Ministers of the King and to bring them to face the
High Court of Justice." I formally ask if in this Chamber,
or outside it, there is any one who wants to make use of Article 47. My speech will then be very clear; it will bring
about an absolute clarification. You can understand this.
After having marched for a long time with comrades to
whom our gratitude always will go out for what they have
done, it is good sense to stop to consider whether the same
route, with the same companions, could be followed in the
future.

Gentlemen, I am the one who brings forth in this hall the
accusations against me.

It has been said that I would have founded a "Cheka."

Where? When? In what way? Nobody is able to say. Russia has executed without trial from one hundred and fifty
thousand to one hundred and sixty thousand people, as
shown by statistics almost official. There has been a Cheka
in Russia which has exercised terror systematically over all
the middle classes and over the individual members of those
classes, a Cheka which said it was the red sword of revolution.
But an Italian Cheka never has had a shadow of existence.

Nobody has ever denied that I am possessed of these three

qualities; a discreet intelligence, a lot of courage and an utter contempt for the lure of money.

If I had founded a Cheka I would have done it following the lines of reasoning that I have always used in defending one kind of violence that can never be eliminated from history.

I have always said—and those who have always followed me in these five years of hard struggle can now remember it—that violence, to be useful in settling anything, must be surgical, intelligent and chivalrous. Now, all the exploits of any so-called Cheka have always been unintelligent, passionate and stupid.

Can you really think that I could order—on the day following the anniversary of Christ's birth when all saintly spirits are hovering near—can you think that I could order an assault at ten o'clock in the morning in the Via Francesco Crispi, in Rome, after the most conciliatory speech that I ever made during my Government?

Please do not think me such an idiot. Would I have planned with the same lack of intelligence the minor assaults against Misuri and Forni? You certainly remember my speech of June 7th. It should be easy for you to go back to that week of ardent political passion when, in this hall, minority and majority clashed every day, so much so that some persons despaired of ever being able to re-establish those terms of political and civil cooperation most necessary between the opposite parties in the Chamber. The shuttles of violent speeches were flying from one side to the other. Finally on June 6th Delcroix with his lyric speech, full of life and passion, broke that storm-charged tension.

The next day I spoke to clear the atmosphere. I said to the opposition, "I recognize your ideal rights, your contingent rights. You may surpass Fascism with your experience; you may put under immediate criticism all the measures of the Fascist Government."

I remember, and I have still before my eyes the vision of this part of the Chamber, where all were attentive, where all felt that I had spoken deep, living words, and that I had established the basis for that necessary living-together without which it is not possible to continue even the existence of any political assembly.

How could I, after a success—let me say that without false or ridiculous modesty—after a success so clamorous that it was admitted by all the Chamber, opposition included, a success because of which the Chamber opened again the next Wednesday in a good atmosphere, how could I think, without being struck with mad extravagance, to order, I won't say a murder, but even the slightest, the most petty offense against that very adversary whom I esteemed because he had a certain courage which looked like my courage, and an obstinacy which appeared like my obstinacy in sustaining a thesis?

They have the minds of crickets who pretend that I was making only cynical gestures on that occasion. Such gestures are the last to be tolerated by me; they are repugnant to the very depths of my conscience. And I feel as strongly against the show of strength.

What strength? Against whom? With what aim? When I think about that, Gentlemen, I remember those strategists who, during the War, while we were eating in the trenches, made strategy with little pins on the maps. But when the problem is to get something done at the place of command and responsibility, things are seen in another light and have a different appearance. And yet on enough occasions, I have proved my energy. I have usually not failed to meet events.

I have settled in six hours a revolt of the Royal Guards. In a few days I have broken an insidious revolt. In forty-eight hours I brought a division of Infantry and half of the fleet to Corfu. These gestures of energy—and the last one amazed even one of the greatest generals of a friendly Nation—are cited here to demonstrate that it is not energy that fails me.

The death punishment? But that is a joke, Gentlemen! First of all, the death punishment must be inflicted under the penal code and, in any case, capital punishment cannot be the reprisal of a Government!

It must be inflicted with restrained, better let us say very restrained, judgment, when the question is the life of a citizen. It was at the end of that month which is carved deeply into my life, that I said, "I want peace for the Italian people and I want to re-establish normal political life."

What was the answer to this policy of mine? First of all the secession of the Aventino—anti-constitutional secession, clearly revolutionary! Then a campaign of the press which lasted throughout the months of June, July and August. A dirty, miserable campaign which dishonored us for three months. The most fantastic, the most terrifying, the most frightful lies were affirmed extensively in the press.

Investigations of underground happenings were also made; they invented things, they knew they were lying, but it was done all the same! I have always been peaceful and calm amid the storm. That storm will be remembered by those who will come after us with a sense of intimate shame. On September eleventh, somebody wanted to revenge a killing and shot one of our best men. He died poor—he had sixty lires in his pocket. But I continue my effort to normalize. I repress illegalities. I state the bare truth when I say that even now in our jails there are hundreds and hundreds of Fascists.

It is the bare truth when I recall to you that I reopened the Parliament on the fixed date and that the discussion covered, with no lack of regularity, almost all the budgets.

It is the bare truth that that oath of which you know is taken by the Militia and that the nomination of all the generals for all the zone commands is conducted as it is.

Finally a question which raised our passions was presented—the question of accepting the resignation of Giunta. The Chamber was excited. I understood the sense of that revolt; however, after forty-eight hours I used my prestige and my influence. To a riotous and reluctant assembly I said: "Accept the resignation," and the resignation was accepted.

But this was not enough; I made a last effort to create normal conditions—the plan for electoral reform. How was that answered? It was answered by an accentuation of the campaign and by the assertion, "Fascism is a horde of barbarians camped on the Nation, and a movement of bandits and marauders." Now they stage, Gentlemen, the moral question! We know the sad history of moral questions in Italy.

But after all, Sirs, what butterflies are we looking for under the arch of Titus? Well, I declare here before this assembly, before all the Italian people, that I assume, I alone, the political, moral, historical responsibility for everything that has happened. If sentences, more or less maimed, are enough to hang a man, out with the noose! If Fascism has only been castor oil or a club, and not a proud passion of the best Italian youth, the blame is on me!

If Fascism has been a criminal association, if all the violence has been the result of a determined historical, political, moral delinquency, the responsibility for this is on me, because I have created it with my propaganda from the time of our intervention in the War to this moment.

In these last days not only the Fascists but many citizens ask themselves: Is there a Government? Have these men dignity as men? Have they dignity also as a Government? I have wanted to reach this determined extreme point. My experience of the life of these six months is rich. I have tried the Fascist Party. Just as to try the temper of some metals it is necessary to hit them with a hammer, so have I tested the temper of certain men. I have seen their value; I have seen for what reasons, at some moment when the wind seems contrary, they turn around the corner. I have tested myself. And be sure that I would not have persisted in measures if they had not been for the interests of the Nation. A people does not respect a Government which allows itself to be scorned. The people want to see their own dignity reflected in a Government, and the people, even before I said it, said, "Enough! The measure is filled."

And why was it filled? Because the revolt of the Aventino has a republican background.

This sedition of the Aventino has had consequences, for

now whoever in Italy is a Fascist risks his life! In the two months of November and December eleven Fascists were killed. One had his head crushed, and another one, an old man seventy-three years old, was killed and thrown from a high wall. Three fires happened in one month, three mysterious fires on the railroads, one in Rome, another in Parma, and the third in Florence. Then came a subversive movement everywhere.

A chief of a squad of the Militia severely wounded by subversives.

A fight between Carabinieri and subversives in Genzano.

An attempted attack against the seat of the Fascists in Tarquinia.

A man wounded by subversives in Verona.

A soldier of the Militia wounded in the Province of Cremona.

Fascists wounded by subversives in Forli.

Communist ambush in San Giorgio di Pesaro.

Subversives who sing the "Red Flag" and attack Fascists in Monzambano.

In the three days of this January, 1925, and in a single zone incidents occurred in Mestre, Pionca, Valombra; fifty subversives armed with rifles strolled through the country singing the "Red Flag" and exploding petards. In Venice the Militiaman Pascai Mario was attacked and wounded. In Cavaso di Treviso another Fascist was hurt. In Crespano, the headquarters of the Carabinieri were invaded by about twenty frantic women, a chief of a detachment of Militia was attacked and thrown into the water. In Favara di Venezia Fascists were attacked by subversives.

I bring your attention to these matters because they are symptoms. The Express train No. 192 was stoned by subversives who broke the windows.

In Moduno di Livenza, a chief of the squad was attacked and beaten. You can see by this situation that the sedition of the Aventino has had deep repercussions throughout the whole Country. And then comes the struggle in which one side says: Enough! When two elements are struggling the solution lies in the test of strength. There never was any other solution in history, and never will be.

Now I dare to say that the problem will be solved. Fascism, the Government, the Party, is at its highest efficiency. Gentlemen, you have deceived yourselves! You thought that Fascism was ended because I was restraining it, that the Party was dead because I was holding it back. If I should use a hundredth part of the energy that I used to compress the Fascists, to loosen them. . . . Oh! You should see, for then . . .

But there will be no need of that, because the Government is strong to break fully and finally this revolt of the Aventino.

Italy, Gentlemen, wants peace, wants quiet, wants work, wants calm; we will give it with love, if that be possible, or with strength, if that be necessary.

You can be sure that in the forty-eight hours following this speech the situation will be clarified in every corner. We all know that this is not a personal fancy, not lust for government, not base passion, but only infinite and powerful love for my Country.

These words, restrained till then, together with my disdain and my force of expression, suddenly awoke Fascist Italy. The situation, as I had foreseen, was clarified in forty-eight hours. The papers of the opposition, which till then had been full of envy, hate and defamatory attacks, began to slink into their holes again. A new situation, full of power and responsibility, was developing. Fascism had now all the attributes—after the long "quartarellista" parenthesis—to enable it to march onward and to govern by itself.

It was on that occasion that the Liberal ministers Sarrocchi and Casati, and also the minister Oviglio, a tepid Fascist, asked to resign from the ministry. I replaced them with three Fascist ministers. We were coming back by the force of events to the historical origins of our movement, back to pure irreconcilableness.

Fascism, after my words full of my faith and my willingness to show audacity, was coming back to its warrior soul. Immediately, all those who were out of Fascism wanted to participate in our movement, but in order not to load too much on our party the membership lists were closed.

Victory was complete. The maneuvre of the former premiers definitely failed and became ridiculous, just as did other artificial structures attempted about that time. One was a movement inspired by Benelli, under the name of the Italian League, to create secessions from Fascism, and another an underhand maneuvre by some shortweight grandchildren of Garibaldi.

At the end of January, 1925, the Aventino, with all our opponents, appeared to have been destroyed, torn to pieces by a thousand internal discords and differences. I was winner again on the whole front and I was getting ready to channel the Fascist revolution into institutions and into constitutional forms.

On October 28th, 1924, the National Militia, which represents the best of Fascism and which has always been my beloved creation, had sworn loyalty to the King. Now it was necessary to bring the Constitution of 1848 up to date and to create new representative institutions, worthy of the new Italy.

With this aim I brought about the nomination of a

commission of eighteen experts on statecraft. I charged
them with the preparation of proposals of reforms to be
presented to our legislative organs.

The commission was then called the Commission of
the Solons. It concluded its work, after a certain time,
suggesting some improvements in the old Constitution
and the creation of new institutions. I afterward used
the recommendations as a base. The commission at the
time did not lay down definite lines, but it contributed
to the reforms which later on I began to see taking
clearer shape and which were approved by the two
branches of the national parliament.

A law against secret societies was voted; so legal
sanction was given to the struggle maintained by Fascism against Masonry. In fact, in 1925, it was ridiculous
to think that there could exist societies constituted for
performing a clandestine public act, outside the control
of the person who has the supreme direction of public
affairs and beyond the control of all who fulfill any
function of the law.

A secret political society in modern, contemporary
life is a thing of nonsense, when it is not a menace. I
settled it that all associations should be known in their
aims, in their formations, membership and developments.

It was at that time that Federzoni, then Minister of
the Interior, prepared with my full approval the new
law on public safety. Then we intrusted the Communes
to the "Podesta," drawing them away from the old electoral patronages, which were no longer suited to our

time and our temper. The Governship of Rome was instituted and there began, because I had made up my mind to it, an inexorable fight against the Mafia in Sicily, the bandits in Sardinia, and against other less widely known forms of crime, which had humiliated entire regions.

In February, 1925, I fell desperately ill. For obvious reasons, and perhaps because of exaggerated apprehension, any exact account of my condition and of my illness was never given out. I admit that the situation was in a certain way very grave. For forty days I could not come out of the house. My enemies now put their great hope in the illusion, revived by their desire, that my end was near. The Fascisti, because of my silence and the contradictory reports that were circulating, were very troubled. Never, so much as then, did I understand that I was indispensable to my men, to my devoted people, to all the great masses of Italian people. I had lively, vibrating and moving manifestations of solidarity, of devotion, of good will. The Black Shirts roared impatiently to see me.

When finally at the end of March, on the sixth anniversary of the foundation of Fascism, I appeared healed on the balcony of the Palazzo Chigi, I had in front of me all of Rome. The sight of me still thin and pale stirred deep emotion. I saluted the multitude in the name of Spring, and among other things I said, "Now will come the best!" This sentence was interpreted in a thousand senses and aroused a wave of plaudits and approbation.

The wise treatment of very clever doctors, such as Professor Bastianelli and Professor Marchiafava, healed me completely. Those miserable persons who had based their hopes upon my illness were baffled. Nothing is more hateful to me than a hope that an illness may end one's adversary. I am more alive and stronger than ever before. I could repeat what I said one day, after an attempt against my life: "The bullets pass, Mussolini remains."

Another train of events which was to mark my complex and difficult existence was the attempts against my life.

Zaniboni initiated the series. He was a vulgar Socialist, who received two checks of 150,000 francs each from the Czechoslovakian Socialists to lead an anti-Fascist struggle. Naturally Zaniboni, a drug addict, used the 300,000 francs to prepare with devilish ability for his attempt against me. He chose the sacred day of the commemoration of the victory. He ambushed himself in a room of the Hotel Dragoni, just in front of the Palazzo Chigi, from the balcony of which I usually review the processions which pass on the way to the altar of the Unknown Soldier to offer their flowers, their vows and their homage.

Having an Austrian rifle with fine sights, the fellow could not miss his aim. Zaniboni, to avoid being suspected, dressed himself in the uniform of a major of the army, and got ready in the morning to accomplish his crime. He was discovered. He had been followed for a long time. A few days before, General Capello had generously given him money and advice. Masonry had made of him its ensign. But by simultaneous action, Zaniboni, General Capello and various less important personages in the plot were arrested one hour before they planned the attempt.

So closed the first chapter.

In 1926, in the month of April, when I inaugurated the International Congress of Medicine, a crazy and megalomaniac woman of English nationality, exalted by fanaticism, came near my motor car and at close range fired a shot that perforated my nostrils. A centimeter's difference and the shot might have been fatal. It was, as I said, a mad, hysterical woman, led on by elements and persons never clearly identified.

I abandoned her to her destiny by putting her beyond the frontier, where she could meditate on her failure and her folly.

Just after the occurrence, before my nose was out of its dressings, I was speaking to a meeting of officials from all parts of Italy. I felt impelled to say, "If I go forward, follow me; if I recoil, kill me; if I die, avenge me!"

Another attempt which might have had grave results was that of an anarchist, called Lucetti, who had come back from France with his soul full of hate and envy against Fascism and against me. He waited for me in the light and large Via Nomentana, in front of Porta Pia. He was able to meditate his crime in silence. He had been eight days in Rome and carried powerful bombs. Lucetti recognized my car, while I was going to the Palazzo Chigi, and as soon as he saw it he hurled at me the infernal machine, which hit an angle of the car and bounced back on the ground, exploding there after I had passed. I was not wounded, but innocent people were hurt and taken to the hospital.

When arrested, the miserable man could justify his crazy act only by his anti-Fascist hate. I did not attach a great importance to the episode. Having to meet the English ambassador, I went directly to the Palazzo Chigi and the conversation with the foreign diplomat continued calmly enough until a great popular demonstration in the streets interrupted us. Only then the English ambassador, somewhat amazed, learned of the attempt against my life.

The last attempt was made on October 31st, 1926. It was in Bologna, after I had lived a day full of life, enthusiasm and pride.

A young anarchist, egged on by secret plotters, at a moment when the whole population was lined up for the salute, came out from the ranks and fired a gun at my car. I was sitting near the "Podesta" of Bologna, Arpinati. The shot burned my coat, but again I was quite safe. The crowd, in the meanwhile. seized by an impulse of exasperated fury, could not be restrained. It administered summary justice to the man.

Other attempts were baffled. The exasperation was now surpassing any limit. I understood that it was time to stop the doleful game of the adversaries. The secret societies, the opposition press, and deceitful political cults had only one aim: it was to hit the chief of Fascism, so that all Fascism should be hit. The entire movement that dominated Italy they believed turned on one pivot, on a name, on a lone man. All the adversaries, from the most hateful ones to the most intelligent, from the slyest ones to the most fanatical, thought that the only way of destroying Fascism was to destroy its chief. The people themselves perceived this and demanded grave punishments for the criminals. The exasperated Fascists wanted to admonish all those who were conspiring in the darkness.

A policy of force was absolutely necessary. I took over the Ministry of Internal Affairs, and launched the laws for the defense of the régime, laws which were to constitute the one essential basis for the new unified national life.

I abolished the subversive press, whose only function was to inflame men's minds. Provincial commissions sent to confinement professional subversives. Not a day goes by that we do not feel in Italian life how much good has been wrought by these measures against the forces of disintegration, disorder and disloyalty.

I must then conclude that a strong policy has yielded really tangible results. Every day the country feels intensely the identification of Fascism with the vital strength of the nation. Nobody suffers ostracism in Italy; everybody is allowed to live under the definite régime of law. Many elements of the old popular subversives understand now to what extent a well regulated life is a benefit, not only for one class, but for every class of the Italian people. Few are those who are still confined, and few are those who intend to disobey. As Minister of the Interior, I distributed a circular on January 6th, 1927, to the Prefects, in which I pointed out what their duty in regard to the population must be.

A new sense of justice, of serious purpose, of harmony and concord guides now the destinies of all the peoples and classes of Italy. There are neither vexations nor violence, but there is exaltation of what is good and exaltation of the virtue of heroism. In every class, among all citizens, nothing is done against the state, nothing is done outside the state.

Many have finally opened their eyes to this serene and severe truth; the Italians feel themselves of one fraternity in a great work of justice. The sense of duty, the necessity of action, the manner of civil life mark now an intense reawakening. The old parties are forever dead. In Fascism politics is fused into a living moral reality; it is a faith. It is one of those spiritual forces which renovates the history of great and enduring peoples.

CHAPTER XI

NEW PATHS

WHEN one watches the building of new structures, when hammers and concrete mixers flash and turn, the occasion is not one for asking the superintendent his opinion about the plays of Bernard Shaw or for expecting the architect to babble discursively on the subject of his preferences between the mountains and the seashore as summer playgrounds.

It is absurd to suppose that I and my life can be separated from that which I have been doing and am doing. The creation of the Fascist state and the passing of the hungry moments from sunrise to the deep profundity of night with its promise of another dawn eager for new labors, cannot be picked apart. I am lockstitched into this fabric. It and myself are woven into one. Other men may find romance in the fluttering of the leaves on a bough; as for me, whatever I might have been, destiny and my own self have made me one whose eyes, ears, whose every sense, every thought, whose entire time, entire energy must be directed at the trunk of the tree of public life.

The poetry of my life has become the poetry of construction. The romance in my existence has become the romance of measures, policies, and the future of a state. These to me are redolent with drama.

So it is that as I look back over nearly six years of leadership I see the solution of problems, each of which is a chapter in my life and a chapter in the life of my country. A chapter, long or short, simple or complex, in the history of the advance and experimentation and pioneering of mankind.

I am not deeply concerned at being misunderstood. It is more or less trivial that conspiracies go on to misinterpret and, indeed, entirely to misrepresent what I have sought and why I have sought it. After all, I have been too busy to hear the murmurs of liars.

He who looks back over his shoulder toward those who lag and those who lie is a waster; it is because I cannot write my life—my daily life, my active life, my thinking life and even my own peculiar, emotional life —without recording the steps I have taken to renew Italy and find a new place for her in the general march of civilization, that I call up one after another the recollection of my recent battles over measures which submerge men, over policies which bury, under their simplicity and weight, everything else I might have lived.

Two fields of my will and action, of my thoughts and my conclusions, stand out as I write and as I record my life itself.

I think of all of them in terms of utter simplicity, stripped of complex phrases. I have seen the futility of those who endlessly speak streams of words. These words are like armies enlisted to go away forever into the night, never to return from a campaign in which the enemies are compromise of principle, and cowardice, inaction, and idealism without realism.

There are those, no doubt, who regard me or have once regarded me as an enemy to the peace of the world. To them there is nothing to say unless it be to recommend my autobiography to them for careful reading. The record of facts is worth more than the accusation of fools.

From the first, I wanted to renovate from bottom to top the foreign policy of Italy. Let it be remembered that I was fully conscious always of the history and the economic and spiritual possibilities of my country in its relation to the world. Such a renovation, such a remaking of policy, was absolutely new for us. It was destined to meet serious preconceptions and misconceptions before it would be clearly understood and appreciated, not only by Italians, but by those responsible for the foreign policies of various nations.

I was fully aware that a new spirit, one of new austerity and dignity, imposed by me to govern every large and small action of my ministry, might create the impression that I wanted to fight to a finish old international political tradition, organization, and existing alliances and the status quo.

What an error! To inaugurate a firm stand does not mean to revolutionize the course of international dealings. To demand a better appraisal of Italy, in accordance with a correct audit of our possibilities as a powerful and prolific nation, was only to re-establish our rightful position.

My problem was to open the eyes of the responsible elements in the various European governments and chanceries. They had gone on rather blindly considering Italy to be in its unstable position after the war.

To open these eyes, sometimes with vigorous calls for attention, was not always easy. I spent months and years in bringing about a realization abroad that Italy's foreign policy had no tricks in it. It was always straightforward, and swerved not. It was always vigilant. It was based on an accurate appraisal of facts, squarely faced, and it demanded equally that others should face facts. This understanding has contributed, naturally, to bringing Italy higher on the horizon of the world's eternal dawn of new events.

A speech on foreign policy delivered by me in the Italian senate in the spring of 1928 reviewed our entire national and international situation, and the part that Italy has played in the many little or great events of world life. It set forth a clear review of my work. It summarized the concrete success won by my ministry. ᵀt brought out that we had correctly insisted upon new appraisals of Italy's part in the world.

But, before this concrete and tangible result was reached, let no one believe that the steps were light and easy. I knew well enough how many would look toward Rome with suspicion, as if it were an irresponsible centre of disturbance. Enemies of our country and of Fascism tried in every way in their power to strengthen, by bad faith, by twisted interpretations, and by false news, all the errors in foreign judgments of what I was trying to do.

But truth usually comes along behind any simple, clear policy and overcomes the obliquity, the conventional mentality, the spirit of opportunism, and the lie-barking of the yesterdays.

There is no country in the world in which foreign policy, though carefully carved out and approved by the nation, is not subject to internal attack based on ignorance or bad faith. Therefore it was no surprise to me to find that even when I had calmed the internal political situation and had established for us the main points of the general policy of Italy within and without, there were those who began an offensive of criticism.

One of them was Count Sforza, who in October, 1922, was in Paris as Italian ambassador.

This man, loquacious and irresponsible as a minister in the past governments, had been a nuisance to the country. He had linked his name with the Adriatic situation, humiliating for our nation. This former minister, an amateur in everything that concerned any perplexity of foreign policy, showed himself so vain that he could not sense the delicacy of his position in Paris. While in Italy events of historic character were maturing, homesickness for lost power made him a bad servant of his own country. He even went to the point of trying to create difficulties for the Fascist government in the French capital. Already political groups there were unfavorable to if not envious of, any new solidarity in Italy. Count Sforza at once began to criticise openly my declaration on foreign and internal policy,

my political method and my concept of Fascist Italy.
I sent him a telegram, and this is what I said:

"I must interpret as a not quite amiable and rather an
awkward gesture, your decision to hand in your resignation
before having officially known my orders as to foreign policy, which I will disclose in the Chamber of Parliament; orders that will not be merely a sum of sentiments and resentments, as you wrongly think. I bid you now formally to
keep your place and not create difficulties for the Government. In this moment, the Government represents the highest expression of the national conscience. I am waiting for a
telegraphic answer and I reserve my later decision as to you.
MUSSOLINI."

To this telegram Count Sforza made an elusive answer. So I called him to Rome and after some explanations which revealed our two minds to be in complete
antithesis, I relieved him of office and dismissed him
from his place. It was time that the central authority
should no longer be debated by those who occupied inferior positions. Italian political life needs command
and organization and discipline. Our representatives
abroad were sometimes shown to have a cold, isolated,
autonomous life, far removed from their primary duties
toward their country.

This first strong gesture of mine was a clear signal;
it undoubtedly served as an example and admonition
for many others of our diplomatic representatives, who
tried to withdraw themselves, with subjective attitudes,
beyond the supreme authority of the state.

Having closed this breach in our diplomacy I dedicated all my energies to the solution of those political

problems which would determine our future. I found
facing me a situation already distorted and prejudiced
by the crass errors of preceding governments. I found
a series of peace treaties which, though in some respects
full of defects, nevertheless constituted as a whole an
unavoidable state of fact squarely to be met.

Still palpitating and open in Italy was the wound of
the Rapallo treaty with Jugoslavia. I wanted to medi-
cate that and heal it. On the delicate ground of treaties
I explained my position and suggestions in a speech
about foreign policy delivered in the chamber, November 16th, 1922. I said then, as I always say, that "treaties, whether bad or good, must be carried out. A respectable nation can have no other programme. But treaties
are neither eternal nor irreparable. They are chapters of
history, not epilogues of history." Speaking of foreign
policy in relation to the different groups of powers, I
summarized my thoughts with this definition: "We cannot allow ourselves either a plan of insane altruism or
one of complete subservience to the plans of the other
peoples. Ours is then a policy of autonomy. It shall be
firm and severe."

In November, 1922, I met, at Lausanne, Poincaré of
France and Curzon of Great Britain. Let it be said that
I re-established then and there, on my first personal
contact with the Allies, our equality. There were some
clear and precise interviews; some went on to a rather
vivacious tune!

For the time had come for Italy, with its record of
sacrifice and with the weight of its history, to enter into

an equality of standing in discussions of an international
nature side by side with England and France.

During my brief stay at Lausanne I held conferences also with the Foreign Minister of Rumania and
with Mr. Richard Washburn Child, Ambassador of the
United States in Rome, and chief of the United States
delegation at the Conference. I eliminated also the question of the Dodecannes.

To sum up my trip to Switzerland; these were the
results:

First, we made clear to foreign diplomats the new
prestige of Italy.

Second, we gave examples of our new style in foreign policy at the moment of initiating a direct contact
between myself and responsible diplomats of the world.

In December of that year, I made other important
declarations to the council of the ministers about our
foreign affairs. I examined again the Treaty of Rapallo. I began a solution of the problems of Fiume and
Dalmatia, making that solution fit in with the situation
created by the preceding treaties to which I had fallen
heir. For the second time I met Lord Curzon, and then
I went on to London, where I stayed for several days.
On that occasion I was received with the most generous
hospitality and found that I was listened to with respect
by the English political world.

Already the question of the Allies' debts was on the
table. I had discussed this with Mr. Child and with the
British ambassador in Rome. I had a plan that I do
not hesitate to claim was one of the most efficacious for

the solution of that problem. My plan aroused a certain interest among the Allies, but some divergencies of a secondary character, and particularly the design of France to occupy the Ruhr, killed that which in my opinion was the most logical solution of the debt question, combined with the problem of the German reparations. It was a solution which might have permitted a quick and powerful restoration of world economy.

Always before me in my foreign policy is the economic aspect of international problems. That was why in 1923 I concluded a series of commercial treaties, with a political background, with a number of nations. It amuses me to be called an anti-pacifist, in the light of our record of treaty-making for peace and for fair international dealings.

These commercial treaties were very helpful in settling our economic position. In February of 1923 I signed the Italian-Swiss treaty, concluded in Zurich; I ratified the Washington treaty for the limitation of naval armaments. Other commercial treaties were concluded with Czechoslovakia, with Poland, with Spain, and, finally, with France. I took the first steps to renew commercial relations with Soviet Russia.

Our record in international affairs discloses a sleepless vigilance to build peace and make friends. More peace, more friends. We yield nothing of our autonomy, nor do we allow our power to be used as a pawn by others. We are idealists in the sense that we endeavor to make and keep peace by building and maintaining, brick by brick, stone by stone, a structure of peace founded on realities rather than on dreams and visionary plans. I have insisted upon being strong, but I have labored to be generous.

For an efficient foreign service, the world requires some housecleaning in its diplomatic machinery, which has grown stale, over-manned, and bureaucratic, and filled with feeble, petty conspiracies to gain place and promotion.

I then began, in the reorganization of our consulates, an elimination of foreign functionaries. That work was long and wide-spread, because it was necessary to re-build our old consular organization. The renovation, complex as were its problems, was completed with un-swerving insistence.

In the midst of this complex task of foreign policy and machinery, and while I was studying the solution of the Adriatic problem, there came the news that the Italian military mission in Albania had been treacher-ously ambushed on a road and massacred in its entirety by bandits from the border. In this tragic happening there were wiped out brave General Enrico Tellini, Surgeon-Major Luigi Corte, Artillery Lieutenant Mario Bonacini, and a soldier, Farneti. The Italian military mission was in Albania, together with other foreign missions, with a well-defined task, laid out by definite international agreements. The offense to Italy and to the Italian name hit the sensibilities of Italy squarely in the face. History furnishes other examples of such outrages and points to accepted standards. I made myself the interpreter of the righteous wrath of

Italians everywhere. I at once sent an ultimatum to Greece.

I demanded an apology. I demanded payment of fifty million lire as indemnity.

Greece turned to us a deaf ear. Pretexts and excuses met my request. There was an attempt by Greece to find allies to aid her to slide away from my demands. I would not play that base game. Without hesitation I sent units of our naval squadron to the Greek island of Corfu. There the Italian marines landed. At the same time I sent a note to the powers. The League of Nations declared itself incompetent to judge and solve the incident. I continued the occupation of Corfu, declaring clearly that Italy would withdraw from the League if we could not obtain there a satisfactory attitude. This was not a mere matter of insult by words; it concerned the lives of Italian officers and soldiers. It was impossible to believe that I could allow this tragic page to be turned over with nothing more than some bureaucratic gesture.

There has been so much misrepresentation and nonsense as to this outrage and the settlement of our demands that I may do well to state the simple facts, which any school child can understand and digest.

The case, when brought for judgment to the Conference of the Ambassadors, received, as was to be expected, a verdict favorable to the Italian position.

Greece gave me all the satisfaction that I had asked. The indemnity was paid. I offered ten millions of this indemnity to the Greek refugees. Thereafter, having obtained full satisfaction, I recalled the squadron from Corfu. The book was closed.

But that month was indeed one of tragic happenings. The new Fascist style of foreign policy had satisfied the sensibility of all the Italians, but I admit that it had hurt the feelings of many foreign elements which saw in my foreign policy something out of the ordinary, disturbing to many and preventing plans opposed to the rights of Italy. I allowed nothing to deflect me. I made important declarations to the senate, both as to the Greek incident and on the question of Fiume. I said then that the most painful inheritance of our foreign policy was Fiume, but that nevertheless I was treating with Jugoslavia to solve, with the slightest possible damage, the very grave Adriatic situation inherited as a consequence of the Treaty of Rapallo.

The senate approved my policies and my acts.

In January, 1924, I was able at last to conclude with Pasic, the great Serb statesman, and with Nincic, the Jugoslav minister, a new treaty between Italy and our neighbor. As a consequence of this treaty Fiume became Italian. Other moves, continued in 1925, brought to signature the Nettuno Conventions, which regulated all the relations of good neighborliness between the two states. It remains for Jugoslavia to ratify.

At the end of all this diplomatic work on a wide field we definitely lost Dalmatia, we lost cities sacred to Italy by the history and the very soul of the populations which live in them. These had been assured us by the pact of London. No better settlement was possible than the one that I, with the good-will and the eagerness that I and Pasic and Nincic put into the negotiations, was able to draw up.

Though there is yet no Jugoslavian ratification of the Nettuno Conventions, our borders are well guarded and sure. Jugoslavia may show its good will; in any case we now can look calmly into the eyes of our troubled neighbor.

The foreign programme in 1924 obtained in the senate three hundred and fifteen favorable votes against six, with twenty-six absent. In December of that same year I had an interview with Chamberlain, new Foreign Minister of the British Empire. In the many events of international character I have always found him a friend of Italy and of Italians.

In 1925 I had to undergo a lively struggle with the government of Afghanistan. In the capital of that distant country one of our countrymen, an engineer, Piperno, who had gone there to work and study, had been slain, as a consequence of some events of internal character. The Afghan government refused to pay an indemnity to the family of Piperno. I had to send something of a demand. Though it was a definite claim for satisfaction, I did not close the door on the resumption of good friendship with the distant state, and indeed, the King of Afghanistan later had in Rome the warmest and most sympathetic of receptions.

The clouds come and pass away, and new clouds come into our skies. A new cloud showed in the anti-Italian propaganda, laid down by Germans in the region of our eastern border. In February, 1926, when the Fascist policy had made its justice, its weight and strength felt in the mixed-population zone of the High Adige, I had to speak clearly as to the problem of our relations with those Germans behind the Brenner Pass. I made two straight-from-the-shoulder speeches that shook many a timid and selfconscious plotter or sentimentalist. These are not practised in the habits of a school of courage and strength. I dismissed on that occasion another ambassador, Bosdari, who, at the centre of an event as significant as was this, one concerning deeply the relations between the Italian and the German people, was not able to behave as we might expect an ambassador of a power like Italy to behave.

The frank speech that I made on that occasion—it was cut from the same cloth as that I used in similar circumstances against the policy of Seipel, Premier of Austria—undoubtedly cleared our relations with the German population behind the borders.

This question of the High Adige, however, was framed in a wide vision of our relations with all other states. It was just at that time that I had a series of important interviews with the Bulgarian, Polish, Greek, Turkish and Rumanian foreign ministers.

Thanks then to this intense political rhythm, Rome became every day more and more a centre of attraction for important political activities and political exchange. The loyal character of my foreign policy, followed and appreciated by all Italians, has given Italy more consideration from other nations. A loyal policy is the one which scores the greatest success. Ambiguities and vagueness are not in my temperament, and consequently they are strangers to any policy of mine. I feel that I can speak with firmness and dignity, because I have behind me a people who, having fulfilled their duties, now have sacred rights to defend and for which to demand respect.

I have sent forth messages of brotherhood and faith to the Italians who live beyond our borders; I did not give them the name of emigrants, because in the past this word has had a humiliating meaning, and it seemed in some way to imply an inferior category of men and women. I have been able, I am glad to say, to protect my countrymen without wounding the susceptibilities of other peoples. This protection is founded on international law and on good sense in all exchanges between nations.

Italy on its part has accorded the greatest hospitality to all those who for business, for religious faith, for pleasure, or even for curiosity have wanted to visit our soil. I have taught Italians to show appropriate respect for foreign representatives in our country; it is never admissible, in fact, for diplomatic controversies to be twisted or troubled by angry popular demonstrations against embassies or consulates. Such disorders belong to an old democratic habit which Fascism has clearly outgrown. There have been delicate moments in Italian affairs during which resentment and protest might easily have been exhibited. I have always held these protests within the limits of Fascist dignity, though often they have been exaggerated in the foreign press. This is no slight undertaking, even for one who has imposed upon himself the task of giving order and discipline to the Italian people.

The foreign policy of Italy as directed by me has been simple, understandable, and rests on these main points:

First, mine is a policy of peace. It is founded not upon words, gestures, and mere paper transactions, but comes from an elevated national prestige and from a whole network of agreements and treaties which cement harmony between peoples.

Second, I have not made any specific alliances with the great powers. Instead, I have negotiated a series of treaties which show a clear and decisive will to assure to Italy a prosperity in its relations with all nations, especially with those of great historical importance, such as England.

Nor have I failed to work out a whole series of treaties with minor powers, so that Italian influence could have its part in general progress. Albania is one case. Hungary and Turkey are others. To assure harmony on the Mediterranean, I have established accord with Spain; to make possible a greater development of our industries and of our foreign trade, I resumed independent commercial relations with Russia.

Stupid indeed are those who fail to see that I have taken a serene, respectful attitude, but not a humble one. The League of Nations and some of the diplomacy inspired by the Locarno treaty are witnesses of that. I made reservations, after meditated discussions, and because of my well-grounded beliefs regarding the disarmament pacts, I noticed some absurdities in them.

I have bettered and completed the consular organization and I have put in it a series of new men born with and grown out of Fascism. They have suffered the passion of the war and the passion of our rebirth. In the meantime I did not fail to bring Fascism also to our colonies, I wanted to extend the standards which demanded discipline and insured full harmony for all Italian initiatives. These must be concentrated from now on in the representatives of our policies.

A sense of new life and pride fills not only the Italians in Italy, but all our countrymen scattered about the world. Italy now enjoys the respect of those nations which evolve and put into effect world policy.

My colonial policy has simple affinity with my foreign policy. Even taking into consideration the virtues of our colonizing peoples, even remembering all the fine human material we have given for the development of entire regions of the African and American worlds, before the war and after, we had failed to realize the potential possibilities of our colonial programme. We had failed to bring it to vigor and fruitfulness.

We missed then that legitimate satisfaction which should have come to us as of right and from duty fulfilled during and after the war.

Colonial development would not have been for us merely a logical consequence of our population problem, but would have provided a formula for the solution of our economic situation. Even now, at this distance of ten years from the war, this problem has still to find its full solution. Our colonies are few, and not all open to extensive improvement. Eritrea, which is the first of our colonies, has not undergone any change. Somaliland has been augmented by British Giubaland, following a diplomatic accord.

Lately, thanks to the wise policies of Governor De Vecchi, we have pacified all Somaliland, and considerable Italian capital is moving toward that colony of ours, to be used for definite objects and to provide work for Italian labor. The Libian colony—which includes Cirenaica and Tripolitania—was reduced during the war to the occupation of the coast and some of the principal cities. Fascism, on assuming power, found grave conditions. These also have been cleared up. Our policy of military occupation, and of course of economic penetration, has assured us the full and uncontested domination of Cirenaica as far as Giarabub, and of Tripolitania as far as the border recognized by treaties of international character.

There is a great fervor of rebirth in both colonies. Tripoli has become one of the most beautiful Mediterranean cities. A congress of medical men has adjudged it a health resort. We have found water for the city and water in the hills for irrigation. I made a visit to the zone of Tripoli, and that gave me a conviction as to all the possibilities for improvements that can be extended to the entire colony. There are zones in Garian which can compete in production and fertility with the better zones of southern Italy. The same can be said about the high plain of Cirenaica. In this last region I have abolished a curious form of parliament created by the weakness of our former governments. Now the governors enjoy complete influence and complete responsibility for the welfare of nations and Italians. These regions are pacified. Immigration continues to go there. Capital goes; laborers go.

These two colonies alone cannot solve our population problem. Mark this well. But with good-will and with the help of the typical colonizing qualities of Italians, we can give value to two regions which once were owned by Rome and which must grow to the greatness of their past and contribute to the new and greatly expanding possibilities of our general economic progress.

Into these labors to rebuild Italy's peaceful position before the world, and to develop as duty dictates every colonial possibility which may help to solve our population problems, I have put my days and some of my sleepless nights. But it would be absurd to suppose that life was quite so easy for me as to allow me to stop with international and colonial questions.

Let us turn to the amazing and dramatic financial situation.

A leader of the Liberal party in parliament, Peano, six months before the March on Rome, had defined the deficit of our budget by a figure of more than six billions!

The financial situation was then, according even to the declaration of our opponents, desperately serious. I knew what a difficult inheritance I had received. It had come down to me as a legacy from the errors and weaknesses of those who had preceded me. In fact, I fully understood that with such an important leak in the hull of the Ship of State, any great voyage of progress would be impossible. Finance, then, was one of the most delicate and urgent problems to be solved, if I wanted to rebuild and elevate our credit abroad and at home.

There were many demands due and waiting; necessity had turned the printing presses to the production of new paper-money, driving down and down the value of Italian currency. An irresponsible and demagogic policy had been followed, which had brought about complex makeshifts. These not only affected the soundness of the budget, but also were undermining all our economic life and the whole efficiency of the state.

I had to deal a smashing blow to useless expenditures, and to those who sought tribute from the treasury. I had to rake up tax-slackers. I had to establish severest economy in every branch of state administration. I had to put a brake on the endless increase of employees. Furthermore, the obligation of settling our debts to foreign powers was staring me in the face. Even if our resources were limited, this supreme act of wisdom and honesty had to be performed.

It goes without discussion that for states as for individual citizens, when a debt has been signed and acknowledged it must be paid, and faith must be kept as to obligations undertaken.

For this work I picked a capable man; I appointed as Minister of Finance the Honorable De Stefani, a Fascist and a Doctor of Political Economy. He was able to curtail expenses, repress abuses, and create new sources of revenue and taxes; in this way the budget was almost balanced within two years.

I demobolized all the economic organization left over from war time; I eliminated the useless bureaucracy of the new provinces, still burdened by the debts and indemnities of war. I settled all these with an issue of bonds, quickly subscribed.

Before launching a policy of severe economy, I wanted to do full justice to the invalids of the war. I fixed, with special privileges and without regard to economy, the obligations that the state was to assume in their favor and in favor of the orphans and widows of those who had died in battle. After having repaired in this way a cruel wrong, and fulfilled a duty toward those who had given their life and their blood to the country, it was easy for me to strike at certain forms of exaggerated and sudden wealth derived from war profits. There is no doubt that I have been very harsh in this matter. But why not? These unjust pocketbook privileges represented an offense against those who had suffered for the war, suffered not only in misery or death, but also in loss of money and property.

While striving to eliminate all that burdened the economy and finance of the state, I tried to promote individual production to the greatest degree. I had to respect honestly accumulated wealth, and make everybody understand the value, not only economic but also moral, of inheritance transmittable in families. Because of this, though I had approved a tax reform of great importance, I restored many basic rights, such as the right of succession.

It was made clear that I would never approve subjecting inheritance to a taxation which had almost assumed a socialistic character of expropriation. Interference with succession strikes a blow at the institution of the family. I aroused controversies, but at last my decision was understood and accepted by the people.

Who knows better than I that the discipline displayed by the Italian people has been worthy of my admiration and of the respect of the world. We have no great natural resources. Nevertheless our citizens subjected themselves to the pressure of taxation so thoroughly that toward the end of 1924 minister De Stefani was able not only to announce to the chamber the balancing of our budget, but also to foresee a surplus of one hundred and seventy millions for the fiscal year 1925–26.

I consider that the corner-stone of all governmental policies is a wise and strong financial policy. And now, supported by the soundness of the budget, this policy was an accomplished fact. The state, through able administration and the disciplined patience of Italian taxpayers, was able to face all its obligations, to liquidate its liabilities and, in 1925 and 1926, to discuss with Washington and London the complex problems of war debts.

We were out of the hole.

We did not stop with the central gòvernment. The state, now self-assured, with its finances reordered, was able, by the strength of its example, to give precise rules for the restoration of the finances of the self-governing units in communes and provinces. But even that was not enough; we had to review the financial situation of many a corporation and industry. Generally, this included all those industries which were quoted on the stock exchange.

By one of those phenomena of national and international speculations, which are not infrequent in modern life, many of our industrial stocks and even government bonds had risen to figures which were hyperbolical and inconceivable, if one considered the relation that should exist between the value of our lira and its purchasing power in regard to gold.

Even in Italy, a wise and honest country, in which excessive speculation was never rampant, and in which the stock exchange was never the object of excessive and unchecked interest from any class of citizens, there arose a madness for stock exchange gambling. Many people, naturally, lost their heads. They shattered patrimonies, caused scandals, provoked bankruptcies; but this was not sufficient to stop the sudden craze for speculation. The Minister of Finance then decided to take steps to watch and to limit the activities of the exchanges. It was necessary to take really serious measures, which of course would run counter to old and rooted business traditions. Perhaps they were too sudden and too unexpected. They provoked in the middle and financial class an opposition which created a disturbance in all markets.

I was following the course of these events. This sudden opposition created by economic and not by political causes might, as was shown afterward, become a real danger, but it gave me a very important field for experience and observations. I brought a counter offensive and tamed those who made the attacks. A more rational policy was instituted but we conceded nothing to the speculators. After a while De Stefani resigned. Volpi succeeded him. In the meantime, after this first difficulty had been dealt with, I concentrated my attention on the war debts.

After settling the state budget and balancing it, I knew that I had come to the task of making an agreement with the United States of America and with England on the reduction of our war debt. I sent a delegation to Washington. The leaders were Count Volpi and the Undersecretary of Foreign Affairs, Grandi. I feel that the negotiations were carried on with great ability. We arrived, I believe, at an agreement that satisfied the American public and safeguarded the interests of Italy.

On January 27th, 1926, by an analogous agreement, with slight modifications due to the different relations that existed between us and England, we were able to settle also our English debts. America and England ratified the agreements; and so did we, with pride, because it is our constant, firm rule, in all our private or public affairs, to keep faith with our given word and to pay to our full ability the last cent we owe, without wailing or complaint.

Then came a gesture of spontaneous national patri-

otism: our people by public subscription and without
the help of the state paid the first installment due the
government of the United States!

I believed then that the security of the budget and
the agreements of Washington and London would be
sufficient evidence to reassure our industrial, commercial and banking classes as to the soundness of the financial policy of the government. I hoped that it would
lead to a gradual revaluation of all our currency and
credit in national and international markets.

Unfortunately, all which appeared to me to grow out
of convincing logic did not follow. In the first six
months of 1926, we were losing an average of ten points
in relation to the pound. The pound sterling naturally
was towing all the other privileged currencies in such
a way that, at a time when our credit should have been
on the upgrade, we were witnessing an opposite phenomenon. Our private economic life was getting thin-
ner and less stable; it was becoming fickle and incon-
stant, through a gradual inflation which might delude
many industrial centres of northern Italy, but was certainly not satisfying to the middle class and to the Italians who saved money.

It was necessary to give a point of support to this gay
finance. It was inconceivable that an orderly, quiet, disciplined state, which had no public agitation as a liabil-
ity and which worked with tenacity, faith and pride,
should abandon these wholesome forces and assets to the
mercy of shark speculators and parasites, eager to en-
rich themselves on the depreciation of the lira, ready to

accept willingly or even to quicken a general bankruptcy so as not to be obliged to settle their private debts, or to face their obligations toward depositors in their banks. A betrayal of the Italian people was being plotted by a class of unworthy citizens. It was a serious betrayal and an injury to moral character, because a ruined people cannot readily be born again in the credit of the world.

I studied for a long time the complex phenomenon of state, private, and individual finance. I was making a comparison between our own economic phase and the situation of analogous countries. I was watching closely the statistical data of our commercial balance. I had in my hand all the evidence for a sure and positive judgment, and was ready to say the word which would influence, in a clear and decisive way, the economic life of Italy.

Thus it happened that in August, 1926, in a square of a beautiful town of central Italy at Pesaro, I made a speech which was to become famous and which was destined to mark the beginning of the revaluation of the lira and our starting-point toward a gold basis.

I had decided for some time to speak out with candor to the Italian people. Foreign exchange had revealed a weakness in our credit abroad. Instability every day, under a régime of giddy and disastrous finance, was a sign of underground work. I had to put speculation back to the wall with a slam. I had to face and defeat that part of a certain class who would have pushed the nation toward bankruptcy. The government could not

ignore them or their machinations. It was not only a
matter touching the financial future of the country; the
very flag of the Italian people was being jeopardized.
In fact, in certain situations, even the soundness of a
currency can assume the dignity of a flag and must be
defended by every open means. One cannot entrench
oneself behind ignorance when the patrimony and the
dignity of an entire people is being threatened.

Fascism, which had put discipline into the nation,
had to put its firm hand on that class of short-sighted
speculators who wanted to bring to nothing the value
of our currency. Fascism, which had won on the political line, now faced, as I could well see, a defeat if it did
not intervene energetically in the financial field.

In this plot against us were joined all the strength
of the international anti-Fascists spurred and aroused
by our eternal foes, inside Italy and out. I understood
that combined with this problem of honesty and rectitude, there was also a problem of will. So I spoke. Here
is the essence of my speech:

You must not be surprised if I make a political declaration of definite importance. It is not the first time that I
have addressed to the people directly, without any official
apparatus, my convictions and my decisions. I must always
be trusted, but especially when I am speaking to the people,
looking into its eyes and listening to the beating of its
heart. I am speaking to you, but in this moment I am speaking to all Italians and my voice for obvious reasons will certainly have an echo behind the Alps, and overseas. Let me
tell you that I will defend the Italian lira to the last gasp! I
will never subject the marvellous Italian people, which for

four years has worked with ascetic discipline, and is ready
for other and harder sacrifices, to the moral shame and economic catastrophe of the bankruptcy of the lira.

The Fascist régime will resist with all its strength the
attempts to suffocate Italy being made by inimical financial forces. We will squash them as soon as they are identified at home. The lira, which is the sign of our economic life,
the symbol of our long sacrifices and of our tenacious work,
will be defended and it will be firmly defended—and at any
cost! When I go among a people that really works, I feel
that in speaking this way I interpret sincerely its sentiment,
its hopes, and its will.

Citizens and Black Shirts! I have already pronounced the
most important part of my speech, destined to dissipate the
fogs of uncertainty and to weaken the eventual attempts of
troublesome defeatism.

My sentences were like whip-lashes for all the speculators hidden in the bourses. The great financial institutions understood that it was not possible to adopt independent policies without having to reckon with the
government. Speculators perceived that they had fallen
into a trap.

On the other hand, I did not want to confine myself
to words. In the council of the ministers on September first, I adopted measures which were to guarantee
my financial policies. These measures can be summed
up: transfer of the Morgan loan of ninety millions of
dollars to the Bank of Italy; regularization of the accounts between the state and the Bank of Italy; reduction of two billion, five hundred millions of the circulation on account of the state; liquidation of the
autonomistic section of the Consorzio Valori.

To all this was to be added a broad simplification of taxation with abolition of certain taxes and a new form of protection for thrift and for banking activities.

In November I floated a loan that I called "The Littorio." It was intended to facilitate cash operations and to give some elasticity to the budget. Since there was a very heavy floating debt, represented by treasury bonds, I decided upon redemption of these bonds and their inscription in the great book of the public debt. These provisions had without doubt a harsh character; they were full of sacrifice. But when the moment and its discomfort had passed, we were able to start on a policy of wise severity; our lira began to climb gradually on the markets of London and Washington and our credit rose again in every part of the world.

To be sure, the passage from a giddy to an austere finance which I had inaugurated with the Pesaro speech was not without its difficulties. Failures and heavy losses were brought about. Business deals begun while the lira was at one hundred and thirty to the pound were closed with the lira at ninety. All this brought with it unavoidable losses which hit hardest those who were the least strong and resistant financially.

The difficulties in returning to a position of financial dignity and austerity were notable; reconstruction was as difficult as inflation had been easy. We had to reduce the budget and state bonds to their simplest expression; we had to start a policy of demobilization of our debts to be able to know our complex financial burden and to determine exactly the interest that had to be paid every year.

But the situation has been cleared and bettered. In order to have a sounder, readier, more agile organization, I had decided on the unification of all the institutions issuing paper money. Only the Bank of Italy has the power to issue paper money; the Bank of Naples and the Bank of Sicily returned to their original functions of guardians and stimulators of the agricultural economic life of southern Italy.

When, after a year of notable difficulties, the financial situation of the budget and of Italian economy had been cleared, I was able to address myself, in 1927, to the new gold basis of the lira, on concrete foundations. In December, 1927, at a meeting of the council of ministers, I was able to announce to the Italian people that the lira was back on a gold basis, on a ratio which technicians and profound experts in financial questions have judged sound.

I felt the pride of a victor. I had not only led the Black Shirts and political forces, but I had solved a complex and difficult problem of national finance, such a problem as sometimes withdraws itself beyond the will and the influence of any political man, and becomes subjected to the tyranny and mechanism of mere material relations under the influence of various and infinite factors. Only a profound knowledge of the economic life and structure of a people can reach, in such an insidious field, conclusions which will be able to satisfy the great majority.

To-day we have a balanced budget. Self-ruling units, the provinces and the communes, have balanced their budgets too. Exports and imports and their relationship are carried in a precise and definite rhythm—that of our stabilized lira. Through solidity and certainty, Fascist Italy is creating a new Italian régime, while the necessary complement of our general policy and the essence of our state organization is being supplied by a new corporative system.

CHAPTER XII

THE FASCIST STATE AND THE FUTURE

AMID the innovations and experiments of the new Fascist civilization, there is one which is of interest to the whole world; it is the corporative organization of the state.

Let me assert at once that before we reached this form of state organization, one which I now consider rounded out, the steps we took were long, and our research, analysis and discussion have been exhaustive. Both the experience and the tests have been full of lessons.

Practical reality itself has been the navigator. First of all, we must remember that the corporative organization was not born from a desire to create mere juridical institutions; in my opinion, it grew out of the special necessities of the Italian situation in particular, and out of those necessities which would be general in any situation where there is economic restriction, and where traditions of work and production have not yet been developed by experience and time. Italy, in its first half-century of united political renaissance, has seen classes armed one against the other, not only because of the desire of one to master the other in political control but also because of the struggle for the limited resources that our surface soil and what was beneath it might be put at the disposition of those who were interested in work and production.

Opposed to the directing middle class, there was another class which I will call, for more easy reference, proletarian. It was influenced by Socialists and anarchists, in an eternal and never-ending struggle with the directing class.

Every year there was a general strike; every year the fertile Po Valley, for instance, was subjected to recurring agitations which imperiled crops and all production. Opposed to that humane sense of harmony which should be a duty upon citizens of the same Fatherland, there was a chronic struggle of interests, egged on by the professional Socialists, the syndicalist organizers, a struggle against a middle class which, in turn, persisted in its position of negation and of expectation of a messiah. Civil life did not move a decisive step forward on the way toward betterment.

A country like ours, which has no rich resources in the earth, which has mountains for half of its area, cannot have great economic possibilities. If, then, the citizens become naturally quarrelsome, if classes have a tendency to strive to annihilate each other, civil life can have none of that rhythm necessary for developing a modern people. The Liberal and Democratic state, in spite of upheavals, recurrent every year, and even at every season, held to a noncommital stand, selecting a characteristic slogan: "Neither reaction, nor revolution,"—as if that phrase had a precise or, indeed, any meaning whatsoever!

It was necessary to emerge from the base, clannish
habit of class competition and to put aside hates and
enmities. After the war, especially following the subversive propaganda of Lenin, ill-will had reached perilous proportions. Agitations and strikes usually were accompanied by fights, with dead and wounded men as the
result. The people went back to work with souls full
of hate against the class of the masters, which, rightly
or wrongly, was considered so idiotically lacking in
vision as to surpass in this regard any other middle class
in the world. Between the peasants and the rising industry of the urban centres there were also the phenomena of unmistakable misunderstanding. All of our
life was dominated by demagogy. Every one was disposed to tolerate, to pretend to understand, to make concessions to the violence of the crowd. But after every
incident of disorder, some new situation promised another and even more difficult problem of conflict.

It was necessary, in my opinion, to create a political
atmosphere which would allow men in government to
have some degree of courage, to speak harsh truths, to
affirm rights, only after having exacted duties, and, if
necessary, imposing these duties. Liberalism and Democracy were only attempted remedies of milk-and-
water character; they exhausted their energies in the
halls of parliament. Leading that agitation were employees of the state, railroad men and postmen and
troublesome elements. The authority of the state was a
kitten handled to death. In such a situation, mere pity
and tolerance would have been criminal. Liberalism and

Democracy, which had abdicated their duty at every turn, failed utterly to appraise and adjust the rights and duties of the various classes in Italian life. Fascism has done it!

The fact is that five years of harmonious work have transformed in its very essentials the economic life and, in consequence, the political and moral life of Italy. Let me add that the discipline that I have imposed is not a forced discipline; it is not born from preconceived ideas, does not obey the selfish interests of groups and of classes. Our discipline has one vision and one end— the welfare and the good name of the Italian nation.

The discipline that I have imposed is enlightened discipline. The humble classes, because they are more numerous and perhaps more deserving of solicitude, are nearest to my heart as a responsible leader. I have seen the men from the countryside in the trenches, and I have understood how much the nation owes to the healthy people of calloused hands. On the other hand, our industrial workers have qualities of sobriety, geniality, stamina, which feed the pride of one who must rule and lead a people. The middle Italian class, too, including the rural class, is much better than its reputation. Our problems arise from a variety and diversity among the various economic interests, which makes difficult the formation of great national groups of producers. None of the Italian producing groups, however, can be rated as "vampires," as they were rated in the superficial terminology of the old Socialist demagogy. The state is no longer ignorant when it confronts facts and the interests of the various classes. Not only does it obviate strife—it tries to find out the origins of clashes and conflicts. By statistics and the help of studious men, we now are able to define what will be the great issues of to-morrow. In the meantime, with the aid not only of the government, but of the bodies locally organized for consultation, we can know precisely what are to be the outlines of the productive programmes of to-morrow.

I have wanted the Fascist government, above all, to give great care to the social legislation needed to carry out our part of agreed international programmes for industry and for those who bear the future of industry. I think that Italy is advanced beyond all the European nations; in fact, it has ratified the laws for the eight-hour day, for obligatory insurance, for regulation of the work of women and children, for assistance and benefit, for after-work diversion and adult education, and finally for obligatory insurance against tuberculosis. All this shows how, in every detail in the field of labor, I stand by the Italian working classes. All that it was possible to do without working an injury to the principle of solidity in our economy I have set out to do, from the minimum wage to the continuity of employment, from insurance against accidents to indemnity against illness, from old age pensions to the proper regulation of military service. There is little which social welfare research has adjudged practical to national economy or wise for social happiness which has not already been advanced by me. I want to give to every man and woman so generous an opportunity that work will be not a painful necessity but a joy of life. But even such a complex programme cannot be said to equal the creation of the corporative system. Nor can the latter equal something even larger. Beyond the corporative system, beyond the state's labors, is Fascism, harmonizer and dominator of Italian life, standing ever as its inspiration.

In 1923, some months after the march on Rome, I insisted on the ratification of the law for an eight-hour day. All the masses which had seen a friend in the legislative policy of Fascism gave their approval to national syndicalism. Instead of the old professional syndicates we substituted Fascist corporations. In a meeting of December 19, 1923, I had occasion to affirm that: "Peace within is primarily a task of government. The government has a clear outline of conduct. Public order must never be troubled for any reason whatsoever. That is the political side. But there is also the economic side; it is one of collaboration. There are other problems, such as that of exportation. I remind Italian industry of these principles. Until now it has been too individualistic. The old system and old ways must be abandoned."

A little further on I said: "Over all conflicts of human and legitimate interests, there is the authority of the government; the government alone is in the right position to see things from the point of view of the general welfare. This government is not at the disposition of this man or that man; it is over everybody, because it takes to itself not only the juridical conscience of the

nation in the present, but also all that the nation represents for the future. The government has shown that
it values at the highest the productive strength of the
nation. A government which follows these principles
has the right to be listened to by every one. It has a task
to fulfill. It will do it. It will do it inexorably for the
defense of the moral and material interests of the nation."

Little by little, the old labor structure and associations were abandoned. We were directed more and more
toward the corporative conception of the state. I did
not want to take away from labor one of its holidays,
and so, instead of the first of May, which had foreign
origins and the imprint of Socialist internationalism, I
fixed on a gay and glorious date in Italian life, April
21st, the birthday of Rome. Rome is the city which has
given legislation to the world. The Roman law is still
the text which governs the relations of civil life. To
celebrate a Labor Day, I could not have selected a more
suggestive and worthy date.

To bring into being, in a precise co-ordination, all the
measures that I had undertaken and that Fascism and
the Corporations had brought about, in all their com-
plexity, I had the Grand Council approve a document.
I do not hesitate to declare it to be of historical character: it is the Labor Charter.

It is composed of thirty paragraphs, each of which
contains a fundamental truth. From the paramount necessity for production arises the need of an equitable
sharing of products, the need of the judgment of

tribunals in case of discord, and, finally, the need of protective legislation.

That document has been welcomed by all the classes of Italy. The labor magistracy represents, in its consecration to duty, something worthy of a strong state, in contrast to the cloudy aspirations in the misty realms of high-sounding Liberalism, Democracy and communistic fantasy. The framing and realization were the tasks of Fascism. Old men of the socialist and syndicalist poses and postures were amazed and perplexed at the daring new reform. Another legend fell: Fascism was not the protector of any one class, but a supreme regulator of the relations between all citizens of a state. The Labor Charter found interpreters and attracted the attention of the studious in every part of the world. It became a formidable pillar of the new constitution of the Fascist State.

As a logical consequence of the Charter of Labor and of all the social legislation and of the magistracy of labor, came the necessity of instituting the Corporations. In this institution are concentrated all the branches of national production. Work in all its complex manifestations and in all its breadth, whether of manual or of intellectual nature, requires equally protection and nourishment. The citizen in the Fascist State is no longer a selfish individual who has the anti-social right of rebelling against any law of the Collectivity. The Fascist State with its corporative conception puts men and their possibilities into productive work and interprets for them the duties they have to fulfil.

In this new conception, which has found its logical
expression in our representative forms, the citizen is valuable because of his productivity, his work and his
thought, and not merely because he is twenty-one years
old and has the right to vote!

In the corporative state all national activities are reflected. It was logical that syndicalistic organizations
should become a part also of the new representative institutions. From this need, imposed by a new political
and social reality, arose the reform of national political representation. Not only does the new political directorate select its candidates with regard for their ca-
pabilities and for the number of citizens represented,
but it is complemented by the work of selection and valuation devoted by the Grand Fascist Council to the task
of creating the best, the most stable, the most truly representative and the most expert national board of di-
rectors.

We have solved a series of problems of no little extent and importance; we have abolished all those peren-
nial troubles and disorders and doubts that poisoned our
national soul. We have given rhythm, law, and protection to Work: we have found in the co-operation of
classes the evidence of our possibilities, of our future
power. We do not waste time in brawls and strikes,
which, while they vex the spirit, imperil our strength
and the solidity of our economy. We regard strife as a
luxury for the rich. We must conserve our strength.
We have exalted work as productive strength; therefore
we have the majority of these elements represented in

the legislative body, and this body is a more worthy and a stronger helmsman for Italian life.

And Capital is not exiled, as in the Russian communistic dream; we consider it an increasingly important actor in the drama of production.

In this, my Autobiography, I have emphasized more than once the fact that I have always tried to weave an organic and coherent character into all the fabric of my political work. I have not confined myself to giving merely an outward veneer or contour to Italian life; I wished to influence the very depths of its spirit. I founded my work on facts and on the real conditions of the Italian people; from such realistic activity I drew valuable lessons. I have been able to bring about useful, immediate results looking toward a new future for our country.

One of the reforms which I have promoted and have closely followed in all its successive developments is the reorganization of the schools. This has been called the Gentile Reform, after the name of the Minister of Public Instruction, whom I appointed immediately following the March on Rome. The gravity and importance of school problems cannot escape the attention of any modern statesman mindful of the destiny of his people. The School must be considered in all its complete expression. Public schools, Intermediate schools, University institutions, all exercise a profound influence on the trend—both moral and economic—of the life of any nation. From the beginning this has been ever in my mind.

Perhaps my early experience as a school teacher increased an unvarying interest in youth and its development. In Italy there were traditions of higher culture, but the public schools had become degraded because of lack of means and, above all, because of lack of spiritual vision.

Although the percentage of illiteracy tended to diminish and even to disappear in certain regions, particularly in Piedmont, the citizens nevertheless were not getting from the school world those broad educational foundations—physical, intellectual and moral—that are possible and humane. The intermediate schools were too crowded because everybody was admitted, even those without merit, through endless sessions of examinations which were reduced often to a spiritless formality. We lacked intelligent systems of selection and vocational and educational valuation of individuals. The mill ground on and on, turning out stock patterns of human beings who ended for the most part by taking tasks in bureaucracy. They lowered the function of the public service by dead and not living personnel. Universities created other puppets in the so-called "free arts," such as law and medicine.

It was time that the delicate machinery which was of such consequence in the spiritual life of the nation be renewed in a precise, definite, organic form. We had to crowd out from the intermediate schools the negative and supercilious elements. We were determined to infuse into the public schools those broad humanistic currents in which our history and our traditions are so rich.

Finally, it was indispensable to impose a new discipline in education—a discipline to which every one must submit, the teachers themselves first of all!

To be sure, teachers draw a very modest wage in Italy, and this is a problem that I am resolved to face and solve as soon as the condition of the budget will allow. Nevertheless, I cannot permit a limited, pinch-penny treatment of education. The niggardly policy is of old and typically Liberal and Democratic origin. It furnished teachers with a good pretext for performing their duties indifferently and for abandoning themselves to subversive thought, even against the state itself. This condition reached its climax in the humiliating fact that many teachers deserted their posts. We had had clamorous examples of such a tendency, not only in the elementary schools, but also in some of the universities.

Fascism put a stop to all this by making discipline supreme, discipline both for the high and for the low, particularly for those who had the high duty of *teaching* order and discipline and of maintaining the highest concepts of human service in the various schools of the régime.

We had an old school law which took its name from Minister Casati, a law that had been enacted in 1859 and had remained the fundamental law even after the successive retouching of Ministers Coppino, Daneo, and Credaro. We had to renew and refashion it, through the ardent will of our Party; we had to give it a broad didactic and moral vision; we had to infuse into it a spirit of vital rebirth which would appeal to the new

Italy. Great ideas and great revolutions always create the right hour for the solution of many problems. The school problem, which had dragged on for many decades, has finally found its solution in the Gentile Reform. This is not the place to explain the reform in detail. I want to indicate, however, those fundamental principles which I myself discussed and settled in a few compact discussions with the Minister of Public Instruction. They can be summarized by the following points:

1st—The state provides schooling only for those who deserve it because of their merits and leaves to other initiatives students who are not entitled to a place in the state's schools.

This throws on the scrap heap the democratic concept which considered a state school as an institution for every one—a basket into which treasure and waste were piled together. The middle class had regarded the school as at its service and therefore did not respect it. They demanded only the greatest possible indulgence in order to achieve as quickly as they could their purely utilitarian aims, such as a degree or a perfunctory passing to promotions.

2nd—The students of the state schools and of the independent schools find themselves under equal conditions when taking the state examinations, before committees appointed by the government.

Thus is encouraged the régime of independent schools analogous to those of England. This régime is advantageous for the Catholics, owners of many schools, but displeases the anti-clericals of the old style. It allows me a free development of scholastic initiative outside of the conventional lines.

3rd—The state watches over the independent schools and promotes a rivalry between independent and state schools which raises the cultural level and the general atmosphere of all schools.

The state does not see its jurisdiction diminished because of the independent schools; on the contrary, it extends its watchfulness over all schools.

4th—Admission to the intermediate schools is now possible only through examinations. The schools are directed toward a broad humanistic culture, but with a standard of scholarship which has eliminated forever the disorder and the easy-going ways of the old democratic schools.

By means of these and other reforms the elementary school comes to have two distinct but co-ordinated purposes. One is that of preparation for the intermediate schools, and the other is a high type of broad popular education complete in itself.

The intermediate schools were broadened by means of the following institutions:

(a) *Complementary schools*. The abolished technical school, complete in itself, was revived along new lines.

(b) *Technical institutes* of higher specialization.

(c) *Scientific Lyceum*, still higher, taking the place of the abolished "Modern Lyceum" and of the Physico-Mathematical departments of the Technical Institute, and preparing the students for the scientific branches of the University.

(d) *Teachers' Institute*, a purely humanistic and philosophical school taking the place of the abolished complementary and normal schools.

(e) *Women's Lyceum*, a general culture school, complete in itself.

(f) *Classical Lyceum*, unchanged in its essential lines, but augmented by the humanistic character of the studies; to it the task of preparing for most university branches has been assigned. To enter the universities, entrance examinations have been instituted. The final examinations of the intermediate schools, of the Classical and the Scientific Lyceum, have been termed Maturity Examinations; all the curricula have been renewed, fitting them for a more modern culture. Latin has been restored in all schools except in the Complementary and Religious Departments of the elementary and intermediate schools.

For all these different types of institutions, one essential rule has been put into practice, that is, every school must be a *unit organism*, with a set number of classes and students; the candidates may enter through a graduated classification, based on the examinations; those who are not admitted must go to independent schools.

The application of this reform, which overthrew the old interests, the old ideas and especially the utilitarian spirit of the population, aroused an unavoidable spirit of ill-feeling. It was used by the opposition press, especially by the *Corriere della Sera*, for controversial purposes; but the reform has been put through with energy under my direction and has marked the beginning of a real rebirth of the Italian schools and of the Italian culture.

The reform of the universities has been co-ordinated with the reforms in the primary and intermediate schools. Its purpose is to divide the university students into different organic institutions, without useless over-lapping. The rule of state examinations is imposed also for the universities, to which both the students of the state and independent schools can be admitted. The Institute of "Libera Docenza," authorities independently attached to certain faculties of the universities, has also been reformed, appointment no longer being made by the individual departments but by central committees in Rome.

On the occasion of a visit by the delegations of the Fascist university groups, I had the opportunity of declaring that the Gentile Reform "is the most revolutionary of all the reforms which we have voted on, because it has completely transformed a state of affairs which had lasted since 1859."

I was the son of a school-mistress; I myself was taught in the elementary and secondary schools. I knew, therefore, the school problem. Because of that, I had wanted to bring it to a concrete conclusion. The Italian school again will take its deserved place in the world. From our university chairs, true scientists and poets will again illuminate Italian thought, while the secondary schools will provide technical and executive elements for our population, and the public schools will create a background of civic education and collective virtue in the masses.

I have willed that, in collaboration with the universities, departments of Fascist economics, of corporative law, and a whole series of fruitful institutes of Fascist culture, should be created. Thus a purely scholastic and academic world is being permeated by Fascism, which is creating a new culture through the fervid and complex activity of real, of theoretical and of spiritual experiences.

But, even closer to my heart than the Institutes of Fascist universities, is a new institution which has all the original marks of the Fascist revolution. It is the National Organization of Balilla. Under the name of a legendary little Genoese hero the new generation of children and of youth was organized. These no longer depend, as in the past, upon various playground associations, scattered political schools and accessory institutions, but are trained through rigid but gay discipline in gymnastic exercises and in the general rules of a well-ordered national life. They are accustomed to obedience and they are made to see a sure vision of the future.

To show the importance that educational revival has in my mind, I myself gave a lecture at the University of Perugia. It has been pronounced by scholars as a broadening of the world's concept of its duty to youth.

Finally, to pay a tribute to culture and to higher culture, and to every one who, in the field of science, art, and letters, has held high the name of Italy, I have created an Italian Academy, with a membership of "immortals."

The armed forces of the state had fallen into degradation in the years 1919, 1920, 1921. The flower of our race had been spurned and humiliated.

Conditions even reached a point where the Minister of War in those "liberal" days had a circular distributed advising officers not to appear in uniform in public, and to refrain from carrying arms, in order not to be subjected to the challenges of gangsters and hoodlums.

This aberration, which it is better to pass over quickly for the sake of one's country, was destined to find its avenger in Fascism. It was one of the factors which created an atmosphere passionately eager for change. To-day, the spirit of the country is much different; today the armed forces of the state are justly considered the secure and worthy and honored defense of the nation.

I had a very clear and decisive programme, when, in 1922, at the moment of the March on Rome, I selected as my collaborators the best leaders of the Victory of 1918. General Armando Diaz, who after Vittorio Veneto had remained aloof in silence, overwhelmed by the difficulty of the moment, and who had issued and had been able to voice an indignant protest in the Senate against the policies of Nitti's Cabinet, had been selected by me as Minister of War. I appoined Admiral Thaon de Revel, the greatest leader of our war on the sea, as Minister of the Navy. On January 5, 1923, General

Diaz presented a complete programme of reform for the army to the Council of Ministers. That was an historic meeting; fundamental decisions for the renewal of the armed forces were taken; and we were able to announce to the country in solemn and explicit fashion that, with that meeting, the army had been given new life, to "accomplish the high mission that had been intrusted to it, in the supreme interests of the nation."

I had fulfilled the first promise I had made to myself and to the Italian people. Immediately after that I dedicated myself to a reorganization of aviation, which had been abandoned to utter decay by the former administrations. The task was not easy; everything had to be done again. The landing fields, the machines, the pilots, the organizers and the technicians all were restored. A feeling of abandonment, of dejection and mistrust had been diffused in Italy by the enemies of aviation; this new type of armed force, many people thought, should be developed only as a sport. Into this situation I put my energy—I gave it personal attention, personal devotion. I have succeeded in my purpose: the successes of De Pinedo, of Maddalena, the flights in squadrons, the great manœuvers, have demonstrated that Italian aviation has recently acquired great expertness and prestige, not only in Italy, but wherever there is air to fly in.

The same can be said of the navy, which has reordered its formation, bettered its units, completed its fleet, and made its discipline efficient. Fourth, but not least, because of its spirit of emulation and daring, comes the Voluntary Militia for the Safety of the Nation, divided into 160 Legions, commanded by distinguished officers and by enthusiastic Fascists. These are magnificent shock troops.

Finally our barracks and our ships can be said to be, in the true sense of the word, refuges of peace and strength; the officers devote their activities to the physical and educational betterment of the men; the training conforms to the modern technic of war. The army is no longer distracted from its functions, as happened too often under the old governments, in order to assume ordinary duties of public order which were exhausting and humiliating, and to which entire Divisions were assigned. I changed all this. For the last five years, the army has left its barracks for its tactical manœuvers and for no other reason.

After some time, General Diaz had been obliged to resign on account of the condition of his health. General Di Giorgio commanded *ad interim*. But later I saw clearly the necessity of gathering all the armed forces of the state under one direction. I assumed the portfolios of War, Navy and Aeronautics. Thanks to this programme, I have created a commander-in-chief of all general staffs, who has the task of shaping, with a complete vision of ensemble, all the plans of the various branches of our forces toward one end: Victory. Our military spirit is lively; it is not aggressive, but it will not be taken by surprise. It is a peaceful spirit, but it is watchful.

To complete the Fascist revival, it was necessary to keep in mind also several lesser problems which, for the sake of the dignity and strength of the life of the nation, were in need of an immediate solution.

The retired employees of the government, who received very small pensions before the war, had seen with alarm the value of their already meager resources diminish because of the successive depreciations of the currency. I had to make a provision of some exceptional nature for their protection, by making their pensions adequate to the necessities of the day and to the current value of money. I made a provision favoring the clergy also; it was a question of a just and necessary disposition. This would have been inconceivable in the days of the Masonic demagogy and social democracy, which was dominated by a superficial and wrathful anticlericalism. Our clergy number about 60,000 in Italy. They are extraneous to the controversy, which I may call historical, between State and Church. They accomplish a wise task and assist the Italian people in all their religious practices, without meddling with political questions, especially since the rise of Fascism. They are reluctant to debase the spiritual character of their mission. The intriguing priest, of course, has to be fought. Instead, the priest who accomplishes his task according to the wise rules of the Gospel and shows the people the great humane and divine truths, will be helped and assisted. Because many of them were living in poverty, we took general measures to better the conditions of their existence.

The policy in regard to public works in Italy had always had an electoral tinge; public works to be done were decided upon here and there, not according to an organic plan or to any plain necessity, but to give sporadic satisfaction to this or that group of voters. I stopped this legalized favoritism. I instituted Bureaus of Public Works, intrusting them to persons in whom I have complete confidence, who obey only the central power of the state, and are immune from pressure by local interests. In this way I was able to better appreciably the conditions of the roads of the South; I mapped out a programme for aqueducts, railroads and ports. All that is just finds in the Italian bureaucracy an immediate comprehension. All the offices of governmental character have received a new impulse and new prestige. The great public utilities of the state, railroads, mails, telegraph, telephone, the monopolies, function again. Certain persons are even sarcastic about the new regularity. And this is easily explained: we should not forget that the Italian people has been for many years rebellious against any discipline; it was accustomed to use its easy-to-hand and clamorous complaints against the work and activity of the government. Some vestiges of the mental attitudes of bygone days still come to the surface. There is even whining because there is efficiency and order in the world. Certain individualistic ambitions would like to slap at our strong achievements of discipline and regularity. But to-day the state is not an abstract and unknowing entity; the government is present everywhere, every day. He who lives in the ambit of the state or outside the state feels in every way the majesty of law. It is not a thing of small mo-

ment that all public utilities are conducted with an efficiency which I might call American, and that the Italian bureaucracy, proverbially slow, has become eager
and agile.

I have given particular attention to the Capital. Rome
is a universal city, dear to the heart of Italians and of
the whole world. It was great in the time of the Roman
Empire and has conserved a universal light. It was the
historical seat and the centre of diffusion of Christianity. Rome is first of all a city with the aura of destiny
and history. It is the Capital of the New Italy. It is
the seat of Christianity. It has taught and will continue
to teach law and art to the whole world.

I could not refuse the resources necessary to make
this magnificent capital a city æsthetically beautiful,
politically ordered, and disciplined by a governor. With
its natural port of Ostia, with its new roads, it will become one of the most orderly and clean cities of Europe.
By isolating the monuments of ancient Rome, the relation between the ancient Romans and the Italians is
made more beautiful and suggestive. This work of revaluation—almost recreation—of the capital was not carried on to the detriment of other Italian cities. Each one
of them has the typical character of an ancient capital.
They are cities like Perugia, Milan, Naples, Florence,
Palermo, Bologna, Turin, Genoa, which have had a sovereign history worthy of high respect; but none of them
thinks now to contest with Rome and its eternal glory.

Some writers who, as keen observers, have followed

point by point the vicissitudes of our political life at a certain moment raised an interesting question. Why did not the National Fascist Party decree its own disbandment or slip into disorganization after the revolutionary victory of October, 1922?

In order to answer this question it is necessary to bring into relief certain essential points. History teaches us that, normally, a revolutionary movement can be channelled into legality only by means of forceful provisions, directed, if necessary, against even the personnel of the movement. Every revolution assumes unforeseen and complex aspects; in certain historical hours, the sacrifice of those who were the well-deserving lieutenants of yesterday might become indispensable for the supreme interest of to-morrow. Nevertheless, in my own life I have never deliberately desired the sacrifice of any one; therefore I have made use of the high influence which I have always had over my followers to stop stagnation or heresies, personal interests and contentions; I have preferred to prevent rather than to repress.

But, when it has been necessary, I have shown myself to be inexorable. In fact, I had to keep in mind that, when one party has shouldered the responsibility of entire power, it has to know how to perform surgery —and major operations, too—against secession. Because of my personal situation, having created the Party, I have always dominated it. The sporadic cases of secession, due not to differences of method but to personal temperament, usually withered under the general loss of esteem and interest, and after the disclosure of selfish ends.

This consciousness of my incontestable domination has given me the ability to make the Party live on. But other considerations also were opposed to the disbandment of the Party. First of all, a sentimental motif had stamped itself upon my soul and upon the grateful spirit of the nation. The Fascisti, particularly the young, had followed me with blind, absolute, and profound devotion. I had led them through the most dramatic vicissitudes, taking them away from universities, from jobs, from factories. The young men had not hesitated when confronted by danger. They had known how to risk their future positions together with their lives and fortunes. I owed and still owe to the militiamen of previous days my strongest gratitude; to disband the Party and retire would have been first of all an act of utter ingratitude.

There was in the end a much more important reason. I considered the formulation of a new Italian method of government as one of the principal duties of Fascism. It was to be created by the vigor of labor, through a well-tested process of selection, without the risky creation of too many improvised military leaders. It was the Party's right to offer me men of our own régime to assume positions of responsibility. In that sense the Party was side by side with the government in the ruling of the new régime. It had to abandon the programme of violent struggle and yet preserve intact its character of proud political intransigentism. Many obvious signs made me understand that it was not possible to patch the old with the new world. I had therefore need of reserves of men for the future. The Chief of the government could very well be the Chief of the Party, just as in every country of the world a representative chief is always the exponent of an aristocracy of wills.

In the meantime, to mark a point fundamental for the public order, my government, in December, 1922, issued an admonition to the Fascists themselves. It was in the following terms:

"Every Fascist must be a guardian of order. Every disturber is an enemy even if he carries in his pocket the identification card of the Party."

Thus, in a few words, were the position and the duty of the Party in the life of the Fascist régime indicated.

We encountered plenty of pitfalls and snares in 1922. The Party had reached a peculiar sensitiveness, through its intense experience. In the moment of its hardest test, it had shown itself to be equipped to guide the interests of the country as a whole. The revolution had not had long, bloody consequences, as in other revolutions, except for the moment of battle. Violence, as I have said before, had been controlled by my will.

Nevertheless, the position of some opposing newspapers was strange indeed. Those of the *Corriere della Sera*, of Liberal-Democratic coloring, and that of the *Avanti*, Socialist, agreed—strange bed-fellows!—in harshly criticising the simultaneous and violent action of Fascism, while they were wishing in their hearts and writing that the Fascist experiment would soon be finished. According to these political diagnosticians, it was a matter of an experiment of short duration, in which Fascism would be destroyed either on the parliamentary rocks or by an obvious inadequacy to direct the complexities of Italian life. We saw later the wretched end of these prophets; but to attain results it had been necessary for me, particularly in the first year, continually to watch the Party. It had always to remain in perfect efficiency, superior to opposing critics and to snares, ready for orders and commands.

One grave danger was threatening the Party: it was the too free admission of new elements. Our small handfuls in the warlike beginnings were now growing to excess, so much so that it was necessary to put a padlock on the door to prevent the influx of further membership. Once the solidity of Fascism had been proved, all the old world wanted to rush into its ranks. If this had happened, we would have come back to the old mentality, the old defects, by overhasty adulteration instead of keeping our growth selective through education and devotion. Otherwise the Party, augmented by all the opportunists of the eleventh hour, would have lost its vibrating and original soul. A check had to be placed upon the old world. It could go and wait with its bed-slippers on, without spoiling a movement of young people for Italian rebirth.

After I had closed, in 1926, the registration in the Party, I used all my force, care and means for the selection and the education of Youth. The Avanguardia was then created, together with the Opera Nazionale Balilla, the organization for boys and girls which, because of its numerous merits and the high value of its educational activities, I have chosen even recently to term "The invaluable pupil of the Fascist Régime."

This programme brought forth unparalleled results; as a result of it the Party-has never encountered a really serious crisis. I believe that I can count among my qualities the ability to act in good season and to strike at the right moment without false sentimentality where the shadow of a weakness or of a trap is hidden.

In this watchful work of prevention, I have always had at my side good secretaries of the Party who have helped me immeasurably. Michele Bianchi had already ably led the Party until the March on Rome. He had been able to balance the particularly violent character of the movement against the demands of political situations which had reality and which must be handled with wisdom. Michele Bianchi has been an excellent political secretary because of this very reason, and to-day he is still with the government, as my greatly appreciated collaborator in internal politics. He has a political mind of the first order, a reflective mind; he is faithful at every hour. The régime can count on him every time.

The Honorable Sansanelli, a courageous participant in the late war, and to-day president of the International Federation of World War Veterans, took his place. The Hon. Sansanelli has been able to face vague secessionist movements, which revealed an origin undoubtedly in the peculiar, pre-Fascist, Italian political Masonry.

There was in that period a reprisal by anti-Fascist forces. The old Liberal world, defeated, but tolerated by the generosity of the régime, was not exactly aware of the new order of things. It regained its wonted haughtiness; Italian Masonry was still developing, with its infinite and uncontrollable tentacles, its practices of corruption and of dissolution. These forces of negation even armed the Communist remnants in the obscurity of ambushes and cellars. A new "direttorio," presided over by the Secretary Hon. Giunta until September, 1924, was formed after the elections. I have already spoken of the Fascist activity of the Hon. Giunta. In the second half of that year, the anti-Fascist movement, aroused by obscure national and international forces, showed itself in growing intensity on all fronts. I threw it down on its nose with my speech of January 3, 1925. But also, following that, I determined that a line of more combatively intransigent nature should be imposed by our party: and with this duty in mind, on February 12, 1925, I appointed the Hon. Roberto Farinacci General Secretary of the Party.

Farinacci knew how to show himself worthy of the task with which I had intrusted him. His accomplishments, considered in their entirety and in the light of the results attained, were those of a well-deserving Secretary. He broke up the residues of the "aventinismo" which had remained here and there in the country; he gave a tone of high and cutting intransigentism, not only political but also moral, to the whole Party, invoked against offenders and plotters those exceptional laws which I had promulgated after four attempted assassinations had demonstrated the criminality of anti-Fascism. I was closely following this movement of vigorous reprisal by the Party and had prepared in time the necessary provisions. The Hon. Farinacci is one of the founders of Italian Fascism. He has followed me faithfully since 1914.

After his task had been accomplished, the Hon. Farinacci left the position of General Secretary to the Hon. Augusto Turati, a courageous veteran of the World War, a man of clear mind and aristocratic temperament, who has been able to give the Party the style of the new times and the consciousness of the new needs. The Hon. Turati has accomplished a great and indispensable work of educational improvement with the Fascist masses. Besides these precious elements in the high positions of the Party of to-day, I must mention the Hon. Renato Ricci for the organization of the "Balilla," Melchiorri for the Militia, Marinelli, a courageous administrative secretary, Starrace, a valorous veteran, and Arpinati, a faithful Black Shirt since March, 1919, and a founder of Fascism in Bologna.

The Party has yielded me new prefects for Fascist Italy, elements for syndicalist organization, and consuls, while various deputies have been appointed Ministers and Under-Secretaries. Little by little, proceeding by degrees, I have given an ever more integral and intransigent line to the whole world of government. Almost all positions of command have to-day been intrusted to Fascist elements. Thus after four years of the régime we have given actuality to the formula: "All the Power to all-Fascism" which I enunciated in June, 1925, at a Fascist meeting in Rome.

I have controlled my impatience. I have avoided leaps into darkness. I do not sleep my way to conclusions, I have blended the pre-existing needs with the formation of a future. Naturally, giving to the state a completely Fascist character and filling all the ganglia of national life with the vitality and newer force of faithful Black Shirts, I not only did not detract from, but constantly added to the importance of the National Fascist Party as the force of the régime. This transfer from political organization to the permanent organization of a state guarantees in the most solid manner the future of the régime. I have laid, with my own hands, the cornerstone of representative reform, based on the interests of Italian unity and the Italian cosmos, and I have arranged that the Grand Fascist Council became a definite constitutional organ for the constancy of the state. Thus the Fascist Party, while remaining independent, is bound by ties of steel to the very essence of the new Fascist state.

A subject that is always interesting and is often misunderstood both by Italians and foreigners is that of the relations between State and Church in Italy. The Law of the Guarantees in 1870, by which the question was believed to be solved, remains a form of relationship which since the rise of Fascism has not caused friction of any great significance. To be sure, the Holy See renews, once in a while, protestations for the supposed rights usurped in Rome by the Italian state, but there are no substantial reasons for apprehension, nor profound differences.

This serenity of relations is a tribute to the Fascist régime. In the past a legend had blossomed around dissensions of historical character tending to foment partisan hatreds; an anti-clerical activity had been developed for a long time in various forms, and it served, through many sections of the so-called "Free thought" groups, to augment the nefarious political influence of our form of Masonry. The idea was diffused that religion was a "private affair," and religion was not admitted in any sort of public act.

If, however, anti-clericalism was superficial and coarse, on the other hand, the Church, with its lack of comprehension of the new Italy, with its tenacity in its intransigent position, had only exasperated its opponents. Anti-Church forces even went so far as to ban every Catholic symbol and even Christian doctrine from the schools. These were periods of Socialist-Masonic audacity. It was necessary that ideas should be clarified. We had to differentiate and separate the principles of political clericalism from the vital essence of the Catholic faith. The situation as it had stood caused, in Italy, dangerous deviations, which ranged from the policy of "abstention" between 1870 and 1900, to the Popular party of baleful memory which was destined to degenerate little by little until in 1925 it took a form of clerical bolshevism which I resolutely liquidated and put into political and intellectual bankruptcy.

This troubled atmosphere, so infested by misunderstandings and superficialities, has been relieved by Fascism. I did not deceive myself as to the seriousness of the crisis which is always opening between State and Church; I had not fooled myself into thinking that I would be able to cure a dissension which involves the highest interests and principles, but I had made a deep study of those lines of set directions and inflexible temperaments which, if softened, were destined to make the principles of religious faith, religious observance, and respect for the forms of worship bloom again, independent of political controversies. They are, in fact, the essential factors of the moral and civic development of a country which is renewing itself.

To be sincere, I must add that high circles of the Vatican have not always been known to appreciate my work, possibly for political reasons, and have not helped me in the steps which appeared wise for all. My labor had not been easy nor light; our Masonry had spun a most intricate net of anti-religious activity; it dominated the currents of thought; it exercised its influence over publishing houses, over teaching, over the administration of justice and even over certain dominant sections of the armed forces.

To give an idea of how far things had gone, this significant example is sufficient. When, in parliament, I delivered my first speech of November 16, 1922, after the Fascist revolution, I concluded by invoking the assistance of God in my difficult task. Well, this sentence of mine seemed to be out of place! In the Italian parliament, a field of action for Italian Masonry, the name of God had been banned for a long time. Not even the Popular party—the so-called Catholic party —had ever thought of speaking of God. In Italy, a political man did not even turn his thoughts to the Divinity. And, even if he had ever thought of doing so, political opportunism and cowardice would have deterred him, particularly in a legislative assembly. It remained for me to make this bold innovation! And in an intense period of revolution! What is the truth? It is that a faith openly professed is a sign of strength.

I have seen the religious spirit bloom again; churches once more are crowded, the ministers of God are themselves invested with new respect. Fascism has done and is doing its duty.

Some ecclesiastical circles have not shown, as I have said, ability to evaluate and understand in all its importance the political and moral rebirth of new Italy.

One of the first symptoms of such lack of comprehension was exhibited at the beginning of Fascist rule: at first the so-called Catholic party wanted to collaborate by having some members in the government, in the new régime. This collaboration, however, began to lead us through a series of reticences and misunderstandings, and after six months I was forced to show the door to the ministers belonging to that party.

I have seen the Popular party allied with Masonry. But when parties have not clashed on the Italian political scene, the troubles between State and Church have been reflected in international politics. The Roman

Question has been once more under discussion. Both historical forces have strengthened their concepts. Journalistic controversies and objective discussions have demonstrated that the problem is not ripe and may be insoluble. Perhaps two mentalities and two worlds are confronting each other in a century-old historic and impracticable opposition. One has its roots in the religion of the fathers and lives by the ethical forces of the Civis Romanus; the other has the universal character of equality of brothers in God.

To-day, with the highest loyalty, Fascism understands and values the Church and its strength: such is the duty of every Catholic citizen. But politics, the defense of national interests, the battles over ourselves and others, must be the work of the modern Fascist Italians who want to see the immortal and irreplaceable Church of Saint Peter respected, and do not wish ever to confound themselves with any political force which has no disclosed outline and knows no patriotism. Whatever the errors of its representatives may be, nobody thinks of taking away from the Church its universal character, but everybody is right in complaining about certain disavowals of some Italian Catholics, and may justly resent political approval of certain middle-European currents, upon which Italy places even now her most ample reservations. Faith in Italy has been strengthened. Fascism gives impulse and vigor to the religion of the country. But it will never be able for any reason to renounce the sovereign rights of the state and of the functions of the state.

CHAPTER XIII

EN ROUTE

SOME readers of my autobiographic record may attribute to these pages of mine the character of a completed life story. If they have believed that story completed they are mistaken. It is absurd to believe that one can conclude a life of battles at the age of forty-five.

Detailed memoirs of intimate and personal character are the attributes of old age and the chimney-corner. I have no intention of writing any "memoirs." They only represent the consciousness of a definitely completed cycle. They do not appear of much importance to a man who is in the most vigorous ardor of his activities!

I was the leader of the revolution and chief of the government at thirty-nine. Not only have I not finished my job, but I often feel that I have not even begun it.

The better part comes toward me. I go toward it at this moment. But I take pride in affirming that I have laid solid foundations for the building of Fascism. Many ask me what my policy in the future will be, and where my final objective lies.

My answers are here. I ask nothing for myself, nor for mine; no material goods, no honors, no testimonials, no resolutions of approval which presume to consecrate me to History. My objective is simple: I want to make

308

Italy great, respected, and feared; I want to render my nation worthy of her noble and ancient traditions. I want to accelerate her evolution toward the highest forms of national co-operation; I want to make a greater prosperity forever possible for the whole people. I want to create a political organization to express, to guarantee, and to safeguard our development. I am tireless in my wish to see newly born and newly reborn Italians. With all my strength, with all my energies, without pause, without interruption, I want to bring to them their fullest opportunities. I do not lose sight of the experience of other peoples, but I build with elements of our own and in harmony with our own possibilities, with our traditions, and with the energy of the Italian people. I have made a profound study of the interests, the aspirations and the tendencies of our masses. I push on toward better forces of life and progress. I weigh them, I launch them, I guide them. I desire our nation to conquer again, with Fascist vigor, some decades or perhaps a century of lost history. Our garrison is the party, which has demonstrated its irreplaceable strength. I have trust in young people. Their spiritual and material life is guided by attentive, quick minds and by ardent hearts. I do not reject advice even from opponents whenever they are honest. I cover with my contempt dishonest and lying opponents, slanderers, deniers of the country and every one who drowns every sense of dignity, every sentiment of national and human solidarity in the filthy cesspool of low grudges. Defeated ones who cluck to the wind, survivors of a building which has toppled forever, accomplices in the ruin and shame into which the country was to have been dragged, sometimes do not even have the dignity of silence.

I am strict with my most faithful followers. I always intervene where excesses and intemperance are revealed. I am near to the heart of the masses and listen to its beats. I read its aspiration and interests. I know the virtue of the race. I probe it in its purity and soundness. I will fight vice and degeneracy and will put them down. The so-called "Liberal institutions" created at other times because of a fallacious appearance of protection are destroyed and divested of their phrases and false idealisms by the new force of Fascism with its idealism planted on realities.

Air and light, strength and energy, shine and vibrate in the infinite sky of Italy! The loftiest civic and national vision to-day leads this people to its goal, this people which is living in its great new springtime. It animates my long labors. I am forty-five and I feel the vigor of my work and my thought. I have annihilated in myself all self-interest: I, like the most devoted of citizens, place upon myself and on every beat of my heart, service to the Italian people. I proclaim myself their servant. I feel that all Italians understand and love me; I know that only he is loved who leads without weakness, without deviation, and with disinterestedness and full faith.

Therefore, going over what I have already done I know that Fascism, being a creation of the Italian race, has met and will meet historical necessities, and so, unconquerable, is destined to make an indelible impression on the twentieth century of history.

INDEX

314 Index

318 # Index

United States, the, 26; Italy's war debt
agreement with the, 265.
Unknown Soldier, altar of the, 237.
Upper Adige, Credaro policy in the, 141;
Salata policy in the, 141.
Utopian illusions, 192.

Valona, 102, 109, 111.
Varano di Costa, 1.
Vassallo, Ernesto, 195.
Vatican, the, 305.
Venetian provinces, the, 36.
Venetian refugees, 218.
Veneto, Vittorio, 107, 194, 290.
Venice, 62, 113, 153, 212.
Vernezzo, 44.
Verona, 14, 15, 112, 232.
Versailles, 74, 80; Treaty of, 57, 75, 76.
Via Paolo da Conuobio, the street of, 65.
Victory of 1918, leaders of, 290.
Vienna, 32, 54, 60; Imperial and Royal
Government of, 18; the children of, 100.

Volpi, Count, 265.
Via Nomentana, 238.
Vicenza, 212.
Victor Emmanuel III, His Majesty, 41,
183, 184, 188, 196.
Voluntary Militia, 207, 291, 292.

War Bulletin, the, 55.
Washington, 263.
Wilson, Woodrow, 62, 74, 101, 103.
Women's Lyceum, 287.
Workers' Chambers, 135.
World War, 102; beginning of the, 22, 29;
end of, 56; Italy's fall in the, 57.

Zababria, 130.
Zanibour, 237, 238.
Zara, 76, 101, 102.
Zenzon, 53.
Zurich, commercial treaties concluded
in, 250.

VOLUME II
MY FALL

PREFACE:

THE MUSSOLINI STORY

BY

MAX ASCOLI

I. TWENTY-FOUR HOURS

THIS BOOK, called by its author *History of a Year*, is actually a long tract on what happened within the span of approximately twenty-four hours, between 5 P.M. of Saturday, July 24, 1943 and 5:20 of the following day. At that time Mussolini, clutching the sides of a stretcher, was driven fast through the streets of Rome in the ambulance that had just picked him up at the door of the King's villa. A captain of the Carabinieri had told him to step in, and inside he had found more carabinieri ready with shotguns. That moment was the climax of the fateful twenty-four hours. The Duce was then just a man in the hands of the police.

The day before, at 5 P.M., he had opened the meeting of the Grand Council. The top leaders of fascism were all there, twenty-eight of them dressed in the black fascist uniform. He could look at each of them, and hardly find a friendly face. In the discussion practically no one had a kind word for him. Some reproached him for being too soft in the conduct of the war and for surrounding himself with heel-clicking morons, others of having led the nation straight to ruin. In the minds of all there was but one question differently phrased: could fascism do without

Mussolini? Was or wasn't Mussolini's dismissal the only guarantee of survival for fascism? What to do with him, that was the question. Get rid of him or patch him up?

What Mussolini said in self-defense, according to his own report in this book, is practically the core of the book itself. Indeed, the hasty reader would do well to start at Chapter V, when Mussolini gives his own summary of the speech. For this book, which is an enlargement of that speech, gains its momentum after its slumbering beginning when the speech is reported—which also means that most probably the report given here bears little resemblance to the speech Mussolini actually delivered, and that the arguments he used then have been strengthened by his afterthoughts. His *apologia pro vita mea* has one theme: my power or your ruin. Il Duce or chaos. It is the usual blackmail of all dictators: I am the only barrier to chaos. In the lengthy rephrasing of his speech that is this book, his argument is re-enforced by the fact that after Mussolini had been dropped the nation did fall into chaos.

The strange thing about the meeting of the Grand Council was that, apparently, no one was afraid of Mussolini— not even Grandi, not even Ciano. Everyone was fearful for his own life, practically every one of them had carried a gun in his pocket. Grandi, if the story is true, had taken along a couple of hand grenades, just in case. At any moment a mob of fanatical fascists might come in and cut their throats. It is said that when the commanding general of the Fascist Militia abruptly left the room, Grandi and Ciano and all the other conspirators looked tensely at each other. Some of them had gone to church in the morning and taken Holy Communion. Then the fascist general came back, with the relieved air of a man who for a short while has evaded the crushing cares of politics.

The men of one faction were afraid of the men of the other factions, and all factions were united in reproaching Mussolini for something. But practically no one was afraid of Mussolini, as if his ties with all factions, even that of his most fanatical supporters, had been cut. He was the pawn of the game, not the one who plays it. Some wanted him reinstated and re-enforced. Some wanted to have him cast aside. Some just plainly didn't know what to do with him.

This book, like his speech at the Grand Council, was Mussolini's desperate attempt to summon the Duce back to power. But in between Mussolini the man and Mussolini the holder of absolute power, there was already such a distance that several times, according to his own report, he mentioned Mussolini as if he had been somebody else— just as in this book the third person which Mussolini uses in writing about himself is at the same time revealing and appropriate. At the Grand Council he tried to convince the leading fascists that no matter how trimmed his power and tarnished his popularity, the Duce was still their only defense from political and possibly physical extinction. But only a few were convinced. The majority, led by

Grandi, ratified the fact that the leadership of fascist Italy had become vacant.

Few of the members of the Grand Council went to their homes that night after the Grand Council adjourned at 2:40 A.M. The fuse of a time bomb had been set but very few of the fascist conspirators knew if, when or where the explosion would occur. Somebody else knew it, above all one man, the Duke of Acquarone, head of the royal household. That night around three o'clock Acquarone received Grandi, fresh from the Grand Council, who told him what had happened.

Acquarone, who for all his Dukedom was a sharp Genoese businessman, had been in touch with practically all the various groups of conspirators. He had been in contact with "respectable" fascists working for a Darlan combination which would deliver Italy to the Allies; he had had connections with the old anti-fascist parliamentary leaders who for two decades had been waiting for just that day. He had been working hand in hand with the head of the General Staff, General Ambrosio, and with a few high officials of the police. Above all, he had been tirelessly acting for the King and on the King. Kings in modern times show their usefulness mainly in a crisis, and here was a crisis of first magnitude—a unique opportunity for the House of Savoy to re-establish itself as the saviour of the Italian nation.

Actually that night everything was ready. Acquarone

and the King had named the new Prime Minister and drafted the list of the new cabinet: the proclamations to the people had been written, announcing Mussolini's "resignation" and warning the people that "the war goes on"; the commander of the carabinieri had been alerted; the former head of the police, Senise, whom Mussolini had dismissed a few months before for serious deficiencies of fascist enthusiasm, was ready at hand to be reinstated.[1] Altogether, there were a handful of men in the know and already posted to act, who had gone so far and had so compromised themselves in the eyes of each other as to have no alternative but to take the next step. The next step was to apprehend Mussolini.

At the General Staff a couple of generals had a clear idea of how the job could be done.[2] Mussolini could have been nabbed while coming back from a military inspection out of town, or else he could have been arrested in the courtyard of the Quirinale, the King's palace. The first solution might have cost some shooting and bloodshed, but it would not have compromised the King. The second was technically easier, but a royal courtyard is hardly a fitting place for a kidnapping job. Moreover, the Quirinale is just in the heart of Rome.

But that Sunday morning of July 25 the shape of things looked like a conspirator's dream. After the top leaders

---

[1] Cf. Senise, C., *Quando ero Capo della Polizia*, Rome, 1946.
[2] Cf. Castellano, G., *Come firmai l'armistizio*, Milan, 1945, p. 59.
Cf. Monelli, P., *Roma 1943*, Rome, 1945.

of fascism had registered Mussolini's default, the King had
no alternative but to countersign the fascist decree. To the
Duce, shorn of his power and returned to private life, the
King's men could easily extend the assistance of the new
government's protective custody. Moreover, the royal family was staying at Villa Ada, the King's middle-class man-
sion in a quiet residential section of the city surrounded
by large parks.

Mussolini himself asked to see the King that very
Sunday. One hour before he entered Villa Ada the head
of the police felt that there was something unusual in the
air and went to inquire of the head of the General Staff.
He was told to wait a while, not to move from the room
and to keep quiet. A few hours later, replaced by the man
who had been his predecessor, the chief of police bowed
gracefully out of office.

At 5 P.M. Mussolini reached Villa Ada and was immediately received by the King. It was a very short interview.
According to the King, the only answer Mussolini gave to
the announcement of his dismissal, was to say over and
over again, "It's my ruin, my complete ruin." At 5:20 he
stepped out of the villa's door. The ambulance was waiting.

That was the moment—the climax of the twenty-four
hours, the end of a regime that had been called a revolution, the hard fact that proved to be like the center of
ever-widening circles. The circles go far into the past and
into the future of Italy and the world—all centered there,

in that moment when that man lifted himself into the big ambulance. At that moment he was just a bundle of tired flesh, an uncomfortable superfluity, as far as Italy was concerned. But what brought that moment, and how far the repercussions of that moment would reach, is something which still cannot be explained without considerable effort. At the time it happened and for several weeks thereafter there was complete astonishment everywhere, in Italy and out of Italy, an astonishment multiplied by the turn of events on each successive day.

For there was no revolt against the King in Italy, not a cry was raised for the Duce, not a single platoon of fascist militiamen decided to go out and die for Mussolini. The people of the country streamed into the streets, tore the fascist buttons from their lapels, and not seeing any fascist symbols on anybody felt that nobody was a fascist, that nobody had ever been a fascist, and the whole thing had been a long ghastly nightmare.

Out of Italy, July 25th appeared as an utterly baffling day—a memorable day, Churchill called it. But the windfall it brought nobody could measure, least of all Churchill. A regime that had been acclaimed or cursed as one of the great political novelties of the twentieth century had, overnight, melted away. It had always been a baffling thing, but nothing it ever did was half as baffling as the way it vanished. Then, a few weeks later, the whole nation too, its treasures and its people, seemed to be on the verge of being swept away.

II. THE PEOPLE

YET the large majority of the men and women, who that night poured into the streets and squares of Italy and went hoarse shouting "death to Mussolini," had been accustomed for years to march through the same streets and squares to the rhythm of the fascist hymns and bellowing "du-ce, du-ce." We cannot, as Burke taught us, indict or acquit a nation. But, if we put our mind to it, we can try to understand.

There are no doubts that Mussolini had been more popular with the people of Italy than any other national leader since the country was unified in 1860. He gripped the imagination and elicited the loyalty of a far larger number of Italians than Garibaldi ever did—Garibaldi, the national hero, who never saw a peasant in his volunteer armies. Indeed, there is no other Italian in the history of Italian politics who has come so close to the large masses of the nation, whose name has meant so much to every single inhabitant of Italy no matter how poor his condition or remote his place of living.

For, first of all, he was one of the people. The exercise of supreme power brought but few changes in his habits and tastes. He learned, or tried to learn, the sports prac-

ticed on the other side of the tracks, like tennis and horseback riding; he came to realize how improper it is to wear
high-top shoes or long underwear. But his inclinations
remained simple throughout. Italian aristocrats and mil-
lionaires, always ready to go the whole way to please him,
never stopped being on the *qui vive* with him for they
knew he was queer and different—and certainly not one
of them. Neither did Mussolini feel at ease with them.
The man who gave away titles of nobility by the score, in
discussing here his relations with the source of all nobility,
the King, has accents strangely remindful of Jim Farley
describing his social relations with President Roosevelt.

He always knew how to speak a language that the people
understood, and he knew how to impress on them the fact
that he was a man of the people who had attained the
highest power. He had all sorts of feelers and antennae
that made him grasp the trend of popular mood and suggested to him the right attitude, the right slogan that could
bring popular passion to a frenzy. Some of these slogans
were outworn clichés of literary rhetoric: like "Italy, the
proletarian nation, the nation for whom nationalism is
class war." Mussolini knew how to use these slogans, how
to dramatize them with the proper gestures in the proper
setting. As a journalist, he had written quite a few newspaper articles on "Italy the proletarian nation." But as a
statesman he nearly succeeded in making this idea the plot
of a great drama of history, with forty-five million people

as protagonists, and the outside world as astonished spectators.

Altogether, fascism was an incredible adventure. The extraordinary thing is that most of the Italians lived it with a sort of dim awareness that there was something unbelievable about it, or unreal, and that at a certain moment it would end. Even the success of the fascist adventures never quite silenced that sense of apprehension. On the other hand the apprehension itself, and the instinctive reaction of the earthy Italian realism, prodded the Italians on the way to adventures, just to see how far they could go. It was as if the fascist era had been a holiday from the hard drudgery of their history—like a carnival that gave to too many people crowded on too poor a land the thrill of a prestige and of a power that are inescapably beyond their means.

Many times the people thought that Mussolini had gone too far, and every time they saw him coming through as the avenger of Italian mediocrity. He had defied the world not once, but on many occasions, from the Corfu incident to the Spanish war. Many times large numbers of people thought that the Duce was wrong, only to have it proved once more that he had been right. No one was more convinced of this good luck than Mussolini himself—he was always inclined to boast about his lucky star and always ready to conjure with all possible anti-evil-eye devices the moment the wheels of fortune turned the other way.

There seemed to be nothing that could stop his adventures. Several times he tried it as hard as he could. Just before becoming Prime Minister he seemed satisfied with the prestige he had gained and was willing to share the government with the two other mass political parties, the Socialists and the Catholics. It was the same idea that made of him the main promoter of Munich: let's restrict the game of power to those who have power, let's build Europe on the basis of the four big nations—or Italy on the strength of the three big parties. Yet he failed in both instances, he could not stop—one of the reasons possibly being that in both cases he did not represent real, but would-be bigness.

The Pact of Steel, as far as the people were concerned, was his wrong turn. It might have been all right to fire Anthony Eden from the British Foreign Office, to treat France like dirt, to impose on Italy the madness of economic self-sufficiency, to close the doors to emigration. Demagoguery and the spirit of carnival could go a long way in making bearable and even exhilarating the most outlandish policies. But the alliance with Hitler was quite a different thing. For the Italians, who have never known racial intolerance, have it in their blood to distrust and fear German power. They have known during twenty centuries that German power tends to fall down on Italy as if by a law of gravity, and that the Germans, in their own way, have an irresistible love for Italy. A powerful Germany will never forget the call of Italy. Hitler himself knew it when he saw Florence.

A new restlessness started creeping all over the nation—

a restlessness that had perhaps been felt since the beginning of the fascist regime but that had somehow been repressed by the thrill of adventure and of marching together and of tasting together what seemed to be the fruit of power. For Mussolini had certainly brought the fact of national existence close to the largest number of people. By imposing his pattern of what an Italian had to be on the immensely variegated nation, he had come closer to making Italians of all the people of Italy than any previous ruler. But he never knew how to leave the people alone. He always wanted something new of them, always had the idea of some new stunt. If not about the number of children the Italians had to bear, it was about the kind of diet that was proper for them, or what use they could make of their leisure—if they could ever find time off from hard work.

There was always a new war. Sometimes it was something like a real war against weaker nations, like Ethiopia, Spain and Albania; or the battle for wheat, the war against flies, the war for straw to increase the sale of straw products. Mussolini, the former grammar school instructor, acted more and more like a schoolteacher gone wild. He imposed one-way traffic for pedestrians in the major thoroughfares of Rome, and the Romans, forced to walk in the hot summer months on the sunny side of the street, felt unhappy. Mussolini himself would take care that his orders were obeyed and scan the street below from his window at Palazzo Venezia, to see whether a pedestrian was strolling on the unlawful side of the street.

Alliance with Germany, however, meant war—not against unlawful pedestrians or even Ethiopians, but real war. From adventure to adventure, not knowing where to stop and not being strong enough to stop, Italy had reached the point where she was going to be ruined no matter whether the Germans won or lost the war. This condition of alarm reawakened the old restrained irritations and apprehensions. The feeling of unreality that never left the Italians or Mussolini himself during the fascist parade through history became acute like the forebodings of immediate ruin. All these pent-up feelings and fears found their outlet in two anti-fascisms. For since the beginning of fascism, there had been two anti-fascisms, one standing against fascism from the outside, the other moving on the inside. One can be called anti-fascism in the proper sense of the term, the other half-fascism. But now the time had come when, in different measure, both anti-fascism and half-fascism could acquire power.

Anti-fascism proper was the movement of the consistent opponents of fascism, the men who found their common identity in denying their confidence to the Regime. The movement had all the weaknesses of a negative position, irreparably tied to a past era that the further passing of time made remote and unappealing. Moreover, anti-fascism had had its chance and missed it when it refused to come down in the streets and fight in June, 1924, at the time all the nation was swept by the horror of Matteotti's assassination.

However, anti-fascism performed two great functions. The first was to force fascism to reveal itself and its murderous nature at the time when near universal acquiescence tended to give to the fascist leaders an air of respectability and statesmanship. From time to time these leaders were forced to betray their origins, and leave their mark in blood. Because of anti-fascism, in the universal confusion of the in-between-wars era, some standards of good were kept by a few good people, while evil men had to confirm their evil.

The second function of anti-fascism was the training of men. Among those who went through the gruelling test of persecutions and jail, some men of unsurpassable moral character had emerged. Some of them, by exposing themselves to the enemy, had been killed; some are active now in public life—not many, to be sure, but they are the kind of men who are the salt of a country. Perhaps in the years spent in jail they have not acquired a good training in practical politics or in administration, but sometimes in the life of a nation there are brief moments when moral character becomes the only qualification for political leadership, as the Resistance proved.

Half-fascism may sometimes have suffered from a superabundance of intellectual or political cleverness, but not of moral character. The original half-fascists were those who, since the beginning of the Regime, thought it was quixotic to fight it out in the open. Rather, they said, the dangerous tendencies of fascism could be checked by working from within. Anything could come out of fascism, neo-bolshevism, rabid nationalism, or an authoritarian middle-of-the-road social democracy. This viewpoint was eloquently expressed by Dino Grandi in 1920 in a letter to a friend, "I would be ashamed to be nothing but a fascist." The struggle of ideologies, for those who did not want to rot in idle opposition, was transferred within the fascist party. The half-fascist was always looking for the substantial filling of another more positive and timely half.

When fascism entrenched itself in power, the ranks of the half-fascists were swollen by the bulk of the government employees, high and low. They could not help serving their country, and if the country had to survive the change of regime, administration must go on. For the General Staff of the Army and for the officers' corps of the Navy, the loyalty was shared between the country and His Majesty the King. And then the leaders of special causes came, the advocates of reforms that only the mighty fascist government could adopt and carry through—be it a reform of education, or of the relationship between capital and labor.

A half-fascist was a fascist with his tongue in his cheek. He was a part-time fascist, and therefore a part-time anti-fascist, but with moderation and care. Italian realism made him keep a running account of the discrepancies between bombastic declarations and the actual state of things, of the remarkable disproportion between the proclaimed reputation of fascist leaders and their real size. This system of double bookkeeping, one for public, the other for private consumption, helped him not to feel utterly silly, even if sometimes he had to act silly. The large scale production of anti-fascist stories was one of the most notable contributions of the half-fascists. Almost identical stories are to be found in every country with a totalitarian leader. Some have all the flavor of spicy Italian humor. For instance, after Mussolini had declared in a speech that every good Italian had to be intelligent, honest and fascist, a story immediately spread all over the country. "It cannot be done," it was said, "for if a man is intelligent and fascist, he is not honest; if he is fascist and honest, he is not intelligent; and if he is intelligent and honest, he is not a fascist."

This condition of double conscience, half good faith and half mental reservations, made life prosperous and easy for many people, as long as things went well. The half or part-time fascist occasionally pretended to be a superfascist, and had sometimes to out-do the most fanatical worshippers in his proclamations of abject devotion to the Duce. This way he could gain indulgence from past and future sins. Two of the men whom Mussolini most bitterly accuses in this book are typical of this category: Grandi, who found the other filling he was looking for in the League of Nations or in the standards of British society, and Badoglio, who on the eve of the March on Rome had been credited with saying that if His Majesty had given him the order, he could have gotten rid of fascism with a few machine guns. But even if he said it, he atoned later and some of his declarations of fealty to the Duce were among the most abject.

Strangely enough both half-fascism and anti-fascism were of some usefulness to the Regime, as long as things went well. Half-fascism let a great deal of steam blow off by the hilarious repetition of harmless jokes. It also represented a healthy adjustment of fascist high-sounding principles to certain irremovable traits of Italian character. Anti-fascism on the other hand, by its very existence, no matter how powerless it had been rendered by police persecutions, justified the huge apparatus of the secret and official police.

But they were not any longer harmless for the Regime when the worst forebodings were confirmed with ever-increasing momentum. Rather, they represented the only possible hopes of some way out. Perhaps the old anti-fascist leaders could be of some use, perhaps those who had power inside fascism could start straightening out things. That was also the time when the fascist half of the half-fascist started withering so fast that on the 26th of July, as Mussolini himself puts it, Italy was reduced to only one fascist, Benito Mussolini. But not even that was quite true, for Mussolini shortly after his arrest wrote a highly deferential letter to Prime Minister Badoglio.[3]

The masses of people, running, singing, shouting in the streets had the answer: *Viva la libertà, viva la pace.* Musso-

---

[3] See text, p. 76.

lini was the one man who had been the cause of all evil, and now he was out. He was still closer to them than any other Italian leader, but this time as an immediate, tangible object of execration. He was down, the *"puzzone."* For some time this was the name he was given, particularly in Central and Southern Italy. It means, translated literally, the stinker. Everything had been centered in him, and he had centered everything in himself. Now everything was over, including war. The most frequently heard cry, aside from "death to Mussolini," was "peace."

In those hours of popular rejoicing the people acted as if, once Mussolini had vanished, his allies, the Germans, had disappeared from the earth.

Yet the Germans were in Italy and from that night on they started pouring in through the Brenner Pass in ever-growing strength.

III. THE KING

ACCORDING to one report, when the ambulance with Mussolini locked inside pulled away from the royal villa, the little old King emerged at the door. He was, it is said, rubbing his hands and chuckling—almost as overjoyed, even if certainly in a more dignified way, as Hitler was at Compiègne, after he received the surrender of the French army.

Undoubtedly, no matter whether the King did his hand rubbing outdoors or indoors, he had every reason to feel happy. He had not risked too much after all. In fact until the very last moment those in charge of the job had a hard time in getting a formal order, written or unwritten, to do it. But no matter who gave the order, it would have been hard to trace it to the King, in case things had turned out wrong. And now there he was, the "*caro Duce*," as the King had called him at the beginning of their last interview— locked in the ambulance like a lamb.

During the previous weeks and months, when everybody around him had been weaving the web of conspiracies, he had played at the same time omnipresent and hard to get. Omnipresent because of the faithful Acquarone, and hard to get because even the few fascist or pre-fascist politicians who had succeeded in reaching him did not succeed in getting much of an answer or an indication of whether, if at all, and in which direction he was going to move. He had listened with that tired patience that had been one of his characteristics in the days when he was a constitutional monarch, with the aloof air of a man who cannot afford personal opinions or political inclinations. "I envy you," he used to say, "who have so many definite ideas. I wish it could be the same with me; but I can't, it is not my job, I must see every side." This was one of his stocks-in-trade in the old days. More recently, with some of the conspirators who had come to see him, he had taken another tack; an old man, very old, very tired, perhaps fearful, perhaps somewhat obtuse. Bonomi, among others, had been positively dejected after one of these interviews.[4]

The fascist rebels who had approached him had thought all along that they were the natural and legitimate heirs to Mussolini's government. Devotion to the monarchy was the keynote of the Grandi resolution adopted by the Grand Council. Devotion to the monarchy had, on the part of the half-fascists, practically reduced the fascist part of the equation to just a name. They had done a magnificent job of pulling the hottest chestnut out of the fire, those monarcho-fascists—but as to giving them the reward they had expected and worked for, that was another matter.

He was not going to abdicate in favor of his son in order to dramatize the break of continuity with the fascist past.

---

[4] Cf. Bonomi, I., *Diario di un anno*, Milan, 1947, p. 7.

That had been the suggestion of Badoglio [5]—a man whom he had never completely trusted. Neither was he going to follow Badoglio's other queer suggestion: to form a cabinet of pre-fascist politicians. Left over from the past, he had called all the Bonomis and Orlandos who after more than twenty years of abstinence from power, considered themselves once more available. A cabinet of trusted civil servants was what the country needed, an efficient, competent government, composed of bureaucrats who had reached the top of their particular branch of the service. He had not overthrown fascism to bring to power the anti-fascists.

For all his efforts in non-committalism, the King had been singularly explicit in talking scornfully of the pre-fascist and anti-fascist politicians to his conspiratorial advisers. Little good could be expected from the obsolete leaders whom fascism had defeated and who had been living a pale, empty life during the years of the fascist regime. Even less good, of course, could come from those who had taken refuge abroad. He had no heart for going back to the old game of party politics, party conventions, party resolutions; he had no desire to meet again hosts of chatty parliamentarians, during the ever recurrent cabinet crises. He had played that game and had respected every single rule of it during the first twenty-two years of his reign. Then, in October, 1922, he had refused to use the power of

---

[5] Cf. Badoglio, P., *L'Italia nella seconda guerra mondiale*, Milan, 1946, p. 63 & p. 74.

the state against the rebel force of fascism, had dismissed the last cabinet made up of representative parliamentarians, and handed the government of Italy to Mussolini.

The Mussolini parenthesis closed, the King could reign according to the constitution as written in 1848, not as interpreted in 1922. In fact, the Piedmontese Constitution of 1848, that in 1860 had been extended to the kingdom of Italy, did not prescribe a cabinet form of government, did not intend to leave the country to the mercy of partisan struggles. It had established the principle of popular representation, in the sense that the people's representatives could give their advisory co-operation to the King, but it had not said that the King's ministers had to be responsible to the people's representatives.

Actually the battle cry, "Let's go back to the constitution," had been raised in Italy every time conservative or reactionary politicians felt that things were moving too fast to the left, and that the King had allowed too much of his power to slip out of his hands. The King could hardly have followed his faithful advisers and gone "back to the constitution" in the period between 1900 and 1922 without risking a royal revolution. But on that day, July 25, 1943, things were quite different. For in 1922 somebody else had given a revolution to the country, and now, the revolutionary cycle closed, the King could bring the country back to the constitution and appear as a liberator to his subjects.

For twenty-one pompous and lean years the King had ruled under fascism. Mussolini had handed him two additional crowns: the imperial crown of Ethiopia and the royal one of Albania. But the piled-up crowns had scarcely increased the King's stature. Mussolini had completely cut off the ties with foreign potentates and foreign countries that had allowed the Italian constitutional monarchs to exert a considerable influence on Italy's foreign affairs. By establishing a one-party system he had eliminated those recurrent crises, those alternations of parties in power or combinations of parties in power that on occasion could give to a constitutional king something more than ceremonial functions. With punctilious pedantry, Mussolini had reached the height of his insolence when he had established that a list had to be kept of the men whom the King could call to the premiership or to cabinet positions. He had even gone so far as to establish that a special new organ of the fascist state had to pass judgment about succession to the throne.

This special organ of the fascist regime however was the Grand Council of fascism. And the Grand Council of fascism, at the first real crisis it had to face, had decided in the night session of July 25 to put the supreme leadership of the country at the King's mercy.

It had been a long endurance game. Who would last longer, the monarchy or fascism, the King or Mussolini? During the twenty-one years of the fascist regime the King, grudgingly or cynically, had done exactly everything Mussolini had wanted him to do, said every single word Mussolini had put in his mouth. In so behaving the King had set an example to all his fellow countrymen. But all along the little man who embodied the institution of the monarchy had quietly fought his endurance game with the big man who embodied a "revolution." Once the "revolution" became solidly entrenched in power, the contest turned into one between two legitimacies. The senior legitimacy had won.

The little old man, in that late afternoon, might have rubbed not only his hands but his eyes. For he was in the saddle. In fact, he was a king.

It was quite incorrect to call him moronic: he was a shrewd, cunning, mean little man, but by no means a moron. He played his little game most cleverly but unfortunately for him both his means and his ends were obsolete. He acted like a prince in Machiavelli's times, aiming at a goal that might have been attainable at the end of the Napoleonic wars. That was the era of restorations, and Victor Emmanuel must have thought that he was a Louis XVI who by sheer patience had aged into a Louis XVIII without ever losing his head. Machiavelli's times were filled with exploits in patience, timeliness, and scientific double-crossing.

Machiavelli himself wrote a special essay on how Caesar Borgia, by deceit and force, had succeeded in liquidating all his enemies, and made himself master of Romagna.

But ours are not the times of Machiavelli, nor of the Talleyrand restoration. The year 1943 was the crucial one of a great war that was a war of life and death, not for a few princes playing the game of power but for all the people of the world. The little King obviously wanted to follow the path from the losing to the winning side that had always been the road to power for the princes of the House of Savoy. But at the head of the winning coalition there were some men whose natural inclination to play the game of power with kingly dynasties was considerably tempered by solemn engagements that they had entered into with their own people. These engagements concerned such things as the unconditional surrender of the fascist enemy, freedom—one freedom or four of them—to be established everywhere in the world, etc. War-making in our times is complicated by the fact that the war potential of the democratic nations is never fully mobilized, unless the leaders tie themselves with exacting commitments with their people. The novelty of our times is that somehow, to a certain extent, the leaders have to abide by their commitments.

Of all this, the King had no notion. He seemed to have had equally no notion of several other things that were much closer to his range of vision. He should have realized that back of Mussolini there were the Germans and that his decision to dismiss Mussolini should have been accompanied or preceded by close negotiations with the Allies. But the King was too much afraid both of Mussolini and the Germans ever to dare send trustworthy emissaries to the Allies. He did use some of the traditional channels of the international demimonde to sound out the Allied leaders through Lisbon or through Madrid or through the

Vatican. But it was in his stingy nature to express himself with half glances and half nods, and his dynastic egoism was satisfied when he received assurances that some, at least, of the Allied leaders would not have been harsh on the House of Savoy. The King cared for his private revenge on Signor Mussolini, the *"caro Duce,"* and for the success of his Machiavellian scheme. His was an experiment in urbane bloodless tyrannicide, with the ultimate aim of making himself, at long last, into a king.

This is one of his two unforgivable crimes—crimes of a lowly, cunning mind, without extenuating circumstances on the count of moronity. His second crime was just as great. The justification for constitutional monarchies, or for that matter, for constitutions, is that both these devices serve to temper and check the swing of popular passions. The King of Italy did not try to apply the laws to stem the turbulent course of Italian politics at the end of the first World War. The Italian monarchy proved then to be not a stabilizing factor, but a weather vane. By acting the way he did, the King at the same time magnified and sanctioned some of the lowest characteristics of his people: the tendency to follow the trend and let it go. Indeed, the worst that can be said of the large majority of Italians is that during fascism the King's behavior was representative of their own.

No wonder that, as soon as fascism fell, an increasing number of Italians started vehemently denouncing the monarchy. For, if the King offered them an ugly mirror of themselves, the first thing to do was to break that mirror, and to have nothing like it ever again in the life of the country.

34

IV. THE ALLIES

IN THE CITY of New York and in the great Eastern region around, July 25, 1943, was just like any other hot, midsummer Sunday. In the morning people in Scarsdale or Larchmont plodded through the bulky main section of the *New York Times* and put aside for the afternoon the thought-provoking feature supplements to be read on the porch, when the sun starts setting and the weather cools off. In the magazine section that Sunday there was a keen, well-balanced piece by Herbert Matthews sent by wireless from Allied Headquarters, North Africa. The title was "Will—Can—Italy Collapse?" More than one *Times* reader might have just been glancing at these words, "But Mussolini must be counted upon to go on fighting until the end," or "And until the last trumpet sounds from an Allied bugle, Mussolini will have the upper hand in Italy. We must always remember that," just when the first radio flash came at around 5 P.M.: "Mussolini is out."

Herbert Matthews is one of the best informed and conscientious American experts on Italian affairs. Probably he had read the latest directives of the American and English political warfare agencies and certainly he was in contact with high political and military experts in the field. His was not a personal opinion, but a careful summary of prevailing authoritative views. That day he proved to have no better idea of what was going on in Italy than his reader in Scarsdale. But President Roosevelt and Prime Minister Churchill did not know any better either.

Let's say it again: Rome was rife with conspiracies; the conspirators were not private characters meeting behind the bushes of Villa Borghese, but the head of the General Staff, the minister of the royal household, some of the top leaders of the Army and the police. Behind the conspirators and working with them there were such personages as the Crown Princess, and noblemen and lawyers and politicians and Vatican prelates. And of course at the knob of the whole network, discreetly but firmly there was His Majesty the King.

In the night of the 25th, not only in Rome but through all the country countless people spent hours at home nervously fidgeting with their radios. Because something was going to come, something had to come. Everybody felt it and everybody had his own little or big crop of hints. The news that the Grand Council had met was no secret, although as to decisions reached at the meeting there were only rumors. Not many people, of course, could imagine that the news which was going to break was as staggering, but some news had to come from the tense thick air. About this countless people had no doubts.

But not the Allies, or their representatives inside the Vatican, or their experts inside and outside the borders of the country who had been trained to keep their ears close to the Italian ground. Not the military leaders of the

Allied armies who, after the invasion of Sicily, were preparing for the occupation of the mainland, and who should have known with the greatest possible degree of precision the political state of affairs of the nation they were set to conquer. At the AMG school of Charlottesburg, Virginia, the prospective administrators of the various Italian towns knew exactly where the carabinieri barracks and the red light districts were. But nobody in condition to influence policies, in London or in Washington or at the Army headquarters seemed to have any remote idea of how the Italians felt about Mussolini.

In all fairness, however, it must be granted that the Allies' gross ignorance was thoroughly matched by the Germans. As it appears from Goebbel's diary, Hitler was no more prepared for the 25th of July than Roosevelt or Churchill or Stalin. Hitler, however, could not help being somewhat blinded by his belief in the supreme virtues of the fascist idea. This consideration could scarcely apply to the leaders of the United Nations.

This thorough black-out of information on Italy across the battle lines can be partly explained by the way in which the Italian situation was seen from abroad. It was shaky, but it had been shaky for so long that it seemed to be stabilized in its shakiness. It was like a tower leaning far more sharply than that of Pisa and defying the law of gravity, as if the law of gravity had taken a holiday. There were rumors around in July, 1943, but there had been rumors for many months, and warnings from people close to the King, and offers from Italian generals wishing to go to the other side. In January 1943, for instance, Badoglio had sent a message to the British through Switzerland proposing to send an emissary to Cyrenaica to discuss with the Allies co-ordinated action inside and outside Italy to overthrow the Regime. But Anthony Eden, with Secretary Hull concurring, had been inclined to drop the matter, for it was better, he thought, to let the situation in Italy remain precarious. If it had further deteriorated, the Germans would have been forced to send additional troops to Italy and to replace the Italian divisions stationed out of the country.

But above all there was everywhere, among the Allies not less than among the Germans, an unshaken reliance on the extraordinary qualities of the great man. Who would deny he was a great man? Certainly not Churchill, who had said it repeatedly and fervently before the war and who found opportunity to say it again during the course of the war. And not Roosevelt, who had sent Sumner Welles to him in the early spring of 1940, as if he and he alone might have the power to stop the cold war of the time— or phony war, as it was called. Sumner Welles was sent to inquire what Mussolini's fee would be for that service to humanity.

Not only was he a great man according to the Allied high spokesmen, but a great Italian, a knower of facts or, as it is said, a realist. His patriotism and his realism were universally acknowledged and flattered by the Allied governments before and after Italy entered the war against them. Above all, his grip on the Italian people was never seriously doubted. It was a queer situation: in the Allies' opinion, Mussolini was the only Italian with whom it would have been worthwhile for them to deal, but he was also the only one with whom they would not deal. At the same time, as long as Mussolini was there, he made it easy for the Allies to consider Italy as an enemy and to treat her as such. Not even at the time when war passions ran highest, could the Allied leaders bring themselves to think of Italy as a criminal nation, object of cold, unforgiving hatred, like Germany and Japan. Rather, she was considered a wayward nation, but even waywardness wouldn't find any other justification than the misled patriotism and misconceived realism of the great man. Actually the Allies needed Mussolini's myth in order to fight Italy as an enemy in the war just as much as they had needed the same myth in order to keep Italy out of the war. For it was impossible to assimilate into the same merciless enmity the Italians and the Germans, but the impossible was nearly achieved once Mussolini was assimilated to Hitler.

In their political warfare, the Anglo-Americans at the same time urged the Italians to overthrow Mussolini and considered such an event as most unlikely. The attack on Italy was to be furiously aimed at one great strategic target that was supposed to be, at least for a long time, thoroughly unbreachable. There was no use taking time off from attacking Mussolini to figure out who could replace him in the most unlikely event of his fall. Actually, as long as Mussolini was there, he offered an excellent reason for not giving any serious thought to Italy.

And then, all of a sudden, on the 25th of July the great mischievous man vanished. There was no longer an heroic target. In fact, there was no "underbelly" at all, but a vacuum. There was an enormous mass of people, a whole nation crying peace, peace and freedom. These people had listened to the Allies' appeals against fascism and its Duce and were furiously tearing away all fascist insignia from their clothes or from their walls or from their streets. They had heard that one man and one man alone was responsible for all the evil they had done. Now the man had been thrown out of power, and to them that meant peace.

Was it shock or was it joy that stunned the Allies on the evening of the 25th of July? Was it legitimate pride to see one of the three main targets collapse, or was it acute embarrassment about what to do once the target had collapsed? Or wasn't the whole thing perhaps a booby trap, a devilish Machiavellian scheme? The Allies had launched an all-out assault to defeat an enemy and to conquer enemy territory. But from the 25th of July on they found a people in front of them. What could they do to or for or against a people?

"The war goes on,"—that was the sentence that Orlando, the elder Italian statesman, had inserted in Badoglio's proclamation to the country announcing the coming into power of the new government. It was an unfortunate expression, but the Italians perhaps couldn't help it for they had the Germans in their midst and several thousand plain-clothes-men of the SS in the city of Rome. They wanted to establish communications with the Allies, and had no time to waste. But the expression "the war goes on" represents far more definitely the frame of mind of the Allied supreme leaders. The war goes on and, if you want to stop it, surrender unconditionally—that was the answer given to the harassed representatives of the Italian government who succeeded in sneaking out of Italy without credentials for fear of being caught by the Germans.

Unconditional surrender—but to whom? For the surrender of a nation means that the arms are laid down by the vanquished and picked up by the winner. It means that the roads, the harbors, the arsenals of the surrendering nation are laid open to the conqueror. It means that the defeated nation breaks its social compact and puts itself, whatever is left of its social structure, and its economic resources at the mercy of the triumphant enemy. The Casablanca formula had its literal application in Germany twenty months later. But in the days immediately following the 25th of July the Italians could surrender only to the Germans. For the Germans were in and the Allies were out.

As Churchill put it in his speech at the House of Commons on September 21, 1943, "the unhappy Badoglio government" could only ask the Allies: "When could they come?" When, and how fast and where? If the Allies had come fast enough, what was left of the Italian army would have joined them and fought against the Germans. There were only thirteen moderately equipped Italian divisions left in the peninsula, for Mussolini had scattered thirty-six divisions in the Balkans, in the Aegean Islands and in Southern France. But the Allies could not bring themselves to trust the Italians enough to tell them when and where and in what strength they were going to land. The Allies could only offer an armistice, the armistice was just a name for surrender, and the surrender had to be unconditional. They could not alter their military time-table—not even if the national territory of the "soft" enemy whose surrender they wanted was going to fall, because of that surrender, into the hands of the hard enemy.

President Roosevelt said it quite crisply in his message to Congress on September 17, 1943. The military time-table could not be upset, the landing in Italy had to proceed as planned exactly in the spot where it had been planned, "armistice or no armistice." He could have added: Italy or no Italy, soft enemy or hard enemy. It did not make much difference whether the military campaign was to knock a minor nation out of the war, or whether it was going to turn into an expensive, most-of-the-time inconclusive diversion favorable to the major enemy who could hold superior Allied forces in check and inflict blows on Allied prestige. It seemed to matter even less if the Italian authorities "with whom we could deal," according to Churchill, at the very moment we dealt with them toppled over as if we had pulled the carpet from under their feet. Because of Mussolini's fall, Italy had turned in a few weeks from a military into a political battleground that would have required the boldest and quickest political aggressiveness. But the civilian leaders of the democratic powers were so taken by the task of fighting the war that they had no patience with political objectives.

The civilian leaders of the two major democratic powers had gained their predominant positions in their respective countries because of their superior skill in playing the game of politics. These two superb politicians put all the power of their office and of their personality back of the purely military effort. They acted with the single-mindedness of politicians who are bent on winning an election at any price, principles or no principles. To win an election you have got to have the votes. To win a war, you have got to have the men and the guns. As democrats, they were weary of programs. A program can always be patched together by a committee on resolutions.

Mr. Churchill's responsibility, as it is becoming increasingly well known, was predominant in deciding the Italian campaign and the line to follow towards Italy. The military supreme commanders in the field, particularly the Americans, had a keen, if somewhat intuitive, realization of how absurd and self-defeating the Allies insistence on long-distance unconditional surrender was. Eisenhower and Bedell Smith tried to do what they could to improve the Italians' lot and to give them the prospect of quick relief through a lightning liberation of the country. But they could not help obeying the orders from above, and in obedience to these orders they had to boast to the Italians of a number of divisions and a military might that they did not have.

So the Italian campaign started, after the Allies had imposed on the largest part of Italy the unconditional surrender to the Germans. The obstinacy and the single-mindedness of the Allied leaders made Italy into what they were afraid Italy could be at the time Mussolini fell: a trap. This trap was manned by the Germans with superior skill, used to drain Allied manpower and material in ever increasing quantity. Yet it was never enough, and every time the Allied armies could gain the initiative and push the enemy back they had to stop because the means either were not adequate or were taken away. For nearly two years the Italian front proved to be not a substitute for the second front, but an expensive secondary front of at least doubtful usefulness. Fighting on the Italian peninsula from Salerno up North, the United States army and air force suffered a total of 109,642 casualties: 19,475 killed, 80,530 wounded, and 9,637 missing.

Incidentally, in German-held Italy fascism had a rebirth and Mussolini had his last taste of vicarious power.

This tragic sequence of errors can be explained only by an all around lack of intelligence: military and political intelligence in the field, preceded much before the war started by an inadequate intelligence of Italy and of fascism. Fascism was never correctly understood by the leading men of the major democracies—fascism in general and more in particular, Italian fascism. It was admired, it was deplored, it was taken seriously. Sometimes the Allied governments offered to fascism the supreme flattery of being afraid of it. But only too seldom was the effort made to see what it was in itself and what it did to the people. In the invasion of Italy the Anglo-Americans paid the penalty for their complacent ignorance of what had gone on in the country during the previous twenty years.

Italian fascism was the superficial result of deep-seated causes. It was superficial, because too many Italians lived it in a condition of double-conscience; but at the same time it gave full play to some of the most dangerous inclinations of the Italian people—dangerous to them and to the world. Rhetoric, first of all, and then cynicism; reliance on cleverness as the best way to regaining past greatness, and a certain lightheartedness that led too many people to share the feeling that, after all, fascism was fun. Mussolini did not invent these inclinations; he worked on them so that the largest number of Italians could become self-deluded and debauched. The outside world offered its powerful co-operation both by admiring the performance and by attributing wondrous qualities to the chief performer. So the grotesque mask of fascism, with its square jaws and big eyes, was thought to be the face and the brains of the nation; and when the mask fell, almost of its own weight, the Allies were left without any idea of what to think or what to do. Except, of course, going on with the Italian campaign, Italy or no Italy.

It took time for the Allies to recover from the shock of Mussolini's fall. But finally they brought themselves to announce an Italian policy and to suggest to the Italian people a line of political development that the nation, for its own good, should have followed. The English were particularly blunt. They made it unmistakably clear to the Italians that the best they could do was to keep the monarchy, for as Mr. Churchill is reputed to have put it, it was inconceivable to have Italy without the House of Savoy.

V. THAT MAN MUSSOLINI

OF COURSE he knew that there were conspiracies going on against him, and of course he was not half as naive about the intentions of the monarchy and of the fascist leaders as he tries to appear in this book. But what could he do to stem the tide? Five days before the meeting of the Grand Council he had gone to Feltre to see Hitler. According to all the reports, his leading military and diplomatic experts had frantically coached him as to what he should tell the Führer: that the Italian divisions abroad had to be repatriated, that Italy needed more German assistance, more guns, more planes, more tanks, or otherwise Italy couldn't stay in the war any longer. He promised he would recite his piece to Hitler; but in the Führer's presence, so the reports go, he hardly opened his mouth. Hitler did all the talking: he said that he had no divisions, no equipment to spare. Of course he found a few weeks later all he needed to stop the Allies at Cassino. But why should he have bolstered the Duce and established a closer partnership with him, when he could so easily establish himself as the master of Italy?

Possibly Mussolini's reluctance to talk was determined by a similar line of reasoning. The more German strength there was in Italy, the more he would appear to his people as the Italian quisling. His major weakness, even more than military deficiency, was his loss of prestige. The more Germans that would pour into Italy, the less popular he would be.

Perhaps, he thought, he could still reconquer the confidence of his people. He had a key, a secret key, as he says in his speech at the Grand Council, that someday he was going to use and things would have thoroughly changed. In the light of what happened later, when he became the puppet republican head of Northern Italy, we know now what his secret weapon was. He would wave again, as in the days of his youth, the red flag of socialism. He would appear once more as the blacksmith's son and talk confiscation of large estates, workers' councils with managerial functions, and soak the rich. By going radical, he could out-flank the anti-fascists on the left and perhaps re-establish his bargaining position in front of the Allies. He had experienced more than once in his career that the powerful and the rich are always inclined to soothe the radicals.

That was the last dream of his life. But actually it was late, too late. The same combination of numbers can seldom come up in the winning tickets of two successive lotteries. Neither had he the opportunity of inventing any new schemes offering unchallengeable solutions to time honored conflicts, like those between church and state, business and politics, or for that matter, monarchy and revolution. Now the great Italian problem was: how to get out of the war and avoid German revenge.

Mussolini had become the only Italian of some importance who could not blackmail or double-cross anybody. Everybody else could conspire, but not he. Almost any one of his lieutenants could offer himself to the Allies as a prospective Darlan, but not Mussolini. He had no other recourse but to go to Hitler, but to Hitler he could not talk. Moreover, he had to be careful even in his silence, for some other lieutenants were ready to boast an even greater subservience to Adolf Hitler. He could watch around him people play games in which he had been a supreme master. But he was out, for his position, his role in Italian history had become the stake of all the games.

And yet, there was nobody in Italy who knew better than he did the art of double-dealing, of blackmailing, of playing one group against the other. All the groups were within the structure of the fascist state and of the fascist party—furiously fighting cliques of extremists against right-wing reformers, of all-out economic planners against industrial magnates, fanatics of the independent air force against big Navy admirals and so on almost ad infinitum. During the two decades of the Regime and particularly since the fascist party established the monopoly of politics, the number of cliques had been steadily mounting and their conflicts increasingly poisoned by violent personal hatreds. Mussolini knew how to keep the fights going and how to hold in his hand the destiny of every fighting clique, because he knew that the people at the head of each one

of them could be threatened, cajoled and always compromised.

He had enjoyed throughout all his life an extraordinary
freedom from consistency and from conscience. In his political career he had espoused almost every possible ideol-
ogy, imitated the verbiage of almost every belief or faith
that in his days had some chance of success. There were
only two exceptions, for he never at any time pretended
tò be either a liberal or a Christian. For a few months,
immediately after he went to power in 1922, he followed
the path of extreme economic liberalism, and decried any
governmental interference with business. In 1929 he made
his peace with the Catholic church. But he never stopped
being contemptuous of political freedom, or having toward
Christ the scornful attitude of a self-made intellectual who
has read some Nietzsche.

With these two exceptions he managed to keep a complete freedom to move swiftly and eloquently all around
the gamut of politics from extreme to extreme. The young
editor of Forlì, who had been jailed for having said "the
flag to the manure pile," could become a champion flag-
waver. A few months before the March on Rome he had
violently opposed daylight saving time that in Italy was
called "state's time" because, he said, everything coming
from or called after the state is detrimental to human
dignity, and then shortly after he coined the expression
"totalitarian state." Voluble mimicry was his greatest
talent: he imitated the most different styles and patterns of

political action just as successfully as when, already a grown man, he discarded his diligent, schoolteacherish handwriting and borrowed the bold heroic penmanship of D'Annunzio. In this he was so successful that he was in turn imitated by most of his followers from Grandi down.

The foot-loose political dilettante had, since his ascent to power, stumbled into a few remarkable discoveries. He found out that the typical institutes of modern democracy, like trade unions, universal education, governmental agencies established for the control of business, can be turned into most effective weapons of twentieth century personal tyranny. Once political freedom is eliminated, the instruments of democracy can be so used to multiply the power of the tyrannical state. This constitutes the essence of fascism, that is democracy without freedom. When a modern government refuses to be accountable to its people, it offers them as compensation the easy, swift solution of the most complex, age-old conflicts.

There were few major problems of our times to which Mussolini did not offer his dazzling answer. When the state becomes totalitarian, the organizations of capital and those of labor become just departments of the same all-embracing administration, and the most irksome difficulties can be solved with the smooth circulation of inter-office memoranda. Administration replaces politics and runs smoothly, provided everything is referred to the supreme administrator. This position suited Mussolini thoroughly. He had

PREFACE

developed since the start of his career as Duce an insatiable,
almost maniacal passion for details.

Nothing was too petty for him. He liked to know everything that could possibly be known about his associates
and all the people who depended on his favors—which
meant the whole upper class of the country. Each man
had a price, and each man could be controlled, if only his
personal files, at the Duce's disposal, were kept in good
order. Mussolini was a master file keeper and, as he shows
in this book, he did not throw away any scrap of evidence
on the men whom he appointed to high office. There was
another file cabinet in his immediate reach that he watched
with equal eagerness. It was on the men who, in jail or in
exile, were his unreconstructed enemies. He was particularly fascinated by those in jail. Didn't they have enough?
Were they ready to send him one of the usual letters of
repentence as the price for their liberation? He wanted to
see every scornful note saying that they did not want his
mercy; he wanted to see every report from the jailers on
the morale of the prisoners, and never did he allow himself
to lose sight of that handful of impossible, unrealistic men
whom he could not break.

All his life Mussolini had played with ideas and it must
have been intolerable to him to admit that in Italy there
were men who liked better to live for their own ideas, even
in the misery of solitary confinement, or eventually to die
for them. But toward the other Italians he had a benevolence that was proportionate to their reasonableness. He

52

wanted a correct external behavior and strict conformity to the fascist ceremonials. But he was not too pedantic about the way his reforms were carried out or about the liberties that men in high office might take with public funds. He wanted to know about the behavior of men so as to have an unlimited control over them; but he, the arch-pragmatist, was not punctilious about literal respect of old moral principles or even of brand-new fascist ethics. He was clever enough to know that his brilliantly improvised solutions of extremely complex problems did not solve much, except on paper. He, who had been in the thick of labor conflicts, could have only a limited reliance on the workability of the system which was pompously called the "corporative state."

His realm was that of the approximative: for after all, the control of men was far more important to him than allegiance to principles, even to his own principles. He had given to totalitarianism not only its name but its definition, "Everything in the state, nothing outside the state, nothing against the state," but he knew what that meant: the result of everything being contained within the state is that the relationships among the various "things" becomes secret, at the mercy of the supreme manipulator. The gap between highly proclaimed standards and actual performances left large room to the private initiative of alert operators. The system was elastic, not stiffened by dogmatists. A certain amount of looseness was to many people a profitable substitute for freedom. Grafting and fixing were tolerated because human nature is notoriously frail, and this tolerance appeared as characteristic of a country that in its old history has had a long acquaintance with sin.

Yet the popularity of the system was by no means restricted to men of the old Italian race. On the contrary, the natural scepticism of the Italians, the underlying feeling that sometime the whole incredible adventure would come to an abrupt end were contradicted by the enthusiasm that fascism and its Duce elicited among foreigners. Mussolini offered his own national solution to worldwide problems: problems of the relationship between capital and labor, government and business, occupational and political organizations, church and state. Any strictly nationalistic solution to worldwide problems cannot help being parochial, stultifying and ultimately disastrous. A few Italians and a few foreigners stuck to this viewpoint, but to a very large number of other men, high and low, the whole thing appeared extremely impressive or even admirable, or even overwhelming. Here, in the old soil of Rome, were the evidences of a new political order, perhaps of a new civilization. Some people from the old democracies of the West wistfully deplored that political freedom could not be so easily exported to countries that were not supposed to have adequate preparation for it, but they were reassured by Mussolini's saying that fascism, too, was no export article. So they could, with peace of mind and equanimity, enjoy the show.

It was like a big world's fair, with temporary structures

set against the background of the old Roman monuments and designed to harmonize with them. The exhibition of the new political machinery devised to overcome the difficulties of our time showed remarkable new features and daring design. Of course they could not show how they worked, if they worked at all, but this seemed not to disturb too many visitors from abroad. The corporative state was a thing to behold. It kept the workers in their place, and at the same time it made them happy. It was, of course, seething with corruption, for it was one of the unwritten rules of the corporative system that one could be punished for political but not for economic misdeeds. The imposing structure of the corporative state was like that of a building that has no trace of sanitary facilities or of sewage. But the nostrils of the visitors from abroad remained largely unaffected.

The visitors came in droves. Mahatma Gandhi, Ramsay MacDonald, and, of course, Churchill. But there is no use filling pages with a list of names. University presidents, great bankers, industrialists, writers—they all went to the fair, admired, were welcomed by Mussolini, agreed that really he was a great man. In the house of many a distinguished American the nail is still there on which the autographed Duce's picture used to hang. Social scientists who by profession have to be noncommittal even if *in pectore* they wish well for freedom, were not unresponsive to the call. They went to Rome, they compared the features of the new regime with those of the other countries past and present, they listed diligently all the paper reforms, and climbed the stairs of Palazzo Venezia. The conclusion of their diligent reports was that one could have doubts as to some of the features of the fascist state, but there were no doubts as to Mussolini's greatness.

His amazing success with foreigners emboldened him to new adventures. His adventures, like his reforms, were of an approximate, showy, but not too risky character. He had talked war all his life, class war at the beginning and then nationalistic war when he became a patriot. He had militarized the nation or at least put the largest number of Italians, men and women, in some kind of military garb. He spoke of eight million bayonets, but failed to modernize the Army and to give air coverage or electronic devices to the Navy, or to use the Air Force for other purposes than stunts or shows. He had no taste for war, but he had a passion for near wars. The defenseless, half-naked Ethiopians or the timid souls at the helm of the League of Nations were the proper target for the kind of war machine he could build.

Dilettante, approximative, and rambling in his views, that were, nevertheless, expressed with magniloquent eloquence, Mussolini was the original half-fascist. His fascism had always been a halfbaked affair, half farcical and half cruel, with enough wide-spread solidarity in murder and in graft to keep together the vast assemblage of major and minor leaders. He had been quick in realizing that fascism was one of the waves of the future. He was eloquent in talking of a new mode of political organization and of living, and he dramatized his half-thought theories by embodying them in his strutting person. Further he could not go. He had tapped an almost miraculous source of power and not being burdened by moral scruples, he went as far as that power could take him. His expensive adventures were made possible by the hard-working, deluded Italians and by gullible foreigners. As every half-fascist, he was ready to go on with the adventure—as long as it would last.

And then he met his Nemesis: Adolf Hitler. At the beginning, he was Hitler's model. He appeared as the Baptist of the fascist religion. But as soon as Nazism entrenched itself in Germany, it became clear that Hitler was not a dilettante in evil, but in a horrible, literal sense evil itself. Hitler's totalitarianism was not elastic and accommodating, but a stiff and unbending machine made to crush the bones and consciences of men. Hitler had no taste for near-war. He climbed to power to bring total war into the world.

The Italian people felt it much before the foreigners: once Hitler's Germany had become the leading power and the arbiter nation of Europe, Mussolini's Italy was doomed. Mussolini had debauched the Italian people, he had forced them to live a fantastic, unreal adventure, and made them unfit for war and for peace. On the background of Hitler's horrible reality, the fascist adventure finally appeared what it had been since the beginning: a hoax played on the nostalgia for greatness of the Italians and on the gullibility of the foreigners.

The Italians have a familiar expression, *"fare fesso,"* that can be translated in American slang, and means "play for a sucker" or "take for a ride." That was a gigantic ride that Mussolini gave to the world. Nationalism, anti-communism, non-interference with other nations' internal affairs, disordered passion for order, sophomoric love for reborn antiquity, all these prejudices and sentiments were catered to, brilliantly satisfied and deluded. The proverbial achievement of selling the Brooklyn Bridge pales in comparison to the fascist deed of having an admiring world viewing the old and new Roman Empire arranged around the re-landscaped Coliseum.

As to Mussolini himself, when he fell so inescapably in Hitler's hands as to be dragged into real war, he appeared to his people as a forlorn, contemptible impostor. The attribute of greatness that was so lavishly poured on him is applicable to only one of his characteristics, which was the predominant one of this character. The Americans have a word for it. He was the greatest "ham" that ever existed, the most intelligent imitation of what, according to him, was political genius. Sometimes he overplayed, sometimes he was astonishingly effective, but a ham he was all throughout. When the wooden, cardboard setting of his corporative state, of his new Roman Empire started crumbling in ruin, he appeared pitifully helpless. He had no stage and no audience.

Maybe he felt relieved when he found himself locked in the big ambulance. Maybe he thought that he was at long last going to have a rest in his big house at Rocca delle Caminate. When Badoglio let him know a day later that he was going to be sent there, he seemed to be satisfied and grateful. Later, on his way to a place of detention, he spoke at length to Admiral Maugeri in whose custody he was. According to what the Admiral reported, he said that he couldn't bear the idea of being rescued by the Germans. "That's the biggest humiliation they could ever inflict upon me. To think that I would ever go to Germany and set up a government there with the support of the Germans! Ah, no! Never! Never that!" [6]

But Hitler thought differently. He grabbed the forlorn old ham, put him on the road again, forced him to go through a new circuit. The repeat performance was a nightmare, both for Italy and for Mussolini. For Italy knew that the played-out mimic was offering them a bloody, gruesome imitation of his old self. And Mussolini knew it, too.

---

[6] Cf. Maugeri, F., *From the Ashes of Disgrace*, New York, 1948, p. 143.

VI. THIS BOOK

THIS BOOK is the story of the fall, written by the man who is falling. For 600 days he re-lived with agonizing slowness the descent from power he experienced during one day. This book is the re-enactment of the first.fall, and was written while the final one was in progress.

Perhaps nothing can give a better description of Mussolini's condition when he was the head of the puppet republican government than the story of what happened to his *History of a Year*. The book appeared in the *Corriere della Sera* of Milan, starting on June 24, 1944. The German censorship got alarmed and heavily edited the first installments. Mussolini fumed and protested, but the only concession he could gain was to have a special censor assigned to his book: the German ambassador to the fascist republican government.

The book later appeared in pamphlet form as a special supplement of the *Corriere della Sera* and later on, in November, 1944, in book form. Mussolini had had serious difficulties in finding a publisher, in spite of the fact that 300,000 copies of the pamphlet had been sold in less than a month and there was still a large demand for it. Until the collapse of the fascist republican regime, the book was a best-seller. Mussolini was particularly anxious to have it translated, but he could not find any publisher in Switzerland, while the Germans refused even to have the book mentioned in their press. The story of how a dictator fell was not considered good reading for the German people in 1944. Finally a French translation was printed in Switzerland, at the expense of a Swiss admirer. Mussolini was anxious to read his book in French, but the first copies were on their way to Milan on exactly the day he was captured.[7] His physical survival had proved to be the major obstacle to the free circulation of the book outside of Northern Italy. Once this obstacle was removed, the Duce's plea for his restoration to power became a historic document of considerable interest.

It would be idle to quarrel with the author at every paragraph, or to heckle him with footnotes at the bottom of every page, pointing out his countless violations of proven facts, or his unprovable assertions. This book is not history, but personal history. The author wants to find out for his readers and above all for himself how it all had happened, how could all this come to pass, that he was betrayed, jailed, humiliated. In giving his explanation, he has to make of the conspiracy that unseated him a link of a long, long chain, a segment of a universal, almost cosmic conspiracy. Of course he could not help accusing the Jews and the Masons and, implicitly, the Vatican. He

---

[7] Cf. Amicucci, E., *I 600 giorni di Mussolini*, Rome, 1948, pp. 167-179.

starts his book by laying the initial responsibility for his fall on the hated French and on General de Gaulle, of all people, whom he made responsible for the Allied landing in North Africa. He sees in every defeat of the Italian army evidence of the universal conspiracy. He never suspects for a moment that he might have some responsibility for the lost war or for his own lost power. Ruined, humiliated every day by the Germans, he is as self-centered and self-hypnotized as he ever was.

Like Augustus in his dying days he cries: "Where are my legions?" Why have the generals lied to him about the military preparedness in Sicily? Of course, a dictator is told by his subordinates only what he likes to hear, and probably he never knew that the soldiers in Sicily lacked many essentials, including shoes. A month before the Allied invasion, quite a few military units had to stay in their camps and abstain from marching to avoid subjecting the soles of the soldiers' shoes to an unnecessary strain.[8] Had Mussolini known about the shoe situation, he would probably have called a group of military leaders to a general assembly, and made a fiery speech. But not even his wrathful eloquence could recover the Army-bought leather that, through fascist channels, had reached the black market.

On the eve of the invasion of Sicily, he had taken care of any military contingency with his "tideland" speech. The Americans and English were quite welcome to Sicily, he had said. They could land at any time, but go no

---

[8] Cf. Roatta, M., *Otto milioni di baionette*, Milan, 1946, pp. 246 & 247.

further than the extreme dry rim of the tideland. They will stay on the Sicilian shores, he said, but all in horizontal positions. Probably the bloodthirsty speaker did not know or did not remember that the defense of the whole Sicilian coastline was entrusted to seventy-five emplaced batteries, mostly of first World War vintage. The second line of defense, where it existed at all, was equally rigid, without self-propelled guns or anti-tank equipment. The mobile units moved around mostly on bicycles.[9]

Still in this book he shows no doubt as to his intuition and to his military foresight. He had foreseen the exact date of the English attack of El Alamein. That was at the time when he had gone to Libya with a white horse ready for his triumphal entrance into the Egyptian capital. One day, he says, flying over Pantelleria he discovered there the Italian Malta.[10] In fact, the fortification of Pantelleria had been the object of a loud press campaign in Italy, years before he decided to make the island into a fortress. An embattled Sicilian writer, Gaspare Ambrosini, had written three books on the subject, and he had no easy time in getting the Duce's ear. Yet the Duce's boastfulness is somewhat understandable. In the war council before the attack on France in June, 1940, one of the leading generals had said that it did not make much difference if the Italians

---

[9] Cf. Roatta, M., *op. cit.*
Cf. Rossi, F., *Come arrivammo all armistizio*, Milan, 1946.
Cf. Favagrossa, C., *Perchè perdemmo la guerra*, Milan, 1946.
[10] See text, p. 13.
Cf. Ambrosini, G., *L'Italia nel Mediterraneo*, Foligno, 1927.

were short in artillery and tanks, for the Duce's genius was on their side.

For twenty years Mussolini had been the prisoner of his self-conceit and of the adulation he had imposed on his lieutenants. In his enormous office at Palazzo Venezia, there was only one chair—his chair. Every visitor, with the exception of important dignitaries from abroad, had to stand up so that Mussolini could enjoy the sight of his uncomfortable posture, just as he had enjoyed his long march through the square-like room, straight-shouldered, chest forward, right arm stiffly raised. As he says in this book, he never had a friend, and he assiduously killed the germ of friendship with any human being. He had created all the conditions that make betrayal inevitable. In this book he denounces his flatterers, but it is late, just as it was late for him to have in his small office on Lake Garda available chairs for prospective visitors.

Yet, as the *History of a Year* proves, there is something left of his old talents in the played-out dictator. He is still coupled, as he had been during his whole life, with an alert newspaperman. He sees the physical background of the tragedy of which he is the protagonist, he finds time to look out of his own self and see the lights in the squares and streets in Rome in the tense hours of his undoing. He uses the skill of a good reporter in selecting or counterfeiting the evidence, so that the final "story" on the men who had overthrown Mussolini would be of the utmost damage to them. Sometimes he brings in evidence that no one can check, as in the case of his interview with Grandi the day before the Grand Council meeting. He asserts that Grandi did not tell him a word about the forthcoming meeting and about the role that he was going to play in it; Grandi on the contrary emphatically says that to Mussolini's face he fully rehearsed the attack he was going to deliver the following day. Here is a clear case of one man's word against an-others, and the truth will probably never be ascertained.

There is an almost Dantesque quality in the violence of his hatred against men who, having prostituted themselves to him, are as politically doomed as he is, although some of them have paid the price for physical survival by be-latedly revolting against him. This applies particularly to Grandi and Badoglio. Mussolini so overstates his case against both of them that he pretends to be the original maker of their political fortunes. Actually neither of them was his creature and both of them were his two best-known rivals in the months immediately preceding the March on Rome—Grandi as an advocate of fascist intransigence against Mussolini's attempt to appease the socialists, Badoglio as the best-known exponent of career militarism alarmed by the new self-made generals of the fascist squads. Both of them later paid the price and received the rewards for their repentance. Grandi was never out of office and never unwatched; Badoglio went so far in what, according to his standards, was his resistance to fascism as to enter the party only at the end of the Ethiopian campaign, when he was given, together with the Dukedom of Addis Ababa, honorary membership in the fascist party.

Even greater than the will to destroy his enemies is Mussolini's urge to rebuild himself. He boasts about his own luck, and in the abjection of his position as a minor quisling he writes about his own star as if it were still undimmed. His escape from Campo Imperatore is for him the latest evidence of his unbreakable luck. In fact, things there were of a far less miraculous character than Mussolini wants us to believe. On September 12, when Skorzeny and his paratroopers arrived, the whole of Italy from the Alps to the Salerno beachhead was a vast no-man's land, that the Germans were set to control. The King and the Badoglio government had fled to the far South, and what was left of the royal government apparatus had melted away. In Rome, however, there was still Badoglio's chief of police, Senise, a very harassed man. The policemen who had Mussolini in their custody had been ordered to kill him the moment the German rescue party arrived. Senise had no doubt that the Germans were on their way to Campo Imperatore and that their revenge on the Italians would have been horrible, had they found Mussolini killed. So, on the 9th, Senise phoned the head of the police detachment and told him that in an emergency he should disregard the previous orders and act "prudently" with Mussolini. The following day, as the Italian divisions seemed strong enough to hold their own against the Germans in Rome, he changed his mind and re-confirmed the order to shoot; but in the morning of the 12th he changed his mind again and wired the police chief at Campo Imperatore to behave "with the utmost prudence." [11]

Yet even boasting of miracles was not enough to re-establish the confidence in a luck that had obviously run out. To find support Mussolini ransacks past history and particularly Italian history. He quotes great men who in their own times were not recognized, and finds in lack of recognition an evidence of greatness, just as a discredited painter who rebels at his mediocrity and uses the history of van Gogh as corroboration to his claim to glory. In his case, as an empire builder who had failed, he cannot avoid summoning the memory of Napoleon, the self-made emperor whose claim to greatness has survived defeat. Napoleon, too, like Mussolini, regained power after having been forced to abdicate. Mussolini had been the co-author of a play on Napoleon's hundred days of restored empire which ended at Waterloo. The man who had mimicked Napoleon throughout his life must have thought, while he was writing this book, that the end of the Napoleonic drama anticipated the pattern of his own future: after the second wind of power, possibly ending in defeat, there would be a resurrection in historical glory.

He had never been so wrong. For the nature of his second call to power was such as to ruin the memory of his past performances even in the most uncritical minds. In the 600 days of the fascist social republic he used up all the

---

[11] Senise, C., *Quando ero Capo della Polizia*, Rome, 1946. P. 251 & 259.

material for myth-making that in generations to come could have appealed to the Italian nostalgia for greatness. That violent inoculation of the most crude Germanic fascism vaccinated the country against future recurrence of the fascist blight. There is still a considerable survival of fascist mentality and habits in present day Italy; there might be in the future stronger groups than there are now working for a return to the fascist past. Yet it is extremely unlikely that a reborn fascism may again grip the country, for Mussolini at the end of his career rendered to his countrymen the service of presenting them with the most sordid, undiluted type of fascism. At the time of the social republic the Italians were much better prepared than in the days of the March on Rome. The Resistance was their answer.

The whole nation resisted. It ignored the native and the external rulers, disobeyed their laws, sheltered the fugitives from religious or racial persecution, shielded the partisans who, whenever action was needed, acted fast and well. The still completely unreported Italian Resistance was, even more than military partisan action, national disobedience. Mussolini and his few remaining acolytes did not rule, for they were constantly made to feel that they had no power, that they were not Italians, that in fact they did not exist. To kill occasionally some Germans or fascists was, of course, a duty. But the most important thing was to make them realize that they were nothing— just a freakish assemblage of doomed men who for some horrid reason were enjoying a too-prolonged stay of execution. But actually they were dead, and they were treated as such: walking, murderous and unburied corpses. Among them the most ludicrous was the former Duce.

The Italian Resistance was the atonement of the nation for more than twenty years of lightheartedness. Not even Mussolini ever succeeded in having the Italians of all classes so united, deliberate and proud. The large majority of the same people, who for two decades had lived with easygoing double conscience, during the Resistance gave all their hearts for the one purpose of bringing the lurid episode to a close. This sudden rebirth of virile dignity is not something new in Italian history; rather it is the dramatic illustration of the two opposite sides of the Italian nature—the fatuous, pompous overacting of a D'Annunzio or of a Mussolini on one side, the passionate integrity of a Verdi or of a Toscanini on the other. During the Resistance, the nation reached so high a pitch of fervid unity, that it could not quite live up to it in the following period of political reconstruction. But the nation succeeded in testing its temper, in performing deeds that memory can leaven, and from which myths can grow.

While the nation was fighting for its own survival, Mussolini lived his haunted life on Lake Garda, and wrote this book. He, too, has his own plan for national survival, and he is still eloquent in the advocacy of his own ideas, as some of these pages prove. Sometimes he has accents of sincerity which sound strange coming from a man who seldom, if ever, knew what good faith is. He has his own principles about national resurrection and national honor, and he has to abide by them. The time of clever playing with ideas and roles in history is well over, as he came to realize when he, too, like the King and Badoglio, had his secret negotiations with the Allies.[12] At the end of his life, cornered as he is by history, his view of things is consistent, and in a strange, inverted way, correct: invariably, what is right for him is wrong for the nation. When he plunged Italy into war, he said that he needed several thousand soldiers killed so that his position would be strong at the peace table. At the end of this book his plea for the Italian participation to the Axis war is based on the argument that there are thousands of Italian soldiers buried in Greece. The nation is fighting for its soul, and he still invokes the days of glory when Italy was conquering Albania. Italy is a nation to be made, and he is nostalgic for the days when Italy could unmake nations. The divorce between Italy and fascism had really become complete.

And, finally, the sinister adventure ends. One April day, the Milanese crowds could see a corpse dangling upside down in Piazza Loreto, the life at last gone out of him. The great adventure in personal and national irresponsibility is finished and the man who had the major personal share of guilt has received the ultimate punishment.

---

[12] Amicucci, E., *I 600 giorni di Mussolini*, Rome, 1948, p. 162.

THIS BOOK

Ruined and sobered, Italy is finding herself. The great prank has ended in tragedy and the incredible story is finished. No reincarnation or returns are to be expected.

For Mussolini and for fascism in Italy, that day was really the end.

EDITOR'S NOTE

THIS BOOK first appeared as a series of nineteen unsigned articles in the newspaper *Corriere della Sera* of Milan, starting on June 24, 1944. In the issue of July 18 that carried the last article, Mussolini acknowledged to be the author of the whole series—a somewhat unnecessary announcement as it had been universally known, since the first articles appeared, who the author was. When the book was issued in pamphlet form, on August 10, 1944, Mussolini gave it the title, *The Time of the Stick and the Carrot,* and the sub-title, "History of a Year, October, 1942—September, 1943." When finally the book edition was published at the beginning of November, title and sub-title were switched around. The book is mostly known in Italy as *History of a Year.*

There were a few changes of no major importance in the various editions. The present translation is based on the text as it appeared in the pamphlet, for it was in pamphlet form that the book had its largest circulation.

An analytical index has been added in the appendix, with some data on the most significant names of Italian people, localities and institutions mentioned in the text.

In editing the book and preparing the appendix I have been greatly helped by my friends Umberto Morra and Carla Pekelis.

M. A.

TABLE OF EVENTS

1942

November 7—The Allies land in North Africa.

1943

January 26—The Casablanca conference is announced. Unconditional surrender is proclaimed to be the only peace term ever to be offered to the Axis.

May 12—End of the war in North Africa.

June 10—Surrender of Pantelleria.

July 10—Allied landing in Sicily.

July 19—Hitler and Mussolini meet in Feltre. First air bombardment of Rome.

July 25—The King dismisses Mussolini and appoints Marshal Badoglio prime minister.

July 28—The Fascist party is dissolved.

September 3—The preliminary (short) armistice between Italy and the Allies is signed.

September 8—The armistice is announced.

September 8—Allied landing at Salerno.

September 9—The King, Badoglio and the highest officers of the Italian government leave Rome to go South.

1943

September 12—Mussolini who was detained at Campo Imperatore, Abbruzzi, is reached by a German rescue party.

September 16—Mussolini becomes the head of the republican Fascist government in German-held Italy.

1944

June 4—Allied occupation of Rome.

TABLE OF EVENTS

June 24—The *Corriere della Sera* of Milan start publication of Mussolini's *History of a Year.*

1945

April 19—The partisans free Milan.

April 25—Mussolini is captured at Dongo near the Swiss border.

April 28—Mussolini is executed.

THE FALL OF MUSSOLINI

FOREWORD

IN RESPONSE to a widespread request the series of articles published in June and July by the *Corriere delle Sera* are collected here.

Their purpose is to make known the events that took place during the most tragic months of contemporary Italian history. We have here a documented account which may (and will) be filled out in more detail at some future time but whose authenticity cannot be questioned because everything in it is a truthful report of what actually happened.

The story itself and its fatal consequences point their own moral.

Today Italy is crucified but on the horizon is the dawn of Resurrection.

M.

I. FROM EL ALAMEIN TO MARETH

ONE FACT has been definitely overlooked in everything that has been written on the Italian catastrophe of the summer of 1943: France originated the catastrophe on a specific date, November 8, 1942. It was France, that so-called Jewish-Masonic-Bolshevik "independent," that opened the gates of the Mediterranean to the Americans. One of the most decisive episodes in the conspiracy against Italy took place in Algiers when, at the dawn of that November day, an American convoy steamed into the harbor. The British stayed offshore for fear of wounding French feelings. The landing of the first cargoes of men and tanks met no resistance but indeed was acclaimed by a triumphal greeting from their accomplices. This betrayal on the part of De Gaulle was a prelude to that perpetrated by Badoglio; these two were links of the same chain. It was clear from the start that the landing of American forces in the Mediterranean was an event of great strategic significance, destined to modify and, in fact, to reverse the balance of military power in this sector, an event which was in Italian opinion if not decisive, certainly very important. The great pincer movement which was under way in the summer of 1942, when the Germans were storming the first bastions of the Caucasus and Rommel's German-Italian armies were at the gates of Alexandria, was now halted with no hope of resumption. There loomed up, on the contrary, an equally vast Allied maneuver designed to close in, from Algeria on one side and Egypt on the other, upon the German-Italian forces deployed in Libya. The Axis took immediate measures to offset the Allied landing by carrying out a total occupation of France, Corsica, and Tunisia.

These countermeasures might have changed the basic strategic situation brought about by the Allied landing if Axis troop re-enforcements and supplies had been moved in fast enough to allow an Axis offensive before the Americans could build up their ultimate strength. But this required an air superiority which we did not possess. Transportation was increasingly and almost completely blocked by the British air and naval forces, which ruled over the shortest sea lane, the Sicilian Channel, well known as the graveyard of the Italian merchant marine.

In brief, the situation was this: progressive strengthening of the Allies and progressive difficulty encountered by the Axis. On October 23, on the eve of the Algiers landing, Montgomery attacked and smashed our positions at El Alamein and the juncture of enemy forces from both east and west began. In Italy there were rapid and deep repercussions following the American landing. All the enemies of Fascism raised their heads and the first traitors, a group of secondary figures even when they held the rank of National Councilors, emerged from the shadows. The nation began to breathe uneasily. As long as England was alone in the Mediterranean, Italy was able, with German aid and ever-increasing sacrifices at home, to hold fast. But America's appearance on the scene disheartened many cowards, increased by millions the already large number of those who listened to enemy radio broadcasts, and provided to traitors who had not yet shown their hand an alibi for their future behavior. The only way to save the situation would have been to attack Montgomery from the rear, a plan which was often discussed but never put into action. The two weeks between October 23 and November 18 were, as successive events have shown, of incalculable importance. From this time on the Allies took and held the initiative.

The attack at El Alamein revealed a crushing British superiority, especially in the air. Rommel's promising attempt to unleash an offensive on August 28 had been paralyzed after three days for lack of gasoline, because the tankers bringing it had gone to the bottom. After this failure it would have been better to abandon the line of El Alamein–El Quattara and to withdraw the Italian troops, which were not motorized, to the Sollum-Halfaya line. When Mussolini left Derna in July he issued written orders to Marshal Bastico and General Barbasetti to strengthen this line and garrison it with idle troops from the rear. Instead the German-Italian command decided to dig in at an advanced position and wait there for the expected enemy attack. Italian infantry units could have withdrawn practi-

cally undisturbed in September, and once they had reached
the Sollum-Halfaya line the motorized Germans could have
safely rejoined them.

In this case there would have been over 250 miles of
desert between ourselves and the enemy, a sufficient distance to delay the enemy's supply service so as to enable us
to strengthen our favorable position on the Sollum-Halfaya
line. As it was, the battle unleashed by Montgomery on
October 23 took on at once a violent and decisive character.
During the first days there was some inevitable wavering
back and forth, but the enemy's air and artillery superiority soon began to tell. The infantry, particularly that of
the Italians, which had no prearranged defensive system
worthy of the name, was submitted for days on end to
deadly cannon fire and uninterrupted bombardment.

Nevertheless the troops stood their ground, some of
them, such as the Folgore Division, heroically. Then the
enemy tanks (for here too there was American armor)
broke through the lines and flanked the Italian infantry
positions. Many soldiers fought bravely, as the enemy
himself was the first to recognize. Retreat followed, but
the Italians were unable to get away because most of their
insufficient motor vehicles were immobilized by enemy fire.
Many prisoners were taken and had to undergo a last
tragic march through the desert to the famous, or rather
infamous, prison cages. The main retreat, one of the greatest known to history, was carried out by Rommel's
armored troops. With the enemy close at his heels on land

and in the air, Rommel managed to keep a jump ahead, without pausing at any of the prearranged halts on the way. The names of Sidi-el-Barrani, Sollum, Tobruk, Derna, Benghazi, all of them so dear to Italian hearts, appeared for the last time in the war communiqués. It was impossible, for lack of arms, to engage a rear action on the El Agheila–Marada line at the border of Tripolitania and the retreat continued to Homs. It was hoped that the Sirte desert would slacken the enemy's pressure, but such was not the case, and the battle for Tripoli actually never took place. All available forces were withdrawn in the direction of Tunisia, where the terrain of the Mareth line lent itself to prolonged resistance. Many men and much matériel did get this far. In the course of the thousand-mile retreat losses of matériel were very small, as is brought out in a detailed report, sent to Rome by General Giglioli, who had charge of supply services in Libya.

Within the brief space of three months the enemy pincer movement had met with extraordinary success. By now it was plain to see that after the battle for Tunisia would come the battle for Sicily. The command of operations in Tunisia was entrusted to General Messe, who was later to betray his country. His task was an extremely difficult one. But he had proved his ability in Albania, where he had blocked a daring Greek attack which threatened Valona, and in Russia, where he headed the Italian Expeditionary Corps, whose soldiers fought bravely under his leadership.

The Expeditionary Corps later turned into a whole army of ten divisions (Julia, Tridentina, Cuneense, Ravenna, Cosseria, Sforzesca, Celere, Pasubio, Torino, Vicenza), and Messe was replaced by General Gariboldi, who had not particularly distinguished himself in either Ethiopia or Libya. This replacement was an error brought about by professional jealousy, by Messe's reputation for being a sincere Fascist, and, above all, by exaggerated respect for the tables of seniority. Now Messe was called to Rome and in spite of the difficulties of the task that lay ahead of him he undertook to perform it and flew straight to Tunisia. He spent his first weeks co-ordinating the equipment of the troops and bolstering up their morale, which had been greatly impaired by the long retreat and by the weariness of thousands of soldiers who had been in Africa for several years in succession. The fate of Tunisia depended upon the availability of supplies to the 300,000 men quartered in its narrow territory. The problem was a critical one, for shipping losses were growing heavier all the time. In April alone 120,000 tons of Italian shipping were sunk and 50,000 tons damaged. Whereas the enemy had almost an excess of supplies, the German and Italian forces were sapped by pernicious anemia. After the failure of the attempted German offensives, which resulted only in widening the enemy bridgehead, the British proceeded to attack the Mareth line.

In Rome there was much discussion of when this attack might fall, and the general opinion was that Montgomery would delay it until he could take advantage of the full moon, as he had done at El Alamein. But he chose, instead, a pitch-black night. In order that the British artillery should not fire upon the advancing infantry, the latter wore white patches on their backs. The Mareth line was strongly fortified to a point some fifteen miles inland from the sea; and the rest of it was considerably weaker and toward the opposite end it amounted to practically nothing. Its defense was in the hands of desert troops which had just taken over his new position after an exhausting march through the wastes of the interior. They had little artillery and no training in how to meet the onset of massed armored units. The Italians quartered on the line, behind a wide antitank trench, put up a brave resistance, and made a counterattack. Montgomery could not break through—let's say it—it is exact to state that on this occasion the British took a beating. The enemy then transferred his attack to the weaker part of the line, at the extreme right of General Messe's position, where by bringing huge armored forces into play he overcame the Italian desert troops and made a flanking movement around them. As a result General Messe had to withdraw some fifty miles to a line situated roughly halfway between Mareth and Tunis. Meanwhile, in the northwest, the Germans were hard pressed by the Americans, who were also much more heavily armed. The iron band was closing in such a way that further resistance was out of the question. The last act of the drama is a matter of history. While in Tunisia

11

the rhythm of events was accelerated and moved on toward a finale, in Rome, Messe was the subject of discussion. Interest centered about his detailed and interesting report on the battle of Mareth, which according to many readers gave excessively high praise to the leaders and men of the British Eighth Army. It was agreed, however, that such praise also brought out the merits of our Italian soldiers for having stood up to such mighty adversaries.

Today, in the light of Messe's particularly shameful betrayal, we may wonder if the flattering terms in which he spoke of the British in this report were not designed to ease the conditions of his coming imprisonment. It is a fact that Messe's report won him favorable attention in the British press and photographs show him received, upon his arrival by plane in the vicinity of London, by a group of generals who appear to treat him not as a mere Italian prisoner but as an honored guest.

When it became obvious that Messe's army had to surrender, we were faced by two alternatives. One was that Messe should be repatriated and take over the command of the troops stationed in Sicily, which was considered a rear-guard position of the African front. The other was that, according to a long-standing tradition of the Italian army, the leader must submit to the same fate as his men and follow them into imprisonment, as the Duke of Aosta had done. This latter solution was favored by Mussolini. It was held that General Messe should be recompensed for his pains by promotion to the rank of marshal. The King disapproved of this step, but only because he was unwilling to have the British capture a marshal after they had already taken prisoner a prince of the royal house.

Since the British held undisputed air and sea control of the channel between Tunisia and Sicily, very few Italians managed to escape capture. Only a few boatloads of hardy navigators put off from the beaches of Cape Bon and landed on the west coast of Sicily. With the close of the Tunisian campaign the curtain was raised on Pantelleria. Soon an assault would be launched against the first strip of our own soil.

Italians knew Pantelleria as an island of detention for political and common criminals. It appeared on the map as an almost insignificant dot, that is, until the day when Mussolini flew over it and saw its possibilities as a challenge to Malta and a fortress set midway in the narrowest point of the Sicilian Channel. The British were justified, after their conquest, in calling it "Mussolini's Island." *

The plan to transform Pantelleria into a naval and air base met with considerable opposition, mostly on the part of technicians, who said that the fortification of this island was not necessary to the defense of the Channel. The reply to this objection was: Is a road better blocked by standing in the middle of it or on the sidelines? If Pantelleria blocks the way for only a few minutes, may not this gain of time be a decisive factor of victory? The technicians

* See Preface, p. 63.

(General Valle among them) dropped their objections and intensive work was begun by thousands of laborers from the mainland. The aim was, within a few years, to deepen the harbor and make it accessible to ships of medium tonnage, to build an airfield and a two-story underground hangar, to set up shore batteries and antiaircraft posts, to lay in stores of food and ammunition; to improve the roads, and to mine short stretches of beach that might be used for enemy landings. This plan was undertaken with admirable energy and the garrison was built up by degrees. On August 18, 1938, a year after work had begun, Mussolini flew to Pantelleria, landed on the still unfinished airfield, inspected the vast underground hangar (the first of its kind), and saw with his own eyes that at least half the job was done.

The British followed with growing and irritated curiosity the construction of this mid-Mediterranean naval and air base. Work on it did not cease with the outbreak of war. Guns, planes, men, and supplies continued moving in. When General Spaatz began his sea and air siege of Pantelleria there were on the island forty gun batteries, several squadrons of pursuit planes, and a garrison of about 12,000 men. Admiral Pavesi was commander of the naval base and General Mattei of the troops.

II. FROM PANTELLERIA TO SICILY

TOWARD the beginning of June, 1943, the air attack went on night and day on a massive scale, frequently accompanied by naval bombardment. Our communiqués numbered 1102 through 1109 all chronicled enemy air raids. Number 1109 stated that: "The garrison at Pantelleria, continuing to resist bravely the enemy's uninterrupted air attack, brought down six planes yesterday." Number 1110 aroused particular attention and feeling among all Italians. It ran as follows: "Yesterday, June 8, the garrison at Pantelleria, although subjected to uninterrupted attack, made no answer to the enemy's appeal for surrender." This same communiqué reported that fifteen enemy planes had been brought down, a fact in which everyone took pride. Number 1111 announced new enemy raids and the downing of eleven more planes. Number 1112 said that: "Powerful formations of enemy bombers and fighters swept over Pantelleria during the whole day and night of June 10. Although hammered by a thousand planes the garrison refused to answer a new appeal for surrender."

On this same day twenty-two enemy planes were brought down by our flyers. The second refusal to General Spaatz's radio ultimatum aroused great enthusiasm among all Italians. Here at last was something to rejoice about! The press in neutral and enemy countries underlined the importance of what was happening. Foreign opinion ran as follows: Italian soldiers had not made a brilliant showing in the war so far because they were fighting away from home, but now that they were defending the sacred ground of their own country, they would, as a Swedish newspaper put it, "astonish the world."

The events of Pantelleria seemed to justify the prophecy of this foreign observer. But a telegram of praise sent from Rome to the commanding admiral crossed a message he had just sent to Rome in which he said that, chiefly on account of a lack of water, resistance was no longer possible. This unexpected change of heart within the course of a few hours was a rude shock to Supreme Headquarters. Admiral Riccardi and Generals Ambrosio and Fougier were called into consultation. The surrender threatened to take place on the anniversary of Italy's entrance into the war and Admiral Pavesi's telegram was addressed to Mussolini himself. To order resistance until the very end would have been a futile gesture and one that had already been unsuccessful on other occasions, at Klisura in Albania and elsewhere. Pavesi's telegram painted the situation as absolutely hopeless; apparently further resistance would have led only to useless bloodshed. But what then was the meaning of the two refusals to surrender twenty-four and forty-eight hours before? Had Pavesi believed that General Spaatz would be moved to such admiration by these acts of defiance that he would suspend his attack?

Or was Pavesi merely indulging in a heroic gesture, of a theatrical rather than a military nature? It was finally decided, amid great bitterness, to send Pavesi the message he was waiting for: "Communicate by radio to Malta that lack of water compels you to end resistance." Large white flags were displayed over the harbor and on various buildings, and all enemy fire ceased. The British made an unopposed landing, although a few Italian soldiers who did not know what was going on fired their guns and wounded two of their number. That was all there was to it.

The capture of Pantelleria, which an English paper said could never have been effected if the garrison had been of a different caliber, cost the invaders only two slightly wounded victims. And what price did Italy pay for the unsuccessful defense of this first outpost of the homeland? The Chief of Staff was called upon to give what indirect information he could (Admiral Pavesi having been extremely reticent) and he reported as follows: In the space of a month there were 56 dead and 116 wounded, almost all of them Blackshirt Fascist militiamen of the antiaircraft service. The soldiers and civilians quartered in the underground hangar suffered hardly any losses at all. The garrison of 12,000 men was captured almost intact. A few weeks later Admiral Jachino drew up an elaborate report in which the number of dead during the month of siege was reduced to 35. The underground hangar, cut out of the rock, had completely thwarted the enemy bombardment and 2,000 tons of bombs had fallen not on human targets but on stone.

It became known later on, from enemy testimony, that water was not lacking. In any case apparatus (made in France) for distilling sea water was on the way.

Communiqué number 1113, announcing the surrender of the island, had the effect of a cold shower upon Italian spirits. It was followed by an attempt to change the object of public interest from Pantelleria to Lampedusa, where "a small garrison was heroically standing its ground." As a matter of fact, here too a white flag had been raised.

Admiral Pavesi had lied; indeed we may now say that he was a traitor. The underground hangar was not blown up and the airfield was ceded to the enemy in almost perfect condition. It is too bad that a firing squad did not catch up with this first of the traitorous admirals, whose successors were only a few months later to indulge in the basest form of betrayal by handing over the whole fleet to the enemy.

After the fall of Pantelleria it was Sicily's turn.

Even before war was declared measures had been taken to strengthen the military defenses of the island. As soon as hostilities were begun the Duce sent Marshal Emilio De Bono, who had been given command of the armies in the south, to inspect these defenses. On June 25, 1940, Marshal De Bono addressed to Marshal Graziani, who was then Chief of Staff, a detailed and acute report of "observations on the disposal of troops and their efficiency, coast patrols and defenses, and antiaircraft installations."

In regard to the efficiency of the troops, Marshal De Bono reported as follows: "Morale is high and a fighting spirit prevails. Troop effectives are nearly at full strength, but vehicles and horses are lacking." Next came some detailed critical remarks on the following subjects: the advanced age of the soldiers in the coastal defense units; missing or incomplete items of equipment; the unfamiliarity with new automatic weapons on the part of some units and the unfinished training of others. As examples of this last weakness De Bono described the case of two officers who had been second lieutenants in the previous world war and now, without having had any training in the intervening twenty years, held the post of battalion commanders. On July 7, 1940, General Roatta, Deputy Chief of Staff, informed Marshal De Bono of "measures taken as a result of your inspection in Sicily," among them "the breakup of twenty-four coastal battalions and their replacement by men on an average of ten years younger." The general defense situation in Sicily had been improved by the addition to the Twelfth Army Corps of the Piemonte Infantry Division. And Roatta concluded: "Reserve supplies and machine guns for coastal defenses will be sent in quantities as large as possible."

The troops in Sicily were under the command first of General Ambrosio, then of General Rosi, later of General Roatta, and finally, after July 1, 1943, of General Guzzoni. During the first three years of the war the island defenses were greatly strengthened. As testimony to this fact we have the diary which General Ambrosio, in the rapidity of his flight,* left behind him. This is a document of no particular value except from an administrative point of view. On May 6, 1942, Ambrosio wrote of having conferred with the Prince of Piedmont, who declared after visiting the island: "The coastal divisions are in good condition; all that is needed is to have the battalions identified by numbers. Military deportment is good and the soldiers salute in a disciplined fashion. Many roads are in very bad shape; there is administrative confusion in Palermo and the troops stationed at Pachino complain of poor postal service." On October 17 General Ambrosio noted in his diary: "Must not talk. There are spies at headquarters. Instances: Transfer of high-ranking officers and Scuero's visit to me. Political situation obscure. The Duce is ill." For November 10, 1942, at five o'clock in the evening, the diary carries a note saying: "Went with Cavallero and Rosi to see the Duce and discuss the defenses of Sicily and Rosi's requirements."

* General Ambrosio, one of the leaders of the conspiracy against Mussolini, left Rome with the King and Badoglio on September 9, immediately after the announcement of the armistice.

For November 11 at twelve o'clock, we find the following entry: "Went to see the Duce in order to complete examination of Sicilian defense problems. Duce ordered me to call up second contingent of conscripts of 1923 so as to raise a force of 40,000 men for service in Sicily. The third contingent will be called up on January 15, 1943." And for November 16: "The Duce has considerable pain from his illness." This note may be closely related to the following significant entry for December 4: "Bonomi called. Badoglio's proposal. His Majesty's abdication. The Crown Prince. Arms. Cavallero."

Here we have the first reference to the coming coup d'état. In spite of his illness Mussolini was giving most of his time to military preparations in Sicily. For January 10, 1943, we read: "Went with Cavallero and Rosi to see the Duce. Rosi said 'The King is satisfied with his visit to Sicily. The troops impressed him favorably: particularly the Livorno Division, with the Assietta and the Napoli next. He was pleased with the coastal divisions and with the extent and execution of defense works, but said that highway communications needed improvement.' " To which the Duce replied that: "Among the conscripts of 1924, only thirty per cent of those sent to Sicily should be native Sicilians and the rest from the mainland of Italy."

It was Mussolini's idea that the defense of Sicily should be entrusted to Italians from all the various regions. In the first World War Sicilians had fought in the Alps and now troops from the mainland should mount watch over the coastline of the south.

With the fall of Tunisia the threat to our main islands was drawing closer and closer and Mussolini sent General Ambrosio on a tour of inspection of Sardinia. He stayed there four days and on May 8, 1943, made a report to the Duce whose essential passages are worthy of attention. After a geographical survey describing the zones most adapted to enemy landings he commented on the island defenses as follows:

"There is a general lack of uniformity in the various sectors of the defense system, due to a succession of conflicting orders from headquarters in the course of recent years. This discrepancy has in turn been caused by a series of new developments in the theory of coastal defense and of new methods of attack based on recently perfected weapons.

"Because for obvious reasons we could not destroy all that had been done in the past and make a completely fresh start, we have had to adapt existing material to new uses and to make such modifications as we could.

"Thus it was that we had in Sardinia rear-line defenses disproportionately strong in contrast to our weak advanced positions. This state of affairs was contrary to the most modern usage, which holds that an enemy landing must be beaten back on the beaches and preferably in the water.

"In order to strengthen both the front and the rear sectors there is a pressing need for both light and heavy artillery pieces to turn against ships, tanks, and landing parties. These serve not only to beat back such of the enemy's motorized columns as may have broken through the first defenses but also, and in fact chiefly, to repulse troops swimming ashore as well as those who have already obtained a toe hold on the beach.

"It is all the more necessary to stop the enemy on the beach before he can make his way inland because we have not enough armored vehicles to cope with his modern equipment once he has put it ashore.

"The present system of defenses, in spite of past mistakes, has been built up into a satisfactory bulwark against attack. Automatic weapons and artillery pieces are being sent in increasing numbers and will further strengthen our position. Work on the fortifications is proceeding with speed and enthusiasm. Morale is high; the commanding officers are ready for their task and the soldiers are well disciplined and prepared to fight to the last ditch.

"During my stay in Sardinia I was led to ask myself once again: Is it likely that the enemy will try to capture this island?

"A landing in Sardinia would be no easy matter. There are only a few suitable stretches of coast, with narrow beaches and arduous terrain immediately behind them. Our air and naval counterattacks would have a good chance of wreaking havoc among the enemy convoys and their later re-enforcements; our ground defenses are far from negligible.

"The enemy, even if he counts on heavy losses, must be quite sure of his eventual success. In this case he

23

cannot be sure and the risk involved is great. Moreover, in view of the heavy losses which he must be prepared to incur, the objective he is storming must be an important one. And, in the general strategic picture of the Mediterranean, Sardinia is not important. To my mind, the difficulties of an invasion are out of proportion to the advantages to be gained, that is, unless the Allies have decided to invade the mainland of Italy, in which case they might carry out a series of sudden attacks and take over the island in order to use it as a springboard to the continent.

"But I do not believe they intend to invade Italy. Its conquest would require too long a time and would have no decisive bearing on the final result of the war. *Italy will resist, even if it is cornered in the Po valley; this the enemy knows very well.*"

It is clear from the above that early in May of 1943 General Ambrosio, our Chief of Staff, did not admit even the remotest possibility of the unconditional surrender that was to take place only four months later. His report on Sardinia is concluded as follows:

"All things considered, I believe that an attack on Sardinia is very unlikely and in any case much less probable than an attempt to invade Sicily, whose strategic position makes it a much greater obstacle to our enemies in the Mediterranean region. The conquest of Sicily does not presuppose a later invasion of the mainland, but may be an objective of sufficient importance for itself alone. It would assure the enemy's freedom of movement, lessen the commitments of his naval forces, and cut the losses of his merchant marine. In short, Sicily is an enemy objective of the greatest significance, worth his running every risk and making every possible effort."

Early in June, General Guzzoni took over command of the troops in Sicily. His first impression of conditions there was conveyed in a telegram complaining of many insufficiencies, particularly in the field of morale. He was asked for a more detailed report, which arrived by courier a few days later. In spite of three years of preparation he saw the situation as a difficult one. Among other things, a clumsily worded proclamation by his predecessor, General Roatta, had understandably wounded the patriotic feeling of the Sicilians. The island was by this time in miserable shape. Whole cities were razed to the ground, their population was wandering half starved over the countryside, and civilian life was almost totally disorganized.

III. THE LANDING IN SICILY

O N JUNE 12, 1943, after the surrender of Pantelleria and a large-scale bombardment of La Spezia, which had severely damaged our fleet, General Ambrosio sent a memorandum to the Duce informing him of the new measures taken to defend the peninsula. The Ravenna, Cosseria, Sassari, Granatieri, Pasubio, and Mantova Divisions were to guard the west coast, with five divisions, Piacenza, Ariete, Piave, the Sixteenth Armored and the Panzergrenadiere. It was planned also to use the First Italian Armored, or M Division, made up of Blackshirt Fascist militiamen, which since the day it was quartered in the zone of Lake Bracciano had been a nightmare to both the royal family and the General Staff.

Taking a lesson from the experience of Pantelleria and Lampedusa, General Ambrosio issued the following orders:

"Bring our Air Force into play at the right moment and take steps in advance to eliminate any possible difficulties it may encounter. Spread our defenses out toward the rear in order not to expose concentrated troop or supply units to enemy bombardment from the

26

air. Be ready to throw in re-enforcements in order to beat the enemy off while his landing forces are still disorganized. Train all units to act on their own initiative when, as is very likely, communication with headquarters is disrupted. Provide stores of supplies for units which may be cut off in the course of combat. *Work up the morale of the troops in such a way that they realize that they must defend inch by inch the sacred ground of their homeland."*

These were very fine words, but nothing more. In reality officers of every rank had never bothered about the morale of their men and at headquarters, the consternation created by the sudden capitulation of Pantelleria had engendered a state of mind not far from that of surrender. Defeatism was once more in the air. The widely heard enemy radio announced an inevitable and, in fact, imminent invasion of Sicily. During the whole month of June enemy planes systematically bombed every city and town, sowing confusion and upsetting the distribution of food, which was already suffering from the interruption of the ferry service to the mainland and of local railroad lines.

On the afternoon of June 14, disobeying his doctor's orders, the Duce summoned to Villa Torlonia the Chief of Staff, the leaders of the three branches of the Armed Forces, and the Minister of War Production. He read to them "a memorandum on Italy's mid-June strategic situation," which ran as follows:

"1. It seems almost superfluous to say at the start that there is at this point no possible political settlement. Surrender would mean the end of Italy as a great power, in fact, as any power at all. Its first effect, aside from the territorial mutilations which come to everyone's mind, would be the dismantlement of all industries directly or indirectly connected with the war.

"2. In the present phase of the war Italian troops simply cannot take the initiative, but must remain strictly on the defensive. The Army has no ground on which to move to the attack; all it can do is to repulse the enemy when he lands and push him back into the sea. Naval activity is limited to the possibilities of our small ships and submarines. In the last few months the Navy has accomplished very little. Our big ships are a dead weight on our hands and exposed to growing danger. The Air Force, too, can do no more than make sporadic attacks on enemy shipping. We have no big bomber fleet and not enough fighters to protect it anyhow, so that what planes we have are restricted to a mere defensive function. In conclusion: all we can do is to defend the mainland. But we must carry on this defense to the last drop of our blood.

"The enemy's tactics, based in part on a war of nerves, are to publicize by press and radio the most absurd and fantastic rumors about a second front. But aside from this rhetorical clamor his strategic conduct of the war depends on the laws of geography and aims at obtaining maximum results with a minimum effort. It was only logical and to be expected that the enemy would attack our mid-Mediterranean islands, and now we may expect him to turn to the larger bases: Sicily, Sardinia, and Rhodes. This is not yet an invasion of the continent, but it is a necessary prologue to such an invasion. This prologue may very well last through 1943.

"It has been said that artillery wins ground and infantry occupies it. Today for artillery we must substitute air power. Pantelleria is a classic and unprecedented example of conquest from the air. We may now ask if the same method can work equally well with a larger island such as Sicily. I do not deny that it may do so. The enemy will first attack all our airfields, destroying planes and installations and disrupting operations in general. When the airfields have been put out of use he will pass without opposition to the destruction of our ground defenses and assure himself of a successful landing. *Our ground defenses are effective only if we have an Air Force to protect them.*

"Under these circumstances our war production must concentrate *entirely* on defensive armaments. And since the most dangerous attack is that made from the air, which opens the way to land invasion, we must bend our every effort to producing:

    a. Fighter planes;

    b. Antiaircraft and antitank guns and their ammunition;

    c. Mines and other weapons of passive defense.

"The production of trucks and other military vehicles can be cut down to essentials. We do not need as many of these as we did during the first phase of the war, when we had to cover enormous distances in Africa. It is equally useless in our present situation to use thousands of workers and much raw material for the construction of bomber planes, of which we could hope, with luck, to obtain no more than a few samples by the latter half of next year.

"Since danger is imminent and our war production cannot be shifted over from one day to the next but will require considerable retooling, it is absolutely necessary that Germany supply us with antiaircraft weapons for our mainland defenses, that is, both fighter planes and guns.

"There is an Italian proverb which says that to go on the defensive is to die. Where a passive defense is concerned this is quite true. But an active defense, on the other hand, may sap the enemy's strength and convince him that his efforts are vain. Today active defense is the job of the Air Force. If ever the enemy holds undisputed sway of our sky nothing is beyond him."

This memorandum was sent to the King on June 12. "It is quite clear," it concluded, "that the repulse of an invasion, especially at the initial stage of the landing, would change the course of the whole war."

In October of 1942 Mussolini already had called a conference of military leaders at Palazzo Venezia in order to discuss strengthening our Air Force. Earlier still, in June of the same year (as we learn from Ambrosio's diary), he had issued the following orders:

Step up the production of planes of the *Centrali Iachino* type.

See to it that we have 3,000 latest-model cannons (90-53 and 75-46 millimeter) and 4,000 smaller-caliber defense guns.

Provide 1,000 high-powered searchlights.

Assign sufficient personnel to antiaircraft service.

Intensify the training of this personnel.

Co-ordinate the functions of the antiaircraft defenses and those of day and night fighter planes.

By the end of June there were many signs that a landing in Sicily was scheduled for the first half of July.

By July 1 we had in Sicily, including the regular Army and the Fascist Militia, 230,000 soldiers, six divisions of which were assigned to the coastal defenses and four (Napoli, Livorno, Assietta, and Aosta) were mobile, plus three German divisions (one of them armored) and our air and naval forces. About 300,000 men in all, supported by a deep defense system. There were no less than 1,500 big guns of every caliber and thousands of machine guns. In short we had everything to make the landing process a difficult one and the possibility, if the worst came to the worst, of delaying the invader by resisting him from the mountainous recesses of the interior.

The landing was prefaced in the usual way by a series of large-scale bombardments, which were regularly described in our communiqués along with the huge number of deaths among the civilian population. From July 1 to

10 the enemy suffered considerable losses in the air, for 312 planes were downed by antiaircraft fire and Axis fighters and much shipping was sunk as well. The attack began on the night of July 9. On the morning of Saturday, July 10, Mussolini had gone to inspect the M Armored Division at Lake Bracciano, where it maneuvered brilliantly under fire. Communiqué number 1141 announced the landing in the following terms: "Last night, supported by powerful air and naval forces and parachute landings, the enemy launched an attack on Sicily. Axis forces are vigorously resisting enemy action and there is fighting along the southeast coast."

The nation held its breath. Various rumors circulated in Rome on Sunday, most of them optimistic, in fact exaggeratedly so, as if defeatists had set them in motion. Communiqué number 1143 of the following day had little to add: "Fierce fighting goes on along the southeast coast of Sicily, where Italian and German troops are energetically opposing and containing the invaders." This communiqué created some uncertainty, for the verb "contain" had been proved by past experience to have a sinister meaning. Monday at one o'clock all Italians waited in suspense to hear the radio and crowds gathered around loud-speakers in the squares. Late the preceding evening it had been announced that Augusta was recaptured from the enemy and that after a counterattack by the Napoli and Göring Divisions a smoke screen sent up by the enemy in the Gela harbor made it look as if the enemy were re-embarking men and supplies. Communiqué 1143 seemed to confirm this rumor:

> "The fighting in Sicily was ceaseless and bitter all day yesterday, when the enemy tried in vain to increase the depth of his narrow coastal holdings. Italian and German troops have definitely begun to counterattack. At several points they have beaten back the enemy and in one sector they forced him to withdraw. Morale is high and the behavior of the civilian population as well as that of the brave Sicilian soldiers among our troops is beyond praise. For a magnificent defense of the positions to which it was assigned special mention should be made of the 206th Coastal Division, under the command of General d'Havet."

Before the release of this communiqué there was a discussion at Palazzo Venezia between the Duce and General Ambrosio, in the presence of other officers. Mussolini thought it was too promising and wanted to tone it down. What was going on in Augusta was far from clear; Guzzoni's telegrams were scanty and his telephone messages couched in vague and hazy terms. General Ambrosio insisted that the news from Guzzoni and his chief assistant, Faldella, justified both the form and content of the communiqué. Needless to say its publication aroused widespread enthusiasm and people imagined that victory was at hand. But the general enthusiasm was dampened by communiqué number 1145, which said: "Continually reenforcing his troops, the enemy has pushed beyond the coastal zone, all the way from Licata to Augusta, into the mountains of southeastern Sicily, overlooking the plain of Catania. Italian and German troops are locked in combat all along the front."

This news was received with astonishment and bitterness. Enthusiasm crumbled and mistrust spread. The discrepancy between the two communiqués was too great. The Italian people's nervous system—although it is not so weak as is generally supposed—had been submitted to too much of a shock. Still they wanted to hope. But number 1147, issued five days after the original landing and speaking already of fighting in the plain of Catania, gave the impression that the game was up. The conquest of all Sicily was inevitable and there was enormous disappointment. Foreign opinion was very severe. The capture almost without a blow of Augusta and Syracuse, the rapid march on Catania and Palermo, and the weak resistance opposed to the early landing were all very mysterious.

IV. INVASION AND CRISIS

WITH FIELD headquarters constantly moving about and communications disrupted it was not easy to size up the situation. There were, however, a few salient facts which are brought out in a memorandum sent on July 14 by the Duce to the Chief of Staff:

"Four days after the enemy landing in Sicily, I consider our situation delicate and disquieting but not irretrievable. We must look at things as they are and decide what it is within our scope to do. Things are at a critical stage, for the reasons outlined below:

"1. The enemy's penetration of the interior has been effected with tremendous speed.

"2. The enemy has crushing superiority in the air.

"3. He has well-trained specialists among his troops (glider pilots and parachutists).

"4. He has complete command of the sea.

"5. His staff work is efficient and adaptable to new situations as they come along.

"Before we decide on a course of action we must know exactly what has happened and what elements, personal and other, brought it about. This is absolutely necessary. The information we have from the enemy (and when he is winning he sticks to the truth) and that received from our German allies both call for a re-examination of what happened during the first days after the landing.

"1. Did our coastal divisions hold out for a long enough time? That is, did they give the minimum of what was expected of them?

"2. Did the second line of defense, with its block-houses, offer resistance or was it too easily swept aside? The enemy seems to have suffered insignificant losses while taking at least 12,000 prisoners.

"3. We must find out what happened at Syracuse, where the enemy found the harbor installations intact, and at Augusta, where there was no resistance worthy of mention and we were led astray by the announcement of the recapture of a base which the enemy had not even occupied.

"4. Were the movements of the mobile Göring, Livorno, and Napoli Divisions made with the necessary promptness and co-ordination? What has become of the Livorno and the Napoli?

"5. Since the enemy is doubtless driving toward the Strait of Messina, have any measures been taken to defend it?

"6. Since the enemy penetration is an accomplished fact, have we the will and the weapons to set up a front in northern Sicily, toward the Tyrrhenian Sea, as was once upon a time considered a possibility?

"7. Have the two remaining divisions, the Assietta and the Aosta, still a chance to do anything in the west and can they handle the situation?

"8. Has something been done or is there any intention of doing something to stop the disorganization among the troops which is added to that among the civilian population after the bombardments rained on the island?

"9. The bad state of communication has given rise to false rumors which have depressed the morale of the country at large.

"In conclusion, we may yet be able to cope with the situation if there is a plan with which to meet it and the courage and equipment to carry it out. The plan must be, in brief, on the following lines:

"1. Resistance at any cost on land.

"2. A blockade of enemy supplies effected by the full power of our fleet and Air Force."

Meanwhile, as preparations were being made to throw up a Tyrrhenian line east of Termini Imerese to protect the Strait of Messina, there were the first rumors of betrayal. Colonel Schmalz, a brigade commander in the German army, sent the following telegram explaining the mystery of Augusta to the German High Command and General Rintelen brought a copy of it to the Duce on July 12:

"Up until today there has been no enemy attack on Augusta. The British have not set foot there at all. In spite of this fact the Italian garrison has blown up guns and munitions and burned a huge gasoline dump. The antiaircraft units at Augusta and Priolo have thrown all their ammunition into the sea and blown up their cannons.

"By the afternoon of July 11 no Italian officers or

soldiers were in the vicinity of the Schmalz brigade. In the morning many officers had abandoned their troops and gone in motor vehicles to Catania and beyond. Many soldiers, alone or in small groups, are roaming the countryside; some of them have thrown away their uniforms and guns and put on civilian clothes."

Amid the plethora of rumors all over the country the commanding admiral of the Navy sent a memorandum (number 28) to the Duce, dated July 15, announcing that there would be an investigation, *which, because of current conditions, would require considerable time*. After making some observations on the previous efficiency of the naval base at Augusta, he admitted that "without doubt the removal and destruction of arms and ammunition north of the town were premature and withdrawal was disorderly."

General Rintelen's note could not go unanswered. On July 18 the Duce sent a message to the Führer, correcting on the basis of the latest information to reach Rome some of the misconceptions of Colonel Schmalz. He said, among other things: "The enemy has opened a second front in Italy and there will now be concentrated the enormous striking power of Britain and the United States, which hope not only to conquer this country but to force their way into the Balkans while Germany is still heavily engaged on the Russian front."

Meanwhile the first eyewitness accounts of recent events were beginning to reach Rome. Here are some excerpts

from a report written by a high official of the Ministry of
Popular Culture who carried out a mission in Sicily from
July 5 to 15. After laying stress on the chaos created by
incessant bombardment, he said:

"In spite of the Sicilians' concern over the present
situation in the interior, I can tell you that up until
July 10 they were resigned (except for outbursts of
wrath against American barbarity) to enduring the
heavy enemy bombardments as an inevitable part of
the war and they had a certain faith in ultimate victory.

"As far as the possibility of an enemy invasion, every
Sicilian declared that any such attempt would be
quickly crushed and all Italy would join in repulsing
an attack on our native land. News of the landing
reached Palermo early in the morning through military
proclamations and later through wall posters and the
newspapers. I can truly say that the population remained calm, and confident that the enemy's attack
would be rapidly overcome. But what did create a certain disturbance was the announcement of a state of
emergency.

"No arrangements had been made in advance to insure the continued functioning of the essential utility
and supply services. Palermo had practically no bread
because the bakers could not buck the flow of refugees
and get through to the city. All transportation was at a
standstill. Finally the civilian and military authorities
agreed to issue a certain number of passes to those wishing to go from one place to another.

"On the third day it was decided to lift the emergency decrees from 5 A. M. to 5 P. M., but it was too late to check the confusion and disorganization caused by the original proclamation. Up to July 12 people were comparatively calm. But the breakdown of telephonic and telegraphic communications and the consequent lack of news soon began to tell. Except for the war communiqués Palermo was cut off from the outside world. Everyone was waiting anxiously to hear a sudden announcement that the enemy had been definitely thrown back, but the communiqués referred only to his being 'contained' by our forces and the general morale began to sink. Even Army officers betrayed a lack of confidence. Weary of waiting for the communiqués, people began to tune in on the London and Algiers radio programs and to absorb news broadcasted by the enemy."

The official tells at this point of his trip from Palermo to Messina and of hearing of the evacuation of Enna. Then he continues:

"On the morning of our arrival in Messina we found the harbor still in flames, the city half destroyed and the population in a state of terror. No one seemed to have foreseen a disaster of such magnitude. At the prefecture, at the commissariat, and on the streets of the untouched higher sections of the city there was open talk of betrayal at Augusta. Everyone, including the military, was in a confused and despairing frame of mind. We were overtaken by an enemy air raid on our way to Punta Faro in search of information from the Germans. On the open road, halfway to our destination, we witnessed four frightful bombardments of Messina,

Villa San Giovanni, and Reggio. Messina was destroyed beneath our very eyes. There was heavy antiaircraft fire, but the aim was poor so that few enemy planes were brought down. Since we could neither go on nor turn back and we were surrounded by straggling, ragged bands of soldiers, sailors, and airmen (particularly the latter two) making their way to the German ferries to the mainland, we thought we might as well cross over the Strait too. There were painful sights in the stations of Scilla and Bagnara. Crowds of soldiers and civilians were storming the trains. Soldiers, sailors, and airmen from Catania, Riposto, and Messina, exhausted from fatigue and hunger, were elbowing their way through the mob, cursing as they went. *Defeat was in the air.* Both at Messina and on the coast of Calabria, Army officers failed to react to the behavior of their men, displaying the same low morale as they did."

This is all we shall quote from the official of the Ministry of Popular Culture. Here is another eyewitness account, from the editor of a newspaper in Palermo:

"In spite of two years of preparation, the military command of Enna, which had its headquarters on an elevation in the center of the island, was not equipped to deal with a simple bombardment and withdrew from the city after the first and last enemy attack from the air. This fact and the rumors about it that spread through the northeastern part of Sicily were bound to create a feeling of abandonment which had the worst possible effects on the spirit of our troops and on our services of supply. In this same region we had a distinct

41

presentiment of a military disaster at the sight of *disorganized troop units* and numbers of individual *sailors and airmen* fleeing in disorderly fashion toward Messina in the hope of getting over to the mainland. The example of Augusta, where no defense was even attempted, and that of several divisions which melted away without ever having engaged in battle are symptomatic of poor leadership. There is something good to be said for the discipline of the Bersaglieri and of the coastal division of Gela. But fatal harm was done by *the Navy and Air Force units which broke up at the mere approach of the enemy.*"

There is a third eyewitness account, relating particularly to Augusta, that of a Fascist Party inspector who gave a report on certain salvage operations. "It is a fact," he said, "that the Augusta base was blown up twenty-four hours before the first British soldier came into view and that before the British arrived, disbanded sailors and airmen had already fled as far as Messina."

We have still another account, given over the telephone by the chief of police of Catania, who said: "Long lines of disbanded and hungry Italian soldiers are streaming into the Mount Etna region, spreading panic and terror before them. The population is afraid of violence and looting."

All over the world the press was surprised by the scanty resistance to the invasion. Here is an editorial which we quote, with due reservations, from the London *Times* (July 22, 1943):

"The Axis armies in Sicily continue to crumble under the Allied blows. Before the invasion it was natural to expect that the Italian troops, who had fought with increasing stubbornness as the Tunisian campaign went against them, would redouble their determination when it came to defending the soil of their native land. That has not been the experience in Sicily. Perhaps they see little point in fighting to save their country for domination by the Germans, perhaps the long-standing unpopularity of Fascism in Sicily has operated on the minds of the garrison as well as of the people; at any rate the resistance of a great part of the defending force has from the first been perfunctory and halfhearted. Especially on the extreme left of the Allied advance the Americans have reported a general readiness to surrender; they have collected thousands of prisoners with very little fighting, and such difficulties as they have encountered in the later stages of their advance have been rather due to the ruggedness of the country than to any resistance by the enemy. Farther to the east, where the invaders have struck deep into the heart of the island, a more resolute attempt has been made to bar their way, since they were approaching the important rail and road junction of Enna, the node of the communications of all the southern part of Sicily. Yesterday, however, this important key city was evacuated by the Italians and immediately occupied by the Canadians and Americans; they have pushed on over the mountainous ridge which forms the backbone of the island and now have only forty miles, though over difficult country, to traverse before reaching the northern shore.

"Some of the defeated Italian troops in these western and central sectors are reported to be streaming away to the northeastward; others are complacently waiting to be rounded up into the Allied prison camps."

A week later the game was up. Among conflicting opinions on the course of events one alone was held unanimously by officers and men, civilians and soldiers alike: Everywhere, and especially in the plain of Catania, the Germans fought with great courage.

V. FROM THE MEETING WITH HITLER AT FELTRE TO THE NIGHT SESSION OF THE FASCIST GRAND COUNCIL

THE MILITARY CRISIS could not fail to bring on a political crisis, which was directed against the Fascist regime in the person of its leader. History, modern history in particular, has shown that no regime falls for purely domestic reasons. Scandals, economic stress, and party strife never endanger the existence of a government. These questions concern not the people as a whole but only limited sectors of public opinion. It is defeat in war that brings about the fall of a regime. The empire of Napoleon III fell after Sedan, those of the Hapsburgs, the Hohenzollerns and the Romanoffs after their defeat in the first World War, and the Third Republic in France after Pétain had signed an armistice. It follows, then, that the Italian monarchy and its accomplices had but one purpose: to bring about, through defeat, the fall of Fascism.

Back of this whole maneuver was the King, who thought that a victorious war under Fascist leadership would further weaken his own position. For twenty years he had waited for just such an occasion. He was now on the alert for an attitude of mind among the general population which one spark would kindle into revolt. With the appointment of Scorza as Secretary of the Fascist Party the Regime had intended to tighten its control. And there was a good start in this direction. The plan was to force the monarchy out of the shadows where it was prudently ambushed and at the same time to win the support of the clergy. To this was joined a new system of promotion from the ranks, of social reform, and of rotation of political and military leaders. But peace and quiet were essential to the carrying out of this long-range plan and instead we were harassed by the vicissitudes of war.

Before the invasion of Sicily the new Party Secretary had arranged to hold a series of regional gatherings where Party leaders would speak. It is a known fact that Grandi repulsed every effort made to induce him to be one of the speakers. Scorza wanted to punish him for this "lack of discipline," but he decided that this was not a propitious time for making an issue of it. Grandi's defection was significant. Nevertheless, after Scorza's radio address of July 18, Grandi sent him a telegram of approval from Bologna, saying that he had recognized "the flaming words and spirit of the great men of the Risorgimento." Grandi had displayed equal enthusiasm after Scorza's May 5 speech in the Adriano Theater. And Grandi, clad in regular Party uniform, was one of the leaders who went with Scorza to Palazzo Venezia from which Mussolini was to speak for the last time to the people of Rome.

On this occasion, indeed, Grandi appeared to be deeply moved and cried out: "What a speech! It is like the old days of the March on Rome! Now we are all born again!" A great crowd filled the square to hear Mussolini's brief speech, but the warmth of the public demonstration was noticeably less than on previous occasions, for the people's enthusiasm was tempered by anxiety. After the Sicilian invasion had begun there was no point in organizing the planned regional gatherings. We had to wait to see the outcome of at least the first phase of military operations. The twelve chosen speakers held several meetings in the Party Secretary's offices in the Palazzo Colonna at Rome and Mussolini was asked to receive them. This he did at eight o'clock in the evening of July 16. Those present, along with the Party Secretary, were Farinacci, De Bono, Giuriati, Teruzzi, Bottai, Acerbo, and De Cicco. Mussolini did not seem to enjoy this occasion, since he had a long-standing aversion to meetings with no program planned in advance.

De Bono was the first to speak, asking for detailed news of operations in Sicily. Then Farinacci called insistently for a meeting of the Fascist Grand Council where everyone could have his say. Bottai supported this view, saying that the meeting was necessary "not in order that anyone should evade his responsibilities, but in order that we should all assume them." Giuriati held forth at length on some constitutional question, to which he returned again in a long letter written the next day. Finally Scorza emphasized the need of a shift of military leadership and proposed the names of several of his own favorites, who later turned out to be traitors. Almost all of those present agreed on the necessity of calling a meeting of the Grand Council in order that Mussolini should impart to top-ranking Party leaders news of a kind that could not be given out to the masses.

At the end of the discussion, which because of the lack of previous planning, did no more than reveal a general attitude of doubt, Mussolini announced that he would call the Grand Council together during the last half of the month.

When this decision became known the tension among political cliques was increased. Some people have laughed off the mention of any such cliques but they did really exist, drawing their membership from the thousands of persons in the capital who belonged vaguely to government circles. Every clique was in turn the center of a constellation, and the frame of mind of these constellations was at certain times the frame of mind of the city and, by reflection, of the nation. Party leaders went to and from the Piazza Colonna in droves and everyone asked himself the question: What will the Grand Council decide? War or peace? For there was a definite atmosphere of weariness and defeat and the bad news from Sicily only served to increase it.

In the late afternoon of Sunday, July 18, Mussolini went by plane to Riccione where he listened to Scorza's radio address, whose content was good although the weakness of the speaker's voice was not in keeping with the violence of his terminology. On the morning of July 19 Mussolini flew to Treviso, where he arrived at 8:30 A. M. Field Marshal Keitel arrived at 9 and the Führer a few minutes later.

The meeting was as cordial as ever, but the attitude of the lined-up Air Force officers and the troops was gloomy. Since the Führer had to return to Germany that same afternoon it would have been better to waste no time. Instead of spending three hours going to and from Feltre the conversation could just as well have been held at the airfield headquarters or at the prefecture of Treviso. But a program had been laid down by protocol and no human force was strong enough to change it.

The Führer and Mussolini and their suites traveled for an hour by train. Then after another hour by car they reached the Villa Gaggia. Here were splendid green lawns and a labyrinthine building, which was to haunt some members of the party. It was like a crossword spelled out in stone. After a few moments of rest the conversation began. Those present were the Führer, the Duce, Undersecretary of Foreign Affairs Bastianini, Ambassadors von Mackensen and Alfieri, Italian Chief of Staff Ambrosio, Marshal Keitel, General Rintelen, General Warlimont, Colonel Montezemolo, and a few others of lesser rank.

It was eleven o'clock when the Führer began to speak.

He began with a systematic inventory of our sources of raw materials and the necessity of defending the places where they were to be found. Then he spoke of the general subject of military aviation and its possibilities, both present and future. Finally he touched on the present operations in Sicily and promised to send additional troops and artillery pieces to the scene. He had been talking for half an hour when a pale and harassed official came into the room. He apologized for interrupting, then went over to Mussolini and said: "At this very moment Rome is undergoing a violent air raid."

Mussolini repeated this piece of news out loud to the Führer and the others present, upon whom it made a very painful impression. At intervals during the rest of the Führer's exposition further details of the attack were made known. After this Mussolini and Hitler had a private conversation in the course of which the former stressed the necessity of sending Italy more aid. This conversation continued during the return trip by car and train. As he took leave of Hitler, Mussolini said: "Führer, we are fighting for a common cause!"

It was five o'clock in the afternoon when the Führer's plane left Treviso and half an hour later when Mussolini took off for Rome. Even before flying over Mount Soratte, Rome appeared to those who were in the Duce's plane to be wreathed in black smoke, which they learned later was coming up from hundreds of burning railroad cars at the

Littorio station. The airfield plant was destroyed and the landing strips, dug up by bomb craters, were out of commission. As the plane flew from the Littorio field to that of Centocelle it seemed as if the bombardment had been a very heavy one and caused considerable damage. A few high officials were at hand to greet Mussolini when he landed. He got into a car and was driven to his residence, the Villa Torlonia. Along the streets a crowd of men, women, and children, loaded with various household belongings, were making their way by car or bicycle or on foot to the suburbs and surrounding countryside. A great multitude, indeed a human flood.

There was no more room for the old illusion that Rome, the holy city, would never be the object of an air attack— or that the best antiaircraft battery was the Vatican; that Myron Taylor had brought the Pope a formal guarantee of immunity from the President of the United States, etc.

All this pack of hopes and wishes had been shattered by a brutal three-hour air raid which had killed thousands of people and destroyed whole sections of the city.

It is not true, as rumor had it, that rocks were thrown at the King when he visited the scenes of the damage but the crowd around him was silent to the point of hostility.

The next day Mussolini visited the Littorio railroad station and airfield, the university campus, and the Ciampino airfield. Everywhere along the way he was received in a friendly fashion. On Wednesday morning he went to give the King an account of his conversation with the Führer.

As he later confided to some of his friends, Mussolini found the King frowning and nervous. "The situation is tense," the King said. "Things can't go on like this for long. Sicily is done for. One of these days the Germans will trick us. Discipline among the troops is very poor. When Ciampino was attacked all the personnel stationed there fled as far as Velletri, under the pretext of 'scattering,' as they called it. I watched the recent raid from the Villa Ada and the enemy planes flew straight overhead. There weren't four hundred of them, as people are saying. No more than half that many, in my opinion. The 'holy city' game is over. We must put our problem up to the Germans. . . ."

The above is a brief summary of what he said in this conversation, which was the last of a long series of bi-weekly interviews held over the years. Ever since November, 1922, Mussolini had gone regularly every Monday and Thursday at half-past ten in the morning, in civilian clothes and a derby, to the Quirinal Palace, accompanied by the undersecretary attached to the Prime Ministry. There were many other unscheduled meetings between them, especially during the Army's summer maneuvers, when they talked almost every day. Mussolini was never the King's guest at his country estate at San Rossore and only once at the Villa Ada, in Rome, when he saw an after-dinner showing of a film of the King's trip to Somaliland. He was invited once to Sant'-Anna di Valdieri and twice to Racconigi, the first time for a wedding and the second in order to report on the negotiations preliminary to the Lateran Treaty.

The King was only once a guest of the Duce at Rocca delle Caminate, and that was after the conquest of the Empire. Their relations were cordial but not friendly, for there was always something between them that prevented any real intimacy. During both wars the King had shown himself to be hesitant and easily influenced. Except in 1940, when he not only raised no objections but considered it absolutely necessary to fight Great Britain and France. In the later part of the war, however, this attitude changed.

Wednesday noon, at the time when he made a regular report, Party Secretary Scorza brought Mussolini the text of a three-page resolution which Grandi and others were planning to set before the Grand Council. Mussolini read it through and returned it, with the comment that it was cowardly and quite inadmissible. Scorza put it back in his brief case without insisting further. At this point Scorza spoke to the Duce in somewhat ambiguous terms of "something fishy, very fishy indeed," to neither of which phrases the Duce paid any particular attention. In the afternoon the Duce saw Grandi, who gave him a volume of the minutes of the London meetings of the Committee of Nonintervention in the Spanish War. Grandi talked of various things, but said not a word of what was hatching.*

* See Preface, p. 65; and Grandi's article in *Life* magazine, February 26, 1945.

The following day, Thursday, Scorza referred again to "something very fishy," but without defining what he meant. Mussolini imagined that he was clamoring as usual for the replacement of high military and political leaders.

On both Thursday and Friday there was much coming and going in the Piazza Colonna, where Scorza had his office. At a certain moment Grandi suggested postponing the Council meeting, a very clever maneuver on his part and one planned to furnish him with an alibi. Scorza telephoned the Duce to hear what he thought of this suggestion. Mussolini replied that it was absolutely necessary to clear the air, that the date had been set and announcements sent out. Of all the governmental organs, such as the Chamber of Deputies and the Senate, whose convocation was discussed at this time, the Grand Council was by far the best suited to discussion of the new military problems arising from the invasion of Italian soil.

Tension increased from hour to hour and in the late afternoon and evening of July 24, Rome was visibly pale. Every city has a countenance of its own, which betrays the feelings that assail it. And on this occasion Rome felt that something grave was in the air. The cars which brought the Council members to the meeting were parked not in the square outside but in an inner courtyard. And the musketeers who always stood guard over Palazzo Venezia were relieved that evening of the task they had long performed so faithfully.

VI. THE GRAND COUNCIL MEETING

I T WAS Mussolini's intention that the Grand Council meeting should be of a confidential character and that everyone should ask questions and obtain answers. Foreseeing a long discussion he had called the meeting for five instead of ten o'clock in the evening.

The members of the Grand Council were all in Fascist uniform. The meeting opened promptly at five o'clock and the Duce ordered Scorza to call the roll. No one was missing. Mussolini, with a stack of papers before him, began to talk. The main points he made, as recorded by one of those present, were the following:

"The war [he said] has come to an extremely critical phase. The invasion of the national territory, which everyone thought was quite out of the question, even after the United States had broken into the Mediterranean, has actually come to pass. We may even say that the real war began for us with the loss of Pantelleria. The peripheral war on the African coast served the purpose of making impossible the invasion of the country. In a situation like the present one, all open and hidden opposition to the Fascist regime is leagued against us and there has already been considerable demoralization even in the Fascist ranks, particularly among those who

have come to have a vested interest in the present setup
and are afraid that their personal position is in danger.
At this moment I am easily the most disliked and, in
fact, hated man in Italy. No wonder that the ignorant
and struggling masses hate me after all they have gone
through in the way of hunger and destruction and demoralizing effects of the 'liberators' ' air raids and radio propaganda. The bitterest criticism is naturally
directed against those who are responsible for the military aspect of the war. Let it be said once and for all
that I never sought for the command of the Armed
Forces which was made over to me by the King on June
10, 1940, when we declared war. This was Marshal
Badoglio's idea.*

"I have here a letter from Badoglio, number 5372,
dated May 3, 1940, referring to organization of the high
command, addressed to the Duce of Fascism and Head
of the Government:
'With my number 5318 of April 15 I had the honor
of calling to your attention the absolute necessity of
obtaining an organization of the high command such
as to define the tasks and responsibilities of the various Army leaders. At a meeting held in your office,
Duce, on that same day, you gave me oral assurance
that this important problem would be settled within
the same week. Since up to date I have received no

* More than two years before receiving the Badoglio letter that Mussolini quotes in the following paragraph, Mussolini in a speech to the
Senate on March 31, 1938, proclaimed, "The war, as it has been in Africa,
will be led, according to the orders of the King, by only one man, the man
who is speaking to you now." See Monelli, *Roma 1943*, Rome, 1945, p. 164.

communication from you on this subject, I venture to set forth my opinion in some detail.'

"Badoglio favored the German solution of this problem rather than the French. This was in accord with the precedent created during the first World War when the King of Italy held the purely nominal post of commander in chief whereas the Chief of Staff actually commanded the Army. Badoglio's letter went on as follows: 'After the last war Italy was the first to recognize the necessity of a unified command. There was created the office of Chief of Staff, but its duties were defined only for time of peace. Now we can no longer delay organizing our high command and defining the powers and responsibilities of the leaders.'

"Badoglio, then, favored the German system because it would make his own position as Chief of Staff one of conspicuous importance. He concluded his letter by saying: 'Duce, I consider it my absolute duty to tell you, as I have always done in the past, exactly what is on my mind. I am not motivated by pride but by a natural concern for the good name which I won for myself at the cost of hard work and sacrifice in the last war and in the Libyan and Ethiopian campaigns. *My only pride lies in the fact that I have always served you faithfully and with unlimited devotion.*'

"On June 4, six days before our entrance into the war, a circular announcement, number 5569, was sent to all the members of the General Staff, to the governors of the various colonies, and to the Minister of Foreign Affairs, entitled *The Structure and Functioning of the*

Supreme Command of the Armed Forces in the Eventuality of War:

" 'There is need for clarification and definition of the structure and functioning of the Supreme Command of the Armed Forces in the eventuality of war.

1. " 'His Majesty the King has delegated to the Duce the post of Commander in Chief of all the Armed Forces, wherever they may be.

2. " 'The Duce exercises this command through the Chief of Staff, who directs the General Staff officers. The duties of the Chief of Staff are as follows: *a.* To keep the Duce informed of the general military situation of the Armed Forces and their strategic possibilities, particularly in relation to the situation of the enemy; hence to receive from the Duce general directives for the conduct of military operations. *b.* To pass on to the General Staff representatives of the various branches of the service directives for the actual carrying out of these operations. *c.* To follow the course of operations and to step in whenever necessary, particularly in order to insure the coordinated and timely use of the Armed Forces.'

"After defining the tasks of the various General Staff officers the announcement concluded:

" 'The organization of the Supreme Command of the Italian Armed Forces, which is different from that of any other nation, is based on the following principles: *a.* There is to be a unified and totalitarian conception of the command delegated by the King to the Duce and personally exercised by him. *b.* The strategic conduct of the war and the co-ordination of action among the various branches of the service and among the various areas involved in the fighting are to be directed by the Duce and carried out by the Chief of Staff. *c.* Practical command of the Armed Forces both at home and abroad is to be exercised by the Chief of Staff or the heads of the various branches of the service. *d. There is to be absolute devotion and obedience to the Duce and disciplined thought and action on the part of all, according to true Fascist custom.'*

"This is how things actually were. Mussolini never assumed the technical direction of military operations, nor was it his job to do so. Only once, because Cavallero was away, did he take over the task of the Staff technicians, and that was on the occasion of the air and naval engagement off Pantelleria on June 15, 1942. This clearcut victory was to the credit of Mussolini alone, which fact is acknowledged in a report to the officers of the Seventh Naval Division by Admiral Riccardi, Naval Chief of Staff, just before Mussolini decorated the officers and men who distinguished themselves in the battle. Indeed, it was at Pantelleria that Great Britain felt for the first time in her own flesh, the sharp teeth of the Roman Wolf.

"When Mussolini fell ill in October of 1942 he thought of giving up his military command and the only reason he did not do so was because he did not wish to abandon the helm in the midst of the storm. He decided to wait for a 'sunny day,' which, alas, has not yet come. This is all there is to say on the subject of military command.

"Some people have thrown doubt on the extent of German aid. But we must honestly admit that the Germans have helped us in a comradely and generous manner. With an eye to the Grand Council meeting Mussolini had asked the Minister of Supplies to give him figures of the amounts of various raw materials sent to us by the Germans in 1940, 1941, 1942, and the first half of 1943. The figures are impressive: coal—40,000,000 tons; steel—2,500,000 tons; buna (synthetic rubber)—22,000 tons; airplane fuel—220,000 tons; naphtha—241,000 tons; without even quoting the lesser amounts of such indispensable metals as nickel. After the heavy bombardments of Milan, Genoa, and Turin in October of 1942 the Führer was asked to bolster our air-raid defenses, and he did so. According to the figures of General Balocco, secretary of the Supreme Commission for Defense, there were 1,500 German big guns in Italy on April 1, 1943. The defeatists are in error when they claim that Germany did not give us sufficient aid. Another defeatist argument is that 'there was no popular feeling for this war.' But as far as that goes there is no popular feeling for any war and never has been, not even, as can be proved by a multitude of documents, for the wars of our Risorgimento. But let us not trouble the great shades of our past; let us look at more recent examples. Take the former World War. Was popular feeling in its favor? Not at all. The people were dragged into the war by a minority which managed to carry three big cities, Milan,

Genoa, and Rome, and a few smaller ones such as Parma. Three men gave rise to the movement on behalf of intervention, Corridoni, D'Annunzio, and Mussolini, but there was no 'sacred unity' of feeling.

"The country was divided between interventionists and isolationists and this division continued even after Caporetto. Was popular feeling back of a war in which there were 535,000 deserters? The present war surely enjoys greater support than that. The truth of the matter is that 'popular feeling' is never enthused about any war at the start. If a war is successful it is popular; otherwise it is not. Our war for Ethiopia became popular only after the victory of Mai Ceu. We must not be influenced by psychological oscillations, even when, as at present, they seem very serious. The masses of the people must be disciplined, that is all that matters.

"War is always the responsibility of the party or political group that brings it on; it is the responsibility of the man who declares it. The war of today is Mussolini's war, just as the war of 1859 was Cavour's war. This is a time for closing ranks and assuming responsibilities. I am perfectly ready to change leaders, to put on the screws, to call upon reserves as yet untapped, all in the name of our invaded country. In 1917 several provinces in the Venetian region were lost, but no one spoke of surrender. There was talk then of moving the government to Sicily; today, if need be, we shall move it to the Po valley.

"Grandi's proposed resolution is an invitation to the Crown; it appeals not to the government but to the King. Now there are two alternatives. The King may say to me:

My dear Mussolini, things have not gone very well of late, but this difficult phase of the war may be followed by something better. You have begun and you must carry on. Or else, as is more likely, the King may say: My Fascist friends, now that you are in hot water you have suddenly remembered Article 5 of the Constitution and the fact that you have a King as well as a Constitution. Very well then, I, Victor Emmanuel, who have been accused of having violated the Constitution for the twenty years of your rule, shall now step up to the footlights and accept your invitation. But since I hold you responsible for the present situation I shall take advantage of the occasion you are giving me to liquidate you one and all.

"That is what reactionary and anti-Fascist circles and all those who favor the Anglo-Saxons will try to persuade the King to do.

"Gentlemen, watch out! Grandi's resolution may endanger the Fascist regime."

These were the highlights of Mussolini's talk as they were jotted down by one of his listeners. There followed a period of discussion. Marshal De Bono spoke first, defending the Army from the charge of having "sabotaged" the war. De Vecchi (one of the original Fascist quadrumvirate), who only a few days before had suddenly intrigued for a military command and obtained that of a coastal division stationed between Civitavecchia and Orbetello, did not back up what De Bono had said. He stated, rather, that many generals and other high-ranking officers had a weary and defeatist attitude which was extremely bad for the morale of the troops.

Next Grandi took the floor and pronounced a violent philippic, the speech of a man who was at last giving vent to a long-suppressed rancor. He bitterly criticized the activities of the Party, particularly under the leadership of Starace (of whom he had once been an enthusiastic supporter). He declared himself equally disappointed in that of Scorza, in spite of its promising beginnings. "My resolution," he said, "aims at creating a united front, such as we have not had so far because the Crown has held itself prudently apart. It is time for the King to step forward and assume his responsibilities. During the last war, after our defeat at Caporetto, he took a firm stand and launched an appeal to the people. Today he is silent. He must assume his share of responsibility before history, in which case he has a right to remain head of the nation, otherwise he himself is a witness to the weakness of the dynasty."

The purpose of Grandi's maneuver, which had been concocted with the aid of Court circles, was quite obvious and his words created a feeling of uneasiness among the members of the Grand Council. The next speaker was Count Ciano, who sketched the diplomatic background of the war, in order to show that Italy had done nothing to provoke war, but had on the contrary done everything possible to prevent its explosion. He concluded by declaring himself in agreement with the Grandi resolution. A reply to Grandi's defeatist strictures was made by General Galbiati, who spoke as a soldier and veteran Black Shirt, in a lyrical rather than a political vein. Roberto Farinacci then proposed a resolution of his own and asked the Grand Council to call for a report from General Ambrosio. This suggestion was not followed.

The next speaker was Suardo, President of the Senate, who said that he did not fully understand Grandi's resolution, especially after the explanation furnished by its author, and that, failing clarification, he intended to refrain from voting on it.

Then came the Minister of Justice, De Marsico, who staged a rhetorical display on the question of the constitutionality of Grandi's resolution. Bottai spoke heatedly in Grandi's favor and Biggini against him.

At midnight Party Secretary Scorza proposed adjourning until the next day. Grandi jumped to his feet, shouting: "No. I am against this proposal. Now that we are here we must finish things up in one session." The Duce agreed, and suspended the discussion for a quarter of an hour while he went to his study and read the latest telegrams from the front.

When the meeting was resumed the first speaker was Bignardi, who spoke of the attitude of the peasants. Frattari spoke on the same theme. Federzoni touched on the "lack of popular feeling for the war" and Bastianini echoed him on this subject, criticizing the efforts of the

Ministry of Propaganda. He deplored the fact that instructions had been issued to minimize the memory of our victory on the Piave during the first World War, and on this point he had a fierce argument with Polverelli. This was the only time when voices were raised during the whole evening.

Cianetti and Bottai spoke again, the latter more excitedly than before. Then came the turn of Scorza, who proposed a resolution not very different from Grandi's. He criticized the General Staff and defended the Fascist Party from Grandi's accusations, saying that it would be the basic element of a united front. After the reading of the Scorza resolution Count Ciano rose and said that any reference to the Vatican would not be well received beyond its bronze doors. The discussion had now lasted almost ten hours, but in spite of the tense atmosphere there had been no violent incidents of a personal nature.

All the rumors of a hand-to-hand scuffle and pointed guns were made up out of whole cloth. The discussion was ordered and gentlemanly and there were no excesses of any kind. But every time the speakers flattered Mussolini to the point of exaggeration he interrupted and begged them to stop.

Before a vote was taken the position of every single member of the Grand Council was clear. There was one group of traitors, who had made a pact with the King, another group of their accomplices, and a third group of innocents who had no idea how serious it all was but cast their vote anyway.

The Party Secretary read the Grandi resolution and called out the names of all those present. Nineteen voted for it and seven against. Suardo did not vote and Farinacci voted alone for his own resolution.*

Mussolini got up and said: *"You have brought the Regime into crisis. The meeting is adjourned!"*

Scorza was about to give the signal for the ritual "Salute to the Duce," but Mussolini raised a hand to stop him and said: "No. I excuse you from that!"

Everyone went away in silence. It was 2:40 A.M. of July 25. The Duce withdrew to his study where he was joined by the group of those who had voted against the Grandi resolution. It was three o'clock when Mussolini left Palazzo Venezia. Scorza went with him to the Villa Torlonia. The streets were empty. But there was in the gray early morning air the feeling of inevitability that is created by the turning wheel of fate, of which men are often the unwitting cogs.**

* The German censor suppressed all references to the Farinacci resolution which, Mussolini had written in his manuscript, "did not differ very much from the one Grandi had proposed." The only mention of the Farinacci resolution the German censor allowed is in the record of the vote. But even here some of Mussolini's words were penciled out by the censor. "Farinacci voted for himself," Mussolini wrote. The German censor thought this expression was unkind to Farinacci and replaced it with the one that appears in the text. See Amicucci, *I 600 giorni di Mussolini*, Rome, 1948, p. 171.

** Text of the Grandi resolution: "The Grand Council of Fascism, reconvened in this hour of supreme trial, turns its thoughts, first of all, to the heroic fighters in every branch of the Army who—side by side with

During this night, which will be remembered as the night of the Grand Council meeting, there had been ten hours of discussion, making it one of the longest sessions of its kind on record. Everyone present spoke at least once and some several times. A crisis might have come on even if this meeting had never taken place, if no discussion had been held and no resolution voted. But history does not take into account mere hypotheses. What happened next happened after the Grand Council meeting. Perhaps the situation was already strained, but this was the straw that broke the camel's back.

the proud people of Sicily, splendid example of the unanimous faith of the Italian people—are renewing the noble traditions of bravery and the indomitable spirit of sacrifice of our glorious Armed Forces;

"Having examined the domestic and international situation and the political and military conduct of the war;

"Proclaims the sacred duty of all Italians to defend at all costs the unity, the independence, the freedom of the fatherland; the fruits of the sacrifices and efforts of four generations from the Risorgimento to the present; the life and future of the Italian people;

"Affirms the necessity of moral and physical unity among all Italians in this grave hour of decision for the destiny of the nation;

"Declares that to achieve that end it is imperative to restore to their original power all the organs of the state and to assign to the Crown, the Grand Council, the Government, the Parliament and the Corporations the tasks and responsibilities established by our basic constitutional laws;

"Invites the Government to beg His Majesty the King—toward whom the whole nation turns a faithful and trusting heart—to assume for the honor and salvation of the fatherland, together with the active command of the Armed Forces on the ground, at sea and in the air, (according to Article 5 of the Constitution of the Realm) that supreme initiative of leadership which our institutions assign to Him and which has always been in our whole history the glorious heritage of our august dynasty of Savoy."

VII. FROM VILLA SAVOIA TO PONZA

ON THE MORNING of Sunday, July 25, Mussolini went to his office, as he had gone for nearly twenty-one years, arriving there at about nine o'clock. Since early in the morning wild rumors had been spread concerning the meeting of the Grand Council, but the outward appearance of the city, flooded by the bright summer sun, was fairly quiet. Scorza did not show up, but he telephoned to say that "the night had brought good counsel and several hotheads had seen the error of their ways." "Too late!" was Mussolini's reply. Indeed, a few minutes later there arrived a letter from Cianetti, saying that he had not realized the serious implications of the Grandi resolution and was sorry to have voted for it. At the same time he resigned from his post as Minister of Corporations and asked to be called up to active duty in his capacity as an artillery captain. This letter, to which Mussolini made no answer, was later to save the life of its author.

Meanwhile Grandi could not be found all morning long. Fascist Militia Headquarters had no news report. General Galbiati was summoned to Palazzo Venezia at one o'clock.

68

At about eleven, Albini, Undersecretary of the Ministry of the Interior, brought the Duce his usual summary of the news of the last twenty-four hours. One remarkable and painful item was the first heavy air raid on Bologna. When Mussolini had finished reading he said to Albini: "Why did you vote last night for Grandi's resolution? You're not a regular member of the Grand Council; you were only a guest at the meeting." Poor Albini seemed embarrassed by this question; he blushed and came out with a flood of protestations: "Perhaps I was wrong. But no one can throw any doubt on my long-standing devotion to your person." Then he went blushing away. Later on, this traitor was to stand in line to beg Badoglio for a post of even the humblest kind, offering himself for any task, no matter how abject. A little later Mussolini told his private secretary to telephone General Puntoni and ask him at what hour of the afternoon the King would receive the Head of the Government, who would come to this appointment in civilian clothes. General Puntoni replied that the King would see Mussolini at the Villa Ada at five o'clock. Party Secretary Scorza called again in order to read the text of a letter which he proposed to send to the members of the Grand Council, saying: "The Duce has asked me to tell you that, having called the Council together in accordance with the law of December 9, 1928, for a consultation on the political situation, he has taken note of the various resolutions proposed at the meeting and of the statement of your point of view." From this letter, which was never sent out (and indeed it would have been quite useless to send it), it appears that Scorza foresaw a normal development of the situation. At about one o'clock Mussolini received a visit from the Japanese ambassador, Hidaka, accompanied by Undersecretary of Foreign Affairs Bastianini, to whom he gave an account of his meeting with Hitler. This conversation lasted for about an hour.

At two o'clock the Duce, with General Galbiati, went to visit the Tiburtino section of Rome, which had been particularly hard hit by the terror raid of July 19. The Duce was surrounded by an applauding crowd of bombed-out people. At three o'clock he went back to the Villa Torlonia.

At ten minutes to five Mussolini's private secretary came to go with him to the Villa Ada. The Duce was completely calm. He took with him a volume containing the Constitution of the Grand Council, Cianetti's letter, and other papers which made it clear that the resolution passed by the Grand Council was not binding upon anyone because of the Council's purely advisory function. Mussolini thought that probably the King would relieve him of the command of the Armed Forces, delegated to him on June 10, 1940, which he had for some time wished to give up. In other words, Mussolini arrived at the Villa Ada without any misgivings. His frame of mind might be called in retrospect positively naive.

At exactly five o'clock the car went through the gate on

the Via Salaria. Around and about there were large numbers of carabinieri, but about this there was nothing unusual. The King, wearing the uniform of a marshal, stood on the steps of the villa. In the hall were two officers. The King was unusually excited, his face was distraught, and he spoke indistinctly. Leading his guest into the drawing room he said: "My dear Duce, it can't go on any longer. Italy is in pieces. Army morale has reached the bottom and the soldiers don't want to fight any longer. The Alpine regiments have a song saying that they are through fighting Mussolini's war." Here he recited in Piedmontese dialect several verses of this song.

"The result of the votes cast by the Grand Council is devastating. Nineteen votes in favor of Grandi's resolution, and four of them cast by holders of the *Collare dell'Annunziata* [Italy's highest decoration]. Surely you have no illusions as to how Italians feel about you at this moment. You are the most hated man in Italy; you have not a single friend left, except for me. You need not worry about your personal security. I shall see to that. I have decided that the man of the hour is Marshal Badoglio. He will form a cabinet of career officials in order to rule the country and go on with the war. Six months from now we shall see. All Rome knows about what went on at the Grand Council meeting and everyone expects drastic changes to be made."

"You are making an extremely grave decision," Mussolini answered. "If you provoke a crisis at a time like this

71

the people will believe that, since you are eliminating the man who declared war, then peace must be at hand. You will strike a serious blow at the morale of the Army. The fact that our troops—the Alpine regiments or the others—won't go on with the war for Mussolini is of no importance, provided they are willing to fight for you. The crisis will be claimed as a personal triumph by both Churchill and Stalin, especially the latter, whose antagonist I have been for the last twenty years. I am perfectly aware that the people hate me. I admitted as much last night before the Grand Council. No one can govern for so long and impose so many sacrifices without incurring more or less bitter resentment. Be that as it may, I wish good luck to my successor."

It was exactly twenty minutes past five when the King escorted Mussolini to the door. His face was livid and he seemed even shorter than usual, as if he had shrunk. He shook hands with Mussolini and went back inside. Mussolini went down a few steps and walked toward his car.

All of a sudden a captain of the Carabinieri stopped him and said these exact words: "His Majesty has charged me with your personal security." Mussolini started to walk on toward his car, but the captain pointed to an ambulance parked near by and said: "No. You must get into this." Mussolini got into the ambulance along with De Cesare, his private secretary. The captain followed them, with a lieutenant, three carabinieri, and two plainclothes men who stood at the door with machine guns. The door was closed and the ambulance started off at high speed. Mussolini still thought that all this was in order to insure what the King had called his "personal security." After half an hour the ambulance came to a stop at some Carabinieri barracks. All the windows of the main building were closed but Mussolini could see that it was surrounded by guards with drawn bayonets and an officer was stationed in the room next to where he waited. An hour later he was taken in the same ambulance to the barracks of the Carabinieri cadets.

It was seven o'clock. The second-in-command of the school seemed to be deeply moved at the sight of Mussolini and murmured vague words of sympathy. Next he was taken to a room which served as the office of the commanding officer, Colonel Tabellini, while an officer mounted guard in the room next door.

During the evening several officers came to see Mussolini, among them Chirico, Bonitatibus, and Santillo, who talked about inconsequential subjects. They continued to speak of protective custody and of how this delicate task had been entrusted to the Carabinieri. Mussolini did not touch any food. He asked to go out of the room and an officer accompanied him down the hall. Mussolini noticed at this time that there were three carabinieri outside the door of this third-floor office. Then for the first time the doubt occurred to him: Is it protection or is it arrest?

Of course the police knew that there were plots against Mussolini's life. But they always maintained—especially under the unfortunate leadership of Chierici—that these were very amateurish affairs of no practical consequence. They were nothing more than expressions of a perfectly understandable discontent. It is worth while noting here that Chierici's appointment as chief of police was strongly supported by Albini.

But Mussolini wondered, what threat against his life could there be in barracks filled with at least two thousand carabinieri cadets? How could any conspirators get at him? What danger was there of "popular fury"? At about eleven o'clock Mussolini put out the light. But a lamp stayed on in the next room, where an officer kept permanent watch and never answered the telephone.

At one o'clock in the morning of July 26 Lieutenant Colonel Chirico came into the Duce's room and said, "General Ferone has just come with a message for you from Marshal Badoglio." Mussolini got up and went into the next room. He had met General Ferone in Albania. Now there was a look of strange satisfaction on his face. The green envelope was from the Ministry of War and was addressed in the Marshal's handwriting to "Cavaliere Benito Mussolini." The letter read:

"YOUR EXCELLENCY, CAVALIERE BENITO MUSSOLINI—
The undersigned Head of the Government wishes to inform Your Excellency that all the measures carried out in connection with you have been inspired by your own interest, since we have information from several

sources of a plot against your life. With all due regret for these circumstances he wishes you to know that he is ready to give orders that you be safely and honorably escorted to whatever locality you may choose.

The Head of the Government:
MARSHAL BADOGLIO."

This letter, of a perfidy unique in history, was designed to convince Mussolini that the King's pledge of his personal security would be maintained and that the crisis would not mean the overthrow of the whole Fascist regime. Badoglio had all too many times recorded his loyalty to the Party, of which he and his wife and family were regularly inscribed members. He had held all too many posts of responsibility under the Regime. He had carried out all too many military and political mandates of the greatest importance. He had accepted all too many honors and all too much money. For all these reasons it was inconceivable that he should have been plotting treason for months past, possibly from the day when he was removed from the rank of Chief of Staff. Since this time he had consented to serve the Regime in the National Research Council, where all he did was to put in a daily appearance in order to read the papers. From the moment when he had entered the cadet barracks Mussolini had had no news of the outside world. He was told only that the King had issued a proclamation and Badoglio another, announcing that the war would go on; that the city was quiet and that the people thought peace was imminent.

75

After reading Badoglio's letter Mussolini dictated a reply to General Ferone, who took it down with his own hand. It consisted of the following points:

"July 26, 1943—one o'clock

"1. I wish to thank Marshal Badoglio for the attentions which he has seen fit to bestow upon me.

"2. The only residence at my disposition is Rocca delle Caminate, where I am ready to be transferred at a moment's notice.

"3. In memory of our former collaboration I wish to assure Marshal Badoglio that I shall not only place no difficulties in his way but that I shall fully co-operate with him.

"4. I am pleased with the decision to go on with the war at the side of our ally as the interests and honor of our country require. I hope that success may crown the grave task which Marshal Badoglio is about to undertake in the name and under the orders of His Majesty the King, whose loyal servant I still am, as I have been for twenty-one years past. Long live Italy!" *

This is the only communication sent by Mussolini to Badoglio. He never sent a single word to the King. In this letter, which Badoglio never dared make public, but which he quoted to his intimates in a mutilated version, Mussolini showed that he believed in all good faith that, although the Marshal might alter the composition of the government, he would not deviate from the policy of continuing the war.

* See Preface, p. 25.

After General Ferone had gone Mussolini retired, staying awake, however, until the early hours of the next morning.

All day Monday the pretense of Mussolini's retirement to a "private residence" was maintained. Various people said at intervals during the day that Rocca delle Caminate was an ideal spot from the standpoint of "personal security," that the general in charge of the Carabinieri in the Bologna region had already inspected the site and declared it admirably suited to this purpose, that orders were expected at any moment specifying the means of transportation, which would probably be effected by air. So the day went by, with no further news. Mussolini was told that everything was all right with his family at the Villa Torlonia, which was not true. In the evening Major Bonitatibus set up an army cot in Colonel Tabellini's office for Mussolini. All the next morning, that of July 27, the same pretense of imminent departure went on, without any practical consequences. But there was an atmosphere of increased watchfulness. At seven o'clock in the evening a platoon of carabinieri and one of city police took up their station near a group of auto vehicles in the courtyard of the barracks, whose opposite wall bore on it in large painted letters the famous watchwords: "Believe, Obey, Fight!" Toward eight o'clock several carloads of officers arrived on the scene.

Finally an officer went to the middle of the courtyard and shouted to the cadets, who were hanging out of their windows, attracted by the unusual commotion below, "Stay in the dormitories! All windows closed!"

It was already dark when an officer came into the room and said to Mussolini, "Orders to go have come through!"

Mussolini went down, accompanied by a group of officers of whom he took leave on the ground floor. As he was getting into a car a general came up and introduced himself:

"Brigadier General Polito, chief of the Military Police attached to General Staff Headquarters!"

Mussolini was convinced that the goal of this night journey was Rocca delle Caminate and asked no questions. The side curtains were pulled down but through a crack Mussolini saw that the car was passing in front of the Santo Spirito Hospital. Apparently it was leaving Rome on the Via Appia rather than the Via Flaminia. At the innumerable road blocks along the way the carabinieri on guard, warned by advance couriers, slowed down the car without stopping it. When they came to the main road to Albano, Mussolini asked:

"Where are we going?"

"South."

"Not to Rocca delle Caminate?"

"That order was countermanded."

"And who are you? I once knew a police inspector by the name of Polito."

"I am he."

"And how did you become a general?"

"It is the military equivalent of my civilian rank."

Mussolini had known Inspector Polito well. He had performed several remarkable feats for the Regime, including the capture of Cesare Rossi at Campione and that of the Pintor band in Sardinia. During the trip he told a host of interesting and unpublicized details of these two cases. After Cisterna the car slackened its pace. Polito, who had been smoking uninterruptedly, lowered a window and asked Colonel Pelaghi of the carabinieri where they were.

"Near Gaeta," was the reply.

"Is Gaeta to be my new home?" Mussolini asked. "Where Mazzini was jailed? I am overcome by the honor."

"It's not yet settled," Polito retorted.

When they arrived at Gaeta, where the streets were empty, a man flagged them with a lantern. The car stopped and a Navy officer called out:

"To the Ciano Pier!"

Admiral Maugeri was waiting at the pier and took Mussolini aboard the corvette *Persefone,* which soon raised anchor and sailed away. Dawn was at hand. Mussolini went below with the officers who had accompanied him. After daybreak the ship stopped within sight of the island of Ventotene and Inspector Polito went ashore to see if it was suitable for Mussolini. Soon he came back with a negative verdict, based on the fact that there was a German garrison on the island. The corvette proceeded to the island of Ponza, anchoring in the harbor at one o'clock in the afternoon of July 28. Polito came over to Mussolini and pointed to a greenish house, half hidden by some beached fishing boats. "There is your temporary home," he said. Meanwhile, by some strange chance, men and women, armed with field glasses, crowded to the windows and balconies and watched the small boat that was put ashore. In an instant the whole island seemed to know of the arrival.

Toward evening several of the inhabitants came to see Mussolini and a gift arrived from the fishermen of Terracina. There was no sign of anything like "popular fury," but with the arrival of more guards there was increased watchfulness and Mussolini was cut off from all connections with the outside world.

It was at Ponza that Mussolini came to understand the wretched conspiracy that had eliminated him from the political scene and began to believe that surrender would be the next step, followed by his delivery into enemy hands.

The days at Ponza dragged slowly by. New officers came, Lieutenant Colonel Meoli and Second Lieutenant Elio di Lorenzo, and Sergeant Antichi. There were a number of anti-Fascist political prisoners and Balkan internees on the island and the local garrison was re-enforced. Mussolini was allowed two swims in a prearranged and carefully guarded spot. He had access to no newspapers and the only communication he received was an eloquent telegram from Göring.

Mussolini spent these days in complete solitude, translating the *Odi barbare* of Carducci into German and reading a *Life of Jesus* by Giuseppe Ricciotti, which he left as a gift to the parish priest.

Ponza cannot be compared to Ischia, much less to Capri. But it has a rustic beauty of its own and a history of famous imprisonments.

Mussolini was informed by someone who knew that such illustrious characters of antiquity as Agrippina the mother of Nero, and Julia, the daughter of Augustus were banished there, not to mention the saintly figure of Flavia Domitilla and, in 538, a pope, Saint Sylvester Martyr. Then, after a lapse of many centuries, such well-known contemporaries as Torrigiani, Grand Master of the Free Masons, General Bencivenga and, very recently, the most modern of all, Ras Imru of Abyssinia!

VIII. FROM PONZA TO LA MADDA-
LENA TO THE GRAN SASSO

IT WAS one o'clock in the morning when Sergeant Antichi burst into Mussolini's room and shouted:

"Danger! We must go away this minute!"

As a matter of fact, ever since the evening before there had been constant searchlight signals from a hill across the way, which gave notice that there was something new in the air.

Mussolini gathered his few belongings together and went with his armed escort to the beach, where a big boat was waiting. The profile of a destroyer was outlined in the distance, at the entrance to the harbor. Mussolini climbed aboard and again met Admiral Maugeri, with whom he had traveled on the *Persefone*. Once more he went down to the Admiral's cabin, followed by Meoli, Di Lorenzo, and Antichi. The ship was the former *Panthère* of the French fleet. Toward dawn the anchor was lifted. Around eight o'clock the sea grew rough, but the *Panthère* kept a steady keel. There were two air-raid alarms of no consequence.

The Duce exchanged a few words with the second-in-

command, an officer from La Spezia, from whom he
learned that Badoglio had dissolved the Fascist Party.

Only after four hours at sea did Mussolini learn that
their goal was La Maddalena. Soon the outline of Sardinia
appeared through the fog. Mussolini disembarked around
two o'clock and was handed over to Admiral Bruno Brivo-
nesi, the base commander. This admiral, married to an
Englishwoman, had been called up to answer for the loss
of a very important convoy, consisting of seven merchant
ships and three warships, with twelve naval escorts, two
of them units of ten thousand tons. This convoy was sunk
by four British light cruisers after a few minutes of combat. The inquiry, which a Navy Board obviously conducted
in a negligent manner, took no more than mild disciplinary
sanctions against this admiral who was directly responsible
for the loss of ten ships and several hundred lives. He was
relieved of his sea command and later assigned to the base
at La Maddalena.

The meeting between this man and Mussolini could
hardly be a cordial one. The villa set aside for Mussolini's
use was outside the village on a rise of land surrounded by
a thick grove of pine trees. The villa had been built by an
Englishman called Webber, who had chosen of all spots in
the world this most solitary and desolate of the islands off
the north coast of Sardinia. Intelligence Service?

The stay at La Maddalena was fairly long and Mussolini's isolation more complete than before. The civilian
population had been evacuated from the island after the

bombardment in May which had caused great damage to the base and sunk two fleet units of medium tonnage. A very mysterious bombardment, apparently planned with exact knowledge of the objectives. Remains of the sunken ships were still visible. From the balcony of the villa there was a view over the harbor toward the steep, bare Gallura mountains, which are somewhat reminiscent of the Dolomites. Mussolini was allowed to write. It seems that he kept a diary of a philosophic, literary, and political character, but no trace of it has been found.* Strict guard was kept at La Maddalena. At least a hundred carabinieri and policemen kept watch night and day over the Webber villa, from which Mussolini went out only once, in order to go for a walk in the woods with Sergeant Antichi.

The hot days went monotonously by without a scrap of news from the outside world. Only around August 20 was the prisoner allowed to receive the war communiqué from the naval base. His isolation was practically complete but it did not satisfy General Antonio Basso, the commander of the Army corps in Sardinia, who wrote on August 11 to the Minister of War, General Sorice, as follows:

"I have lately heard that a very important person is now residing in a house with a view over the harbor.

"I call to your attention the fact that there are many German naval units—and very few of our own—in these

* Later, (p. 131) Mussolini seems to have found Mussolini's diary.

waters, which are engaged in maritime traffic with Corsica and the defense of the supply base at Palau.

"This situation may be a cause of inconvenience.

"I think it advisable for the person in question to be transferred to some other place. If it is necessary that he remain in these islands he would be safer in a mountain village of the interior where he could be more carefully watched."

On the margin of this sheet of paper is written in red ink: "What a discovery! B."

The one surprise of this period was a gift from the Führer of a complete set of the works of Nietzsche, with an autograph dedication. A marvel of German publishing skill.

With this gift came a letter from Marshal Kesselring which said: "Duce, the Führer has asked me to send you, through the good offices of His Excellency Marshal Badoglio, this birthday present. The Führer will be happy if this masterpiece of German literature gives you any pleasure and if you will consider it as a mark of his personal devotion. May I add my own personal respects. Field Marshal Kesselring, Headquarters, August 7, 1943."

Mussolini had time to read the first four volumes, containing Nietzsche's fine youthful poems and his early philological works on the Greek and Latin languages, which he knew as well as his own.

Another surprise was the unexpected appearance at

eight o'clock one evening of a German plane flying from Corsica at a very low altitude, perhaps a hundred and fifty feet above the ground. It was so low that Mussolini could see the pilot's face and wave to him in greeting. Mussolini had an idea that this flight would cause his removal from La Maddalena. And indeed on the evening of August 27 Captain Faiola (who had taken the place of Meoli) announced:

"Tomorrow we're off!"

A Red Cross seaplane had lain for several hours in the harbor, almost across from the Webber villa.

Mussolini was awakened at four o'clock in the morning of August 28 and went down to the harbor. He got into the plane which, because of the heavy load it was carrying, took off with some difficulty and only after skimming for quite a distance across the water. An hour and a half later the plane arrived at Vigna di Valle on Lake Bracciano. A major of the Carabinieri and Police Inspector Gueli were waiting here with the usual ambulance, which set out on the Via Cassia in the direction of Rome. On the outskirts of the city, however, it turned left onto the Via Flaminia. After the bridge across the Tiber it became evident that it was going in the direction of the Sabine mountains.

The Duce had been well acquainted with this road ever since he "discovered" and developed the sport facilities of Mount Terminillo, which came to be known as the "mountain of Rome."

Beyond Rieti and Cittaducale, in the vicinity of Aquila, the trip was interrupted by an air-raid alarm and every one had to get out. A squadron of enemy planes was flying by, so high that they could hardly be distinguished. But the behavior of the troops in the neighborhood gave clear indications that the Army was in a state of almost complete disintegration. Groups of half-clad soldiers ran shouting in every direction, followed by the civilian population. Nor did their officers set any better example. A pitiful sight! When the all clear was sounded the ambulance drove on, but a short way beyond Aquila it was stopped by some slight trouble with the motor.

While the ambulance windows were lowered a man came up to the Duce and said: "I am a Fascist from Bologna. They've done away with everything. But they won't last. Everyone's disgusted with the new government because it hasn't brought peace."

Beyond the village of Assergi the cars arrived at the station of the funicular railway to the top of the Gran Sasso. Mussolini and his guards (Captain Faiola and Inspector Gueli of Trieste) were lodged in a small house, with an even greater number of sentinels than before thrown around it. Mussolini was allowed to read the government newspaper, *La gazzetta ufficiale,* including back numbers. One day he asked Gueli:

"Have you any idea of why I am here?"

"You are considered an ordinary prisoner," Gueli replied.

"And what is your job, then?"

"The same as before. To see to it that you don't try to get away and, above all, that no one tries either to free you or to do you harm."

Nothing unusual happened during the few days Mussolini spent at La Villetta, as the house was called.

Mussolini could listen to the radio but he had neither books nor papers. In the square outside there was a radio transmitter and receiving apparatus. One morning a police guard came up to Mussolini and said:

"The locomotives coming through the Brenner Pass have your picture painted on them and the railroad cars are covered with inscriptions bearing your name. Something big is going to happen. Rome is in a state of complete confusion. No one would be surprised if the cabinet ministers were to scatter in every direction. There are dire rumors of what the Germans will do if Badoglio betrays them."

Another morning an inspector from Trieste, walking with a brace of police dogs, managed to approach Mussolini and say:

"Duce, I'm a Fascist from the region of Treviso. Do you know what happened yesterday in Rome? They killed Muti.* The Carabinieri did it. We must be ready to avenge him." And he walked away.

---

* Muti was a former secretary of the Fascist party who had become a Fascist hero fighting against the Loyalists in the Spanish Civil War.

This is how Mussolini heard of Muti's brutal assasination. Later Gueli told him the same thing.

After a few more days tents were struck for the last time and Mussolini was taken to a lodge known as the Gran Sasso Hospice, some 6,000 feet above sea level. The highest prison in the world, as Mussolini described it to his guards.

He was taken there on the funicular railway, which climbs 3,000 feet, passing over two arches. Both the funicular and the lodge were built during the twenty years of the Fascist regime. The tragic August of 1943, the first month of Mussolini's imprisonment, was now at an end.

IX. THE DYNASTY SOUNDS A FIRST CALL OF ALARM

BEFORE narrating the events of the first half of September we must examine the coup d'état more closely. One must grant that, thoroughly and painstakingly planned, its technique was nothing short of perfect. If Italian generals had shown the same enthusiasm during the war, our side would have won in short order.

As soon as the Duce was arrested, at five-thirty in the afternoon of July 25, all telephone connections were cut off except for a group of wires that had been installed several days in advance in the office of the traitor, Badoglio. This abrupt halt in service naturally attracted wide notice. By seven o'clock the city was in a state of unusual excitement. The news was given in a radio bulletin at half-past ten and repeated at intervals. As if by a pre-arranged signal there were outbursts of popular feeling, whose effervescence was increased by the element of surprise. Who, we may wonder, made up the throngs of demonstrators? But perhaps this is a superfluous question. The "people," or shall we say the "mob"? Thousands of persons acclaimed the King and the Marshal. The Fascists were taken completely by surprise. Their meeting places were closed and they could not gather to defend them. The anti-Fascist character of the coup was clear from its very first announcement. The Fascists looked bewildered. What they saw was a complete about-face. Within half an hour a whole people changed its thoughts and feelings and the course of its history.

The contents and form of the news bulletins only increased the general confusion. They gave the impression that the crisis was a purely constitutional one, a normal transfer of power. Even some Fascists did not comprehend. The radio sent out a sort of smoke screen, which was most effective in spreading uncertainty. The masses believed that peace was near at hand; they called for it and saw it just around the corner. Mussolini was gone and he alone had wanted to go on with the war! Others believed that the change meant an intensification of the war, a new Fascist government, or something close to it, minus the Duce. Was not Marshal Badoglio a regular Party member?

This *may* (but it is mentioned only as a possibility) explain the declarations of loyalty sent by wire and by mail to the Marshal. But if there was some doubt on the evening of July 25 about the real nature of the coup, it was due to be dissipated the next morning.

That morning the "mob" poured through the streets under the protection of the Carabinieri, who had been the instruments of the whole upheaval, sacking the offices of

Fascist organizations, destroying Fascist ensigns, laying violent hands on individuals, and wiping out with a stupid and ferocious spirit of iconoclasm every reminder of Mussolini and his regime.

Thousands of busts and pictures of Mussolini were broken and every shop window was adorned with images of Victor Emmanuel and Pietro Badoglio.

What are we to say of a people that makes a spectacle of itself before the rest of the world, by such a sudden and almost hysterical change of heart? Of course some of those who wired their allegiance to Badoglio were taken in by the ambiguous tone of the first news bulletins, which announced that "the war would go on," and that there were to be no reprisals or recriminations against the Fascists, stressing the need for patriotic unity and the military character of the new government.

And yet a few minutes of reflection should have caused some doubt to arise as to how matters really stood. The real meaning of what had happened was "imprisonment of the Duce and preliminaries of capitulation." Wasn't it strange that the announcement of the Duce's resignation was not accompanied by a single word of appreciation or gratitude for his services? It was not merely a question of the stereotype signed letters which the King used to send to his generals. Here was a man who had served his country in war and peace for twenty-one years and who, after the conquest of Ethiopia, had been given the highest military decoration. Did he not deserve at least the kind words of farewell to which even a mediocre servant is entitled?

And even if Mussolini received no recognition in the bulletins, why was he not allowed to take leave of the troops, to say a word to the people? Why was there no mention of the transfer of his power to the new head of the government? What was the meaning of this sudden silence? Why did he disappear completely from view?

Of course there were rumors of the most fantastic kind. One of these, spread by Court circles, was to the effect that Mussolini was a guest of the King in some unspecified place and that in a few days, when popular feeling had died down, he would return to circulation. The efficacy of the new government's highly successful effort to create confusion was over by the early morning of July 26, when the dregs of the population gave themselves up to wild excesses, which the newspapers described with relish.

After the morning of July 26 no Fascist could be in doubt as to the character and purposes of the Badoglio government. It aimed simply at the destruction of every idea, institution, and accomplishment of the twenty years of Fascism. And men lent themselves to this miserable task who up until 10:29 of the evening of July 25 were sworn Fascists, even if they had belonged to the Party for different lengths of time. Indeed some of the betrayers had been Fascists from the earliest days of the movement. Meanwhile orders were to ignore Mussolini completely. Around his name reigned the silence of the grave. He was to all effects a dead man, but no one was willing to announce his death. Thus began the month of August, a month of infamy, betrayal, and surrender. No part of Fascism was respected, not even its martyrs. The instruments of Badoglio's policy (and they put a refined cruelty into their work of which no one would have suspected them) were the officers and men of the Carabinieri, a branch of the Armed Forces which Mussolini had always praised and protected and whose effectives during the first half of 1943 came to 156,000 men.

This was the month of "freedom." A freedom marked by martial law and the curfew, freedom to desecrate everything Fascist. No one was spared. Even the most unimportant Fascist leaders were accused of having concealed gold ingots and food supplies in their cellars. The British hailed the fall of Mussolini as the greatest political victory of the war and during the whole month they conducted air raids of particular violence, aimed at "softening up" the resistance of the people and paving the way for surrender, of which there was already talk in the air. Moral and material disorder reached such a high pitch that Court circles were worried.

Among the many papers which the fugitives of September did not succeed in hiding in the vicinity of the Swiss frontier, as planned, was one of especial significance. It bore this title in Badoglio's own hand:

THE DYNASTY SOUNDS A FIRST CALL OF ALARM

"A memorandum which His Majesty the King gave me at the audience of August 16 as of his own composition—Badoglio."

Here is the complete text of the memorandum:

"The present government must keep up on every occasion its character as a 'military government' such as was described in the proclamation of July 25 and such as can be evidenced by its personnel. Marshal Badoglio, Head of the Government. Career officials in all the ministries.

"Political problems must be the province of another government of a later date when the fate of the nation can be decided under different and calmer circumstances.

"We must keep faith with the promise made in the King's proclamation and repeated by Marshal Badoglio —'not to countenance any recriminations.'

"The process of general elimination of all former Fascist Party members from public activity must be brought to an end.

"All Italians of good will must have the same right and the same duty to serve King and Country.

"The examination of individual cases must be conscientiously carried out in order to eliminate those who are really guilty and undeserving of public office.

"No political party such as that of the Republicans or Labor Democrats should be allowed to organize openly or to publicize itself with posters and pamphlets. Many such writings in current circulation are of easily discernible origin 'which is subject to severe punishment by the law.'

95

"Tolerance means weakness and weakness is anti-patriotic.

"The investigative commissions appointed in large numbers to the various ministries have been unfavorably received by the healthiest sections of public opinion. It might be thought both at home and abroad that every part of our public administration was tainted. People will think that with every change of government existing laws and institutions may be shaken.

"If this trend continues the King himself will stand condemned.

"If the honest majority of former members of Party organizations are suddenly for no good reason prevented from carrying on any activity, they will transfer their organizing abilities to the extremist parties and make trouble for future governments based on law and order.

"The majority of former Fascists, seeing themselves abandoned by the King, persecuted by the government, misjudged and insulted by the old political parties which for twenty years consented to bow their necks and disguise their opinions, will soon reappear on the scene in order to defend the bourgeoisie against Communism. But this time they will stand very much to the Left and oppose the monarchy.

"This is a difficult time. The government will endure more easily if Italians, no longer fearful of new punitive measures, but judged by a single severe standard, can resume their normal lives, which began afresh for all honest men on July 25, as the King solemnly promised."

This is the end of the royal memorandum, whose meaning is clear to all. We do not know what was the reply of the Marshal, to whom this note was personally delivered. It is plain that by the middle of this unhappy August, Victor Emmanuel had begun to have misgivings about his own future. He had set a landslide in motion and now, seeing it gain ground too fast, he was trying to slow it down. Too late! The King seems in these lines to regret having thrown overboard a regime in whose ranks he had found numerous and sincere defenders. But now the die was cast. Even if he had wanted to, Badoglio could not have freed himself from the parties which had helped him pull off the coup d'état and in whose grasp he was now a hostage. He had to go along with them willy-nilly until surrender.

The royal document of August 16 is an unsuccessful effort on the part of the King to discharge himself of all responsibility, without closing the door behind him. The reference to the revival of Communism is eloquent in this regard.

Did Victor Emmanuel "feel in his bones" the approach of someone called Palmiro Togliatti?

To imagine that forces such as those he had unleashed could be harnessed to a legal status, especially under a government of worn-out career officials, was a pitiful illusion.

The Marshal put this memorandum into the "records," and there it was later found. Perhaps we might call it "the dynasty's first call of alarm."

X. TOWARD SURRENDER

By THE MIDDLE of August the flags which had flown for two weeks as if in triumphal celebration had been hauled down and the hymns to reconquered liberty had died away. The country was under heavy pounding from the air and the food situation was precarious. The government had to "distract" public opinion and so it was that it set into motion a fortnight of scandalous revelations about its predecessors.

First came the charge of profiteering. All the Fascist leaders were gougers and thieves. Not even Diogenes with his lantern could find an honest man among them. It was calculated that they had robbed the Italian people of exactly 120,000,000,000 liras.

If this sum were returned to the treasury there would be a balanced budget instead of huge public debt! Were it not recorded in black and white it would be difficult to believe in the existence of such a fantastic theory! The attics and cellars of Fascist leaders' homes were found to be overflowing with hoarded foods. A strange collective psychosis, centered around gold ingots and hams, took hold of the Italian people.

This campaign was aimed at arousing the lowest instincts of the mob. One of the families singled out for attack by the famous Committee of Investigation headed by the traitor Casati was that of Ciano.

This was an indirect way of hitting at the Duce, who was uppermost in many people's thoughts although Badoglio's censorship forbade any mention of his name. The family fortune of Count Galeazzo Ciano was spoken of as amounting to billions. The letter on this subject written by Count Ciano to Marshal Badoglio on August 23, 1943, is not a private document but one that belongs to the public domain.

Rome, August 23, 1943

"Illustrious Marshal,

"I have read with great bitterness an article in the *Corriere della Sera* which outrages my father's memory. I shall not stoop to argue with anonymous newspaper reporters who are engaged in a campaign of mudslinging which does not spare even the dead. But while awaiting the findings of the committee of investigation I wish to inform Your Excellency of the exact nature of the estate left by my father to my late sister and myself. At the time of my father's death he owned the following:

1. A three-fourths interest in the printing and editorial plant of the newspaper *Il Telegrafo* of Leghorn.
2. Four buildings in Rome of a value (at that time) of about 5,000,000 liras.
3. Industrial stocks as follows: Rome Electric—

1,400 shares; Terni—500 shares; Montecatini—2,000 shares; Valdagno—1,000 shares; Metallurgica—1,000 shares; Navigazione Generale—300 shares; Ilva—500 shares; Anic—1,000 shares; Monte Amiata—1,000 shares; I.M.I.—100 shares; Consorzio Credito Opere Pubbliche—24 shares; Treasury bonds—1,000,000 liras; Cash—355,089 liras; Postal Savings—32,975 liras.

"I have, of course, documentary proof of what I have stated above, which is at Your Excellency's disposal.

"I am sure that these figures, which are remote from the astronomical fabrications of anonymous scandalmongers, will represent to Your Excellency's fair judgment not the dishonorable booty of a profiteer but the honestly earned rewards of a very busy life.

"For this reason, Your Excellency, I appeal to Marshal Badoglio to safeguard the memory and good name of a patriot.

GALEAZZO CIANO"

Churchill's speech of September 22* proves that the principal terms of unconditional surrender were settled at Lisbon toward the end of August. One of its clauses provided for handing Mussolini over to the enemy, a procedure unprecedented in the history of mankind! During the hectic September days after Mussolini's rescue from the Gran Sasso there was not space in the newspapers for the full text of Churchill's speech. But even at this late date it is worth reprinting as a historical document. Speak-

---

* Actually September 21.

ing of Italian affairs to the House of Commons on this date, Churchill said:

"Unconditional surrender of course comprises everything. But not only was a specific provision for the surrender of war criminals included in the larger terms, but particular stipulation was made for the surrender of Signor Mussolini. It was not however possible for him to be delivered specially and separately before the armistice and our main landing took place, for this would certainly have disclosed the intention of the Italian Government to the enemy [Germany]. . . .

"The Italian position had been that, although an internal revolution had taken place in Italy, they were still the allies of Germany carrying on a common cause with them. This was a position very difficult to maintain day after day with the pistols of the Gestapo pointing at the napes of so many necks.

"We have every reason to believe that Mussolini was being kept under strong guard in a secure place. Certainly it was very much in the interests of the Badoglio government to make sure he did not escape.

"Mussolini himself was reported to have declared he believed he was being delivered to the Allies. This was certainly the intention and would have taken place but for circumstances unhappily beyond our control. The measures which the Badoglio government took were carefully conceived and the best they could do to hold Mussolini, but they did not provide against so heavy a parachute descent as the Germans made at the particular point where he was confined.

"It will be noted that they sent him some books of

Nietzsche and leaflets to console him and diversify his confinement, and no doubt they were fully acquainted with where he was and the conditions in which he was, but the stroke was one of great daring and was conducted with a heavy force and certainly shows there may be possibilities of this kind which are open in modern war.

"I do not think there was any slackness or breach of faith on the part of the Badoglio government, and they had one card up their sleeve—Carabinieri guards had orders to shoot Mussolini if there was any attempt at a rescue—but they failed in their duty, having regard to the larger and considerable German forces who descended upon them from the air who undoubtedly would have held them responsible for his health and safety.

"So much for that . . ."

This is the text transmitted by the Reuter News Agency at 7 P.M. of September 22, 1943.*

The fact that Marshal Badoglio had "carefully" worked out plans for insuring Mussolini's captivity and then handing him over to the enemy is confirmed in a letter signed by his own hand addressed to Chief of Police Senise:

ROME, August 16, 1943

"YOUR EXCELLENCY:

"This morning I sent the following message to His Excellency, Commanding General Cerica of the Carabi-

Actually September 21.

nieri: 'Inspector General Polito of the Police is responsible for the custody of the former Head of the Government, Benito Mussolini.

" 'He is personally responsible to the Government for seeing to it that the above mentioned Mussolini neither escapes nor is released from detention.

" 'General Polito will ask Carabinieri Headquarters and the Chief of Police for whatever personnel he requires and may specify the names of the men he prefers to have with him.

" 'He is to be given everything he requests. Inspector Polito will keep me constantly informed.'

BADOGLIO"

After the decision to hand Mussolini over to the British had been made and the terms worked out in detail, the government felt it must launch a campaign of mudslinging against his name. If he were covered with ridicule and infamy the already forgetful people would be indifferent to his delivery to the enemy, considering him a man not only politically finished but physically and morally done for as well.

Gossip and scandal were given full rein. To five per cent of truth was added ninety-five per cent of extravagant invention which had however a certain appeal to the petty curiosity of the masses. No one was in a position to throw the first stone, none of the great or small men of the past and none of those of the present, least of all Marshal Badoglio. But the deed was done.

Mussolini had to be killed, first with silence and then

with ridicule. The campaign lasted two days but that was quite enough. Many people deplored these tactics and expected a "boomerang." But they deceived themselves. The campaign had had its effect. The Jesuits, who are well acquainted with the human soul, are credited with the famous maxim: "Go ahead, calumniate! Some mud will always stick where you have slung it!" In this case it is all too true that some mud did stick.

During the last days of August capitulation was in the air. A crime was about to be committed which will cast its shadow over the history of our country for centuries to come. Italy was to be made a bloody battleground disputed by foreign armies.

Only a fool could have imagined any other result, a fool who had neglected to read the telephone and telegraph messages reporting every morning to Rome from the frontier the passage of German troops and arms. These messages were found left on the desks of the officials who fled from Rome on September 8. Every day since the morning of July 26 news from the Brenner, Tarvisio, and Ventimiglia frontier posts had described the southward sweep of German divisions, hundreds of trucks, tanks, armored vehicles, and soldiers. Germany realized from the start that the plan of the Badoglio government was first to surrender and then to take up arms against its former ally. It is true that on July 28 Marshal Badoglio was shameless enough to send Hitler the following telegram, which failed to deceive anyone:

"FÜHRER: My new cabinet took office today with an oath of allegiance to His Majesty the King and Emperor. As I said in my first proclamation to the Italian people, which was officially communicated to your ambassador, the war goes on for us in the spirit of alliance. I wish to repeat this to you and to ask you to receive General Marras, whom I am sending to your headquarters with a personal message. I am happy to have this opportunity, Führer, to extend to you my cordial greetings.

BADOGLIO."

German observers in Lisbon and Rome could not fail to see at this time what direction the policy of the King and Badoglio was taking. This policy could lead to only one thing: surrender.

Among the most suspicious symptoms of what was going on was the request to German Headquarters to withdraw a number of Italian army units in service abroad. Territory bought dear with Italian blood was abandoned for the purpose of getting soldiers home and turning them against the Germans. Here is a telegram signed by Guariglia, dated August 10, and couched in the following plainly hypocritical terms:

"ROYAL ITALIAN EMBASSY, BERLIN:
Make immediate contact with the Auswärtigesamt and relay the following message:

"As was stated at the meeting at Tarvisio on August 6, the Italian Command has decided to recall the entire Fourth Army, presently in France, and one army corps from the three divisions now in Croatia and Slovenia.

"There are various reasons, which were set forth at Tarvisio, for this decision.

"First, the Supreme Command believes it necessary to strengthen the defenses of our home territory. It seems advisable, moreover, that our units should stand beside the German divisions now operating in Italy. Their task seems to be limited to the defense of only certain zones, whereas it is plain to us that our whole territory must be defended. There are political and moral considerations, as I explained to Herr von Ribbentrop, which make it important for the Italian people to feel that their national defense is entrusted not only to the troops of their ally but to Italian troops, in even greater numbers, as well.

"Make use of these arguments and whatever others occur to you in order to convince t he Auswärtigesamt of the cogency of our decision.

"We realize that, as von Ribbentrop said, the recall of these units raises certain political questions, but we are firmly convinced that everything can be solved in a way satisfactory to both parties.

"The contacts necessary for the achievement of this purpose must be made by the proper military personnel as soon as possible.

GUARIGLIA."

XI. SEPTEMBER ON THE GRAN SASSO D'ITALIA

IN HIS TALK to the Grand Council, Mussolini said, apropos of "popular" and "unpopular" wars, that he did not wish to disturb the great shades of our past, that is, he did not want to go back over the whole nineteenth century to see which wars were "popular" and which "unpopular" at the time of the Risorgimento.

Here is what he might have said on this subject had lack of time not forced him to condense it into a few words.

Mussolini began by recalling the first World War, which Italy entered in 1915 in an atmosphere akin to that of civil strife, with interventionists and isolationists at each other's throats. This split continued until Caporetto and, after a ten-month lull during the stand on the Piave River, it cropped up again as soon as the war was over and the false peace of Versailles was signed. Was this a "popular" war? It was called the "Milanese war" and many soldiers had to disguise the fact that they came from Milan in order to escape the insults of their comrades.

Let the volunteers of that time (I hope some of them are still alive!) tell us of all the annoyances to which they were subject. "Are you a 'volunteer'?" they were asked. "Then you got into it 'voluntarily,' of your own free will!" Even the *irredenti* who came from Austrian-held territory to join the Italian army found very little brotherly feeling. Men like Battisti and Sauro suffered a disillusionment that only their unbounded love for Italy enabled them to overcome.

Volunteers did lead a charge from the trenches in October of 1915, following a heroic impulse which stemmed in part from their exasperation and disgust with the hostile atmosphere around them. The Italian army has never had any use for volunteers. The Army has always been considered an appendage of the dynasty, with the job of defending national institutions rather than of making war. When war did come the officers considered it not the longed-for crowning glory of their career, but a bothersome bit of bad luck which every one of them was anxious to avoid.

Already by October, 1915, the elite of Italian volunteers, from Corridoni to Deffenu, had been cut down in the trenches on the slopes of the Carso, beyond Isonzo. In all likelihood there were no volunteers left alive in the Italian army when, after the martyrdom of Battisti on August 14, 1916, General Cadorna finally sent around a two-page circular suggesting that they should be objects of respect on the part of officers and soldiers rather than of derision.

The war of 1915–18 was not "popular" among the aristocracy or Court circles, and even less so among priests and politicians. It was because of strong feeling among the masses; because of the famous manifesto, "Either War or a Republic," which Mussolini improvised after a meeting in Palermo with the chiefs of the interventionist movement; and because of the gigantic demonstrations organized by D'Annunzio in Rome that the three hundred deputies who had formerly held out for Giolitti's bargaining with both sides failed to appear in the Chamber and let the declaration of war be voted by default. It is a law of history that when there are two opposing currents in a nation, one for war and one for peace, the latter is inevitably defeated even if it musters a majority of supporters. The reasons for this law are not hard to find. The "interventionists" form a young, eager and dynamic minority, which acts as a leaven upon the sluggish masses.

Were the wars of the Risorgimento "popular"?

The history of the Risorgimento is still to be written. A synthesis must be made of the version made up by the monarchists, who succeeded in obtaining a mortgage on it, and that of the Republicans. It must be settled how much was due to the people and how much to the monarchy, what came out of revolution and what out of diplomacy. Among the cheap prints that influenced our childhood there stands out one, formerly very popular, representing the four leaders of the Risorgimento. Victor Emmanuel, wearing very long trousers and spurs sticking out below them, with a thick moustache that gave him a rustic air. Cavour, with eyeglasses diplomatically veiling his expression and a short beard framing his face, giving him the appearance of a distinguished old gentleman. These two, then, standing for dynasty and diplomacy. Then the fiery, great-hearted, and generous Garibaldi, the eternal adventurer, smitten by a love for Italy as flaming as that of his followers' red shirts, naive and "boisterous," as he unaffectedly described himself, a true specimen of the old Ligurian stock. And finally Mazzini, born on the shores of the same sea, absorbed in his own thoughts and fanatically tenacious in his republican orthodoxy which was to remain for so long impracticable. The last two made the wars of the Risorgimento possible, even if they were not "popular" wars. In those days public opinion could not make itself felt as it can today. We have only to remember the attitude of the various Italian parliamentary bodies toward the series of wars between 1848 and 1870, which eventually brought the House of Savoy to Rome.

The war of 1848 seems to have been fairly "popular." But even at the start certain deputies did not hesitate to criticize, particularly Brofferio, who on May 29, in the course of a discussion as to what answer to make to a speech on the part of the Crown, touched on the painful subject of the way the generals were conducting the war. At a later meeting Deputies Moffa di Lisio and Grossi made further criticisms, which became all the more lively when military operations took an unfavorable turn. The stupidity of the generals was continually under attack, which proved very embarrassing to Cesare Balbo, who was premier at the time.

Agitation increased until, coincidentally with an especially difficult phase of the war, there was a government crisis. The new cabinet headed by Casati proclaimed at a meeting of July 17, 1848, that "the war was to go on," just as Badoglio did on July 26, 1943. But the first steps had been taken toward an armistice, which was then too termed a "betrayal."

"If you insist on making a disastrous peace," cried Brofferio, *"We shall answer you with cannons instead of courtesies. The people's representatives will turn against you and declare stubborn, tireless, unending war."* Casati's government could not last and he was succeeded by Gioberti, who in his turn was unable to master the rising wave of feeling and had to dissolve the Chamber. Three cabinets in the course of nine months! Gioberti stayed only two months at the helm. The war began again in March of 1849, in a hostile atmosphere, and lasted little more than a week. Carlo Alberto abdicated, setting an example which his future grandson, in far graver circumstances, has so far shown no desire to follow!

Even less "popular" was the Crimean War, or rather the Piedmontese intervention in the war between Turkey and Russia. The treaty of alliance between Piedmont and the great powers (England and France), a masterpiece of Cavour's diplomacy, was presented to the Chamber for approval on February 3, 1855, and ran into strong opposition from left and right alike.

Brofferio, among others, accused Cavour of having no definite political aims and no "respect for constitutional conventions and morality." The treaty, he maintained was both useless and untimely. *"The alliance with Turkey is an offense to Piedmont and a dishonor to Italy. We have braved all kinds of privations, we have submitted to odious taxation, we have faced national bankruptcy, all in the hope of returning one day to the struggle with the battle cry of 'Away with foreign conquerors!' And then what? We seem to have endured all this only in order to spend millions of liras and Italian lives in Crimea, for the benefit of our enemies. . . . If you ratify this treaty the prostration of Piedmont and the ruin of Italy will be complete."*

Even Cavour's brother Gustavo, who was one of the deputies, voted against ratification. This was the occasion of one of Cavour's best speeches.

The treaty was approved by a vote of only 101 to 60. The war of 1859 also aroused strong opposition. Cavour practically sent the Chamber packing and just before its dispersal he obtained extraordinary powers, by a vote of 110 to 23. Everyone knows the tremendous indignation, the wave of popular fury aroused all over Italy by the announcement of the "betrayal" perpetrated by Napoleon III at Villafranca. Feeling ran unusually high and yet Napoleon's "betrayal" had nothing of the character and importance of that perpetrated by the House of Savoy on September 8, 1943. Besides, Napoleon was a foreign king!

The Italians never forgave Napoleon and for years and years his statue was left abandoned like a piece of rubbish in the Senate courtyard of Milan.

From the point of view of comfort Mussolini's imprisonment was never a hard one, except at La Maddalena, on account of the natural poverty of the island and its general inconveniences. Officers and soldiers always treated him with respect. But from the beginning of September on things were "eased" even more. He still ate all his meals alone, but in the evening he could listen to the radio, read the newspapers, and play cards with his guards. This softening appeared to him suspicious. Was it not reminiscent of the last-minute favors accorded to a man awaiting execution?

Rumors from Aquila were more and more confused. The official communiqués made it increasingly clear that the war was a farce.

On September 1 Mussolini heard a radio speech by the Pope, whose pacifist tone was part of the advance propaganda for the approaching event. At the mountain lodge everything was quiet. The prisoner left the building only in the early hours of the afternoon and walked within a radius of only about ten yards, in the company of a non-commissioned officer. One morning machine guns were placed on either side of the front door, and later there was heavy machine-gun practice on the surrounding heights.

From an "esthetic" point of view the Gran Sasso is truly fascinating. One cannot easily forget the jagged profile of this mountain, which rises in the very heart of Italy to a height of 9,000 feet. Most of the mountain is made up of bare rock, but at the foot of the highest peak a plateau extends for at least ten miles toward the southeast. This is called the Campo Imperatore (Emperor Field) and its gentle slope makes it an ideal spot for winter sports.

Early in September flocks of sheep were pastured on this and the adjacent plateaux, having come up in the spring from the Agro Romano, or flatlands around Rome, to where they were now gradually preparing to return. Sometimes the sheep owners made a brief appearance on horseback and then disappeared over the mountain tops, standing out against the sky like figures from another age.

There is an indefinable something about the country and people of the Abruzzo region that tugs at one's heart. One day a shepherd came up to Mussolini and said in a low voice: "Your Excellency, the Germans are at the gates of Rome. If the government hasn't fled already it will very soon. Here in the country we're still Fascists. No one has disturbed the villages, except for closing our meeting places, and we've talked about you right along. Some thought you had fled to Spain, others said that they had killed you, that you had died during an operation in

Rome, and they had shot you at Fort Boccea. I believe that when the Germans hear where you are they'll come to free you. I'm going to take my sheep down to the flatlands and I'll tell them about you. It won't be long now, because the sheep go by train. When I tell my wife that I've seen you she'll think I'm quite mad. . . . Now the sergeant is coming. Good luck and good-by!"

XII. THE CROWN COUNCIL AND SURRENDER

IT WAS seven o'clock in the evening of September 8 when Mussolini heard the announcement of the armistice, after which he listened to all the news coming over the radio. From this time on the watch over him was increased and a sentinel was posted in front of his door at night. The inspector in charge of the guards seemed more worried every day. The guards themselves had greeted the armistice without any particular enthusiasm. Then came news from Rome about the flight of the King and Badoglio and the disintegration of the Armed Forces and indeed of the whole nation. The so-called "grapevine" was working to perfection. On the evening of September 10 at eight o'clock, Mussolini came downstairs and turned on the radio. He happened to be tuned in to Berlin and heard transmitted from there a news item from Algiers, which said: "Allied Headquarters officially announces that the surrender of Mussolini is among the terms of the armistice." A discussion among those present followed.

One of the men said: "That was announced once before, and then London denied it." But Mussolini was convinced that the news was true. He was resolved not to give himself up alive either to the British or, above all, to the Americans. The commander of the Carabinieri, who had been a prisoner of the British in Egypt and seemed to detest them cordially, said to the Duce: "If anything of the sort happens I'll see that you are warned an hour in advance and can get away. I swear it on the head of my only son."

These words, which he pronounced with tears in his eyes, were a sincere expression of devotion but there was no guarantee that he might not be taken by surprise and find himself unable to carry out his pledge. Many of the younger guards had an unconcealed liking for Mussolini, but four or five deceitful and evasive-looking fellows were obviously hirelings of the lowest type.

By September 15 all the news and rumors from Rome indicated that confusion was complete and that German troops were proceeding with a total occupation. During the morning the guard leaders went down to Aquila where they conferred with the local prefect and had a telephone conversation with the Chief of Police, who was still in the Palazzo Viminale in Rome.

There was no exact statement of the armistice terms. All that was known was that capitulation had taken place. Many versions have been given of the events of September 7 and 8. Here is the most reliable account we have, given by an eyewitness:

"In the late afternoon of September 7 a strapping young American general, called Taylor, accompanied by an elderly colonel, arrived at the Palazzo Caprara in an ambulance from Gaeta, where they had been landed from an Italian warship.

"General Taylor was received by my informant, who had expected his arrival and announced it to General Roatta. General Roatta refused to see the visitor and so did General Rossi, Assistant Chief of Staff. Both of these men were unwilling to assume any responsibility. General Carboni finally did see him and asked his leading staff officer for the map showing the positions of Italian and German troops in the vicinity of Rome.

"The American general was very much irritated at having to wait so long.

"Their conversation went on for over three hours. Apparently Carboni made it quite clear that the Italian troops could hold off the Germans around Rome for no longer than five hours. General Taylor retorted that when General Castellano had signed the armistice on September 3, he had stressed the ability of the Italians to stand up against the Germans, either with or without Allied aid, around Rome or anywhere else in Italy. They would give the Germans a thorough beating or at least put them in such a difficult position that Italy would be strategically assured to the British and Americans.

"It was on this basis, fearful lest the Italians change their minds again and contribute (as they well might have done) effective aid to the Germans, that Eisenhower had required an immediate signature of the armistice, which Castellano, by virtue of the powers vested in him, consented to give.

"Taylor was convinced by what General Carboni had to say and, after one of the sumptuous dinners for which the General Staff is famous, the two of them went to Badoglio's private residence, where they talked until three o'clock in the morning.

"Badoglio asked General Taylor to take back word that the Italian troops would be in a very bad situation if the armistice were announced too soon, and they agreed that no such step should be taken before September 16.*

"For some reason or other the American general and his aide stayed in Rome until four o'clock in the afternoon of September 8, when they left in a plane of the Italian air force. My informant gave them civilian clothes to wear to the airfield.

"General Taylor was taken by surprise on his way back to headquarters by the announcement of the armistice.

"Why then had General Eisenhower entrusted him with this mission?

"General Roatta and his aide, Lieutenant Colonel Fenazzi, went in an armored car to take refuge in the Palazzo Caprara, where late at night the rest of the General Staff joined them.

"At four o'clock in the morning General Carboni came out with a pale face from a conversation with Badoglio, who was at the Ministry of War, and gave orders that the armored corps should be detached from its position and fall back on Tivoli.

"His Chief of Staff objected that it would be impos-

---

* Actually there was no such agreement.

sible to carry out this order without endangering the troop units already fighting the Germans.

"Carboni answered that the King was at Tivoli, and this argument was all-persuasive. The written order was signed by General de Stefanis, who was the only ranking officer left by five or six o'clock in the morning. Carboni disappeared from view until the evening of September 9.

"The troops were caught up in a tragic tangle of orders and counterorders. Calvi took command of the Army corps and confirmed the original order.

"Carboni returned on the evening of the 9th, convinced that we should negotiate with the Germans. Negotiations were begun, with the intervention of Caviglia. During the morning of September 10 negotiations were broken off. Carboni decided to fight. Calvi came into the picture again and Carboni disappeared.

"The troops disbanded, while various generals disguised themselves and fled.

"Meanwhile at 5 P.M. of September 8 General de Stefanis received a telephone call from Badoglio's office ordering him to go at once to the Quirinal to take the place of General Roatta, who was keeping an engagement with Marshal Kesselring to discuss the normal course of military operations.

"General de Stefanis telephoned to the Quirinal to make sure that he was expected there, for it seemed to him strange that he should be summoned so urgently to the royal palace. The summons was confirmed.

"When he reached the Quirinal at half-past five he

found that he had been called to attend a secret Crown Council.

"Suddenly he found himself in the same room as the King. Those present besides himself were Badoglio, Acquarone, Ambrosio, Sorice, Sandalli, De Courten, and Guariglia. Carboni was apparently not there.

"Badoglio took the floor and said that in view of the desperate situation the King had called them in to advise him.

"To the patent surprise of all those present Ambrosio told them that an armistice had been signed with the British and Americans on September 3, and he read them its terms, adding that the victors had, contrary to expectations, announced it prematurely. This information was for the benefit of the Chiefs of Staff of the Army, Navy, and Air Force.

"Guariglia registered a protest against the fact that he had not been informed earlier of what was going on. De Stefanis demurred at the absence of Roatta and did not commit himself beyond saying that personally he was opposed to the whole thing. Acquarone insisted that the armistice be accepted immediately.

"Badoglio was in a state of nervous depression.

"A majority of those present dissented.

"At this point it seems that Badoglio exclaimed: 'Then I and my government must go.'

"At quarter past six a radio message came from Eisenhower, which was to all intents and purposes a two-hour ultimatum.

"Faced with this ultimatum all those present were overtaken by uncertainty and panic.

"Upon a second request Eisenhower radioed back

that guaranties would be made for the future with full understanding of the situation of Italy and the Italian government.

"At seven o'clock the King stood up, said that he had decided to accept the armistice, and asked the others to compose the Italian announcement which was to be sent over the radio at eight o'clock, the hour when the ultimatum expired.

"De Stefanis objected to the last part of this announcement, which was worded 'by whatever Power hostilities are undertaken. . . .'

"The King himself approved his argument and this last part was omitted.

"At half-past seven the Crown Council broke up.

"At nine o'clock, at his mess in Monterotondo, in the presence of Generals Mariotti, Utili Surdi, and Parone, De Stefanis expressed his surprise and disappointment that the sentence about hostilities with Germany, which the King and his Council had decided to omit, had apparently been restored.

"It seems that at the last minute Badoglio had inserted it, entirely on his own initiative.

"De Stefanis and the other staff officers stayed at Monterotondo until midnight.

"Meanwhile the Germans made a request through the Italian military command of Sardinia to be allowed to evacuate this island, taking with them the 88-millimeter antiaircraft guns which they had given to our units. De Stefanis consented and ordered that the Germans be allowed to embark in safety.

"After this the staff officers went to the Palazzo Baracchini and the Palazzo Caprara in Rome.

"At six-thirty in the afternoon of September 9 De Stefanis and Mariotti left for Carsoli in the Abruzzo region, where they found orders from Ambrosio to go on to Chieti. De Stefanis went to Avezzano, where his family had come by car from Mantua to join him. Then, at half-past three, with Lieutenant Colonel Guido Perone of the General Staff, he set out for Chieti, saying that he would be back by evening.

"At six o'clock he reached Chieti, where Ambrosio was presiding over a General Staff meeting. Those present were Generals Roatta, Mariotti, Utili, Armellini, Salazar, and others (including Lieutenant General Braida and Captain Barone, who are now in Rome).

"At half-past nine, after sharing the garrison mess and hearing Roatta order General Olmi, a divisional commander, to take command of the Chieti region, they all went hurriedly and mysteriously away, with their headlights off and their cars keeping close to one another in order that they should not get lost on the way to their mysterious destination.

"By midnight their column reached Ortona a Mare, where they were joined a few hours later by a few other cars containing the King, the Queen, and Prince Umberto, together with a small suite.

"The Queen was upset and kept taking drops of some kind. The Prince stood alone at one side, racked by a cough.

"The King conferred with Ambrosio, Sandalli, and De Courten. Soon a tugboat docked at the pier. In the bay the corvette *Gleno* was waiting. The fugitives embarked in the pitch darkness. Fifty thousand liras were distributed among the carabinieri who had guarded them. A few high-ranking officers remained on land, among them General Cener of the Bureau of Transportation."

The preceding is an eyewitness account. We may add that the royal family had hidden in the Ministry of War, whence they had fled when news came that German tanks were about to enter the Piazza Venezia. So rapid was their flight that many documents and papers were left in desks and bookcases, but chests that had contained money were found thoroughly emptied. This unique and unprecedented example of desertion to the enemy marked the ignominious end of the Savoy monarchy, born after the Treaty of Utrecht in 1713 out of a diplomatic agreement among the great powers, and enthroned first in Sicily and then in Sardinia.

Nor will the judgment of history be different from that of the Italian people.

XIII. ECLIPSE OR DECLINE?

DID THE PERPETRATORS of this betrayal, their ringleader, the King, the fugitive generals, and the rest have any idea of what they were doing? Were they or were they not aware of their crime? Surely the consequences were easy to foresee. It was perfectly clear that at the magic word "armistice" the Italian armed forces would crumble into pieces and the Germans would take measures to strip them to the last cartridge, that Italy would be rent asunder and turned into first a battle field and then a piece of "scorched earth," that the long prepared betrayal of our ally would be a lasting disgrace to our people and the word "Italian" would become a synonym of "traitor," that confusion and humiliation would be unbounded.

After the enormous cloud of dust raised by the collapse of the whole framework of the nation had faded away and the looting of military supplies by soldiers and civilian mobs was over, two points stood out clearly in the national conscience. First, the monarchy was done for. A King who goes over to the enemy, who commits the unprecedented act of handing his country over to foreigners —allies in the north and enemies in the south—has condemned himself to the scorn of future generations.

Second, military stores were found to be overflowing with arms and equipment of every kind, mostly of the very latest type, which had never been distributed to the troops. On April 22, 1943, three months before the crisis, Agostino Rocca, the engineer who was head of the Ansaldo steel works, sent the Duce the following report:

"Duce, I should like to inform you about Ansaldo's artillery production. During the first thirty-one months of the war (July, 1940, to January, 1943) our plants turned out 5,049 pieces of artillery. In a corresponding period of the last war (June, 1915, to December, 1917) the glorious old Giovanni Ansaldo firm produced 3,699 pieces.

"From the enclosed chart you will see that we accomplished this in 15,000,000 working hours as opposed to 6,000,000 working hours required for the production of the corresponding period of the last war.

"This chart shows that modern artillery, on account of the greater power needed to create the higher initial velocity of its projectiles, requires far more time to manufacture in spite of the aid of modern tools and machinery. You will see that our productive capacity was much greater at the beginning of the war in 1940 than it was in 1915 because of farsighted measures taken during the preceding year. In this and all other branches of Italian industry the Fascist regime's policy of economic self-sufficiency led to a much more advanced state of preparedness than there was before the other war. The same chart shows that production was at a peak in 1941 and slightly declined in 1942 although plant conditions would have allowed it to double at this time.

"All this goes to prove that the stepping-up of production facilities approved by you in 1939–40 and executed by the *Istituto Ricostruzione Industriale* made it possible to completely supply the needs of our Armed Forces."

So one company had produced 5,000 artillery pieces! *

Our fall was truly what the Spanish call a "vertical" one. What a poignant contrast there is between the Italy of 1940 and that of today's unconditional surrender, which was greeted by an unworthy people with shouts of joy whose echo reached even the hospice of the Gran Sasso. In 1940 Italy was an empire; now it is not even a nation. Then its flag flew from Tripoli to Mogadiscio, from Bastia to Rhodes and Tirana; now that flag has come down and even over our homeland enemy flags are flying. Once Italians were at Addis Ababa; now Africans are encamped in Rome.

Let all Italians—old and young, men and women, workers, peasants and intellectuals—ask themselves whether it was worth while to undergo the infamy of this surrender? If there had been no capitulation and the war

* No matter what the production of the Ansaldo works might have been, this rosy picture is flatly contradicted by General Favagrossa, who was Mussolini's minister of war production. According to Favagrossa, only 24% of the artillery that the Italian armed forces needed could be provided, even at the peak of war production. See Favagrossa, *Perchè perdemmo la guerra*, Milan, 1946, p. 49.

had gone on as before, would Italy be any worse off than it has been since September 8, 1943?

The catastrophe has been a material as well as a moral one. No Italian can fail to feel the fatal consequences of the decision to surrender; no family has escaped being drawn into the whirlpool. And the survivors of our 300,-000 war dead must wonder if the sacrifice of their own flesh and blood was made in vain.

By frequent repetition the word "betrayal" may lose all meaning, until we come to doubt its very existence. But is it not a classical example of betrayal to plant a dagger in the back of those with whom, up to the very last war communiqué, one has been fighting side by side? And when one's ally begins to doubt and question, to answer with lies, even when the enemy radio had already announced the surrender, is this not the blackest deceit? There is one very sore point that must be called to Italians' attention; that is, their responsibility before the world for this betrayal. Specific responsibility may fall upon certain groups and individuals, but in foreign eyes the shame of it is shared by us all. The geographical, historical, moral, political entity known as Italy is to blame. The atmosphere in which the betrayal was brought to a head was Italian and all of us, in greater or lesser degree, contributed to its creation, including the millions who listened to the London radio broadcasts and are responsible for having developed in themselves and others our present state of heedless apathy. History has its give and take, its credits and debits. Italians may be proud to belong to the country of Caesar, Dante, Leonardo, and Napoleon; a ray of their glory shines on every one of us. But the same thing is true of our shame and dishonor; here too each one of us must bear his part. If we are to wipe out our recent disgrace and bring the balance back to normal we must go through the trial of trials, trial by blood.

Thus and only thus can we answer a no less painful question—is our country in temporary eclipse or definite decline?

In the history of every nation there are periods like that which Italy is going through today. Russia must have been in somewhat the same condition after the peace of Brest-Litovsk, when six years of chaos fostered the success of Lenin. But subsequent events proved that Russia was in anything but a decline. Prussia, too, went into only a temporary eclipse after the battle of Jena, where the Germans fought as valiantly as usual and lost what was called "the flower of the Prussian army," besides their commander in chief, the Duke of Brunswick.

Italian intellectuals of today have struck an attitude not unlike that of Johannes von Müller, the German Tacitus. Even Hegel greeted Napoleon as the "soul of the world" when he went through Jena. The standard-bearers of the school of Illuminism in Berlin hailed him as "liberator." Even the present Prince Doria Pamphili of Rome had his counterpart in Count von der Schulemburg-Kehnert.

But, I repeat, this was only an eclipse. Prussian national feeling had a rapid and powerful revival. The tradition of Frederick the Great was not dormant for long.

Men like Stein, Gneisenau, and Schaarnhorst were the heralds of this recovery. And the philosopher Fichte with his *Addresses to the German Nation* would be a tonic piece of reading for Italian intellectuals today. Hear in what terms this great German philosopher speaks of the ancient Romans:

"What was it that inspired the noble Romans (whose ideas and ways of thinking still live and breathe among us in the monuments they left behind them)? What made them endure such labor and sacrifice and suffering for the sake of their country? They have told us quite clearly themselves. It was their absolute confidence in the eternity of Rome, their assurance that they too would live on in the shadow of this eternity. Because this confidence of theirs was justified, and took the best possible form, it did not deceive them. All that was truly eternal in their eternal Rome still lives today (and they along with it) and will go on living until the end of the world."

As a result of the great expiation we are now going through it is necessary that this spirit of the ancient Romans be breathed into the Italians of today. That is, Italians must have confidence that Italy will not die. Italians must ask themselves the questions that Fichte asked the Germans. "We must come to an agreement," he said, "on the following questions: (1) whether a German nation really exists, and if so, whether there is a serious threat to its survival as an individual and independent unit; (2) whether or not it deserves to be saved; (3) whether there is any sure way of saving it, and what this way may be."

Prussia answered Fichte's questions with Blücher's divisions at Waterloo. As far as Italy is concerned, we may answer that an Italian nation does and will exist and that it is indeed worth saving. In order to save it, it is necessary to wipe out the defeat and the shame (above all, the latter) which weigh down its conscience today. And the only way to do this is to rejoin our ally, or rather our allies, in the field of battle. We must raise again, once and for all, the old banner of the Fascist Revolution, the banner which has divided the world into two enemy camps. The phase of the war that was fought to obtain a German "corridor" inside a Polish "corridor" is long since over. The war of today is a religious war, which affects the fate of whole nations and peoples and continents.

In a sort of diary Mussolini wrote at La Maddalena, which may yet see the light of day, it is written: "It is not surprising that the people should destroy the idols of their own creation. Perhaps this is the only way to restore them to human proportions." And further on:

"After a while Fascism will once more light up the horizon. First, because the 'liberals' will persecute it,

131

proving that liberty is what a man claims for himself but denies to others; second, because of a nostalgia for the 'happy days' of the past, which little by little will return to torment the Italian soul. This nostalgia will affect the veterans of the European and African wars, especially the latter. 'The call of Africa' will spread like an epidemic.

"When Napoleon brought his drama to a close, by naively counting on the chivalry of the British, the twenty years of his reign were cursed and denied by his subjects. Most Frenchmen of his day—and many of our day too—condemned him as a wicked man, who for the sake of his own wild dreams of domination led millions of his countrymen to slaughter. Even his political accomplishments were misjudged and the empire that he had created was said to be an anachronism in French history. Years went by, and the balm of time soothed all mourning and passion. France began to live (even more intensely after 1840) in the aura of the Napoleonic tradition. The twenty years of Napoleon's reign are no longer just a matter of history; they have become an indissoluble part of the French national tradition. Perhaps something of the sort will happen in Italy. The decade from the Lateran Treaty to the end of the Civil War in Spain, the decade that brought Italy to the rank of a great empire, the Fascist decade, when our people all over the world were able to raise their heads and unblushingly proclaim themselves 'Italians,' will return to thrill the young men of the second half of our century, even if there are those today who are trying to obliterate its memory."

132

Elsewhere in the diary we find these words:

"We must suffer if we are to achieve redemption. Millions of Italians today and tomorrow must see and feel in their bones the meaning of defeat and dishonor. They must know what it means to lose one's independence, to become the slaves rather than the masters of their political fate, to be completely disarmed and powerless to resist. We must drink this bitter cup to the dregs. Only after we have touched bottom can we hope to rise again. Only intolerance of their humiliation will endow Italians with the strength to rise above it."

XIV. A "STORK" ON THE
GRAN SASSO

IN THE HISTORY of every nation there are tales of daring and romantic escapes from prison. But the rescue of Mussolini, even now that it is over, seems the boldest and most extraordinary of its kind, besides being completely modern in planning and execution. It has, indeed, all the makings of a legend.* Mussolini had never believed that Italians, even Fascist Italians, would free him. There were, of course, those who wished to do so, and certain courageous groups went so far as to draw up plans for his liberation, which they were unable to put into action. The individuals and groups capable of carrying out such plans were under strict watch and they had no means at their disposal.

But from the very beginning Mussolini had a feeling that the Führer would do everything in his power in order to set him free. Immediately after the arrest von Mackensen went to the King and voiced the Führer's desire that he, as the German ambassador, should be allowed to visit Mussolini. This request was refused by the following note: "His Majesty the King transmitted the Führer's message to

* On the "legendary escape," see Preface, p. 66.

Marshal Badoglio. The Marshal reported that His Excellency Mussolini is in good health and satisfied with his treatment. He regrets that it is to the best interest of His Excellency Mussolini himself that he refuse permission to visit him at this time. But the Marshal will be glad to transmit any letter that His Excellency the Ambassador may wish to send and to deliver an answer." This was on July 29, 1943. A high official of the Ministry of Foreign Affairs went to call on the German ambassador and reported on his conversation to Marshal Badoglio.

Because the Italian government was still pretending to be an ally and to go on with the war, Berlin could not demand Mussolini's liberation. Such a step at this time might have disturbed the relationship between the two governments and have brought on a premature crisis. Already Berlin had serious doubts about the eventual aims of Badoglio, but diplomatic practice forbade mentioning them without some concrete provocation. Mussolini's birthday, July 29, went by totally unnoticed. But there was one exception. Marshal Hermann Göring sent the Duce a telegram, which was brought to Ponza by an officer of the Carabinieri and which read as follows:

"DUCE:
"My wife and I send on this day our heartiest good wishes. Circumstances prevent my coming to Rome to bring you a bust of Frederick the Great as a birthday present, but this only strengthens the loyalty and

brotherly friendship which I wish to express to you on this occasion. Your statesmanship will go down in the history of our two nations, which are destined to march on to a common goal. I wish to tell you that our thoughts are constantly with you, to thank you for the hospitality you have shown me, and to assure you that my faith in you is boundless. Your devoted

GÖRING."

A little later, when Mussolini was confined at La Maddalena, he saw signs of German activity around him. The Germans had a base at Palau, across the straits, and they had indeed worked out a plan of landing men disguised as British sailors from a pretended British submarine to carry him away. They were about to put this plan into execution when Mussolini was transferred to the Gran Sasso.

On the evening of Saturday, September 11, an atmosphere of uncertainty and expectation seemed to hang over the Gran Sasso. It was thoroughly known by now that the government had fled along with the King and that the King had abdicated. The leaders of Mussolini's guard seemed embarrassed, as if they were faced with some particularly unpleasant duty. At about two in the morning Mussolini got up and wrote a letter to the captain, saying that the British would never take him alive. Captain Faiola removed all sharp metal objects from the Duce's room, including razor blades, and then repeated what he had said once before: "The British captured me when I was

136

wounded at Tobruk and I can bear witness to the cruel way they treated Italians. I'll never turn an Italian over to them." And he cried as he had on the previous occasion.

The rest of the night went by without incident.

Early in the morning of September 12, the top of the Gran Sasso was covered by heavy white clouds, but airplanes could be heard overhead. Mussolini had a presentiment that this day would be a decisive one. Toward noon the sun broke through the clouds and there was a September brightness in the air.

At exactly two o'clock in the afternoon Mussolini was sitting with folded arms in front of an open window when a glider landed about a hundred yards away. Four or five men in khaki uniforms got out, set up two machine guns, and then advanced toward the lodge. A few seconds later other gliders came down and the same maneuver was repeated. Mussolini did not think for even a minute that these were British soldiers. To kidnap him and carry him off to Salerno would have required no such dangerous undertaking. Then the alarm sounded. Carabinieri and policemen rushed out of the hospice with drawn arms and lined up against their attackers. Meanwhile Captain Faiola burst into the Duce's room and said:

"Shut the window and stay where you are!"

But Mussolini looked out the window and saw another larger group of Germans, who had taken possession of the funicular railway and were marching resolutely up toward the hospice with Skorzeny at their head. The carabinieri had already raised their guns to fire when Mussolini spied among the Germans an Italian officer whom he recognized when they drew nearer as General Soleti of the Police.

Mussolini broke the ominous silence preceding the order to fire by a loud shout:

"What are you doing? There's an Italian general! Don't shoot! Everything's in good order!"

At the sight of the Italian general the guards lowered their guns.

This was what had happened. General Soleti had been kidnapped early in the morning by the Skorzeny group, without being told where they were taking him. He was disarmed and set out with them for an unknown destination. When he found out, at the very last moment, what they were doing he was extremely happy to take part in Mussolini's liberation and to prevent by his presence a bit of unnecessary bloodshed. Soleti told Mussolini that it was inadvisable for him to go to Rome, where there was an atmosphere of civil war, and gave him the latest news of the flight of government and King. When Captain Skorzeny thanked him for his part in the expedition he asked that his pistol be returned and that he be allowed to follow Mussolini wherever he might go. These requests were granted.

In all this rapid succession of events Inspector Gueli played no part; in fact, he appeared on the scene only when it was all over. After Skorzeny's men had taken over the machine guns guarding the lodge entrance they all went up together to the Duce's room. Perspiring and deeply touched by the solemnity of the occasion, Skorzeny drew himself up to attention and said: "The Führer brooded night after night, when you were taken prisoner, as to how you could be freed. Then he entrusted me with this mission. I managed, under tremendous difficulties, to keep up with your movements everywhere that they took you. Today, by freeing you, I am happy to have accomplished my mission."

The Duce answered: "I knew all along that the Führer would give me this proof of his friendship. I thank him, and with him, you and your comrades in this daring enterprise."

Then the talk fell upon other subjects while Mussolini's papers and belongings were gathered together.

On the ground floor the guards were engaged in friendly conversation with the Germans, some of whom had suffered light wounds in landing. By three o'clock everything was ready for departure. As he went out the door Mussolini addressed warm words to these men and then all together, including the Italians, they set out for a field a short way below where a "Stork" plane was in waiting.

The extremely youthful captain who was the pilot of the plane introduced himself. His name was Gerlach. He was an ace. Before climbing into the plane Mussolini turned to say good-by to his guards, who seemed to be still in a daze. Many of them were deeply moved and some had tears in their eyes.

The space from which the "Stork" had to take off was extremely narrow. First it was backed up in order to gain a few yards. At the other end of the field there was a steep descent. The pilot took his place, with Skorzeny and Mussolini behind him. It was three o'clock. The propellers began to turn, the plane swayed and started across the stony field. Barely a yard from the precipice, with a jerk of the stick, it took off into the air. There were shouts from below and arms waving good-by. Then the silence of the upper air. After a few minutes the plane flew over Aquila and an hour later it glided quietly down to the airfield at Pratica di Mare, where a big trimotor plane was all ready to proceed further. Mussolini climbed in and the plane set out for Vienna. It arrived late at night, but there were men there to receive it. Mussolini was taken for the night to the Continental Hotel and flew the next day at noon to Munich.

On the morning of the day after, he was greeted at the Führer's headquarters with brotherly affection.

Mussolini's liberation by a group of German daredevils was enthusiastically applauded by the Germans; indeed the great deed was celebrated in every home in the land. The radio laid the stage for a very important announcement and when the news was given out at 10 P.M. the listeners' expectations were not disappointed. The event was generally considered as of exceptional significance.

Hundreds of letters and telegrams and verses were sent to Mussolini from every part of the Reich. But in Italy there was no such reaction. These were days of chaos, destruction, looting, and degradation and this piece of news was an unwelcome surprise which caused only bitterness and agitation. First of all it was denied altogether. They said the whole thing was a farce, that Mussolini was dead, that he had been handed over to the British, that a double had spoken for him at Munich. This rumor continued to go the rounds for months afterwards; perhaps it was indicative of a subconscious desire to be rid of him.

Although since this day hundreds of people have seen Mussolini in the flesh, the rumor of his death still persists. It cannot be explained away merely by the fact that the enemy radio threw doubts on Mussolini's health and spoke of frequent attempts on his life which supposedly caused him to move from one part of Germany to another. No, the explanation of this rumor's popularity must be sought elsewhere, perhaps in the elementary psychology of some Italians, who are "gifted" rather than really "intelligent."

From this viewpoint Mussolini has proved to have as many lives as a cat. More than once he has been at death's door. In March, 1917, when he was at the military hospital at Ronchi, with shell fragments all through his body, he was given up for dead and told that the best he

141

could expect was the amputation of his leg. But instead he lived to tell the tale and kept his leg to boot. After the war, in 1920, coming back from a Fascist meeting in Florence his car ran into and smashed the lowered bars of a railway crossing near Faenza, but Mussolini was only momentarily dazed. His bullet-proof skull withstood the blow. The airplane accident in which Mussolini was involved on the airfield of Arcore was an interesting one. The plane fell so fast that Mussolini had just time enough to think, "We are falling!" To fall a straight 150 feet even in a plane as well built as the unforgettable Aviati is no joke. The crash on the ground was a noisy one and there was a loud screech from the wings and cockpit. Men came running from all over the field. The instructor-pilot, that fine enthusiastic fellow, Cesare Redaelli, was only slightly wounded and Mussolini had no more than a bruise on one knee and a scratch on his "armor-plated" head between the nose and temples. Another very adventurous flight taken by the Duce was from Ostia to Salerno, on the day of his famous and long unpublished speech at Eboli in June, 1935. It was hurricane weather and just before landing the plane was grazed by lightning, which put its radio out of commission. It doesn't happen so frequently to a human being to be struck by lightning 9,000 feet above the ocean and to come out of it unscathed.

And what of the many duels that Mussolini fought? Even when the weapon chosen was the broadsword they were no more than harmless games.

Less harmless but more tedious were the various attempts on his life in the years 1925–26. Bombs and revolver shots, by men and women, native and foreign, and other sundry efforts of unknown origin—that was all in the day's work.

Let us pass now from the realm of external shock and violence to that of constitutional or organic infirmity. For twenty years, ever since February 15, 1925, Mussolini has had a neat little duodenal ulcer, whose history is told in great detail (among 70,000 other case histories) in the files of Professor Frugoni. Mussolini derived an understandable and intimate satisfaction from seeing this ulcer in X-ray pictures taken by the very honest and able Dr. Aristide Busi, head of the Medical College of Rome. From what we have said above it is clear that Mussolini may be considered a "die-hard" where death is concerned.

How, then, are we to explain the widespread public opinion that Mussolini was dead?

There have been several political incarnations of Mussolini. Even from the political viewpoint he had nine lives. In 1914 when he was expelled from the Socialist Party at its memorable assembly in the *Teatro del Popolo*, almost all the party members thought he was completely done for, crushed by the overwhelming vote of the rank and file, who wanted to disgrace him not only on political but on moral grounds. But a few months later the isolationist Socialists were hooted out of the public squares.

Then, when the war was over, came the threat of Bol-

143

shevism. In the election of 1919 (when Mussolini had the honor of running on the same ticket with Arturo Toscanini), he received only 4,000 votes against the millions cast for his opponents. The Reds swept the field. Drunk with victory they staged a mock funeral of Mussolini, and the coffin containing his effigy, followed by a crowd of noisy mourners, passed right in front of the house where he lived, on the Foro Bonaparte, Number 38, top floor.

It was out of this coffin that the Mussolini of 1921–22 arose. Something like this burial of 1919 was attempted again in July of 1943. This time they meant to finish up the job. His physical and political demises were to coincide. But the inscrutable ruler of fickle human fate thought differently. The Mussolini of today contains the Mussolini of yesterday, just as the Mussolini of yesterday contained the Mussolini of today. Now he lives at the Villa delle Orsoline instead of Palazzo Venezia; he has put himself in harness and gone to work with the same energy as before. And so you see, you doubting Thomases, that if he works he must be at least alive!

A Greek philosopher, Thales, used to thank the gods for making him a human being and not a beast, a man and not a woman, a Greek and not a barbarian. Mussolini thanks the gods for sparing him a clamorous trial at Madison Square Garden (a fate worse than being hung in the Tower of London) and for letting him, along with the best of his countrymen, live out the fifth and last act of the drama that involves his native land.

144

XV. ONE OF THE MANY: THE COUNT OF MORDANO

O N THE MORNING of July 25 Count Dino Grandi of Mordano was nowhere to be found. He was neither at the Chamber of Deputies nor at his luxurious villa at Frascati, where the servants said that he had left by car for Bologna. But a telephone call to his newspaper, *Il Resto del Carlino*, of Bologna, failed to unearth him there. Actually he was hiding in Rome, waiting for the coup d'état, and there he stayed for several days.

As soon as he heard of the formation of the Badoglio government he wrote a letter to the Marshal, saying that the new cabinet seemed to him a "solid" one and that "the ministers could not have been better chosen."

After several days of vain expectation Grandi assumed the name of Domenico Galli and fled to Spain. He was received with peculiar hospitality by the Italian consul at Seville, but feeling that his position was unsafe under the Franco regime he soon went to Estoril, in the vicinity of Lisbon.

His attitude before and during the Fascist Grand Council meeting of July 24 and his escape from Italy by plane under the protection of a passport issued by Badoglio leave little doubt as to the leading role he played in the conspiracy.

Grandi had held a great number of offices under the Fascist regime. He was Undersecretary of the Interior, Undersecretary and then Minister of Foreign Affairs, Ambassador to London, and finally Minister of Justice, and President of the Fascist Chamber of Corporations. And he had been given the title of Count of Mordano. Surely these honors should have contented him. But not so.

Early in March 1943 Grandi came to call on Mussolini at Palazzo Venezia, bearing with him the yearbook of the Ministry of Foreign Affairs.

"This is not the first time I have felt embarrassed in your presence," he said, "but under the circumstances it is particularly embarrassing to ask you a favor. You know that after ambassadors have been in service for a certain length of time, especially if they have been accredited for many years to the Court of St. James, they are invariably decorated with the *Collare dell'Annunziata*. It seems to me that I have fulfilled these conditions. Would you say a good word for me to the King?"

Mussolini had always intensely disliked this sort of talk. When the *Collare dell'Annunziata* was first offered to him he had turned it down in favor of Tommaso Tittoni.

"Very well," he answered dryly. "I'll mention it next time I see him."

And so he did. But the King showed little enthusiasm.

146

"First of all," the King said, "the ambassador to London is not necessarily dean of the diplomatic corps and hence automatically entitled to this decoration. Nor has he brought new territory under Italian rule. His only claim is as President of the Chamber. But if we decorate him in this capacity we must also decorate the President of the Senate, Count Suardo. And this would be a most inopportune step at this time, after all the gossip there has been about senators feeding information to the police."

Mussolini interposed that an investigation of this matter had shown that no such information had been given.

Mussolini brought the question up again at his next audience with the King and this time he met with no objections. In fact the King observed that Grandi's elevation to the post of Keeper of the Seals, which went along with the Ministry of Justice, entitled him to the collar. This change of heart within the space of forty-eight hours seemed suspicious. In any case, the date chosen for the award of the decoration was the feast of the Annunciation. Thus it was that on March 25, 1943, Count Dino Grandi won the right to be an honorary cousin of Victor Emmanuel of Savoy.

The papers carried this news without any particular comment.

A few days later Grandi turned up again at Palazzo Venezia and made declarations of devotion and loyalty to the Duce so vehement as to shake the walls of the building.

Was the award of this decoration perhaps connected in some way with the plot against Mussolini?

Who could ever have doubted the sincerity of Grandi's Fascist faith? Some people did doubt it, but no one paid them any attention. In the files containing all there is to know about 200,000 important Italians, Grandi's folder is especially voluminous. It would take hundreds of pages to record the oral and written public statements in which he boasted of his Fascist "orthodoxy" and his allegiance to the Duce. Had not Mussolini found him in an obscure editorial job on the *Resto del Carlino* and given him Party office and nationwide importance? *

"Where would I be today," Grandi often said to Mussolini, "if I had not met you? The most I could have hoped for was to be an unknown provincial lawyer."

Let us look at Grandi's folder, whose contents were not meant for the public eye and hence should have real documentary value. In March, 1923, after the March on Rome, Grandi was called to the capital to resume his political activity. On this occasion he wrote to the Duce in the following terms:

"Thank you for your kind words, which have restored my capacity to fight and work. I reproach myself for all the time I have wasted in sterile silence. I know my *own faults very well: they are grave ones and there are*

* Actually Grandi had gained a position of national importance in his struggles with Mussolini before the March on Rome. See Preface, p. 65.

many of them. But you, my chief, will see what I can do when put to the test. You will see that Dino Grandi is all loyalty and devotion."

In May, 1925, Mussolini made Dino Grandi Under-secretary of Foreign Affairs. Grandi had never hidden his desire for this post and he thanked the Duce in these words:

"Frankly and without false modesty I must tell you that my unexpected appointment gives me enormous pleasure, most of all because this important job will bring me close to you. This is my highest ambition, the greatest reward that I could hope for. *You already know my boundless and unconditional loyalty* and the fact that I ask nothing but to obey you. Do with me whatever you think best at any time, since you are in a position to judge how I can be most useful."

On December 14, 1927, Grandi wrote in a letter to the Duce:

"A few months ago you ordered me back to my job. I obeyed and in so doing I wish to give you passionate assurance of what amounts to an oath of loyalty. *I want you to know that my loyalty is blind, absolute, and in-destructible.* I consider it as a spiritual conquest won from silence and meditation. *Put me to the test and you will see."*

After he had held the post of Minister of Foreign Affairs for a number of years it was given to someone else. How did this happen? Because Grandi's frequent visits to Geneva had an extremely bad influence upon him and he came to espouse the cause of the League of Nations. During this period he made quite a name for himself abroad. He visited almost every European capital, including Ankara, and he was generally considered to have democratic tendencies and a moderating influence upon Italian foreign policy. After the failure of the Four-Power Pact, the Fascist government took quite another tack. One fine day Grandi was demoted to the post of Ambassador to London. It is reasonable to suppose that at this time he might have begun to harbor a certain resentment, which might eventually lead him to rebel. But if so he hid it very successfully.

On February 20, 1935, when new developments in Africa were in the air, he wrote from London:

"I have come back to my job with a picture of Fascist Italy such as I never had before. This is the Italy of your creation, marching with keen judgment toward the the future, immune to worry on the one hand and to hysterical enthusiasm on the other, but with a clear vision of things as they are. The wise old Romans would have called this period one blessed by the deity known as *Fortuna virilis*. I think you can be proud of the way Italy has responded to your marching orders."

Every now and then the Ambassador came to renew his contact with his country and its Regime. Never either in public or in his private correspondence did he make the slightest criticism; in fact he always sang its praises.

In February of 1939, after visiting some Fascist Militia barracks, Grandi wrote: "I have come away deeply impressed. Guidonia is a mighty powerhouse of strength for our future war. *Among all your creations perhaps this one gives the most plastic evidence of Genius and Power.*"

This was the year when the so-called "Roman parade step" was introduced, first into the Militia and then into the regular Army, giving rise to a great deal of useless discussion. The fact is that the Italian army was the only one without a marching "style" of its own. It is obvious that a parade step is the crowning accomplishment of close formation drill and that it has a tremendous disciplinary value. Everyone knows what happened at Waterloo. At one point of the battle some Prussian units, surprised by massed French artillery fire, began to waver. They were rallied by Blücher's order to close ranks in "goose step," after which they fearlessly re-entered the fray.

During one of his periodical visits to Rome, Grandi had occasion to see the first parades executed in this step, and he was positively electrified with enthusiasm. Here is part of an ecstatic letter which he wrote to Mussolini at this time, containing an interpretation of this step from both an auditory and spiritual point of view:

"The ground trembled under the thud, or rather the hammering, of the legionnaires' feet. I looked from close by at our Black Shirts. When they march in 'Roman step' their eyes sparkle, the line of their mouths is hard and narrow and there is a new expression on their faces, which is not just conventionally martial but reflects the pride of a warrior who splits and crushes the enemy's head beneath his heel. Indeed it is only after ten or twelve steps that the hammering becomes steadily louder, because its echo sounds in the marchers' ears and makes them pound with intensified vigor. *Among the necessary changes which you have brought about in our way of doing things the Roman step, along with the new uniform and the substitution of* voi *for* lei, *is the most powerful instrument of Fascist education.* I only wonder whether in a parade of this kind music may not be superfluous. Don't think me presumptuous to make such a suggestion, but it seems to me that in this case band music distracts the spectator's attention. Silence, broken only by the rolling of drums, is the best background for the vibration of this powerful, rhythmical, collective hammering, with its resonance of bronze."

These were the years in which the Fascist Party proposed to recast Italian habits. This was the purpose back of the introduction of the ceremony of the change of the guard.

The change of the guard had become with time one of the dullest of military ceremonials. No one was interested enough to look at it. The change of the King's guard at the Quirinal Palace was now improved by the accompaniment of a military band. The same improvement was carried out at Palazzo Venezia and thereafter an increasingly large crowd of both Italians and foreigners came to look on.

One day Grandi happened to see the change of the guard at Palazzo Venezia, which he described as "superb and formidable," going on to say:

"I witnessed the same ceremony in Berlin not long ago and in London I see it frequently. But this was far superior to both. The close-formation drill which you have taught your soldiers is unique and marvelous. The steel color of your soldiers is surely matched by hearts and muscles and tendons of steel. They have not the 'ballet step' of the British or the 'catapult' formation of the Germans. Instead they form a massive block of steel, just as heavy as that of the Germans, but of a metal more supple than the German cast iron. *This drill is the most powerful instrument of popular education that you have yet forged.*"

In these days of disaster everyone has belittled and condemned former Fascist Party Secretary Starace. At the last Great Council meeting Grandi spoke up violently against him. And yet in 1938, after a visit to the Farnesina, he said in a letter to Mussolini that "Starace was working wonders." On this same occasion, speaking of his imminent departure for London, he said that he would make a point of traveling through Germany rather than France. *"In all my seven years in London,"* he wrote, *"I have not once spent so much as a single night in Paris. I hate the place."*

When Albania was occupied Grandi wrote from London in the following terms:

"The events of today have *electrified* me. Duce, you are pushing the Revolution ahead with the fatal and pitiless rhythm of a powerful machine. First Adua was avenged and now Valona. As your devoted collaborator, who for eight years was privileged to bear witness to your daily work, I know that you have never flagged for a second in the pursuit of this goal. This new victory makes the Adriatic, strategically speaking, an Italian sea and opens to Mussolini's Italy the ancient roads of Roman conquest in the East."

As for the present war, Count Grandi was at the beginning highly enthusiastic. On August 9, 1940, he sent the Duce a photostat of an article he had written twenty-six years before (December, 1914), which showed that his interventionist sympathies had the same essential idealistic and political basis in the case of both wars.

"I am one of those who under your guidance, Duce, have thought all along that Italy's real, revolutionary, people's war was yet to come and that it would be waged between Italy, Germany, and Russia on the one side and Britain and France on the other. *From the very beginning we looked upon the latter as our real enemies, even if we were then preparing to join them.*"

After war was declared, when Grandi came back from London, where he had acquired a certain prestige, he was made Minister of Justice and Keeper of the Seals and in this capacity hastened the completion of the new codes, to which he himself gave the name of "Mussolinian." He was given at the same time the presidency of the Fascist Chamber of Corporations and this inspired him to write to the Duce on March 27, 1941:

> "I am deeply grateful to you for the kind words you said to me this evening. Oh to be every day more intensely one of the new type of Italians that you are hammering out of steel! This is the one aim of my life and faith and spirit, which for twenty-five years, Duce, have belonged to you."

On December 2, 1942, the Duce spoke to the Chamber on the political and military situation. Grandi was presiding. The assembly was enthusiastic and there seemed to be complete unity of feeling. The next day the Duce received a letter, signed "A Woman," which ran like this: "Two or three of the leaders are plotting against you. I followed yesterday's meeting from the press gallery and saw the impenetrable expression on Grandi's face. His applause was perfunctory. He stayed in London too long! Someone who knows him warns you to look out!"

Grandi's case is not an isolated example. There are many more just like it. It is a historical fact that in time of crisis the higher-ups give way and betray, while the little people hold firm and keep faith. With the former shrewdness (that is, intelligence) is uppermost; with the latter simple, spontaneous feeling prevails. Such a complete about-face as that of Grandi (documented above in letters which are only a small part of a large collection in the same vein) explains Mussolini's skepticism, due in part to the fact that all his life he never had any friends.

Was this a good thing or a bad one? He gave considerable thought to this problem when he was at La Maddalena, where he wrote: "Good or bad, it doesn't matter, for now it is too late. Someone in the Bible said, 'Woe unto the lonely!' But there was a saying during the Renaissance, 'Be alone and you will be your own master.' If I had any friends now would be the time for them to sympathize, literally to 'suffer with' me. But since I have none my misfortunes remain within the closed circle of my own life."

XVI. THE DRAMA OF DUAL RULE

From the March on Rome to the Speech of January Third

IN THE MIDST of such vast historical events as war and revolution it is no easy matter to pin down the causes that first set them in motion, especially from a chronological point of view. We risk looking in some prehistorical period for the origins of contemporary happenings, since the search for one motive invariably leads to another still more remote in time. In order not to wander so far afield we must set some definite point of departure for the chain of events we wish to study.

The beginnings of Fascism go back to 1914–15, to the time of the first World War, when the *Fasci di Azione Rivoluzionaria* (Fascist Groups for Revolutionary Action) took up the cause of intervention. These were reborn on March 23, 1919, under the name of *Fasci di Combattimento* (Fascist Combat Groups). Three years later came the March on Rome. It is from this day, October 28, 1922, that we must date our survey of the twenty years of Fascism and look for the causes of the coup d'état of July, 1943.

What was the nature of the March on Rome? Was it a mere government crisis, a normal change of cabinet? No, it was much more than this; it was an insurrection, which had its ups and downs for two years before it was successful. Did this insurrection amount to a revolution? No, it did not, that is if by revolution we mean not only a reversal of the existing government, but a sweeping change of governmental institutions. In this case the monarchy, which had existed before Fascism, was left undisturbed. Mussolini once said jokingly that there was one error in the itinerary of the Black Shirts' triumphal parade through the streets of Rome on October 31, 1922: they should have marched through the Quirinal Palace instead of in front of it. But at the time such action would have seemed impractical and absurd.

How could one attack a monarchy which not only failed to bar the gates but indeed left them wide open? The King had revoked Premier Facta's last-minute proclamation of a state of siege; he had not listened to the suggestions attributed by some people to Marshal Badoglio, which provoked violent comment in the Fascist *Popolo d'Italia;* he had asked Mussolini to form a cabinet which (except for the absence of the intransigent left wing) was symbolic of a new era of national unity and of the Fascist victory.

To proclaim out of a clear sky that the March on Rome aimed at setting up a republic would only have made for complications. In his speech at Udine in September, 1922,

Mussolini had already shelved any such idea. But we must look at the very beginnings of the Fascist movement if we wish to see its attitude toward the existing form of government. Paragraph D of the first program issued by the Fascist Combat Groups in 1919, from their headquarters at Via Paolo da Cannobio 37, proposed *"the convocation of a three-year session of a National Assembly whose first task shall be to establish the constitutional form of the government."* There is in these words no commitment to a republic. A year later, at the national congress held in the Teatro Lirico of Milan, May 24 and 25, 1920, came the announcement of various Fascist aims, which were summarized by the pamphlet entitled *Technical Theories and Practical Directives of Fascism* (issued by headquarters in Via Monte di Pietà). Here we find a statement that the Fascists "do not oppose the debatable doctrines of Socialism as such, but do oppose their theoretical and practical degeneration into what is called Bolshevism." Then, going on to the problem of forms of government, we read:

"In Fascist opinion the form of government is subordinate to the present and future interests of the Nation, both material and spiritual. For this reason Fascists have no prejudice either for or against present institutions. This does not mean that the movement can be said to have a monarchical or dynastic trend. If the best future interests of the Nation call for a change in the form of government the Fascists will be ready to effect it, not as a matter of principle but on a basis of strictly factual considerations. All forms of government are not indiscriminately suited to all peoples. The Phrygian cap does not fit every head. Each nation has it own requirements. In England old forms survive, but the actual government is democratic, whereas the so-called Soviet republics are ferociously aristocratic in character. Today Fascists do not consider themselves committed to our present monarchical institutions."

We can see from this declaration that the Fascist approach was a strictly pragmatic one, and it did not substantially change during the years 1921–22. At the time of the insurrection the idea of a republic was far from the people's minds. Ever since the death of Giuseppe Mazzini and his disciples (the last of whom, Aurelio Saffi, died in 1890) the Republican Party had lived only in its "sacred memories," caught between the monarchy on the one side and the new doctrines of Socialism on the other.

Three figures stand out in the Republican decline: Dario Papa, Giovanni Bovio, and Arcangelo Ghisleri. This last was of such stalwart faith that he refused election to the Chamber of Deputies in order not to be obliged to take an oath of allegiance to the King. But the other Republican leaders, corrupted by parliamentary privilege, had come to terms with the monarchy and during the first World War they even accepted posts in the cabinet.

This sort of Masonic Republicanism was represented by the Jew Salvatore Barzilai. The monarchy and the Masons between them had to all intents and purposes emasculated the ideals of the Republican Party. The liberation of Trento and Trieste as a result of the war meant that the historical function of the party was over. After a century of sacrifice, struggle, and martyrdom, a dream had come true, and the Republicans, who had held the torch lighted all this time, deserved full credit for its accomplishment. In the postwar period, except on the occasion of the Red "parade" at the re-opening of the Chamber after the elections of November, 1919, no one spoke again, even on the Left, of a republic.

From the day when the King called the Socialist leader Turati to confer with him in the Quirinal and Turati (even if in street clothes and an old felt hat) consented to go, any mention of the Republic seemed a thing of the past. The war victory had thoroughly consolidated the monarchy's position.

Among the Fascist quadrumvirate, De Vecchi was an ardent monarchist and defender of the House of Savoy and De Bono, at bottom, shared his feelings. Only Italo Balbo had had republican leanings in his youth. As for Michele Bianchi, the "brains" of the group, who came to Fascism from revolutionary syndicalism, he too considered the question of the monarchy of secondary importance.

In view of these historical and political conditions the March on Rome could not lead to the installation of a republic. The people were completely unprepared for any such drastic change and an untimely effort to force it upon them would have handicapped and perhaps endangered the outcome of the Fascist insurrection.

The monarchy remained, but Fascism felt almost immediately the need of creating institutions of its own such as the Grand Council and the Militia.

It was at a meeting at the Grand Hotel of Rome in January, 1923, that these two bodies came into being and along with them a political system which might be called "dual rule," or divided command. Mussolini observed, with unintentional humor, that it was like twin beds, which, according to Balzac's *Physiology of Marriage*, are a very bad system indeed.

Little by little dual role acquired definite status, even if there was no special legislation to cover it. At the top of the ladder were the King and the Duce, and whenever troops under review gave a vocal salute, they hailed both names. There was a time, after a conquest of the Empire, when the volcanically exuberant General Baistrocchi ordered a triple salute, but Mussolini enjoined him not to introduce any such "litany" into the Army. In addition to the Army, which took orders from the King, there was the Fascist Militia, commanded by the Duce. The King's bodyguard was composed of extra-tall carabinieri; later Gino Calza-Bini set up a similar guard, made up of "musketeers," for Mussolini.

The Cabinet was a constitutional body, but the Grand Council, created by the Revolution, came to outrank it. The martial and dashing Fascist song, *Giovinezza*, had the same ceremonial status as Gabetti's *Marcia reale*, a noisy national anthem, whose repetitive strains put both musicians and audience to sleep. In order not to prolong unduly the time required to listen to the two tunes in succession, only a few bars of each were sounded.

The form of military salute fell, too, under dual rule. The old form was retained when a cap was worn, but the Roman or Fascist raised-arm salute was given by bareheaded men. (As if they had changed heads in the meantime!)

Of the three branches of the Armed Forces the Army was most loyal to the King, followed closely by the Navy, particularly the General Staff. Only the Air Force, which was built up, or rather rebuilt, by the new government, went in for Fascist insignia.

One section of the Army, the Carabinieri, had a strictly dynastic character. These were the King's men. Here too Fascism sought to create a police organization to insure political security and at the same time it started a new secret police called the *Ovra.*

But the dynasty had a domestic police force and information service of its own made up of retired Army officers and civil servants living in the provinces. The King had also a skeleton diplomatic corps which gathered him information from abroad. When accredited diplomatic representatives came back from their foreign posts they invariably called at the Quirinal. Then the King availed himself of his relationship to royal and princely families all over Europe and of the once-powerful "Kings' International," which is now reduced to a few pale ghosts.

The General Staff of the Army was "royalist" to the core. It was a closed, practically impenetrable caste upon which the dynasty could completely rely. The Chamber was a representative Fascist Party organ, but the Senate, whose members were chosen by the King and included an impressive number of admirals and generals, exercised a strong political and moral influence in the monarchy's behalf.

The nobility, first the "White" faction and then, after the reconciliation with the Church, the "Black" as well, made up another group loyal to the monarchy. After the Lateran Pact, Vatican and clerical circles came into the royal orbit and religious ceremonies came to include a prayer for the King.

The wealthy bourgeoisie—bankers, businessmen, and landowners—although they displayed their sympathies in a less conspicuous manner—were nevertheless on the King's side. Freemasons considered the King as an "honorary brother" and so did the Jews. The Crown Prince had a Jew, Professor Polacco, for a tutor.

Now, in order for the system of dual rule to endure, its two parallel structures had to balance one another perfectly.

The year of 1923, when the Fascists exercised "full power," went by uneventfully except for the incident of

164

Corfu, which was settled by the League of Nations to the entire satisfaction of the Italian government.

But 1924 was a year of crisis. The Regime had to face the consequences of a crime which, all other considerations aside, was ill-timed, clumsily executed, and hence a political error.

During the summer of 1924 the Aventine group had considerable influence in Court circles and the Opposition went so far as to advance formal proposals to the King. The King gave the petitioners some vague reassurances of a purely juridical kind, but hesitated to follow them into any political action.

The King was not particularly impressed by the famous confession of Cesare Rossi, which the government itself published at the end of December before the Opposition could turn it to their own ends. The Opposition staked everything on a moral question to which there could be no solution in their favor, and by withdrawing from the political arena they left the way clear for the Regime to counterattack them whenever it saw fit. The counterattack came with Mussolini's speech of January 3 and the drastic measures taken in the forty-eight hours that followed. Although the King had stood up with a certain firmness against the preceding maneuvers on the part of the Opposition, he did not seem pleased with the revolutionary action of January 3, which suppressed all political parties and laid the foundations of a totalitarian state.

This was the first clash between the two partners of the

dual rule. The King felt that from now on the monarchy had lost its constitutional character. No longer could he choose his ministers; the disappearance of the political parties meant that they would no longer alternate in power. The monarchy had less and less of a function to perform. Once upon a time cabinet crises, along with national calamities and New Year's receptions, had given the King the only occasions on which to make himself known to his people as anything beside a fanatical collector of old coins. Cabinet crises, in particular, when candidates for the premiership flocked to the royal palace, had made the King the center of public attention. Now all this was gone. From 1925 on, any change in government leadership was a strictly Party affair.

The year 1925 was one of repressive measures. The next year, 1926, witnessed the passage of constructive social legislation. But toward November the Chamber, which now frankly called itself Fascist, expelled the decadent fugitives of the Aventine. This new tightening of the Regime's totalitarian grip could not fail to be noticed at Court. People began to speak of the monarchy as a prisoner of the Party and to feel sorry for the King because he was relegated to second place.

But on the whole the years 1925–26 went by quietly enough.

*From the Establishment of the Grand Council
to the Conspiracy of July, 1943*

T HE LAW defining the functions and prerogatives of the Fascist Grand Council and legalizing its position as the most important government organ was at the root of the first serious differences between the monarchy and Fascism. The Council acquired the right to keep an up-to-date list of persons suitable for government office (Mussolini once did present such a list to the King) and, in addition to this, to determine the succession to the throne. The shock to Court circles was great. This new law was a death blow to the old Constitution, which heretofore had automatically ensured that the crown should be passed down from father to son. It was even insinuated that the move was of Republican inspiration or at least that it was aimed at preventing Prince Humbert from ascending the throne and putting the Duke of Apulia in his place.

From this day on Victor Emmanuel detested Mussolini and nursed a tremendous hate for Fascism. "The Regime has no business meddling with these things," he said one day. "The basic law of the land had already provided for them. Under a monarchical form of government if a single party claims to decide upon the succession to the throne, then the monarchy is done for. There is only one watchword where succession is concerned, and that is: 'The King is dead! Long live the King!' "

The crisis provoked by the law strengthening the Grand Council lasted for several months, although relations between the two camps remained superficially cordial.

The conciliation between Church and State effected in 1929 blew away this access of bad feeling and normal relations once more prevailed. At first the King was skeptical of the possibilities of solving the "Roman question" and later he harbored doubts as to the sincerity of the Vatican. But eventually the idea of freeing Rome from the mortgage left behind by the last Pope to hold temporal power came to attract him. He was flattered by the prospect of an exchange of calls between two sovereigns and saw in the whole thing a re-enforcement of existing institutions. Even the Concordat did not displease him although his well-known anticlerical sentiments made him wary. But when the bishops marched by to swear him allegiance he came to the conclusion that he had received a fair exchange for the concessions made to the Vatican.

Nineteen twenty-nine, then, was a fortunate year. Not long after the signing of the Lateran Treaties the King said to Mussolini in the course of one of their regular conversations: "First you succeeded in doing something that other men would have neither undertaken nor carried through. Then in your speeches before Parliament you corrected the unfounded presumptions of certain clerical groups. This is a real accomplishment. I don't know how to make a public demonstration of my gratitude. I really don't know. . . . You received the *Collare dell'Annunziata* after the annexation of Fiume. Perhaps a title of nobility . . ."

"No," Mussolini interrupted, "a title of that kind would make me ridiculous. I couldn't look at myself in the mirror. I shan't be so vain as to say: '*Roi ne puis, prince ne daigne, Rohan je suis,*' but I beg of you not to insist. Everyone must cut out a distinctive pattern for himself."

The King understood and did not pursue the subject further.

It would take too long at this point to tell of all the occasions when dual rule was submitted to severe strain. There was, of course, a comic aspect of the affair when the sacred, inscrutable regulations of "protocol" came into play. The height of complication was reached when the Führer visited Rome, and the paradox of dual rule was exhibited to the public for a whole week, in a series of unforeseen episodes, which were irritating and amusing in turn. In 1937 Mussolini had made a trip to Germany, where both Berlin and Munich had given him a memorable reception. Millions of Berliners crowded the Maifeld in order to hear the Führer and the Duce speak, and world opinion was greatly impressed. In May of 1938, then, the Führer came to Rome. It was no easy task to plan the details of his visit, but it was clear that his chief intention was to see Mussolini's Rome.

When the German train pulled into the new San Paolo station the Duce was there with the King to meet him. Then the Führer got into the royal coach beside the King and they set out for the Quirinal. The crowd lining the Via dei Trionfi, Via dell'Impero, and Piazza Venezia looked for the Duce in vain. He had returned by side streets of the Testaccio section to his own office.

This seemed to hurt the Führer's feelings. The following days were marked by alternate hospitality. The King escorted the Führer in the morning and Mussolini escorted him in the afternoon, or vice versa, according to the degree of Fascist character of the various ceremonies they went to attend.

In the freezing atmosphere of the Quirinal, where various details of his physical comfort were neglected, the Führer felt ill at ease. At the great military parade in the Via dei Trionfi members of his suite noticed that the Queen and her ladies-in-waiting made deep reverences to the Army flags but appeared not to see the banners of the Fascist Militia.

At the ceremonies which King and Duce attended together the Duce stepped back in order to allow the King's aides to take front place. This was particularly noticeable at the costumed celebration held in the Piazza di Siena, one of the most picturesque and spectacular shows of recent years in Rome. Finally the Führer invited the Duce to take his place beside him in the front row.*

At last the visit to Rome came to an end. When the Führer had escaped from what one Berliner called the "stuffiness of the royal catacombs" and arrived in Florence, his mood improved. He had been struck by the majesty of Rome, but the beauty of Florence aroused in him even greater enthusiasm and he would have liked to stay longer. "This is the city of my dreams," he said.

The week of the Führer's visit to Rome revealed certain contradictory aspects of the etiquette of dual rule, but a later episode, the law creating the two first "Marshals of the Empire," brought on a really serious crisis. This law was passed upon the spontaneous initiative of a group of deputies and senators after a speech by Mussolini that particularly aroused their enthusiasm. After both branches of Parliament had approved it the King very nearly refused his signature. In a conversation held soon afterward he appeared to be in a state of great agitation.

"After the privileges given the Grand Council," he said, "here is another law that deals a mortal blow to my

* According to Mussolini's original manuscript, Hitler told him, the first time they met after the trip to Italy, "You know what I did as soon as I came back to Germany after my trip to Rome? I immediately doubled the pensions to the former ministers of the social democratic era. It was out of sheer gratitude. After having realized what it means to have a monarchy and what a dynasty is, I thought that those old Social Democrats deserved my thanks for having got rid of the Hohenzollerns." The German censor definitely did not like the sentence and struck it out. See Amicucci, *I 600 giorni di Mussolini*, p. 172.

royal prerogatives. There is no rank that I could have refused you as a testimony of my admiration. But this equalization puts me in an impossible position, because it is another patent violation of the Constitution."

"You know that I have no hankering for titles and trappings," Mussolini replied. "The promoters of this law thought that if they conferred such a rank on me, you too must automatically receive it."

"But the two Houses have no right to take steps of this kind!"

The King was pale with anger and his chin trembled.

"This is the last straw. Because of the tense international situation I don't wish to add fuel to the flames, but at any other time I should have abdicated rather than submit to such an insult. I'd like to tear these things up!" And he looked scornfully at the new cap and sleeve insignia.

Mussolini was surprised by this outburst and asked the opinion of Professor Santi Romano, president of the Council of State and an eminent scholar of constitutional law. Santi Romano prepared a memorandum in which he proved that the Parliament was quite within its rights and that if an unprecedented rank in the military hierarchy had been conferred upon the Duce it must also be conferred, by virtue of his supreme leadership, upon the King as well. When Mussolini showed this memorandum to the King the latter had another fit of anger.

"Professors of constitutional law, especially when they are faint-hearted opportunists like Professor Santi Romano, can find arguments to justify the most absurd propositions. That is, in fact, their job. But I stick to my guns. And I have already told the Presidents of the two Houses what I think, with the request that they transmit my opinions to the promoters of the new law. This affront to the Crown must be the last of its kind."

From this time on Victor Emmanuel swore revenge. It was only a question of waiting for an opportune time.

In the spring and summer of 1943 the relationship between the two elements of the dual rule had undergone a deep change. The whole Fascist "machine"—government, Party, syndicates, and administration—was showing wear and tear from the effects of war. Tens of thousands of Fascists had fallen in the field, among them two thousand leaders. (This is a fact that it would be criminal to forget.) A million Fascists were under arms—from Varo to Rhodes, from Ajaccio to Athens. Few Party members were left in Italy and they were occupied almost exclusively with war relief. Then came unsuccessful military operations, the loss of our colonies in Africa, terroristic bombardments of our cities from the air, and food shortages.

The next thing was a subtle, well-planned, continuous attempt to sap the nation's morale. Everything was turned to this end. When there were no facts to go on, facts were invented or embroidered. At a certain moment there was a widespread impression that the whole structure was mined from within and that the slightest blow would cause it to crumble. The main thing was to demoralize our youth. Two rival forces, both of them international in scope, worked against us in every sector of political and economic life. The long-dormant Masons saw that their hour had come and resumed activity in the circles where they had the most influence: the professions and the civilian and military bureaucracies. Through Lisbon, contacts with the Anglo-Saxon lodges were re-established. A wave of mysterious and elusive sabotage spread throughout the Armed Forces. Wild rumors were on every tongue. Of course this sudden activity did not fail to arouse attention inside the bronze doors of the Vatican. Here, too, a no less insidious and demoralizing campaign, based on different grounds, was launched to obtain the same ends. The watchword was pacifism, above all considerations of nationality, and preached in the Italian tongue on Italian ground it had great effect upon the population, especially in some districts. The maneuvers of these two large organizations were seconded, of course, by the efforts of the anti-Fascist parties, old and new, whose program was one of simple revenge.

When the landing in Sicily made all hope of military success fade away, the dual rule was bound to burst apart in brutal fashion. Seeing the discomfiture of the Fascists, the monarchy called upon the forces it had held in reserve among its traditional supporters and passed to the attack.

In July of 1943, when the Crown was sure of holding

the upper hand, its motive was sheer self-preservation. The course of the war and the future of the nation had no part in its plans. Pure personal egotism inspired the action of the King, as is clear in the "posthumous" declaration he made from Bari to the effect that he had wanted "to get rid of Fascism."

But the King's calculations were mistaken and now a crucified nation is paying for his betrayal.

Fascism must pay for the generous and romantic error it made in October 1922, when instead of making a clean, totalitarian sweep of old institutions, it tried a compromise solution which the experience of history has shown to be a precarious compromise.

The Fascist Revolution stopped short of the throne. At the time this course seemed inevitable. As things have turned out, the Crown has expiated with its fall the dagger it stuck in the back of the Fascist regime and the unpardonable crime it perpetrated upon the nation.

But the nation can come to life again only under the auspices of a republic.

XVIII. ONE OF THE MANY:
THE EXECUTIONER

ON APRIL 2, 1925, Mussolini, just recovered from an illness, made a speech on military matters during the Senate discussion of the proposed Di Giorgio law. By unanimous acclamation, the Senators ordered that the speech be posted in every town and village of the land. A few days later the Duce took over the Ministry of War. On April 10 General Pietro Badoglio cabled him from Rio de Janeiro, where he was then Italian ambassador:

> "Upon the occasion of your taking over the direction of the Ministry of War, accept my warmest greetings as a general of the Army and a soldier of our victorious and respected country."

Badoglio had been made ambassador to Brazil after the March on Rome. Not long before the Fascist insurrection certain statements attributed to him had provoked a violent note in the *Popolo d'Italia* of October 14, 1922.

Badoglio seemed willing to accept the post of ambassador and set out for his new destination, where he remained for several years without distinguishing himself in any way. When he came home, after the Regime had successfully emerged from the difficulties of 1924, his loyalty seemed unquestionable. At this time he went around saying: *"I'll go wherever I'm sent; whenever you give me orders you will find Badoglio ready."*

In the spring of 1925 came a decision to create the rank of Chief of Staff with a view to the co-ordination of all the Armed Forces. General Badoglio was strongly backed by Court circles for this post and the King himself declared that from a professional point of view he had by far the "best brains" among all the candidates.

What has become of Senator Edoardo Rotigliano, a lawyer from Florence who passed from the nationalist group to the Fascist movement? His last public utterance was a somewhat irreverent speech made before the Senate in the spring of 1943, recalling the King's attitude at the time of the rout at Caporetto during the last war.

On April 4, 1925, the then ex-Deputy Rotigliano sent to the Head of the Government the following significant and almost prophetic letter:

"YOUR EXCELLENCY:
There was much talk in the Chamber today of the appointment of General Badoglio to the post of Chief of Staff. I hope that this talk is unfounded. I had occasion to know General Badoglio during the war and to study his behavior at close range. I can assure you that he has not the necessary qualifications for this post. Many people know that Badoglio was chiefly responsi-

ble for Caporetto, but few are acquainted with his disgraceful conduct immediately after the defeat, when he left three of the four divisions of his 27th Army Corps on the left bank of the Isonzo river with no one to command them and rushed to Udine and Padua in order to clear himself of blame and to intrigue for the post of Deputy Chief of Staff. He is a man of insatiable ambition. If he were to be at the head of the Army, I feel sure he would use his office to get hold of the government. I am not backing any other candidate; in fact, I consider that none of the generals in the public eye is unswervingly loyal to our Regime. But from this point of view, Badoglio is the worst possible choice. Forgive me, Your Excellency, but I consider it my duty to express my opinion. It is based on direct experience of which I should be glad to give you a more detailed account. With assurances of my unfailing devotion,

E. ROTIGLIANO."

There followed a typewritten postscript:

"He tried, by means of a forged telegram, to make it appear that he had been transferred to another command before the smashup of his Army corps."

Rotigliano's letter received due attention and led to further research and consultations. During a conversation that Mussolini held with Rotigliano he got the impression that the latter's position was a partisan one, for the nationalist group had always stood up for Cadorna. In a letter written from Villar Pellice on September 12, 1919, to the editor of *Vita Italiana*, Cadorna had written:

"Yesterday the *Gazzetta del Popolo* published the results of the investigation of Caporetto. . . . It would take a whole volume to reply. . . . Responsibility is loaded on Generals Porro, Capello, Montuori, Bongiovanni, Cavaciocchi, and myself, without a single word about Badoglio, who deserves a great share of the blame. It was his Army corps (the 27th) which was smashed across from Tolmino, losing three lines of defense in the course of a single day, although the day before (October 23) he had told me personally that he was sure of resisting and he had said the same thing on October 19 to Colonel Calcagno, whom I had sent to investigate the condition and needs of his troops. The smashing of this corps brought on the disintegration of the entire front. And yet Badoglio has wriggled out of it so easily! The Masons must have something to do with it, and other influences besides, considering the honors that have since been showered upon him. And that is all I have to say!"

By "other influences" Cadorna meant the monarchy. Speaking of Caporetto, there are in the War Museum in Milan three unpublished manuscripts by General Cavaciocchi, which his daughter presented to the Duce fifteen years ago through the intermediary of General Segato with a view to eventual publication.

This political and military controversy was finally resolved, largely through the influence of Marshal Diaz, in Badoglio's favor. When it came to choosing his Deputy Chief of Staff, Badoglio eliminated Grazioli as "slippery,"

Vaccari as "doddering," Ferrari as "having lost his prestige," and he finally settled on General Scipioni, in spite of his druggist's appearance. Writing to the Duce on this subject on May 1, 1925, Badoglio concluded: "I have said above exactly what I think. *But no matter who is my deputy I shall go ahead on my own and Your Excellency will have the Army he desires. For this reason I am willing to leave the decision in Your Excellency's hands.*"

A series of conferences were held at this time at the Ministry of War, under Mussolini's chairmanship and in the presence of Bonzani and Thaon di Revel, with the aim of making the Air Force into a separate branch of the service.

After Zaniboni's unsuccessful attempt on Mussolini's life, Badoglio sent the following message to the Duce, dated November 7, 1925:

"Having received confirmation of the fact that ex-member of Parliament Zaniboni was wearing the uniform of a major in the Alpine troops when he made his criminal attempt on your life I wish as Chief of Staff and a faithful government servant to protest, in the name of all who wear the Italian uniform, against the heinous act of a man who, forgetful of the laws of honor, sought to cover up with decorations of the past the most vile and hideous misdeed of the present. *God has saved Your Excellency and Italy.* Amid the emotion of the nation, which has gathered around you during these days of alternate distress and joy, Your Excellency has surely recognized the heartbeat of all of us who bear arms in the service of our country and who are, in the august name of the King, your respectful and loyal followers.

BADOGLIO."

It is ironic, at a distance of almost twenty years, to hear the word "honor" on the Marshal's lips! And it is a curious fact that among the first people appointed to high office by the Bari government, born of surrender, should be Zaniboni, the unsuccessful assassin of 1925!

After he had entered upon his new functions Badoglio attended to military affairs from somewhat of a distance, giving out orders of only the most general kind. He rarely attended the annual maneuvers, for fear of meeting persons whom he particularly disliked, such as Cavallero. But on December 24, 1926, Badoglio sent the Duce his "deepest and most sincere greetings along with the wish that under the Duce's energetic leadership the Army may attain the greatest possible efficiency," adding: "I promise Your Excellency that in this great task we shall be your tireless and most loyal collaborators."

In the autumn of 1928 Badoglio was made Governor of Libya, succeeding De Bono, who had greatly forwarded the colony's agricultural development. It was agreed that Badoglio should retain his post as Chief of Staff, that barring unforeseen events he should stay in Libya for five years, and that he should continue to receive full Army pay in addition to his stipend as Governor, which he insisted should be no less than what he had received as ambassador to Brazil.

It was at this time that he raised the question of the title of Marquis of Sabotino. In a letter dated September 12, 1928 (Year VI of Fascism), he wrote:

"Everyone knows how generously Your Excellency rewards his faithful collaborators. For this reason I am presuming to ask Your Excellency to propose to His Majesty the King that he award me an hereditary title of nobility under a name referring to my military action on Mt. Sabotino. I should be grateful to Your Excellency for acknowledging the receipt of this letter. As I said yesterday in the course of conversation, *Your Excellency can always count on my complete and absolute devotion.*

PIETRO BADOGLIO, *Marshal of Italy.*"

This is not the place to examine the political, military, and economic accomplishments of Badoglio's five-year term as Governor of Libya. The strict objectivity of this account requires the statement that he carried out De Bono's previous undertakings on an even larger scale. From time to time, in order to show that Libya was not a "weak link" in Italy's economic setup, Badoglio sent the Duce gifts of fresh fruits and vegetables from the land which thousands of hard-working Italians had tilled and made fertile.

In 1933 all hope was lost of bringing about an understanding among the Western powers that should allow for the political and social development of Europe. It now became clear that in order to survive Italy had to win living space in Africa. On December 30, 1934, Mussolini sent to his most important political and military chiefs a memorandum setting forth his plan for the conquest of Ethiopia.

This document still exists, along with the hundreds of signed telegrams with which Mussolini directed the preparation of the campaign and every step of its execution. Which one of us who lived through those stirring days can forget the great national meetings of October 2, 1935, of May 5 and 9, 1936? Who is not proud to remember how we withstood the siege declared against us by the League of Nations? Who can fail to be moved by the memory of the day when Italian men and women gave their gold wedding rings to their country? No one can tear out these great pages from Italian history. In the prefaces which he wrote to the books of the three great soldiers of the Empire, Mussolini gave each one of them his due. The war was taking on large proportions, with the Italian expeditionary force numbering, between soldiers and civilians, over half a million men (all of them transported to East Africa by Italian ships in spite of the British navy!). Mussolini thought therefore that the Chief of Staff should be called upon to direct it. In September, when the British fleet steamed into the Mediterranean, Marshal Badoglio was very upset and considered that the game was up.

He wrote a letter imploring the Duce, "who had done so much for Italy, to make some gesture to avoid a clash with Great Britain," to which Mussolini replied that Italy would not start any trouble in the Mediterranean, but would stand its ground in the face of blackmail and defend itself if it were attacked.

The British steamed through the Mediterranean without firing a shot, and the much-feared crisis was over. Badoglio made no objections to the orders which sent him to Africa. Before leaving Naples, on November 18, 1935, he sent the Duce the following telegram:

"As I leave for Eritrea I wish to express to Your Excellency my gratitude for having given me another chance to serve the cause of Fascist Italy overseas, under Your Excellency's orders. The job which has already begun under such favorable auspices will be carried out according to the Duce's will, with an effort that binds soldiers, Black Shirts, and the Italian people into a single unit of faith and passion."

During the war and the victory celebrations of May, 1936, Marshal Badoglio did not conceal his Fascist feelings; in fact, he conspicuously displayed them. Everywhere Fascists paid him tribute as if he were one of their own. Meanwhile he presented his bill. First in July, 1936, as soon as he returned from Addis Ababa, he asked for another title of nobility. Fedele, who was head of the

Council of Heraldry, favored giving him the title of Duke, but objected to the name of Addis Ababa and to the privilege of transmitting the title which Badoglio claimed to his daughter as well as to his sons. Badoglio asked moreover for full war pay for the rest of his life and for reimbursement from the Premier's office of all expenses connected with the *motu proprio* necessary for obtaining his title. The King raised some objections, principally to the use of the name of Addis Ababa, but finally gave in. As for Mussolini, he simply let things take their course. Thus it was that the Duke of Addis Ababa was born.

Badoglio resumed his office as Chief of Staff and left to others the thankless task of pacifying the Empire. Badoglio had a "clan" of his own in Rome, which took care to preserve a halo of glory around his head. When Sem Benelli, at the end of his book, *Africa and I,* gave Mussolini credit for the speed of the Ethiopian victory, Badoglio sent him a strongly worded protest, which the writer answered in very definite terms. In 1940 a book came out by Alberto Cappa on *Total War,* which Colonel Gandin, an aide to Marshal Badoglio, called to the Duce's attention in these disdainful terms: "In case you have not already seen it, I am sending you the enclosed book, which contains vile accusations against the person of Marshal Badoglio. I believe it is my duty to mention it since the Marshal does not intend to do anything about it."

This book spoke of the battle of Caporetto and had a preface by Enrico Caviglia, which said:

"This study deserves reading and meditation on the part of all those who are concerned with military and political affairs. Those who have military or political responsibilities today cannot afford to be ignorant of the workings of total war, which are such as to involve a whole nation."

Through 1938–39 Badoglio's relations with Mussolini were apparently cordial. On September 21, 1938, when the Duce visited the province of Alessandria, Badoglio offered to put him up at his villa or at least to give a tea in his honor, *"which would be an honor to me and a cause of satisfaction to the whole province."*

Badoglio accepted the war against France with seeming enthusiasm, although he wished to postpone it as long as possible. It is true that when Badoglio presented armistice terms to the French at Villa Incisa near Rome there were tears in his eyes.

As late as 1940, on the anniversary of the foundation of the Fascist Party, the Marshal sent the Duce his *"warmest good wishes."* In the preceding rapid survey of the twenty years of the Fascist regime the figure of the consistently traitorous Marshal has been exposed in all its ignominy. He drew apart from the Regime and began to meditate revenge against it after the beginning of the campaign in Greece, when he was relieved of the post of Chief of Staff.

XIX. THE MEETING OF OCTOBER 15, 1940, AT PALAZZO VENEZIA

AT ONE TIME a rumor was cleverly spread to the effect that Marshal Badoglio was opposed to the war against Greece. It is time to put this matter straight once and for all. In view of our present situation we may open our "steel cabinets" and publish the essential parts of documents which belong to history. It was indeed a historical meeting that took place on October 15, 1940, at eleven o'clock in the morning in the Duce's study at Palazzo Venezia. Those present were Badoglio, Ciano, Soddu, Jacomoni, Roatta, and Visconti Prasca. Lieutenant Colonel Trombetti acted as secretary and took down the proceedings in shorthand.*

* There are a number of different and contradictory reports of this historic meeting. According to Roatta who was present, Mussolini opened the discussion by announcing he had decided to attack Greece and had set the day on which the operations had to start, the 26th of October. This meant that nine days were left to complete the military and political preparations, while the day before, Roatta reports, Mussolini had agreed with him and Badoglio that at least three months were needed before starting the war on Greece. Moreover, at the beginning of October 300,000 soldiers had been demobilized. It was exactly at that time, with nine days' preparation and a half-demobilized Army, that Mussolini decided to attack Greece.

No matter how reliable or unreliable Roatta and Badoglio may be, there seems to be no doubt that in the report of the meeting published here Mussolini omitted his opening speech. See Roatta, *Otto milioni di baionette*, Milan, 1946, pp. 117-31.

187

The Duce announced the subject of the discussion, which was one of a series that had gone on all summer long. First he reviewed the list of provocations offered by Greece in its capacity as a vassal of Great Britain. Then he went over the general political and military situation with particular reference to Italy, Greece, and Albania and called for the views of Governor General Jacomoni of Albania.

Jacomoni: "In Albania they are waiting impatiently for us to start action. The nation is highly enthusiastic, so much so that there is almost a feeling of disappointment over our delay.

"We have taken thorough measures to insure adequate supplies. Of course if the harbor of Durazzo were to be bombed we might have some difficulty in replenishing them. The condition of the roads has been greatly improved although they are not yet in entirely satisfactory condiction."

Duce: "What do Albanians think of the situation in Greece?"

Jacomoni: "It is not easy to say. Public opinion is apparently indifferent. We published the news that a niece of an already martyred Albanian patriot had been murdered by the Greeks, but they denied it. Our informants tell us that whereas two months ago the Greeks did not seem inclined to put up a fight, now they appear to be determined to resist us.

"I believe that the extent of Greek resistance will be determined by the vigor of our attack. The more rapidly and decisively we go about it, the less opposition they will offer.

"Then we must take into consideration the aid that the Greeks may receive by sea from the British."

Duce: "I am absolutely sure that they will not send any troops."

Jacomoni: "The only hazardous thing would be to attempt a partial rather than a total occupation. In this case, if the British had a sufficient number of planes, they could attack southern Italy and Albania from airfields in the south of Greece. The Greeks themselves have an air force of only 144 planes, which is nothing to worry about."

Duce: "How is the morale of the Greek people?"

Jacomoni: "Very low."

Ciano: "There is a wide rift between the people and their plutocratic political leaders, who support the British cause and are back of whatever spirit of resistance there is in the country. These leaders form a small and wealthy minority, while the people in general are indifferent to everything, including our invasion."

Jacomoni: "The Greek people were very much impressed by my revelation of the high wage levels in Albania."

The *Duce* asks General Visconti Prasca, commander of Italian troops in Albania, to set forth the military situation.

Visconti Prasca: "We have prepared an operation against the Epirus, which we should be ready to begin on the twenty-sixth of this month with excellent chances of success.

"The geography of the Epirus is such as to make it difficult for Greek re-enforcements to reach it. On one side is the sea and on the other a chain of impenetrable mountains. This terrain favors a series of encircling movements. We should be able to take care of the Greek forces, which we calculate as numbering about 30,000 men, and complete the occupation of the region in ten days or two weeks.

"This operation, which should lead to the liquidation of all the Greek forces, has been worked out in every detail and is, as far as is humanly possible, free of any possible error. Its success would better our strategic position and give us a stronger frontier; moreover, we should come into possession of the harbor of Prevesa, which would make for a drastic improvement in our situation.

"This is the first phase of the operation, which we must see through to the best of our ability. But the whole undertaking depends on the weather. A few weeks from now rains may raise great difficulties in the way of our conquest of both the Epirus and Prevesa."

Duce: "Then the date of the operation may be moved up, but it cannot be delayed."

Visconti Prasca: "The morale of the troops is excellent and their enthusiasm is at a high pitch. I've never had any complaints to make about the troops in Albania. The only lack of discipline of which officers and men are guilty is overanxiousness to get into the fight."

Duce: "How many men have you?"

Visconti Prasca: "About 70,000, not counting the specialist battalions. We outnumber the enemy's approximately 30,000 men by two to one."

Duce: "What about the enemy's tanks and defensive weapons?"

Visconti Prasca: "We have nothing to worry about

except British planes, since I consider the Greek air corps as practically nonexistent. I have some doubts about the Salonika front because of the weather. But we are ready to go into action in the Epirus."

Duce: "But we must see to it that Salonika doesn't become a British base."

Visconti Prasca: "To move on Salonika would take time. We should have to land at Durazzo, which is 150 miles away. I calculate that it would take several months."

Duce: "But there must be a way of preventing a British landing at Salonika. We must get two divisions to that front. Their presence might induce the Bulgarians to help us." ʻ

Visconti Prasca: "If we are to march on Athens, our whole strategy hinges on the occupation of the Epirus and the harbor of Prevesa."

Duce: "And the three islands of Zante, Cefalonia, and Corfu."

Visconti Prasca: "Certainly."

Duce: "These drives must all be made at the same time. What do you know about the morale of the Greek army?"

Visconti Prasca: "They don't like to fight. We've planned our operation so as to impress them with the fact that we can crush them within the space of a few days. I've ordered our battalions to attack relentlessly even if they have to go against a division."

Badoglio: "We have two subjects to consider: that of Greece and that of British aid. I agree with you completely, Duce, that a British landing is almost out of the question. They are more concerned with Egypt than with Greece and they are unwilling to risk their men on Navy transports in the Mediterranean. Hence the only aid they can give is that of their Air Force. We might prevent this by a simultaneous offensive at Marsa Matruk. Under such circumstances it is unlikely that they would take planes away from Egypt and send them to Greece. We can perfectly well do this because Graziani, too, can be ready by the twenty-sixth of this month.

"Now, coming to the Greek problem, I say that to stop with the conquest of the Epirus is not enough. I am not overstating the case when I say that if we are to occupy Greece we must occupy Candia and the Peloponesos as well. Visconti Prasca's plan for the Epirus is a good one. If our left flank is secure the enemy shouldn't give us much trouble. We have enough planes . . ."

Duce: "We shall throw in at least 400 planes, in order to make allowance for British intervention."

Badoglio: "We must occupy the whole of Greece to make the campaign worth while." *

Roatta: "With this in mind we shall need eleven divisions. If we are not to stop at the Epirus we must send more re-enforcements. Another reason for keeping up our strength is to prevent the enemy from thinking that we haven't stamina enough to push on.

* According to the report of the October 15 meeting published by the newspaper *Il Tempo* of Rome on July 18, 1944, Badoglio added, "But we need about twenty divisions, while in Albania we have only nine, plus a cavalry division. It is obvious that in these conditions we need three months to be ready." See Silvestri, C. *I Responsabili della Catastrofe Italiana.* Milan, 1946, p. 121.

"Let us say then that our program is to plan for a total occupation of Greece."

Duce: "If we agree to start operations on the twenty-sixth of this month and count on cleaning up the Epirus by November 10–15 we have a month ahead of us in which to send re-enforcements."

Visconti Praca: "The despatch of re-enforcements depends on the progress of our campaign. We can't send them until the Epirus is completely ours.

"We must aim less at speed than at security. At this season we can't fight anywhere except in the south of Greece. If we use Durazzo as a base for landing troops to send against Salonika, we must count on a month for every division we send over."

Duce: "In order to clarify our discussion I should like to ask just how you expect to proceed with the march on Athens after the conquest of the Epirus."

Visconti Prasca: "I don't foresee much difficulty. Five or six divisions ought to be enough."

Badoglio: "I think it is more urgent to march on Athens than on Salonika, especially in view of the fact that a British landing at Salonika is unlikely."

Ciano: "And in view of the fact that the Bulgarians might join us."

Roatta: "We must bring some pressure to bear there too."

Duce: "Are two divisions enough?"

Roatta: "Yes."

Duce: "It seems to me that now our ideas are clearer. First the operation in the Epirus. Salonika. A close watch on future developments in case the Bulgarians come in, as I think it very likely they will.

"I am in complete agreement as to the occupation of Athens."

Visconti Prasca: "After all, from Athens we can cut Greece in two and march on to Salonika."

Duce: "How far is it from the edge of the Epirus to Athens?"

Visconti Prasca: "About 125 miles, by roads that are in only fair condition."

Duce: "And how is the terrain?"

Visconti Prasca: "High, bare hills."

Duce: "And how do the valleys go?"

Visconti Prasca: "From east to west, in the direction of Athens."

Duce: "That's an important factor."

Roatta (showing the Duce a map): "Up to a certain point. We have to go over a chain of mountains 6,000 feet high."

Visconti Prasca: "But there are plenty of mule paths."

Duce: "Have you ever been over them?"

Visconti Prasca: "Yes, many times."

Duce: "Now there are two more questions. Having settled all this, how many extra divisions do you think we must send to Albania in order to occupy all the territory on the way to Athens?"

Visconti Prasca: "Three divisions of mountain troops would do to start with. Later on we shall see. We could transport that many men to Arta in one night."

Duce: "Another thing—how many regular soldiers and guerrilla bands can the Albanians contribute to the campaign? I consider their participation important."

Visconti Prasca: "We have drawn up a plan for that.

We want to organize bands of 2,500 and 3,000 men each with our officers to lead them."

Jacomoni: "There are a great many applications for enlistment. But we mustn't use too many Moslems because of their vengeful behavior."

Duce: "Then you can organize a certain number of such bands?"

Visconti Prasca: "Everything is ready. I have already wired them to be on the alert and to call in their individual members."

Duce: "How are you going to arm them?"

Visconti Prasca: "With light machine guns and hand grenades."

Duce: "One more aspect of the picture. What preparations have you made along the Yugoslav border?"

Visconti Prasca: "We have two divisions plus a battalion of carabinieri and customs guards. In other words, the line is covered."

Duce: "I don't believe we'll be attacked from that end. And beside the troops are backed up by fortifications."

Visconti Prasca: "The terrain lends itself to defense. A few small groups might filter through the woods, but there's nothing to fear because the whole border area is well protected. There is a customs post every five or six hundred yards."

Jacomoni: "In Albania they'd like to call up several classes of conscripts."

Duce: "How many men would there be in every class?"

Jacomoni: "About 7,000 men."

Duce: "That's something to be taken into consideration. It would be a good idea to let a certain number of Albanians in on it, as long as their absence doesn't disturb the rest of the population. I'd call up two or three classes. Antiaircraft defenses should be the object of our particular attention. We must avoid, as far as possible, bombardment of the oil wells and the Albanian cities. We don't want them to make unfavorable comparisons between the defense of our South Italian cities and their own. We must prepare antiaircraft defenses on a large scale."

Soddu: "I've already arranged to send some Skoda 75's from Germany."

Visconti Prasca: "We have only two antiaircraft groups in Tirana and five for the whole of Albania."

Duce: "We need to have at least a hundred pieces of antiaircraft artillery in Albania in order to keep off demoralizing daylight raids. Send all the Skodas, and the Oerlikons besides."

Soddu: "We haven't yet got them all. I'll send them as soon as they come. As for the Oerlikons, I'll send them by plane."

Duce: "We must have fighter planes on the spot too. Fortunately we have plenty of them. On October 1 there were 52 planes in Albania all ready for use and 15 waiting to be made ready. 67 planes in all."

Ciano: "The 74th Squadron is on its way."

Duce: "It seems to me that we've examined every angle of the problem."

Badoglio: "Details of the operations will be settled by the General Staff."

Thirteen days after this (two days later, unfortunately,

196

than had been planned) came the start of the war against Greece, which was never so disastrous as certain people tried to make it appear. It was not an overwhelming and crushing affair such as General Visconti Prasca intended, but it is a positive fact that by the end of December the Greeks had lost all possibility of taking the initiative. It is equally sure that even without German help, as the Führer himself frankly declared, Greece was certain to receive a decisive beating in the battle planned for the coming April. The operations around Klisura during the month of March had already exhausted Greek resources.

When Giolitti was in power and Valona was abandoned in 1920 there was great lamentation. Who can fail to remember Mussolini's article entitled "Farewell, Valona!"? Twenty years later we set out again on the ancient road, whose course is marked not only by history but by the eternal laws of geography as well. Flying across in a few minutes' time from Bari or Brindisi the traveler sees the indented Albanian coast beyond Valona, the Scindeli mountain chain, the Trebiscines, and the bloody Golico, while wrapped in mist in the distance rises the rugged and severe Tomori. What a profusion of public works were accomplished within the space of a few years in Albania! And according to the old Roman custom Albanians were endowed with all the rights and duties of Italian citizenship! Look at the highway from Durazzo to Tirana, the new buildings in the capital, the reclamation of the Musachia region, the oil wells at Devoli (Italy's only source of supply), the mines supplying iron, bitumen, copper, coal, and chromium. Look at the nearly completed railroad line from Durazzo to Elbassan whose continuation beyond Lake Ocrida would have put us in direct communication with Sofia and the Black Sea. Italian agricultural, business, industrial, banking, and commercial enterprises were proceeding to change the face of this land, which had for centuries gravitated toward Italy and the West, from the days of Teuta, queen of the Illyrians, to those of Skanderbeg, to whom a monument was recently erected in Rome. Of all this nothing now remains, nothing at all. On the ill-famed date of September 8 all was lost.

Our soldiers overseas, who laid down their arms and accepted the terms of surrender instead of going over with their flags unfurled and their honor intact to the Germans, committed, willingly or no, a great crime.

In lands bathed with Italian sweat and blood our country's flag should never have come down. Italian soldiers should never have exposed themselves to ridicule or, worse yet, to the ironical compassion of the people of the Balkans. They should never have left to their fate thousands of Italian civilians—men, women, and children—who had gone overseas trusting in the protection of the Italian armed forces and who now found themselves abandoned to the murderous violence of enemy mobs.

Nothing is left of the Ninth and Eleventh Armies except men interned in Germany, wandering bands in the mountains of Greece, and workers packed off to Siberia.

In Albania there are still 8,000 suspected and defenseless Italians who are trying to "patch up" their miserable situation. The anxiety and hard work of "beginning all over again" seem to be the privilege and punishment of the Italian people.

Is there anyone left to look after the cemeteries where our brothers are sleeping? Who is watching over the truly holy ground of Hill 731? The mountains where once battle raged, where in a storm of fire and steel men fought against men, are now wrapped in deep silence. But the 400,000 Italian soldiers who fought in Albania still cherish these places in their hearts. Let us set out again on our way, with our eyes on the road before us.

History is a sequence of eternal returns. The phases in the lives of nations are measured in terms of decades. Sometimes of centuries.

APPENDIX

STEFANI NEWS AGENCY
ROME, September 16, 1943
Year XXII of Fascism
12:15 A.M.

No. 7—Berlin, September 16.—The semiofficial German news agency, *Deutsches Nachrichten Bureau,* announces:

Today Benito Mussolini has resumed the leadership of Fascism in Italy.

The Duce released under the date of September 15, 1943, the six following government edicts:

Government Edict No. 1

To my faithful comrades all over Italy—

As of today, Sept. 15, 1943, I resume the leadership of Fascism in Italy.

MUSSOLINI

Government Edict No. 2

I name Alessandro Pavolini as temporary Secretary of the National Fascist Party, which shall henceforth be known as the Fascist Republican Party.

MUSSOLINI

APPENDIX

Government Edict No. 3

I order all military, political, administrative, and scholastic authorities, along with all others relieved of their functions by the Surrender Government, to resume their offices and activities.

MUSSOLINI

Government Edict No. 4

I order the immediate restoration of all Party institutions, in order to perform the following tasks:

1. To give active comradely aid to the German army, which is engaged in combat on Italian soil against our common enemy.

2. To give immediate moral and material aid to the people.

3. To review the status of Party members with reference to the coup d'état, which led to surrender and dishonor, to mete out exemplary punishment to all cowardly traitors.

MUSSOLINI

Government Edict No. 5

I order the reorganization of all divisions and groups of the Fascist Militia.

MUSSOLINI

Government Edict No. 6

In completion of the edicts of the preceding days I have made Lieutenant General Renato Ricci commander of the Fascist Militia.

MUSSOLINI

KEY TO NAMES AND PLACES

ACERBO, Giacomo, (1888-   ), Fascist Member of the Chamber of Deputies, 1921. Undersecretary to the Presidency of the Council of Ministers, October 1922—July 1924. Later President of the International Institute of Agriculture. Was granted the title of Barone dell'Aterno.

ACQUARONE, Count Pietro, (1890-1946), A former cavalry officer, Minister of the Royal Household. A member of the Royal Senate, he was made Duke by the King.

ADUA, Locality in North Ethiopia, where the forces of Emperor Menelek defeated Italian troops, March 1, 1896.

ALFIERI, Dino, (1890-   ), Ambassador to Berlin from 1939 to September, 1943.

ALPINES, Mountain troops.

AMBROSIO, General Vittorio, (1879-   ), Chief of General Staff from 1943 to 1945. Member of the Royal Senate.

AOSTA, Amedeo di Savoia Duke of, (1898-1942), The former Duke of Apulia, son of Emanuele Filiberto, cousin of King Victor Emmanuel III. Became Duke of Aosta at his father's death in 1931. Was Viceroy of Ethiopia, died while a prisoner of the English in 1942.

AUGUSTA, Town and harbor located in Eastern Sicily, on a small peninsula, of great strategic importance.

BADOGLIO, Marshal Pietro, (1871-   ), Deputy-chief of the Army Staff in World War I, 1917-18. Chief of the Army Staff, 1919-21. Ambassador to Brazil, 1924-25. Chief of the General Staff, 1926-40. Governor General in Lybia, 1929-33. Commander of the Expedition in Ethiopia, 1935-36. Viceroy of Ethiopia, 1937. Prime Minister, July 1943—July 1944. Made Marquis of the Sabotino and later Duke of Addis Ababa by Mussolini.

BAISTROCCHI, General Federico, (1871-   ), Undersecretary of State for War, 1933. Member of the Royal Senate.

BALBO, Cesare, (1789-1853), Piedmontese historian and statesman. Was head of the first Constitutional Government in Piedmont under King Carlo Alberto, from March 1848 to July 1848.

BALBO, Italo, (1896-1940), One of the four leaders of the March on Rome, October 1922. Commander-in-Chief of the Fascist Militia, 1923-24. Undersecretary of State and then Minister of the Air Force, 1926-33. Air Marshal, 1933. Governor of Lybia since 1933. Killed in a rather dubious air accident.

BARBASETTI, Curio, (1885-   ), A general in the Army. At one time, Military Attaché in Paris.

BARZILAI, Salvatore, (1860-1939), Member of the Chamber of Deputies since 1890, Republican Party. Minister in the Salandra Cabinet, 1915. One of the Italian Delegates at Versailles. Member of the Royal Senate.

BASTIANINI, Giuseppe, (1899-   ), Fascist boss of Perugia. Undersecretary of Foreign Affairs, 1934-39. Ambassador in London, 1939-40. Again Undersecretary of Foreign Affairs in 1943, till the 25th of July.

BASTICO, Marshal Ettore, (1876-   ), Commander-in-Chief of the troops in Lybia for a time during World War II. Member of the Royal Senate.

BATTISTI, Cesare, (1875-1916), Socialist representative of Trento in the Austrian Parliament, advocated the annexation of South Tyrol to Italy. At the beginning of World War I, volunteered in the Italian army. Wounded first, then captured, he was hanged by the Austrians, July 12, 1916.

BENCIVENGA, General Ugo, (1872-   ), Was on the Italian General Staff at the end of World War I. Antifascist Member of the Chamber of Deputies in 1922. Frequently arrested during the Fascist regime, was one of the leaders of the Resistance movement in 1943, 1944. At present one of the spokesmen of the Monarchic Party in the Republican Senate.

BENELLI, Sem, (1875-   ), Dramatist and poet. Member of the Chamber of Deputies, 1921.

BERSAGLIERI, Light mobile infantry.

BIANCHI, Michele, (1883-1930), Formerly a Revolutionary Syndicalist. General Secretary of the Fascist Party, 1921. One of the

KEY TO NAMES AND PLACES

four leaders of the March on Rome, Oct. 1922. Undersecretary at the Ministry of the Interior, 1927. Minister of Public Works, 1929.

BONGIOVANNI, General Luigi, (1866-   ), Governor of Cirenaica, 1920-24. Member of the Royal Senate, 1929.

BONOMI, Ivanoe, (1873-   ), Socialist Member of the Chamber of Deputies since 1909. Several times a Minister after 1916. Prime Minister, June 1921—February 1922. At the head of the Committee for National Liberation in Rome, Sept. 1943—June 1944. Prime Minister, June 1944—May 1945. Since April 1948, President of the Republican Senate.

BOTTAI, Giuseppe, (1895-   ), Fascist Member of the Chamber of Deputies, 1921. Minister of Corporations, 1929-32. Governor of Rome, 1935-36. Minister of Education, 1936—Feb. 1943. Escaped from Italy and volunteered in the French Foreign Legion, 1944. Returned to Italy after acquittal from all political charges, 1948.

BOVIO, Giovanni, (1841-1903), Philosopher, professor at the University of Naples, member of the Chamber of Deputies, leader of the Republican Party.

BRACCIANO, Lake of, Small lake north of Rome, in the Lazio region.

BROFFERIO, Angelo, (1802-1866), Political writer and politician. A fanatic Republican, he opposed the Crimean War and alliance with France.

CALCAGNO, Riccardo, (1872-   ), A general in the Army. Commander of an Army Corps, 1932. Member of the Royal Senate.

CALVI DI BERGOLO, Count Giorgio, (1887-   ), Married in 1923 Princess Jolanda of Savoy, eldest daughter of King Victor Emmanuel III. A general in the Army. For a few days (Sept. 1943) Commander of the "Free City" of Rome.

CALZA-BINI, Gino, (1886-   ), A general of the Fascist Militia.

CAPELLO, General Luigi, (1859-   ), Commander-in-Chief of the Second Army at the battle of Caporetto, Oct. 1917. Involved in a plot against Mussolini and sentenced for life, 1925. Died in custody.

CAPORETTO, Locality on the Isonzo river. In the Caporetto region, German and Austrian armies inflicted a crushing defeat on the Italians, October 1917.

205

CARABINIERI, National uniformed police, the main organ for the maintenance of public order.

CARBONI, General Giacomo, (1889-   ), Commander of an Armored Corps supposed to defend Rome, September 1943.

CARDUCCI, Giosué, (1835-1907), The best known Italian poet in the period between the Risorgimento and the beginning of the century.

CASATI, Ettore, (1873-   ), Judge of the Italian Supreme Court.

CASTELLANO, Giuseppe, (1893-   ), A general attached to the Army Staff, was the most active member of the anti-Mussolini conspiracy. Sent to Lisbon to get in touch with the Allies, Aug. 1943. Signed the Armistice at Cassibile, Sicily, on Sept. 3, 1943.

CAVACIOCCHI, General Alberto, (1862-1925), Commander of the Fourth Army Corps at the battle of Caporetto, Oct. 1917.

CAVALLERO, Ugo, (1880-1943), An Army marshal. Undersecretary of War, 1925-28. Member of the Royal Senate, 1926. Commander-in-Chief in Oriental Africa, 1937. Chief of the General Staff from 1941 till the Winter of 1943. Committed suicide or was killed by the Germans, Sept. 1943.

CAVIGLIA, Enrico, (1862-1945), An Army marshal. Commander of the Eighth Army in World War I, 1918. Minister of War, 1919. Member of the Royal Senate. Commanded the operations against D'Annunzio in Fiume, Dec. 1920. Took the command of the defense of Rome against the Germans for one day in Sept. 1943.

CIANETTI, Tullio, (1899-   ), Minister of Corporations in 1943. Voted for the Grandi resolution at the Grand Council's session, July 1943. Prosecuted at the Verona trial in 1944, but escaped death sentence.

CIANO, Count Galeazzo, (1903-1944), Entered the Diplomatic Service, 1925. Married Edda, Mussolini's daughter, 1930. Minister of Press and Propaganda, 1935. Minister of Foreign Affairs, 1936 —Winter 1943. Ambassador to the Holy See, 1943. Executed in Verona, 1944.

COLLARE DELL'ANNUNZIATA, Highest Italian decoration at the time of the Monarchy. A Knight of the Annunziata became an honorary cousin of the King.

CORRIDONI, Filippo, (1888-1915), A Revolutionary Syndicalist leader, was for the intervention of Italy in the first World War. Volunteered in the Army and was killed in action.

KEY TO NAMES AND PLACES

DE BONO, Marshal Emilio, (1866-1944), Commander of an Army Corps during World War I, 1918. One of the four leaders of the Fascist March on Rome, Oct. 1922. Chief of Police, 1922-24. Commander-in-Chief at the beginning of the Ethiopian Campaign, 1935. Voted for the Grandi resolution. Was executed in Verona by the Fascist Republicans, 1944.

DE VECCHI, Cesare Maria, (1884-   ), One of the four leaders of the March on Rome, Oct. 1922. Governor of Somaliland, 1923-29. Member of the Royal Senate. First Ambassador to the Holy See, 1929. Minister of Education, 1935. General Governor of the Aegean Islands, 1936. Made Count of Val Cismon. At present, lives in Latin America.

DIAZ, Marshal Armando, (1861-1928), Commander-in-Chief of the Italian army in World War I, 1917-18. Minister of War, Oct. 1922-24. Member of the Royal Senate. Made Duke della Vittoria.

DI REVEL, Admiral Paolo Thaon (1859-1946), Chief of the Navy General Staff, 1913. Commander-in-Chief of the Navy during World War I, 1917. Minister of the Navy, Oct. 1922-25. Was made a Duke, with the title of Duca del Mare.

DORIA PAMPHILJ, Prince Filippo, (1886-   ), Sent to "confino" by the Fascist regime, 1940. Mayor of Rome, 1944-46.

FACTA, Luigi, (1861-1930), Member of the Chamber of Deputies since 1892. Several times a Minister. Prime Minister from February to October 1922. Member of the Royal Senate.

FARINACCI, Roberto, (1892-1945), Started as a Socialist, Fascist Member of the Chamber of Deputies, 1921. Secretary of the Fascist Party, 1925-26. Was the leader of the most extreme pro-German faction of Fascists. Killed by Partisans in Northern Italy.

FEDELE, Pietro, (1873-1942), Professor of History. Member of the Chamber of Deputies, 1924. Minister of Education, 1925-28. Member of the Royal Senate, 1928.

FEDERZONI, Luigi, (1878-   ), Nationalist Member of the Chamber of Deputies, 1913. Minister of Colonies, October 1922—June 1924 and again 1926-28. Minister of Internal Affairs, 1924-26. President of the Senate, 1929-38. President of the Italian Academy, 1938-43. Escaped after the liberation of Rome, 1944. Returned to Italy after acquittal from all political charges, 1948.

207

FRUGONI, Professor Cesare, (1881-   ), Well-known physician. Was Mussolini's doctor.

GALBIATI, General Enzo, Commander-in-Chief of the Fascist Militia, 1943.

GIOBERTI, Vincenzo, (1805-1852), Philosopher and political writer. Was Prime Minister of the Piedmontese government for a short time in 1849.

GIOLITTI, Giovanni, (1842-1928), The boss of Italian politics for 25 years, he was an insuperable master of parliamentary manipulations.

GIURIATI, Giovanni, (1876-   ), Member of the Chamber of Deputies. Minister of Public Works, 1925-29. President of the Chamber of Deputies, 1929. Secretary of the Fascist Party, 1930-31.

GRANDI, Dino, (1895-   ), Fascist Member of the Chamber of Deputies. Undersecretary and then Minister of Foreign Affairs, 1926-32. Ambassador in London, 1932-39. Escaped from Italy to Portugal immediately after Mussolini's fall. At present in business in San Paulo, Brazil.

GRAZIANI, Marshal Rodolfo, (1882-   ), Governor of Somaliland, 1935, Viceroy of Oriental Africa, 1936-37. Commander-in-Chief in Lybia during World War II, 1940-41. For a while Chief of the General Staff. Minister of Defense in Mussolini's Northern Italian Government, Oct. 1943. At present in jail, pending trial.

GRAZIOLI, Francesco Saverio, (1869-   ), Commander of an Army Corps during World War I. Member of the Royal Senate.

GUARIGLIA, Raffaele, (1889-   ), A diplomat. Successively Ambassador in Madrid, Buenos Aires, Paris and the Holy See. Minister of Foreign Affairs in Badoglio's Cabinet, July to Sept. 1943.

GUZZONI, General Alfredo, (1877-   ), Minister of War during World War II. Commander-in-Chief of the Army in Sicily at the time of the Allied landing, July 1943.

HUMBERT OF SAVOY, Prince of Piedmont, (1904-   ), Lieutenant General of the Realm, June 1944. Acceded to the throne as Humbert II upon abdication of his father, May 1946. Was king for one month.

IL RESTO DEL CARLINO, Daily newspaper in Bologna.

KEY TO NAMES AND PLACES

I.R.I., ISTITUTO RICOSTRUZIONE INDUSTRIALE, A governmental agency, founded in 1933 for the control of industrial holdings, somewhat along the lines of the Reconstruction Finance Corporation.

IRREDENTI, IRREDENTISMO, Movement directed towards the liberation of that part of Italy that was still under Austrian domination after 1866.

JACOMONI, Francesco, (1893-   ), A diplomat. Minister in Tirana, 1934. High Commissioner in Albania, 1939.

LAMPEDUSA, Small island in the Mediterranean, southwest of Sicily, between Malta and Tunis. Was used as a penal island.

LATERAN PACTS, Signed in 1929 by Cardinal Pacelli and Mussolini, had brought to an end the rift which existed between the Italian government and the Vatican since the Italian occupation of Rome in 1870.

MATTEOTTI, Giacomo, (1885-1924), Socialist Member of Parliament, one of the most courageous opponents of the Fascist regime. Was kidnapped and murdered on June 10, 1924 by a gang organized by Mussolini's closest associates. The chief executioner of this gang was Amerigo Dumini, an Italian American gangster, born in St. Louis, Mo.

MAUGERI, Admiral Franco, (1898-   ), Head of the Italian Navy Intelligence 1941-44. One of the leaders of the Resistance in Rome, 1943-44. At present Chief of Staff of the Italian navy.

MESSE, Marshal Giovanni, (1883-   ), Commander-in-Chief of the Expeditionary Corps in Russia, 1941-42. Commander-in-Chief of the Italian troops in Tunisia, 1943. A prisoner of war, 1943-44. Chief of General Staff, 1944-45.

MONTEZEMOLO, Colonel Giuseppe, (1901-1944), Actively engaged in the Resistance Movement in Rome, 1943-44. Killed in the massacre of the "Fosse Ardeatine" in Rome.

MUSSOLINI, Benito, (1883-1945), Son of a blacksmith and a grammar-school teacher, became a schoolteacher himself in 1902. A revolutionary Socialist since his first youth, he escaped to Switzerland to avoid the draft. Returned to Italy in 1904, became Editor of the Socialist paper *Avanti* in 1912. In 1914 he was expelled from the Socialist Party.

OVRA, Fascist secret police, the Italian equivalent of the Gestapo.

PALAZZO VIDONI, Seat of the Fascist Party.

PALAZZO VIMINALE, Seat of the Ministry of the Interior.

PANTELLERIA, Mediterranean island, southwest of Sicily.

PAVOLINI, Alessandro, (1900-1945), Minister of Popular Culture. Took part in Mussolini's government in the North as Secretary of the Fascist Party. Executed by the Partisans in April. 1945.

PIAZZA VENEZIA, Large square in the center of Rome, where Mussolini used to address the crowds from the balcony of Palazzo Venezia.

POLACCO, Professor Vittorio, (1859-1926), An eminent legal scholar. Member of the Royal Senate.

PONZA, Small volcanic island in the Mediterranean, west of Naples. It was one of the most ill-famed penal islands.

POPOLO D'ITALIA, Daily paper in Milan. Organ of the Fascist Party, launched by Mussolini in 1914.

RACCONIGI, The castle near Racconigi, small town in the province of Turin, was one of the favorite residences of the King's family.

RICCI, Renato, (1896-   ), Head of the Youth Organization of the Fascist Party. General of the Fascist Militia.

RICCIONE, Beach resort on the Adriatic coast, patronized by the members of Mussolini's family.

ROATTA, General Mario, (1887-   ), Commanded the Fascist forces in the Spanish Civil War, 1937-38. Held a high command in Yugoslavia, 1941-42. Chief of the Army General Staff, 1943. Escaped from jail in 1945.

ROCCA DELLE CAMINATE, Mussolini's estate near Forlì, Romagna.

ROMANO, Professor Santi, (1875-1946), Legal scholar. Member of the Royal Senate. President of the Council of State, 1928-43.

ROSI, General Ezio, (1882-   ), For a time Chief of the Army General Staff during World War II.

ROSSI, Cesare, Chief of Mussolini's Press Office, 1922-24. Involved in the Matteotti murder, June 1924. Escaped from Italy and then dealt with anti-Fascists abroad. While in Switzerland, was kidnapped by the Fascist Police and taken back to Italy, 1931. Kept in jail and "confino" until 1943.

ROTIGLIANO, Edoardo, (1880-   ), Member of the Fascist Chamber of Deputies. Member of the Royal Senate.

KEY TO NAMES AND PLACES

SAFFI, Aurelio, (1819-1890), Follower of Mazzini. Was one of the leaders of the Republican Party.

SAN PAOLO STATION, One of Rome's railroad stations, located near the San Paolo Basilica. Was only half built at the time of Hitler's visit, but with good stage setting it could look like a real station.

SAN ROSSORE, Summer residence of the Royal Family near Pisa.

SANT'ANNA DI VALDIERI, Another summer residence of the King's family, near Cuneo, Piedmont.

SAURO, Nazario, (1880-1916), A native of Istria, volunteered as an Italian naval officer in World War I. He was caught by the Austrians and hanged.

SCORZA, Carlo, (1893-   ), Secretary of the Fascist Party, 1943. At present lives in Latin America.

SCUERO, Antonio, (1885-   ), A general in the Army. Undersecretary of War, 1942.

SENISE, Carmine, (1883-   ), Chief of Police, 1940—Winter 1943 and again July-Sept. 1943.

SKORZENY, Lt. Col. Otto, Lt. Colonel in Hitler's Elite Guard. Surrendered to U.S. troops at Salzburg, 1945. His war crimes trial resulted in acquittal. Held in custody while waiting examination by a denazification court, he escaped, July 1948.

SODDU, Ubaldo, (1883-   ), A general in the Army. Undersecretary of War, 1939. For a time Commander-in-Chief of the Expeditionary Corps against Greece, fall 1940.

SORICE, General Antonio, (1897-   ), Undersecretary of War, 1943. Minister of War in the Badoglio Cabinet, July-Sept. 1943.

STARACE, Achille, (1889-1945), Was Secretary of the Fascist Party for eight years, from 1931 to 1939, the longest term of office in a particularly delicate job. Starace was the champion heel-clicker and the inventor of the most celebrated Fascist propaganda stunts, such as the Battle of the Flies, the Campaign against starched collars, etc.

SUARDO, Count Giacomo, (1883-   ), President of the Royal Senate since 1939.

TERRACINA, Town in Southern Italy, on the Tyrrhenian coast.

TERUZZI, Attilio, (1887-   ), A high officer in the Fascist Militia. At one time Minister of Colonies and Governor in Cirenaica. At present, in jail.

TITTONI, Tommaso, (1855-1931), Minister of Foreign Affairs almost without interruption from 1903 to 1910, and again in 1919. Ambassador in Paris, 1910-16. President of the Italian Academy, 1929-30.

TURATI, Augusto, (1888-   ), Fascist Member of the Chamber of Deputies. Secretary of the Fascist Party, 1926-29. Later in disgrace.

VALLE, General Giuseppe, (1886-   ), Chief of the Air Force General Staff, 1930. Undersecretary of Air, 1933-1940.

VENTOTENE, One of the "Isole Pontine," between Ischia and Ponza.

VICTOR EMMANUEL OF SAVOY, (1869-1947), Succeeded his father Humbert I to the throne, in 1900. Abdicated in favor of his son, Humbert II in 1946.

VILLA ADA, Private residence of King Victor Emmanuel III, located in the "Quartiere Salario" of Rome.

VILLA TORLONIA, Private residence of Mussolini and his family in Rome.

VISCONTI PRASCA, General Sebastiano, (1883-   ), Was the first commander of the Expedition against Greece, Nov. 1940.

ZANIBONI, Tito, (1883-   ), Socialist Member of the Chamber of Deputies. Awarded the Gold Medal during World War I. Sentenced for life after an attempt to kill Mussolini, 1925. Freed in 1943.